TILTING
AT
MORTALITY

TILTING AT MORTALITY

Narrative Strategies in

Joseph Heller's

Fiction

DAVID M. CRAIG

 Wayne State University Press Detroit

Library of Congress Cataloging-in-Publication Data

Craig, David M., 1948–

   Tilting at mortality : narrative strategies in Joseph Heller's fiction / David M. Craig.

      p.   cm. — (Humor in life and letters)

   Includes bibliographical references and index.

   ISBN 0-8143-2653-6

   1. Heller, Joseph—Technique. 2. Humorous stories, American—History and

criticism. 3. Narration (Rhetoric) 4. Fiction—Technique. I. Title. II. Series.

   PS3558.E476Z6 1977   96–44560

   813'.54—dc21

THE AUTHOR WISHES TO THANK THE FOLLOWING PUBLISHERS AND ORGANIZATIONS FOR
PERMISSION TO QUOTE FROM THE WORKS OF JOSEPH HELLER: SIMON & SCHUSTER AND
SCAPEGOAT PRODUCTIONS FOR *CATCH-22, GOOD AS GOLD,* AND *CLOSING TIME*; ALFRED A.
KNOPF FOR *SOMETHING HAPPENED* (BRITISH COMMONWEALTH RIGHTS DONADIO-ASHWORTH
AGENCY) AND *GOD KNOWS*; AND G. P. PUTNAM'S SONS FOR *PICTURE THIS.*

HUMOR IN LIFE AND LETTERS SERIES

A complete listing of the books in this series can be found at the back of this volume.

General Editor
Sarah Blacher Cohen
State University of New York, Albany

Advisory Editors
Joseph Boskin
Boston University

Alan Dundes
University of California, Berkeley

William F. Fry, Jr.
Stanford University Medical School

Gerald Gardner
Author and lecturer

Jeffrey H. Goldstein
Temple University and London University

Don L. F. Nilsen
Arizona State University

June Sochen
Northeastern Illinois University

FOR THE CRAIG FAMILY

GEORGE (1916–1995), CHERYL, AND RANDALL
KRISTIN, JENNIFER, AND ELLEN

[who may] be stimulated to reflect with
poignancy on some incidents of a family nature
that once took place between us. . . .

JOSEPH HELLER

Do not go gentle into that good night,
Old age should burn and rave at close of day;
Rage, rage against the dying of the light.

DYLAN THOMAS, "Do Not Go Gentle into That Good Night"

The secret cause of suffering is mortality itself, which is a prime condition of life. It cannot be denied if life is to be affirmed.

JOSEPH CAMPBELL, *The Power of Myth*

Death is the mother of beauty.

WALLACE STEVENS, "Sunday Morning"

Death sometimes changes people for the worse.

JOSEPH HELLER, *God Knows*

CONTENTS

PREFACE

It is necessary to me not
simply to *be* but to *utter*.

GEORGE ELIOT, letter

■

    For Joseph Heller, silence partakes of the stillness of the grave, and words do not so much fill silence as push it back, much as a lamp forces the night shadows into the corners of a room. He finds silence and the inability to speak unnerving. Typically, in this respect, Heller remembers a recurrent nightmare that he had while teaching at Penn State, his first teaching job, a dream in which he was in a classroom with fifteen minutes left and had nothing to say.[1] In a world that threatens, like his dream, to resolve into wordlessness, Heller finds power in speech. Looking back on his days in the intensive care unit of Mount Sinai Hospital, a victim of Guillain-Barré syndrome, he asserts, "Conversation was all that prevented me from going mad. I wisecracked boisterously, commented, interrupted, counseled" (*No Laughing Matter* 8).[2] So do his fictional protagonists, affirming through their words their presence in an ever-threatening world. But speechlessness always intrudes in Heller's fiction, as certain as the silent, "sleepless, bedridden nights" in which Yossarian finds himself a prisoner in *Catch-22* (426). In *Something Happened*, Slocum fears that his life will lead to an insensate end and refers incessantly to his retarded son's speechlessness. Even the compulsively oral King David, the narrator-protagonist of *God Knows*, dreads his speechless nights and the silence of dreams and memories that they bring. For Heller and his protagonists, words provide the necessary remedy, confirming existence, even if only temporarily.

As a novelist, Heller is quite a talker.[3] *Something Happened, God Knows*, and *Closing Time* have the cadences of speech: Slocum's incessant monologue, King David's bumptious oral autobiography, and the oral histories of Sammy Singer, Lew Rabinowitz, and his wife Claire. Even the more cinematic *Catch-22* gives the impression of being spoken, a quality that Whitney Balliett responds to when he says *Catch-22* "doesn't seem to have been written; instead it gives the impression of having been shouted on to paper."[4] Some of the harshest critiques of Heller's work have come from reviewers and critics who are put off by his orality. A. Alvarez's review of *God Knows* illustrates the point: "*God Knows* has . . . a King David re-created in the image of an aging Jewish funnyman. It is the Gospel according to Henny Youngman, entertaining and not quite coherent, unless you postulate an audience that merely wants a novel to be a vehicle for a performance."[5] Indeed, many of its jokes, like those of Heller's other novels, have their source in the routines of stand-up comics and approximate the "performance-oriented" patterns of speech.[6] In describing his writing talent, Heller himself alludes both to the oral and response-oriented qualities of his fiction: "I can be funny, and given enough time with any dialogue I write, I can have somebody make a remark which will produce a response. And it will be funny."[7] It is dialogue—writing that pretends to be speech—that supplies much of the comedy of Heller's novels as well as much of their bulk.

Speech itself always plays an important role in Heller's fiction, but its meaning changes in the later work. In his early work, most notably his stories, speaking or not speaking chiefly symbolizes ethical choices.[8] The pattern is a simple one: while speaking out is the ethically correct thing to do, it also brings personal danger. The endings to *Catch-22*, *Something Happened*, and *Good as Gold* work variations on this motif, with the extension that ethical speech confirms one's identity, while false speech or silence is identity-destroying. Yossarian saves himself by rejecting the chance to "[s]ay nice things about [Cathcart and Korn]" (416). By contrast, Slocum extinguishes an independent sense of his identity when he will not admit killing his son but will give the three-minute speech at the annual company convention. Like Yossarian, Gold saves himself with his words, specifically by turning down the deal which will make him secretary of state and by saying Kaddish for his brother Sid. In Heller's fiction, to speak is to act, and such action necessarily involves ethical choices and responsibilities.

After *Catch-22*, speech does not simply stand for the ethics of existence; it comes to stand for existence itself and against the silence of the grave. *Something Happened* exemplifies this equation. The novel's speechless characters—Slocum's retarded son Derek, his senile mother, and dead father—represent the trajectory of Slocum's life: "I can see myself all mapped out inanimately in stages around that dining room table, from mute beginning (Derek) to mute, fatal, bovine end (Mother), passive and submissive as a cow, and even beyond through my missing father (Dad)" (401). Origins and ends are mute, partaking of the silence of the universe. No wonder Slocum speaks so compulsively and so unceasingly in the novel, trying to push back the quiet, a quiet out of which he was born and into which he will pass. This cast of mind will lead in *Good as Gold* and *God Knows* to Heller's writer-heroes, Bruce Gold and King David, as well as, in *Picture This*, to his Aristotle. Each records his life in order to preserve the space between the muteness of origins and ends and thereby to confirm existence in an otherwise still universe.

As Heller's career has progressed, this space becomes more tenuous, even suspect, as does his confidence in the language by which it is expressed. *Good as Gold*, which is Bruce Gold's "study of the contemporary Jewish Experience in America" (15), operates narcissistically. Gold cannot see his subject, Jewish life, as distinct from himself. King David's authorial mode is braggadocio: "I honestly think I've got the best story in the Bible" (13), and to prove it he writes *God Knows*. As *Picture This* suggests, Heller himself comes to doubt the storyteller's capacity to narrate truthfully. Debunking the Socrates myth, Heller remarks: "Death by hemlock is not as peaceful and painless as [Plato] portrays: there is retching, slurring of speech, convulsions, and uncontrollable vomiting" (350). Yet the silent agony of such a death is too great to bear, so Heller himself, in the manner of author-protagonists Gold and David, constructs a better story, the tale of Asclepius, a leather merchant to whom Socrates owes a cock. Heller's account of Asclepius refigures Socratic irony as farce: instead of a cock being offered to the god of healing, a gesture that makes death the cure for life, Heller's Socrates repays a debt to a merchant, a repayment that results in Asclepius's arrest, trial, and death. The scene in which all this occurs resembles Clevinger's trial in *Catch-22*, except that there is nothing to prevent the Athenian Assembly, as there was the bloated colonel, from invoking the death sentence. The result may move readers to echo Yorick at the end of the *Tristram Shandy*—"a COCK and a BULL . . . And one of the best of its kind, I ever heard."[9] Like Sterne, albeit with darker, more menacing humor, Heller inserts his novel in the space between origins and ends. For Heller, as author and as man, "words, after speech, reach into the silence."[10] Such silence—the inescapable reminder of mortality—is unbearable for Heller and his protagonists, and so he writes about the way they speak.

This study pursues two related tracks: examining mortality as theme and raison d'être of Heller's fiction, and exploring his narrative strategies. It did not begin with these foci, but as an introduction to his fiction in the absence of a comprehensive account of his career. This bears mention because, since I began, Robert Merrill, David Seed, Sanford Pinsker, and Judith Ruderman have published books on Heller; Stephen Pott's book on *Catch-22* has appeared; and James Nagel has edited an anthology that provides an overview of his work.[11] In order not to replicate the overviews of each novel provided by Merrill, Seed, Pinsker, and Ruderman, I had to abandon my original approach. Something of my introductory format remains, however, in that I inquire into a variety of issues: for instance, into Heller's style, especially style as oral and performative; into the correspondences between his fiction and his life (although the limited biographical information available restricts this inquiry); into the published and unpublished stories that anticipate the concerns of his novels. Out of this diversity, I hope to present a coherent picture of Heller the novelist: my study explicates his war with mortality and the narrative techniques by which he wages it.

Chapter 1 looks at Heller's stories, his apprenticeship efforts, for what they reveal about his development as a writer. Read by the light of *Catch-22* and *Something Happened* as they inevitably are today, they are surprisingly ungainly, like ugly ducklings. And yet, they hold the distinctive germ of his imagination: manifesting his stylistic and narrative preferences, foreshadowing his preference for comedy that juxtaposes the serious and the farcical, and announcing his principal themes. They also document the process by which he set aside the models of Hemingway, O'Hara, and Shaw, among others, and achieved his own distinctive fictional voice. The stories also explain why Heller traded in the realist's for the anti-realist's art. In the stories, reality—the characters' economic, social, and cultural environments—is always more powerful than the stories are themselves, and the more imaginative the character, the more painful his or her failure. In anti-realism, Heller would find a way to unleash both his own and his characters' imaginations.

The second and third chapters discuss *Catch-22* and *Something Happened*, the novels on which Heller's reputation rests and will continue to rest. Of the relationship between the two novels Heller says, "I put everything I knew about the external world into *Catch-22* and everything I knew about the interior into *Something Happened*."[12] Indeed, the novels are companion pieces, though the relationship between the internal and the external worlds is more complicated than Heller's characterization of his aims suggests. While *Catch-22* is about the external world, or, more accurately, about 1950s America, over the course of the novel Heller attends equally to the way this world is perceived. As the Snowden death scene illustrates, Heller makes the meaning of external events dependent upon the mind that perceives them. Knowledge is doubly embodied: as Yossarian's famous meditation on Snowden's entrails reveals, mortality—and by extension knowledge about it—resides in matter, in the flesh. If *Catch-22* can be said to move from the world into the mind, then *Something Happened* moves from the mind into the world. While Heller constructs the novel as an interior monologue, the protagonist Bob Slocum's consciousness comes to represent America itself. Slocum's identity partakes of the America in which he lives. His desires, dreams (and nightmares), and aspirations are all products of suburban, middle-class life; his life its synecdochic representation.

Catch-22 is Heller's story, as distinctive in theme and method as F. Scott Fitzgerald's tales of youthful aspirations or Dickens's of emotionally abandoned children. Its defining elements are announced in two unpublished war stories, both set at Avignon, and recur with variation in each subsequent novel: guilt, bad faith, secret knowledge, and the death of children (or, alternatively, wounded innocents). The narrative core of this story is the death of a child, this death controlling each novel as Snowden's controls *Catch-22*. The desolation of this death provides the impetus to narrate, propelling both the story and discourse of *Catch-22*. The story might be summarized in Yossarian's vow "to live forever or die in the attempt" (29); he must learn how to live in a world whose governing principle—Catch-22—ensures that threats to life and identity are its only certainty. Heller's style and comic narrative strategies are the discourse counterpart to Yossarian's efforts, defusing death with ridiculing laughter.

Heller's use of the monologue form in *Something Happened* is as startling today as it was to its initial readers, who expected to find *Catch-22* set in suburbia and, instead, found themselves confined in Slocum's claustrophobic consciousness. Heller's theme is common enough: the stultifying conformity of corporate and suburban America. But Heller uses the monologue to implicate his readers in this theme. He requires readers to participate in Slocum's consciousness so that it becomes a mirror for themselves. Slocum's concerns are uncomfortably familiar. In this, Heller works the turn that Freud argues for in the Oedipus myth: the myth occurs inside the self. Yet, Slocum's story, Heller insists, is also enacted daily in contemporary America. *Something Happened* is its fable. Similarly, Heller uses the monologue form to involve the reader in the construction of the novel. Like the magician who explains his tricks, Heller lets his readers observe his performance, see how he works order and interest out of a mind that drones, whines, and trivializes.

Good as Gold and *God Knows*, the subjects of chapters 4 and 5, naturally fall together: both are about Jewish life, concern the protagonist's
ethical education, and work self-consciously. In each text, the authorial
process is foregrounded as the reader reads about a man composing an account of his life. The critics' scorn for these novels is well known; each
provided new ammunition for those who viewed Heller as another American one-novel novelist. These novels, while flawed, reveal an author extending himself into new territory and experimenting with new narrative
techniques and strategies. In this way, these novels illuminate the development of the novelist and his increasing anxiety about his art. Their author-
protagonists are not admirable characters, though each is endowed with
the trademark wit of a Heller hero. For both Gold and David, writing is, in
large part, self-aggrandizement. Because Heller conceives their "writings"
as self-conscious texts, he calls attention to the workings of his own novels, in the process ironically calling into question the fictional undertaking
itself.

The fourth chapter explores Heller's self-conscious method in *Good
as Gold* and what it enables him to say about Jewish life. From his early
stories, Jews have been a fictional subject that both stimulates and constrains Heller's imagination. On the one hand, he associates Jewish characters with moral values and ethical courage, and, on the other, he finds
the plots that they occasion neither free nor unconstrained. For Heller,
Jewish characters carry baggage—a certain cast of mind and point of
view, inherent limitation in the roles that society allows them to play, and
a long cultural tradition that life in America frays. In effect, Jews, as fictional subjects, lead Heller toward the kind of realism that he abandoned
when he began writing novels. However, by employing the literary device
of a book about an author writing a book, Heller turns the limitation that
he found in Jewish characters into an advantage. *Good as Gold* is about
plotting Jewish life, though, predictably, the resulting plot turns upon a
death. This self-consciousness makes the Jewish experience in America
and writing about this experience two strands of a single tale. Both are stories of seeing, of looking at the world through the eyes of a Jew; Heller's
novel guides his reader toward this point of view.

In the biblical story of David, Heller already had many of the catalytic
agents for his imagination: dead children, guilt, and bad faith. Because
most readers, like Heller himself, know the main lines of this story, his authorial task is to interest his readers in what they already know. He solves
the problem by designing the novel as deathbed recollection, a solution
that places the reader at David's side as he reviews his career. Death im-
pinges on the narrative as it does on David himself, its pressure simultaneously occasioning and shaping his life story. True to form, Heller makes
his ending out of the death of children, in this case the deaths of Absalom

and David's unnamed son by Bathsheba. They provide the climax and the occasion for narrative clarification. David's reminiscences cast new light on Heller's subject, human mortality. Heller presents the human condition as an unceasing interchange between possibility and restraint. Physically embodied, David as desiring subject (and author) finds that possibility exists only within boundaries. David, whose playful imagination purportedly conceives *God Knows*, cannot escape the deathbed stench of his own mortality.

After *Good as Gold* and *God Knows*, *Picture This* marks a change of course. It is, in equal parts, novel and crib course in Western history. Particulars multiply as the narrator continually wanders from his ostensible subject, Rembrandt painting his masterpiece, *Aristotle Contemplating the Bust of Homer*. But wherever the narrative goes, be it Periclean Athens or present-day America, the same story is told: human beings are talented self-deceivers who mythologize their history in order to protect themselves from painful truths. For Heller, the story of Cold War America—which he tracked in different guises in *Catch-22*, *Something Happened*, and *Good as Gold*—has already occurred, in ancient Greece and Rembrandt's Holland. In all these places, economic wealth and power have bred tyranny, which masks itself as democracy and produces a constant state of war or imminent war ("Peace on earth would mean the end of civilization as we know it" [*Picture This* 100]). Heller's original title for the novel, *Poetics*, conveys something about his method as well as about his subject. In effect, Heller turns Aristotle's *Poetics* on its head. Instead of Aristotle's dispassionate, magisterial logic, which divides the world into nuances, shades, and categories ("I propose to treat of Poetry in itself and of its various kinds, noting the essential quality of each"), Heller limns a world in which everything is the same ("There are outrages and there are outrages, and some are more outrageous than others" [350]).[13] Thus, his narrative task involves finding unforeseen routes to the same destination, to surprise his readers even as they say "that again."

Closing Time constitutes a summing-up, Heller's reflection upon *Catch-22* and, to a lesser extent, his subsequent career. He confirms the dark thematic vision of *Picture This*, in which humans exert little control over human events and history follows its own autonomous course independent of its actors. Using the transformation of the Coney Island neighborhood in which he grew up and the experience of friends who have gone into business, Heller argues that American capitalism transforms childhood delight into middle-aged malaise and converts vital urban neighborhoods into blighted cityscape. Yet, against a future that he can only conceive in apocalyptic terms, Heller holds out the power of the comic spirit, a spirit figured by the paunchy, white-haired, worldly worn, and ethically compromised Yossarian. Yossarian has changed as well as aged. As

Heller draws him, he is no longer an antihero, but only a man, albeit one blessed with the hope that a comic vision affords. At novel's end, as nuclear missiles fly, Yossarian eschews safety and walks into the night in search of the woman he loves. Of this ending, one might say: Joseph Heller tilts at death with the intensity of Don Quixote, while mocking his efforts with the comic realism of Sancho Panza.

I wish that there were a muse to invoke for these acknowledgments, preferably one with an Aristotelian sense of proportion, manner, and means, so that I could adequately express my gratitude for the generosity of many people who have given me support, inspiration, and commentary. Clarkson University, the Center for Liberal Studies, and the Mellon Foundation provided research grants under which this study was written. Deans Owen Brady and Jerry Gravander compounded the value of their professional support with their personal thoughtfulness.

Material from this book has been previously published in somewhat different form, and I gratefully acknowledge permission for its reuse. Parts of chapter 2 appeared in: "Closure Resisted: Style and Form in Joseph Heller's Novels," *The Centennial Review* 30 (Spring 1986): 238–50; "Battlefield Messages: Joseph Heller's 'Catch-22 Revisited,'" *War, Literature, and the Arts* 1 (1989–1990): 33–41; and "From Avignon to *Catch-22*," *War, Literature, and the Arts* 6 (Fall/Winter 1994): 27–54. "Closure Resisted" also contains material from chapter 3. A section of chapter 7 first appeared in "Revising a Classic and Thinking about a Life: Joseph Heller's *Closing Time*," *CEA Critic* 58 (Spring/Summer 1996): 15–30. I also wish to acknowledge the staff of Wayne State University Press for their unfailing kindness and helpfulness in the production of this book, especially Arthur Evans, Kathryn Wildfong, Alice Nigoghosian, and Ann Schwartz, as well as the copy editor, Mary Gillis, and the proofreader, Hope Steele. I firmly believe that it is a better book for their efforts.

The Clarkson interlibrary loan staff has been typically responsive to my many requests, and in particular I wish to thank Gayle Berry, James Nolte, and Barbara Osgood. In the Special Collections Department of Brandeis University Library I was made to feel like a distinguished visiting scholar; I am especially indebted for the assistance of Charles Cutter, Victor Berch, John Favreman, and Nancy Zibman. As people here at Clarkson know, Judy Grant tranforms secretarial and editorial assistance into acts of friendship. It is a pleasure to make her generosity known outside the university.

Albert Guerard, Avrom Fleishman, and James Phelan directed NEH Summer Seminars that I attended, and each became to my mind a model of academic excellence. I hope the spirit of their seminars is appropriately conveyed by these pages. Joseph Heller has been considerate and kind, especially given my many queries and the burdens that they must have imposed. He trusted me with copies of his early unpublished work, and I hope my treatment of this material repays his trust.

Without the help of my colleagues and friends, Peter Freitag, John Serio, Linda Van Buskirk, Donald Purcell, and Mary Lay, this project would never have been completed. They shared their ideas (so frequently that I have been unable accurately to reflect their contributions in the notes), shaped unshapely arguments, and have become editors and proofreaders. Each has read all or part of the manuscript as if it were his or her own, which in a sense it is. From the earliest moments of this undertaking, John Serio and Peter Freitag, in particular, counseled, coaxed, cajoled, and encouraged me toward its completion.

In this project, as in my life, the greatest debts incurred and those most joyfully acknowledged are familial, and making my family dedicatees declares what I feel but am unable to express. Without their lessons in mortality, I would not be writing about those of Joseph Heller.

1

THE SHORT STORIES
UNCERTAIN FIRST STEPS

His mind presents the world
And in his mind the world revolves.
WALLACE STEVENS, "The Sail of Ulysses"

Like many first works, Joseph Heller's short stories are imitative, appropriating others' styles, themes, and methods. Yet they also contain in embryo the distinctive cast of his imagination. They reveal his fondness for plot over character and for dialogue as a primary means of narrative development. Stylistically, they rely heavily on repetition. And while most are essentially serious, they foreshadow Heller's preference for comedy, particularly in dealing with an oppressive reality or with the emotionally painful. Juxtaposing the serious and the farcical, a few stories fracture reality and already make use of mordant humor—both identifying marks of Heller the novelist. They also announce his fictional values: his emphasis upon ethics, courage, and integrity as well as his critique of middle-class life. Largely unknown today, these stories provide the opportunity to peer backward at the genesis of a novelist and to observe his characteristic way with words. Almost inevitably for contemporary readers, they derive much of their meaning from an acquaintance with—and suffer by a comparison to—*Catch-22* or *Something Happened.*[1]

From this vantage point, the stories constitute youthful performances, caught as if by the flickering light of old home movies. Familiar characters appear, most notably Marvin B. Winkler ("Bang the Bangtails" and "The Art of Keeping Your Mouth Shut"); Winkler is the prototype for Milo Minderbinder and appears as a character in his own right in *Closing Time*. As do comic situations—buying high, selling low, and still making a profit ("The Polar Bear in the Ice Box")—and early versions of well-known scenes—a veteran refusing to wear his clothes ("I Don't Love You Any More"). The hallmarks of Heller's style are immediately and forcefully recognizable: the self-negating sentences, the repetitions, and the preponderance of dialogue. Yet from the perspective of the later work, the stories appear somewhat strange. Unlike the novels, they are largely realistic and have simple, linear plots. Heller has not learned to use discourse to displace story in order to undercut the logic of chronological progression (*Catch-22*), to transform the limitations of the narrative mind into an authorial resource (*Something Happened*), *not* to tell the story, but to reflect upon its production (*Good as Gold*), to exploit memory fully as a narrative method (*God Knows*), to cast into doubt the very enterprise of fiction making (*Picture This*), or to follow the Modernists' lead in using allusions as a device for narrative progression (*Closing Time*).[2] While most of the stories cannot bear much critical pressure, they can illustrate the choices made and the lessons learned—the roads, detours, and wanderings by which Heller got to *Catch-22* and beyond.

Between 1945 and 1953—while in the army and later in college at the University of Southern California and New York University, at Oxford University on a Fulbright Fellowship, teaching at Pennsylvania State University, and working for *Time* magazine—Heller wrote approximately twenty-five stories, eight of which would eventually be published.[3] He had been writing stories and submitting them for publication since he was a child, sending them to places like the *New York Daily News*, *Liberty*, and *Collier's*. He also dreamed of becoming a dramatist and in high school aspired to writing comedies like those of Moss Hart and George S. Kaufman. Although secondary to his interest in fiction, his interest in drama continued: he did his master's thesis on Pulitzer Prize–winning plays and in the hiatus years between his stories and the beginning of *Catch-22* collaborated on a play, "The Bird in the Fevverbloom Suit," with his friend George Mandel.[4] These dramatic interests foretold his work as a screenwriter: he contributed to the screenplays for *Sex and the Single Girl* and *Dirty Dingus Magee*, as well as to the pilot for *McHale's Navy*.[5] His first publishing success came in 1945 when his story, "I Don't Love You Any More," appeared in *Story* magazine, the magazine which also first published Truman Capote, J. D. Salinger, Carson McCullers, John Cheever, Erskine Caldwell, and William Saroyan, among others. It was a special issue devoted to servicemen recounting their war experiences.[6] While attending college, Heller had his writing aspirations reinforced by his composition and creative writing teachers, who encouraged him to submit his work for publication; in particular, Maurice Baudin's comments guided Heller's revisions. Erasing the A from his freshman essay, "Beating the Bangtails," he took the advice and submitted it to *Esquire* where it appeared as "Bookies, Beware!" While in college, he would have two more stories published by *Esquire* as well as two by *The Atlantic Monthly*. Of these stories, "Castle of Snow" was selected by Martha Foley (who together with Whit Burnett edited *Story*) for inclusion in *The Best Stories of 1949*.

If these stories marked Heller as a promising writer, they did not, as he himself realized, signify a writer who had found his subject or voice. Nor did those published offer him a clear sense of direction in commercial terms. Looking back on these early efforts, Heller observes, "I didn't have any concept of what I should write. . . . I would read a story in a magazine like *Good Housekeeping* or *Women's Home Companion*, and then I would try to write a story for them. I was not very good at it."[7] To find models for his more ambitious efforts, he read and studied the stories of Irwin Shaw, John O'Hara, and Ernest Hemingway. Retrospectively, he realized that the resulting stories were not written out of his "own experiences as much as out of [his] experience reading other people's work."[8] The plots, styles, and themes of stories such as "I Don't Love You Any More," "Nothing to Be Done," and "Girl from Greenwich" demonstrate the accuracy of Heller's self-assessment. Significantly, after these early efforts Heller never returned to the short story form. Stories such as "MacAdam's Log" and "World Full of Great Cities," although published in the fifties and sixties, were written in the forties, and the short story–like "Love, Dad" (*Playboy*, Dec. 1969) was originally a chapter from *Catch-22*. Only in the novel has Heller found a form consonant with his imagination.

Many of Heller's early stories, including his first published effort, "I Don't Love You Any More" (*Story*, Sept.–Oct. 1945), concern marital discord. In their handling of the topic, they have the familiar resonance of Hemingway's "Cat in the Rain," "Mr. and Mrs. Eliot," or "Hills Like White Elephants" or Shaw's "The Girls in Their Summer Dresses." In Heller's stories, marriage is confining (as it also will be in his novels), and his male protagonists yearn for freedom and excitement. Hence the plots work as quests, or rather as aborted quests, with the hero leaving the home to seek a better life. Wives stand in the way, restricting rather than occasioning desire. The world, which Heller represents after the fashion of Hemingway, is also inhospitable to the protagonists' yearnings. The protagonists fail and learn little, their experiences serving at most as a mirror in which they can see their own ineffectuality. Only when Heller casts marital discord as farce do the patterns change: the quest plot gives way to the romance plot and the warring partners are happily reunited.

"I Don't Love You Any More" tells of a married couple who quarrel and fall out of love without entirely realizing what is happening to them or understanding the sources of their dissatisfaction. Like Hemingway, Heller conveys the action of the story by dialogue which places the reader as a slightly embarrassed auditor to the marital quarrel. Also like Hemingway, Heller handles the plot as a slice of life, characters caught in a moment identifying their core concerns and attitudes. In "I Don't Love You Any More," the marital dispute grows out of a war veteran's realization after three days at home that he no longer cares for his wife. Heller's gritty dialogue conveys the escalating conflict with sparse, but evocative detail:

> "You aren't being very considerate, you know," she said quietly.
> "I know," he replied, "I'm sorry."
> "I don't believe you are sorry," she said. She waited for him to answer but he remained silent. "Are you?"
> "No," he said. "I'm not." (40)

Neither character acts upon this emotional impasse. The veteran simply keeps asking his wife to get him a pitcher of beer, and his wife responds with puzzled questions and with assertions that she is doing her best. Finally, she packs and leaves, and, now alone, he calls her mother's home to ask his wife to return. At story's end, she does come back, pitcher of beer in hand. With this thrust of his narrative knife, Heller confirms that the three days of marital strife will continue undiminished and uninterrupted.

While Heller's reliance on Hemingway is unmistakable, there are also indications of the direction his later fiction will take. As Melanie Young notes, his portrait of marriage in "I Don't Love You Any More" foreshadows his presentation of Slocum's marriage in *Something Happened*.[9] Similarly, the germ for Yossarian's refusal to wear clothes appears in the veteran's refusal to put on clothes for company. And with his title, Heller announces the love theme that is an undercurrent in much of his fiction, a theme I will take up in connection with *God Knows*. But the most important intimations that "I Don't Love You Any More" hold for Heller's development as a writer are stylistic, particularly in his use of repetition. Repeated lines punctuate the story—the husband's requests for beer and his wife's assertion, "you know it hasn't been easy for me"—rendering its rhythms as insistent as those of a march. Heller's reliance on repetition has mixed results though. When the wife returns home with beer and a sheepish look, the story turns flat. Even so, the repetitions heighten the emotional drama, disclosing the bleakness of a marriage in which the couple can speak to each other only with formulaic lines. Like the refrain of a ballad, these restated lines carry emotional force disproportionate to their literal meaning. Also, they anticipate Heller's variations on "Catch-22" in *Catch-22* or his use of lines like "Something bad is going to happen" in *Something Happened* to convey the claustrophobic world of Slocum's consciousness.

Two unpublished stories about marital disharmony—"The Death of the Dying Swan" and "The Polar Bear in the Ice Box"—deserve attention for the way in which they presage the themes, style, and fictional techniques of the novels.[10] In "The Death of the Dying Swan," another story heavily influenced by Hemingway, the protagonist, Sidney Cooper, perceives his wife, Louise, as an obstacle to the life he hoped to have lived and as an emblem of his faded dreams.[11] The story recounts a moment of release, as Cooper leaves a party to get the mustard his wife needs. On the street, he meets Harry Schwoll, a man-of-the-world brassiere manufacturer who is sympathetic to his yearnings, and they go off for a drink together. In the bar, Cooper is attracted to a young widow who had once dreamed of becoming a ballerina. In response to her sadness, he persuades her to dance a section of *Swan Lake*. But as the dance ends, Cooper remembers the mustard for his wife and rushes out and back into marital captivity.

The story is about mortality and dreams. Depressed by the sterile, artificial party talk, Cooper "long[ed]" for people who were real, people who lived with honest passions and found vigorous pleasure in the mere event of existing, people for whom death came too soon." Responding to Cooper's sympathetic queries, the widow tells him, "Nothing's the matter. We're all dying. From the day we're born, we begin to die. They get candles and coffins from the same tree." In preliminary form, this is the sensibility of the novels: of the mother of the dead soldier whom Yossarian impersonates, who tells Yossarian that he is dying, and of Slocum who sardonically jokes that he has "exchanged the position of the fetus for the position of the corpse." These mortality-bound visions of life stand in contrast to the cocktail party, a world whose mores are articulated by Louise Cooper when she sends Sidney off on his errand: "Darling, something terrible has happened. I'm all ready to serve the cold cuts and there's no mustard."[12] In Heller's fiction, spouses and lovers reside in the comfortably middle-class world, refusing to consider death or to learn the lessons of mortality. "Lot's Wife," another story involving the Coopers, explicitly turns on this refusal, in that Louise will not look at or speak to the man she has injured in a car accident. At this point in his career, Heller offers *carpe diem* as the only antidote to characters of Cooper's cast of mind; the rebellion against death itself awaits a protagonist of the heroic (or anti-heroic) stature of Yossarian.

As its title implies, "The Polar Bear in the Ice Box" is a farce with Heller playing marital discord for its comic effects. The story uses the formulaic plot of the comic hero's education at the hands of a discerning woman. Dr. Amos Thackett, the eminent but money-foolish economist, has been writing romantic pulp fiction under his wife's name to earn extra income. But his wife, Em, whom Thackett sees as a "homespun country girl," will not sign over the most recent royalty check to him. When a Hollywood agent wants to buy the story and to hire its author to write the screenplay, Thackett forgives Em's obstinacy about the royalty check and sends his reluctant wife off to Hollywood, masquerading as his sister. In Hollywood, Em's talents emerge. She vanquishes its most feared movie mogul, charms even the jaded members of the party set, and is pursued by the town's most eligible bachelors. The now jealous Thackett wants Em to admit that he has written the story and to return to being his academic wife. Wisely, she resists, at least until she solves the scriptwriting problem that results from turning the story into a film—how to get the polar bear out of the ice box (Em's solution: defrost the fridge). Even Thackett appreciates her ingenuity and begins to see the woman whom Hollywood has already detected—at which point comic harmony is restored and the story can end.

Readers of Heller's novels will recognize the stylistic mannerisms and the characteristic plot rhythms of "Polar Bear." "It was impossible not to like him—but I had achieved the impossible before. I succeeded in loathing him, particularly since he renewed our friendship by apologizing for his knavery at the party." This is an early version of Heller's self-negating sentences, statements that deny the meaning they have just advanced. In *Catch-22* and Heller's subsequent novels, the pattern recurs, but the sentences are compressed, their force heightened: "The Texan turned out to be good-natured, generous, and likable. In three days no one could stand him" (*Catch-22* 10). Similarly, the plot of "Polar Bear" relies on the kind of reversal structures that propel his novels: the homespun Em turns out to be both ravishing and intelligent, and so on. Additionally, one scene in the story uses the premise for one of Heller's most famous comic sequences, in which Milo makes a profit while buying eggs for seven cents and selling them for five; in "Polar Bear," Dr. Thackett tries to persuade a Hollywood starlet that she will make more money by taking a cut in salary. As "The Death of the Dying Swan" and "The Polar Bear in the Ice Box" illustrate, Heller's short stories mark the incubation period of the novelist.

For Heller, stories about low life—pool rooms, bookies, drugs, and city streets—propel their protagonists into a world of danger, excitement, and possibility. As in his marriage tales, Heller relies upon quest plots, with the hero sallying forth in search of adventure. However, the world, like that of literary naturalism, is more powerful than the individual, its forces shaping, even determining, an individual's values and choices. As in Hemingway, successful protagonists have mastered the ethos of the streets and exhibit stoic grace and endurance. Similarly, they fail when they cannot muster the requisite will or when they are undone by the latent violence of life. Either kind of failure signifies weakness (defeat itself can be ennobling if the protagonist acts in the manner of Hemingway's code heroes). As this suggests, it is a man's world in which women play bit parts. Unlike the characters of the marriage stories, these protagonists can, at least potentially, relate to others directly; the rules for conversation and relationships are mutually understood. This world is uncomplicated, but violent. Heller's direct, unadorned style and straightforward narratives purport to mirror reality, when in fact, as he later recognizes, they reflect Hemingway.

In "Nothing to Be Done" (*Esquire*, Aug. 1948), Heller loosely follows the model of Hemingway's "The Killers."[13] The plot is spare and simple: a small-time mobster's winning bet has been lost and a bookie and his two runners now wait in a poolroom for the mobster to have his revenge.[14] Nat, the college student runner who thinks he has misplaced the bet, waits with the stoic grace of Hemingway's Ole Andreson. By contrast, Carl the bookie passes the time with tired indifference, rousing himself only momentarily to try to persuade Nat to flee, while Hank, the other runner, sweats profusely, trying ineffectually to think of ways to help Nat. After watching the mobster and his thugs beat up Nat, Carl goes upstairs, tears up the bet (which he had forgotten to place until it was too late), and flushes the shreds down the toilet. Alone, the bookie absolves himself of guilt and responsibility by "trying to figure out if there was anything that could be done and realizing all the time there wasn't" (131). Such failures in moral responsibility and courage will become motifs in many Heller plots, from *Catch-22*'s Doc Daneeka to *Good as Gold*'s Ralph Newsome.

The story begins and ends at an impasse, for, as Heller's title tells the reader, there is "nothing to be done." Heller's presentation of his characters and their low-life code limits what they can do. Carl believes that the mobster's revenge is unavoidable, and so he holds the bet without acknowledging his responsibility for what will follow. Steeling himself to Nat's beating, he remains outwardly calm. What he cannot still is his own dissatisfaction; nor can he voice it. Using Hemingway's touch, Heller alerts the reader to Carl's emotional state by having his protagonist repeatedly refer to the imminence of rain ("It's going to rain like hell"). At first Carl dreads the coming rain, but at story's end he wishes for it—as if the rain will cleanse his mood along with the weather. It won't. Having read the story, the reader recognizes the irony of Heller's title; of course something can be done. Paradoxically, Nat's choice to do nothing illustrates the possibilities for both choice and action. In this sense, the title "Nothing to

Be Done" proclaims and denies its meaning; as do the titles of *Catch-22,*
*Something Happened, We Bombed in New Haven, Good as Gold, God
Knows, No Laughing Matter, Picture This,* and *Closing Time.*

In "Bookies, Beware!" (*Esquire,* May 1947), another story about
gambling, Heller uses the low-life atmosphere for humorous effect. As a
freshman essay, the story shows why Heller earned an A; as a story, it is a
slight piece of a work. Essentially the tale works as an extended joke:
Marvin B. Winkler (Heller borrows the name of a childhood friend for his
protagonist) uses science to predict the winners at Santa Anita racetrack.[15]
He expostulates on his method to a dubious bookie: " 'I mean pure science,' Mr. Winkler said with a deprecating smile, as he computed the den-
sity of the ultraviolet rays. 'I have determined the dew point, the
barometric pressure, the resistance of air and wind, the cubic weight of
moisture in the air, and the surface tension of the turf. Upon looking over
the entries in the first race, I find that only one horse has ever before raced
under these conditions, and then it did quite well. I conclude, therefore,
that this horse will win by two and three-sixteenths lengths' " (98). Since
Winkler's pick is a hopeless also-ran, his prediction brings derisive laughter, most notably from the horse's jockey (himself rumored to have bet on
another horse) who dies laughing, necessitating an emergency replace-
ment. Predictably, the horse wins by exactly two and three-sixteenths
lengths, a triumph of "the pure science method," the narrator laconically
announces. The pseudo-scientific language with which Heller lards the
story alerts the reader familiar with Heller's novels to his partiality for language effects and wordplay. The characteristic marks of Heller's sense of
humor also abound in the story, as, for example, the scientists too busy
testifying before congressional committees to investigate Winkler's
theory. The farcical—that which elicits groans or scorn from highbrow
readers—energizes Heller's imagination.

In "A Man Named Flute" (*Atlantic,* Aug. 1948), another story with a
bookmaker as its protagonist, Heller still relies on the model of Hemingway, but also announces his own fictional concerns. The most ambitious
of the bookmaker stories, "Flute" locates the reader in bookie Dave Murdock's mind and directs the authorial audience's attention to the gap between Murdock's understanding of his situation and the way in which he
acts.[16] Again the plot is simple. Murdock's bookmaking operation has
temporarily been closed by the police, but he avoids the consequences of
this by having someone else arrested in his place and rigging alternative
contacts with his customers. While "out of business," Murdock learns that
his son is smoking marijuana and goes to confront the pusher, "a man
named Flute." In the confrontation, he receives two unpleasant lessons:
that he has overestimated his physical prowess and that Flute's activities
parallel his own. Lest he miss the parallels, his friend, poolroom owner

Marty Bell, tells Murdock in terms strikingly similar to those Murdock has just used to justify his profession to his wife: "There are a dozen guys in the neighborhood who would sell tea to your kid if he wants it. If Flute didn't do it, somebody else would. It's just like your business" (70). Like other Heller protagonists, Murdock cannot assimilate the disquieting knowledge. As the story ends, he is eating with his family, unable to taste his food or to look at his wife.

Heller's handling of character relationships in "Flute," especially between Murdock and his son, and of point of view illustrate the maturation of his storytelling skills. To himself, Murdock can say upon learning that his son is smoking dope, "Dick was a good boy," and everything could be settled by a serious talk (67). But in practice, Murdock neither acts as if his son is good, nor is able to talk to his son at all. Without telling his son the reason for his anger, Murdock insists that he must go to military school, and later, when Dick lies about the kind of cigarettes he smokes, he hits him. Murdock sees no contradictions in any of this; his anger and self-assurance blind him. Locating the narrative audience in Murdock's mind, Heller creates eddies of dissonance, evoking sympathy for Murdock, while simultaneously inviting readers to condemn his actions, especially beating his son.[17] Judging Murdock, however, carries its own risks: if readers believe that they would handle their own children better than Murdock does, they run the risk of falling into the frame of mind that brings Murdock trouble—his assumption that his son is good and that any differences can be worked out with a serious talk. When he creates such conflicting planes of understanding, Heller makes an important turn in his apprenticeship as a writer; he has begun to attend to discourse as well as to story.

In several of the unpublished stories, drugs also figure prominently as the complication that propels the action and raises issues of choice and ethical responsibility. In each, violence flares as suddenly as Murdock's blow to his son. A mood piece, "The Coward" relates the protagonist Sid's trip to a boxing match. On the way, his friends smoke reefers and offer him one, but he rejects it with moral self-assurance. Yet Sid becomes increasingly anxious, especially amidst the raucous boxing match crowd. When the crowd riots, Sid joins the frenzy, with a "wild flare of exultancy" crashing a chair down on the head of a neatly dressed man in a gray flannel suit. "To Laugh in the Morning" and "A Day in the Country" are variants of the same motif, the drug addict's predicament. In "To Laugh in the Morning," Nathan Schwoll, the well-meaning, malleable protagonist, returns home from the federal drug treatment center, but once again in the old haunts drifts back into the same associations and way of life that originally led to his addiction. In "A Day in the Country," Nathan is driven by his addiction, becoming so strung-out and crazed that he takes money his seriously ill mother needs for her heart medication and, after that, throttles the family doctor in order to get the drugs that he craves. Of Nathan's state of mind while attacking the doctor, the narrator says, "he was trapped like an innocent stranger inside the grotesque and demonic blur which flashed by him on every side and which he was no longer able to control and powerless to understand." While occasionally Heller's prose tends toward the melodramatic, his stance does not. He neither sensationalizes nor moralizes, but rather presents his story with the graininess of cinema verité. Given the aims of Heller the novelist, this strength holds a limitation: he seeks to reconstruct reality, not, by a faithful reflection, to testify to its power.

In "Castle of Snow" (*Atlantic*, Mar. 1948) and "MacAdam's Log" (*Gentlemen's Quarterly*, Dec. 1959), Heller moves away from the preformed plots which predominated in his earlier stories. More important to the development of the novelist, he discovers the narrative effects of memory. For Heller, memory complicates and enriches the narrative progression: plots can move back and forth in time; events take their meaning in anticipation of what will come or from the residue of what has been; and, most critically, memory itself shapes "the story." The story comes to reside not in what happened, but in its recollection. This reseeing narrativizes experience, a lesson that Heller puts to good use in Snowden's death in *Catch-22* as well as in each subsequent novel. "Castle of Snow" and "MacAdam's Log" do share features with Heller's other short stories. Both use marriage as plot complication, with women again serving as the voice of the world and as impediment to male desire, although in these stories this plot lies more in the background. And, as in all Heller's short stories, the world is more powerful than the imaginative individual. But the stories mark a breakthrough for Heller: memory enhances the narrative, educating the sensibility of teller and told alike, just as it does for novelists like Thomas Wolfe and poets like William Wordsworth.

"Castle of Snow" takes place during the Depression, with its actualities—evictions, lost jobs, and sold possessions—serving as important plot details. In this way, setting becomes integral to, rather than backdrop for, the action. Heller's realist technique, however, is not what makes the story memorable.[18] What is distinctive—in addition to his use of memory—is the way in which Heller conjoins pathos and humor in the same scene, and juxtaposes the realistic and the fantastic. Thus the story has a variegated texture, one more complex than the other stories so far examined, but anticipatory of his novels. Heller also makes his narrator a character in the story for the first time and relies upon his interpretation in order to impart the story's meaning.

"Castle of Snow" has two centers of interest: the events in the life of its protagonist, Uncle David, once he loses his job, and the memories of his nephew, who narrates David's story. A resolute idealist who fled czarist Russia in order to maintain his socialist vision, David retains his vision-ary fervor by reading voraciously and sympathizing with others' Depression-caused hardships. When David himself loses his job, the fami-ly's fortunes rapidly deteriorate. Guided by Aunt Sarah's pragmatism, the family sells first items of furniture and household goods, later David's books—the latter a gesture that he voluntarily undertakes, saving only his copy of *The Canterbury Tales*. When David gets a job as a loading inspec-tor at a bakery, family fortunes momentarily seem to turn, but darken when the nephew finds his uncle playing in the snow with children on what is supposed to be his first day of work. Sensing trouble, the nephew gets his aunt and together they bring David home. His wife can sympa-thize with David's quitting the bakery job because it would mean scab la-bor, but cannot understand how he can demean himself by playing in the snow like a child. Recollecting his uncle's story, the nephew learns from it, appreciating David's choice of Chaucer's earthy humor over the Bible's "comforting promise" (54). But, unlike his uncle, he can "understand the implacable laws of economics and the harsh punishments of poverty" that have determined family fortunes (52).

Restrained and unadorned, Heller's language controls the sentimental-ity of his plot. Instead of the language effects to which he is so partial, Heller emphasizes contrasting moods and points of view, a family at har-mony when it is well off, but distant and estranged when financial difficul-ties occur. He also writes to an authorial audience via the limitations of the narrator, while respecting his point of view. The narrator remembers the gentle marriage of his uncle's and aunt's contrasting personalities as "a perfect and harmonious relationship" (52). The two exist in distinct, but complementary, worlds, David reading, his wife performing the household rituals; they come together in shared, comfortable conversation. But when David loses his job, the couple lose their mode of relating to one another. David's embarrassment over his inability to provide for the family drives him into the kitchen to do his reading and Sarah, frustrated when he shows no awareness of her concern for him, grows distant and silent. In time of hardship, the snow castle creates an unbridgeable chasm. Sarah simply "cannot understand why a grown man should want to act like a child" (55), and for his part, David builds the castle in order to recreate a mem-ory in which he and Sarah had gone into the woods together and David had built one for her (another example of the repetition of which Heller is so fond). And so David's and Sarah's moods stand in contrast: his una-bashed enthusiasm while playing in the snow and the pathos of his cries to Sarah to remember the earlier castle ("Do you remember, Sarah? Try to remember" [55]) set against her cold, distant anger and hot embarrass-ment. In the nephew who witnesses the scene, the different moods blend together, and in his narration they blend as well. Even in memory, the nephew cannot finally understand his uncle's and aunt's different points of view, leaving it to his readers (and Heller's authorial audience) to apprehend "The Castle of Snow."

Heller looks upon "Castle of Snow" as the "one good story" among all those he published and fondly remembers the conjunction of the imagined and the real in the snow castle episode.[19] In some ways, however, his memory tells more about what he comes to value in his novels than it does about the story. Certainly, the snow castle scene conjoins the imagined— Uncle David's attempt to relive the memories of his youth—and the real— represented in the story by Aunt Sarah and the narrator's views of David's snow escapades. Yet the union affirms the power of the real. David's fantasy, while rendered sympathetically, is treated as the dreamer's ineffectual response to the world's unaccommodating actuality. Only when Heller stopped writing realistic stories did he take up David's cause, unleashing the powers of imagination and fantasy on the purportedly real. As the opening chapter of *Catch-22* announces with details like the soldier in white's interchangeable urine and drip jars and Yossarian's rambunctious censorship, Heller attacks the power of reality.

In "MacAdam's Log" (*Gentlemen's Quarterly*, Dec. 1959), Heller interweaves the imagined and the real in the most complex fashion of all his stories. This story also has the most complicated plot, with more episodes, and the most elaborate temporal structure. The plot unfolds in Walter Mittyish fashion in that the protagonist, usually identified as the Captain, increasingly begins to live in his mind by taking imagined voyages across the Atlantic. The stimulus for the voyages is his unhappy home life. For example, he sets mental sail on the *Niew Amsterdam* after being rebuked by his son-in-law Neil for amusing his grandchildren with a game of drilling imaginary oil wells. At sea, the Captain can act the part that continually gets him into trouble at home, that of the kindly, solicitous old man, as he does helping an Austrian girl orphaned by the *Anschluss*. The Captain's imagined journeys are aided when he makes the acquaintance of an actual seaman, Mr. Simpson. Meeting Simpson each time his ship comes to port, the Captain gains new material for fashioning his own ocean adventures and gets to spend time on Simpson's ship. Of course, the Captain's voyages get him into further trouble at home, particularly when he injects details from them into family affairs. The climax of the story occurs as the result of one such moment, when the Captain argues with a dinner guest about whether the Blue Grotto is in Capri or Genoa. Incensed that her father would bring his concerns to the dinner table when one of her husband's influential clients is there, the daughter forces him to admit that all of his voyages were fictitious. Disoriented by this enforced dose of reality, the Captain does go down to the harbor where he surreptitiously boards Simpson's ship. The ship's crew finds him, and he receives yet another sample of the world's hostility to dreamers when he learns that Simpson has been arrested for smuggling and that he himself is now considered an unwanted intruder. Disillusioned, the Captain announces plans to his family for a last voyage to visit his dying sister, a voyage that readers know foretells the imminence of his death.

Interlayering the imaginary and the real, Heller constructs his most ambitious narrative and demands more of the reader than in his other stories. As implicitly announced by the opening passage, Heller entangles the two in such a way that the reader, particularly on first reading, cannot easily disentangle them.

> The Captain's first voyage, the beginning of a long and distinguished career on the high seas, had taken place a number of years earlier when his sister, the last surviving relative of his own generation, had sailed back to Scotland to die. She did not give that as her purpose, of course, substituting instead some obstinate nonsense about a girlhood friend now alone and in failing health; but the Captain, whose recollection of the many vast and shambling decades behind remained surprisingly acute, remembered clearly that he himself was but nine years old when his father, a burly shipwright with a ringing laugh that sounded frequently now in the Captain's thoughts, had uprooted his mother, his wife, and his seven 'bairn' in one gigantic impulse that carried them all swiftly from Glasgow over the ocean to Portland, Maine. . . .
>
> It was the day she [the Captain's sister] sailed that first provided the Captain with the grand inspiration that ultimately sent him to sea. The Captain had not been aboard ship since that eventful time nearly fifty years before [the time of his childhood departure], and he was left breathless now by the sudden spectacle of the broad and massive vessel with all its ornate luxury glittering endlessly in every direction and its noble air of dignified and compact strength. (112)

The story's opening sentence seems to announce an essentially realistic narrative, the sister's death and a variety of temporal references confirming readers' impression of a world corresponding to their own. But by the third paragraph, readers know something is amiss, for the distinguished career announced in the opening sentence could not begin until the Captain was almost sixty. This stylistic method, in which readers can decode the meaning of the details they are given only long after they first appear, controls the entire story.[20] Initially, Heller works the method so as to invest individual sentences with particulars that seem to proclaim their verisimilitude only to provide additional information a few sentences or paragraphs later that undermines their apparent realism. For example, the Captain's detailed description of the harbor at Cobh—its shoals and tides

—later founders, when the reader realizes he has mislocated the harbor in one of the low countries, "Belgium, Holland, or Norway" (169). Later, Heller reverses the process so that details that first appear to be part of the Captain's fantasies, as for example Mr. Simpson and the Captain's experiences on Simpson's ship, in fact turn out to be actual events. By using a style that initially frustrates readers' ability to assimilate information, to distinguish real and imagined, Heller merges the actual and the fantasied, thereby aligning readers' experience with the Captain's.

Heller uses plot as well as style to reveal the relationship between the Captain's actual life and the nature of his imaginary voyages. Like many a fictional dreamer, the Captain uses his fantasies to remedy the dissatisfactions of his life. His travels correspond to the actual circumstances of his life, as when, for example, his attacks of gastritis are transformed into the rough seas of the *Washington's* passage.[21] The Captain also enriches his life by fashioning voyages to historical places or by modeling them after actual ones, notably wartime ones he has read about in the newspaper. The interpenetration of real and imagined also works the other way in that the Captain's understanding of the events of his actual life is shaped by what happens in his voyages—for example, the sea voyages not only help him pass the time of his gastritis attacks but also to learn how to weather them. In Heller's novels, this two-way interpenetration of fantasy and actual events will become an essential technique. Most of the bombing sequences from *Catch-22*, Slocum's "lost child" myth in *Something Happened*, and the sentient Aristotle of *Picture This* depend upon the imagined and the real becoming coextensive realms.

Although marred by its sentimentality and its Walter Mittyish vision, "MacAdam's Log" is nevertheless an important story for Heller's development as a writer and for the reader retracing the steps of this development. A style that relies on delayed decoding of details becomes an essential Heller narrative technique. This technique presents details—the Snowden references in *Catch-22* or the "something bad is going to happen" lines in *Something Happened*—so that they become intelligible in relation to what occurs later in the narrative. Previously, as in "Nothing to Be Done," Heller would withhold information (for instance, the knowledge that Carl the bookie, not Nat, had mishandled the bet)—thereby inviting the reader to reevaluate each character's behavior in light of the new information. But, in "MacAdam's Log" and to a much larger extent in the novels, Heller makes details fully comprehensible only in relation to what is narrated later. With delayed decoding, he can also construct an intelligible narrative from a character's or narrator's confusion, as he will do in *Something Happened* when Slocum verges on nervous breakdown and his tale tumbles out in almost inchoate shards. In such narratives, the act of reading can never be simply linear; reading proceeds backwards as well as forwards, as readers must continually reinterpret details which they thought they understood. Thus, they process the story as they do life experiences, continually adjusting its interpretation to take into account new or partially understood or misunderstood information. The construction of a text with such an intricate temporal structure marks a crucial moment in Heller's maturation as a writer.

Writers and aspiring writers supply the subject for some of Heller's least successful stories, though they are stories that hold considerably more interest for what they indicate about his own attitudes—and perhaps his anxiety—about his art. These stories prefigure the questionable or divided motives of the writers and artists of his novels: Slocum, Gold, David, Rembrandt, and Yossarian. Already Heller conceives a tension between the process of production (which partakes of the commercial circumstances of the times and of the psychology of the artist) and the product (which purports to exist unsullied by worldly concerns). Like the marriage and street stories, they use variants on the quest plot, with the difference that a text serves as the goal. Women play crucial roles, either as obstructions to the act of writing or as the subject that occasions it. The writer-protagonist must differentiate among these women, but typically fails to do so. The plots are more overtly sexual than the marriage plots in that Heller entangles sexual and authorial desire. Alluring women distract the writer and deaden his creativity; by contrast, innocent women, whose innocence is signified by their victimization, awaken desire and creativity. For the writer's quest to be fulfilled, the woman must remain the object of chaste, distant love, as in the case of Dante's Beatrice. These stories embody a curious paradox: the protagonists' failure to write occasions Heller's "success," their inability to produce a text begetting his own.

In "Girl from Greenwich" (*Esquire*, June 1948), one of his slightest works, Heller uses a literary party—an event which at this point in his career he had not yet attended[22]—to tell a story of social mores, the hero's education, and the eternal triangle. Duke, a young writer, meets Arlene, an attractive young author who has just learned that her first novel will certainly be a commercial success (which, as yet, Duke can only dream about). Their conversation is interrupted when she is called away to talk to a trench-coated stranger who has just appeared at the party. When Duke and Arlene get together again, they decide to leave the party so that he can initiate her into the wonders of New York. Who should reappear when they leave the party but the man in the trench coat, who insists on talking to Arlene despite her objections. Duke intervenes, prompting the stranger to sucker punch him. Responding in anger, (the aptly named) Duke fights the man, ignoring his protests and tears that he does not want to fight. In the aftermath, he learns that the man is Arlene's husband. Despite

Arlene's protestations that they continue their walk, Duke leaves her, advising her to return to the glitz of the party.

"Girl from Greenwich" is a social comedy, and this form—with its reliance on deft, witty dialogue and social mores—takes Heller away from his own strengths. As in many such comedies, Heller centers the story on his protagonist's education. While Duke has mastered the social surface, he has not learned to see beneath its glitter. He can rescue the distressed Arlene from the mysterious visitor with a convenient lie about a phone call for her or expediently praise a fellow author's book in deference to his publisher's wishes. But he does not know how to read relationships—the most notable instance of this being his misperception of the stranger. Playing the part of the gracious man of the world, he fails to attend to the cues that would reveal the stranger's relationship to Arlene—as for instance his earnestness in talking with her. Many authors have made such an initiation story work; the difficulty for Heller in "Girl from Greenwich" lies in his handling of it. His exposition of Duke's realization of his perception is dull and flat: "All the pieces fell together in a horrible pattern, and in the center he could see the man's pale face reeling with punches as the tears streamed down his cheeks" (143). His closing line is even flatter: Duke admonishes Arlene to "[g]o back to the party and drink some more martinis" (143).

Duke is also the protagonist of the unpublished "Young Girl on a Train," which also turns upon his interest in a beautiful young woman.[23] When he has trouble writing, Duke visits his friend Charlie, who works at the train station. On this night, Duke finds an unexpected commotion because a passenger has died of a heart attack while on the train to New York. His beautiful nineteen-year-old wife has sat alone on a train with her husband without telling the conductor of his death. All the men at the rural station respond to the woman. The doctor, who diagnoses her shock, sees her as the ideal daughter. Bystanders stare as if she were a centerfold. Recognizing her helplessness and attracted by her beauty, Duke thinks that he should buy a ticket and travel with her to New York, but stops himself because the fourteen-hour journey is too long for him. He needs to write. When the train leaves, Duke tells Charlie, "I'd like to write about her, but I don't know how." In this context, writing about her would constitute a kind of violation, as Charlie seems to realize because he asks Duke not to do it. As in "Girl from Greenwich," Duke's failures as writer originate in his character.

"World Full of Great Cities" (*Nelson Algren's Own Book of Lonesome Monsters*, 1963) works discordantly, combining a sexually titillating plot with heavy-handed psychological moralizing. The plot has a ritualized movement to it: Sidney, a Western Union messenger, is called to a luxurious apartment where he has three encounters—first with the beautiful Helen, then with her writer husband, and finally with the couple together.[24] Each conversation becomes increasingly sexual, until the third reveals that the couple have brought Sidney to the apartment not to take a message, but to make love to Helen. In explaining the request, the writer says that he and his wife miss their dead son (Helen has earlier called the dead child her stepchild) and that Sidney's making love to her will make her stop missing him. Even the naive Sidney apprehends the kinkiness of this proposal, yet he reluctantly agrees to kiss her as he would one of his "fast girlfriends." Neither the kiss nor Helen's revealing nightgown excites Sidney, and their love-making quickly breaks down. With an extravagant tip, Sidney is sent back to Western Union with the injunction "to forget all about it" (19).

This plot echoes the myth of the fisher king. The present is sterile, the environment partaking of the king's, or in this case the writer's, sterility. It can be reinvigorated only with the entrance of the hero, the potent outsider. But in Heller's ironic displacement of the story, the hero is offered the king's wife rather than his daughter, hence to participate in an adultery rather than a marriage story. Since accepting the invitation also means to assume the place of the dead son, Sidney would also be acting out an Oedipal drama—a conception to which Heller will return in *Something Happened* and *God Knows*. Heller has frequently admitted his "trouble with literary language," and among other things, "World Full of Great Cities" demonstrates the aptness of his assessment. As if to balance the sexually titillating plot, Heller uses the language of psychological drama. In this vein, the husband does not simply proposition Sidney, but glosses the meaning of urban experience: " 'It's a hell of a feeling being lost in a great city,' the man said slowly. 'And the world is full of great cities.' His voice was deep and solemn. He spoke slowly, staring straight ahead, and his words seemed to emanate from a trance. 'The human mind is a great city in which a guy is always lost. He spends his lifetime groping, trying to locate himself' " (15). The ponderous rhetoric does not change the character of the story, nor make it any less prurient. In fact the opaque moralizing leaves the reader as well as Sidney to puzzle over the meaning of such insights as "[w]e're still strangers when we die . . . lost in a great city" (15). Fortunately, Heller discovers his medium in the novel and devises a vehicle to express a similar vision in "The Eternal City" chapter of *Catch-22*. In Yossarian's night journey with its surrealistic distortion, Heller combines a highly charged sexual atmosphere with a psychological exploration of urban experience.

Heller's unpublished story "Early Frost" works through issues similar to those of "World Full of Great Cities" in more mature and interesting fashion. In a plot reminiscent of F. Scott Fitzgerald's *Tender Is the Night*, "Early Frost" recounts David Everts's relationship with the Wilson family

—Paul, Miriam, and their daughter Ellie—and their friend Betty. Initially, Everts, who is a recently divorced writer, is befriended by the gregarious Paul Wilson, who is surrounded by a social circle similar to the one Fitzgerald's Dick Diver heads. As the story develops, Everts and the Wilsons' daughter Ellie are gradually thrown together until they form a friendship that is simultaneously innocent and latently sexual (a friendship reminiscent of that between Dick Diver and Rosemary Hoyt). Initially, the Wilsons strongly encourage the friendship, but eventually Miriam forbids Everts to see Ellie when he does not pay sufficient homage to her own charms. In agreeing not to see Ellie and in lying to her about the reason, he fails to live up to the advice he had previously given to her: Of her parents and their social set, Everts says, "They're afraid or insensitive, and they're unable to see what a magnificent creature a person can be if he would only learn to act without fear and shame." In the aftermath, Everts fails both Ellie and Betty, who, while sexually promiscuous, possesses a well-honed moral sensibility. Everts proposes spending the night with Betty but, remembering the jokes and comments associated with her reputation, spurns the friendship she offers. Like Duke as well as later protagonists such as Slocum, Gold, and Rembrandt, Everts fails ethically; he knows what he should do, but guides his actions by a more worldly compass.

If he had written more stories in the vein of "Early Frost," Heller might have had a career like those of Irwin Shaw and John O'Hara. The story explores contemporary social mores in a way that enables readers to endorse the story's values without questioning their own. Although it has structural flaws (for example, the conflict between Everts and Miriam Wilson is awkwardly handled), the story is well crafted; it demonstrates the plotting skills Heller has been accused of lacking. The form of "Early Frost" allows Heller to use his skill at constructing dialogue. The story also reveals an aspect of Heller's talent that does emerge in the novels: he uses nature imagistically, especially to convey emotional nuances. For example, the gray, swirling, ocean fog with which the story opens communicates to the reader what Everts does not realize about himself, his lack of orientation as man and writer. Everts himself thinks imagistically: "he watched the waves spring from the darkness, the crests boiling with hissing foam, and suddenly the fire went out, leaving him with cold exhaustion." In this case, watching the ocean enables Everts to chart the feelings he experiences after agreeing not to see Ellie anymore. And when she does make a last visit, her footsteps crash with the force of high tide in his ears. While this is not the Heller of *Catch-22*, the story signals the more conventionally successful career that he might have had and the writer's voice he might have acquired.

Essentially realistic, often imitative in style, plot, and technique, Heller's short stories are the products of a young writer who has not yet discovered his fictional voice nor realized that anti-realism—not realism—is his *métier*. Except for "Castle of Snow" and, to a lesser extent, "A Man Named Flute" and "MacAdam's Log," they reveal Heller's greatness as a writer only as pale anticipations of the novels that will follow. Yet read as they now are in light of *Catch-22* and *Something Happened*, they unfold the development of an artist—his love of language and language play, his preference for a fictional world in which the imagined and the purportedly real interpenetrate, his stylistic (to become his narrative) predisposition toward details that become fully comprehensible only in retrospect, his fondness for disclosing the comic in the serious, his valuing courage and integrity, and his criticism of middle-class conformity. They also reveal an orientation that continues in his novels: Heller's is a male world in which women all too frequently are assigned the role of Eve. And finally, the stories foretell his essential theme, his assault on reality, a reality that Heller will figure in his novels as mortality, the one irreducible element of the human situation.

When Uncle David builds his snow castle or the Captain embarks on his voyages, Heller depicts characters tilting at reality. While these characters fail in their attempts to infuse their lives with the vitality of imagination, Yossarian will succeed. Imagining Yossarian's determination "to live forever or die in the attempt" (29), Heller will succeed as well. In *Catch-22*, Heller unleashes the power of imagination, no longer constraining it as he does in Uncle David's and the Captain's failures. Like his hero Yossarian, Heller will refuse to accept the inescapable logic of Catch-22 and the certain death that it holds. While conceiving Yossarian caught by Catch-22 or King David lying near death—or while recovering from Guillain-Barré syndrome himself—Heller writes, and of this writing it might be said: his "perspective is that of a man fearing extinction, of a man for whom the very act of inscription (as opposed to any particular text he produces) assures him so long as he writes he is alive."[25] His stories document the beginnings of this imaginative life.

2

CATCH-22

LOCATING THE WOUND, TELLING THE TALE

> Myselves
> The grievers
> Grieve
> Among streets burned to timeless death
> A child of a few hours
> With its kneading mouth
> Charred on the black breast of the grave
> The mother dug, and its arms full of fires
>
> DYLAN THOMAS, "Ceremony after a Fire Raid"

FROM AVIGNON TO CATCH-22

Joseph Heller's experiences as a bombardier over Avignon during World War II were catalytic to his career as a writer. In them *Catch-22* begins. Their spark was not to his desire to be an author, for that had burned unabated since childhood. Nor did the reaction that they occasioned occur quickly, regularly, or consciously. Rather, Avignon provided in highly compressed form his essential subject, human mortality, and engaged his imagination in a way in which this subject could eventually be given expression. No *Catch-22* reader is likely to forget the result, the Snowden death scene over Avignon or the secret of his entrails: "[m]an was matter. . . . Drop him out a window and he'll fall. Set fire to him and he'll burn. Bury him and he'll rot, like other kinds of garbage" (429–30). While the evidence for the importance of Avignon is unmistakable, many pieces of the story are unknown or missing today. Heller's public accounts of these experiences come long after Avignon began to feature in his writing, and, predictably, these accounts partake of the persona of Joseph Hel-

ler, author of *Catch-22*.[1] The accounts are couched in jokes that distance
the experience from the man.

Heller's early writing furnishes some of the links between his experience and *Catch-22*, and these early fictional versions of Avignon illuminate the novel as if by ultraviolet light, defamiliarizing the familiar.
Avignon serves as the setting for two unpublished stories, "The Miracle of
Danrossane" and "Crippled Phoenix," his only short stories about the
war.[2] It also figures prominently in the planning material for *Catch-22*.[3]
The role that Avignon plays in this early writing reveals the process by
which Heller draws upon and gains control over personal experience and
reveals its "increasingly conscious transformation into writing."[4] The same
concerns occur in each version: guilt, secret knowledge, bad faith, and the
death of children (or, alternatively, of wounded innocents). Also, each account—"The Miracle of Danrossane," "Crippled Phoenix," the early manuscript, the published, and even, as I will show, the autobiographical
retelling in "'Catch-22' Revisited"—has built into it the struggle of how
to voice the story. The plots of "Danrossane" and "Crippled Phoenix" depend upon retelling what has happened at Avignon—or, more accurately,
upon working out what can and cannot be told and what can and cannot be
confronted. In an early version of the Snowden death scene, Yossarian endeavors to have the chaplain understand his own reactions to what happened, not the event itself. Finally, in *Catch-22* itself, Yossarian endeavors
to unlock the significance of Snowden's dying words and, in so doing, to
plumb the meaning of death itself. As in the previous versions, Yossarian's understanding hinges upon telling the story of what happened, albeit
to himself. In each story of Avignon, Heller makes the telling as important
as what is told, as if the repeated tellings will help the author himself to
understand what happened there.

Heller flew two missions to Avignon, just as there are two missions in
the novel itself. Before the Avignon mission, he had, by his own account,
romanticized war: "I wanted action, not security. I wanted a sky full of
dogfights, daredevils and billowing parachutes. I was twenty-one years
old. I was dumb" ("'Catch-22' Revisited," 51). Avignon shatters this.
"*There* was the war, in Avignon, not in Rome or Île Rousse or Poggibonsi
or even Ferrara" ("'Catch-22' Revisited," 141).[5] On the August 8, 1944,
mission to bomb a railroad bridge, Heller saw a plane shot down for the
first time. As a bombardier on one of the lead planes which had been assigned to drop metallic paper to disrupt the radar for the antiaircraft guns,
Heller could look back on what was happening to the rest of the squadron.
He saw a plane on fire go into an uncontrollable spin and crash. Parachutes billowed and opened: he would later learn that three men had gotten out, while three others were killed in the crash. One of the three
survivors was found by members of the Avignon underground, hidden and

eventually smuggled back across enemy lines. This mission provides the basis for the "Crippled Phoenix" and, presumably, the inspiration for the survivor's guilt that its protagonist Dan Cramer experiences.

On August 15, Heller's squadron returned to Avignon to bomb another railroad bridge over the Rhone, and this mission would later provide the model for the Snowden death scene. For both Heller and Yossarian, it was their thirty-seventh mission. In notes Heller made about the mission in 1966, he records: "Man wounded in leg. Wohlstein and Moon killed."[6] According to Heller, the details from the novel correspond "perhaps ninety percent to what I did experience. I did have a co-pilot go berserk and grab the controls. The earphones did pull out. I did think I was dying for what seemed like thirty minutes but was actually three-hundredths of a second. When I did plug my earphones in, there was a guy sobbing on the intercom, 'Help the bombardier, but the gunner was only shot in the leg.'"[7] In recounting the experience, Heller confines the correspondences between the actual and the novelistic Avignon missions to "physical details" and denies any similarity between Yossarian's emotional reactions and his own.[8]

His own explanation as well as his fictional use of Avignon indicate that more than physical details are at play. Whether factual or fictional, each account that Heller gives of Avignon has an Ur-plot that turns upon an intense experience of personal mortality. In answering interviewers' questions about his own experience, he repeatedly dwells on his sensation that he had died over Avignon. He remembers pressing the talk button of his headset, hearing nothing, and thinking he was already dead. He stresses his sense of distorted time—of events which unfolded in microseconds seeming to last much longer.[9] His change of habits after this Avignon mission also testifies to its effects; from then on, he carried a personal first-aid kit and took a vow never to fly once his combat missions were over (a vow he kept until 1960, when a twenty-four hour train ride convinced him to reassess the dangers of flying).[10] The comic "'Catch-22' Revisited" retelling sheds more light on Heller's reactions in that he makes himself, not the wounded airman, the victim. "I went to the hospital the next day. He looked fine. They had given him blood, and he was going to be all right. But I was in terrible shape, and I had twenty-three more missions to fly."[11] Of course, the wound becomes mortal in *Catch-22*, or as Heller laconically describes the change: "He was shot through the leg. . . . But I added to it and had him shot in the middle."[12]

"The Miracle of Danrossane" and "Crippled Phoenix" mark the artistic steps by which the wound gets relocated. Together with the early draft of the Snowden death scene, and *Catch-22* itself, the stories offer a complex range of reactions to death: denial, confusion, immersion, and understanding. While all of these reactions figure in each work, one predominates in each, as if designating stages in Heller's thinking, from denial in "The Miracle of Danrossane" to understanding in *Catch-22*. As this progression indicates, the stories and manuscript draft of the death scene provided the vehicle by which Heller worked out his masterplot and determined that death could serve as thrust and destination for his narratives. In the stories, the journey toward this death is spatial and temporal, a visit to Avignon in "Danrossane" and a return to it in "Crippled Phoenix." In *Catch-22* and the novels that follow, the journey becomes psychological and emotional, one culminating in a death that surfaces, like Snowden's does, as if from the protagonist's subconscious.

"The Miracle of Danrossane," the slighter of the two unpublished war stories, recounts a correspondent's visit to the village outside Avignon where his father was born. Its plot turns upon a father denying his sons' deaths. The correspondent is intrigued by the name of the inn in which he stays, L'Auberge des Sept Fils. While Durland, the innkeeper, will not talk about the name, the mayor will and tells Durland's story—which provides the principal plot of "Danrossane." Even though Durland had been a Nazi collaborator during the war, his seven sons had been killed by the Nazis as a reprisal for the death of two of their soldiers. Durland himself bears responsibility for their deaths, because he neglected to protect them. The story is irony-laden: the Nazis' random selection of reprisal victims results in the deaths of all seven of Durland's sons (hence the darkly ironic title); one of Durland's sons had been involved in killing the Nazi soldiers as revenge for the rape of a village girl by the soldiers; one of the other killers goes free even though he volunteers to turn himself over to the Nazis and despite the fact that the mayor informs on him. Durland himself never comes to terms with his sons' deaths; in fact, he tells the correspondent that they are out working in the fields.

In this earliest Avignon story, Heller announces the already listed concerns that characterize his subsequent accounts as well as his novels: guilt, secret knowledge, bad faith, and most crucially the death of children. The underlying structure of this story has the primitive, evocative force of a folktale. A young man, who is symbolically looking for his father and thus for his own origins, finds a surrogate whose act of bad faith has caused the death of his sons. Refusing to acknowledge their deaths or his own complicity in them, the father lives "respectably" in a house memorializing the dead sons. When the young man gains the father's secret knowledge, he returns from where he came and, as artist, transforms it into story. Thus conceived, the story the reader has just read originates in guilty, concealed knowledge—a conception which aligns it with such myths as those of Prometheus and the Garden of Eden. The architecture of "Danrossane," particularly the crucial element of the sons' deaths, is striking for the way it anticipates the design of Heller's novels.

Although unpublished, "Crippled Phoenix" marks another step on Heller's journey toward *Catch-22*. Like the novel, it features death, guilt-caused confusion, and a protagonist who has been wounded in the leg. Evidently, Heller spent considerable time on the story, for there are three versions of it in the Brandeis University Library Heller collection and he tried placing it with different literary agents. Possessing clear affinities with *Catch-22* as well as with *Something Happened*, "Crippled Phoenix" tells a double story of guilty conscience: that of Dan Cramer, an American airman who feels guilty for surviving the crash in which his crew died, and of Morain, a French peasant who aided Cramer's escape after the crash. Cramer has returned to Avignon to see Morain, to whom he feels grateful for hiding him and about whom he feels guilty because Morain's son had been killed when a bombardier with only one mission left to fly dropped his bombs too early.[13] Cramer has another reason for his guilt in that he has been unfaithful to his wife during a recent stay in London, and, even in bed with her in Avignon, he finds his mind wandering back to Luciana, a wartime liaison in Rome.[14] More crucially to the action of the story, he fails to come to terms with this guilt. First, although Cramer goes to see Morain with the intention "of help[ing] him in some way," he cannot provide the support that Morain wants—comfort for his own wartime guilt. Morain confesses to Cramer that he was afraid his daughter would be taken away to a Nazi work camp and so he forced her to become the mistress of a German official (which ruins her life and that of her child, born of the relationship). Although Morain explicitly asks him to visit again, Cramer, even after agreeing to, cannot bring himself to do so. Second, he fails to come to terms with his wife, although sharing some of the details of the crash with her offers the chance for reconciliation. Convinced that she is too superficial to understand his feelings, especially about the war, he allows her to believe that their marital difficulties have been reconciled, while despising her.

Significantly, Cramer, who stands in Yossarian's position as participant in the events of the past, cannot fully disclose his story and thus remains isolated and tormented.[15] In a symbolically resonant moment, Heller communicates the moral wilderness that Cramer has brought himself into with his inability to confront his guilt; he also conveys the way in which Cramer has deliberately estranged himself from his wife: "Suddenly, though, [Cramer] was frightened. The forest was immediately before them [his guide, his wife, and himself], and he realized that Katherine belonged only on the fringe of his emotions, and he knew that everything might still be all right if he kept her there. But they were already between the trees." The passage forecasts the role that Avignon will play in *Catch-22* (as well as anticipating Slocum's marriage in *Something Happened*). It locates the wilderness within the self, that wilderness which, as Conrad demonstrates in *Heart of Darkness*, is the territory of the modern condition. While the same elements—dead children, secret knowledge, guilt, and bad faith—constitute the story, Heller relocates them. In "Danrossane," Durland's history is part of public discourse, unknown only to the correspondent, the outsider. In "Crippled Phoenix," Cramer and Morain's past is secret, disclosed in the vain hope of confessional relief. Both disclosures fail because they look to others for relief of their own inner guilt: Morain to Cramer when the injured party is his daughter and Cramer to his wife when he cannot accept his own actions. The guilty knowledge of what happened at Avignon isolates and estranges, at least until what happened there can be fully confronted and related. This is what *Catch-22* is about.

An early manuscript draft of the Snowden scene documents his evolving conception of Avignon and dramatizes the imperative for reporting what happened there. Yossarian not only sees death but also immerses himself in it.

> "Dirty hands," Yossarian said. "Yesterday they touched a dead man's flesh." The chaplain attempts to comfort him. "A dead man's private parts. I spoke to Doc Daneeker [the original name for Doc Daneeka]. Probably his lungs, his pancreas, his liver, his stomach, and some canned tomatoes that he had for breakfast. I hate canned tomatoes." The chaplain tries again. "But you don't understand. I enjoyed it. I actually enjoyed touching the graying flesh, the clotting blood. I actually enjoyed touching his lungs, his pancreas, his liver, his stomach and some canned tomatoes from his breakfast, even though I hate canned tomatoes. I made excuses to myself to touch every shriveling shred." The chaplain tries again. "But even that's not the worst of it. I rubbed blood all over myself. And do you know why I rubbed blood all over myself? To impress people. To impress those God damned Red Cross biddies with the smiles and doughnuts . . . and by God, it impressed, even Doc Daneeker, who broke down and gave me some codeine and told me about Cathcart and a tour of duty."[16]

There are many noteworthy differences between this early version and the published one. Snowden's mortal wound is open, displaying what Heller calls in the novel "God's plenty" (429). Yossarian is compelled to touch the viscera, then compelled to relate his enjoyment of doing so to the chaplain. He has previously told Doc Daneeker about this. In *Catch-22*, Yossarian tells no one, although his recollections have the quality of telling the story to himself. The time works differently as well. In the manuscript, the experience, only a day old, has the immediacy of the here and now, while in the novel version it emerges as though from Yossarian's subconscious. In *Catch-22*, the intensity of Yossarian's remembrance erupts into the present: "liver, lungs, kidneys, ribs, stomach and bits of

. . . stewed tomatoes" (429). The same message is embedded in both—
man is matter—but in the manuscript Yossarian, and perhaps Heller, has
not yet apprehended its significance.

The early version is at the same time more public and more private
than the Avignon of the published *Catch-22*. Heller's appropriation of the
dirty hands motif from *Macbeth* dissociates this version from himself,
connecting it to a literary past rather than a personal one.[17] Also, having
Yossarian report the story, Heller publicizes Avignon in a way that third-
person narration would not. This recounting of Avignon proclaims Yossarian's guilty consciousness, whereas the novel displaces it into the tree-
of-life episode, in which Yossarian's nakedness reveals his feelings of
guilt (his guilt likewise triggered by Snowden's blood). Simultaneously,
this early version is more private, more evocative of the Heller who experienced Avignon and of the author who repeatedly sets key scenes there.
The confessional quality of the scene with Yossarian trying to make the
chaplain understand what he has done directs attention to the personal basis of the scene. Finally, Yossarian's revelation that, on one level, he enjoyed the experience points to the complexity of Heller's own experience
over Avignon. This early version illustrates the attraction of the horrifying
—an attraction that he seems compelled to specify.

Significantly, before the idea for *Catch-22* came to him, Heller had
virtually given up writing. Of the time between the short stories and the
novel, Heller later said, "I wanted to write something that was very good
and I had nothing good to write. So I wrote nothing."[18] Out of the silence
—a silence that he partially filled with reading—came a new method of
writing, anti-realist and comic in orientation. Reading "the comic novels
of Evelyn Waugh and Céline's *Journey to the End of the Night*, and
Nathaniel West's *Miss Lonelyhearts*, and I remember Nabokov's *Laughter
in the Dark* particularly," Heller says, "I was comprehending for the first
time that there were different ways to tell a story, and the methods these
people used were much more compatible with my own technical ability
. . . with my own imagination."[19] The realization that there are many different ways to tell a story is what Heller's evolving use of Avignon documents.[20] The discovery was long in coming, though, for he did not publish
Catch-22 until 1961, sixteen years after the publication of his first story.
By then he was thirty-eight, the same age as George Eliot and Willa
Cather when they published their first novels.[21]

Heller's key discovery involves discourse, not story, the how of narrative rather than the what. His Avignon short stories (as did most of his
other short stories) have linear plots that unfold on a single narrative level.
In each, characters journey to Avignon (or nearby Danrossane) to learn
something from the past. Heller's narrative method is straightforward, the
plots proceeding forward until access is gained to characters who hold and

will disclose crucial, secret knowledge from the past. In *Catch-22*, Heller makes discourse—the narrative act itself—part of the story as well as the means of its transmission. The Avignon mission on which Snowden dies can illustrate this. As is well-known, Heller's narrator distributes references to the mission throughout the novel; sometimes cryptically, as in the first reference: "Where are the Snowdens of yesteryear?" (35); sometimes explicitly, as in: "the way Snowden had frozen to death after spilling his secret to Yossarian in the back of the plane" (165). In effect, the narrator dissects the Avignon plot as if he were performing a narrative autopsy on Snowden. This creates a much richer narrative progression than that of the Avignon stories, one that depends upon discourse—the vertical narrative axis—as well as upon story—its horizontal axis.[22] Three effects follow from this: first, the meaning of Snowden's secret depends upon the interplay between narrative levels and involves the contrast of tragic and comic perspectives; second, Heller uses the synthetic dimension of narrative to complicate his story;[23] and third, he can make the text the verbal embodiment of Snowden's secret, which is that mortality exists in the conjunction of mind and matter.

Heller's first reference to Avignon typifies the way that he takes advantage of the interplay between the narrative levels. Yossarian's question about the Snowdens of yesteryear has complementary roles in the novel's story and discourse, in each case providing the pathway to Snowden and to the secret of his entrails. For Yossarian, it speaks to both an actual and a linguistic quest. Like the protagonist of the Avignon stories, Yossarian must unlock a secret from the past, a secret of which Snowden is the embodiment (potentially, this knowledge is already available to him because he has already ministered to the dying Snowden). But the question is also about language as well as about history, as becomes clear when Yossarian translates it into French: *"Où sont les Neigedens d'antan?"* (35). Heller underscores the seriousness of this linguistic dimension with the narrator's comment about Yossarian's willingness "to pursue [the corporal of whom he asked his question] through all the words in the world" (35). The narrator knows the answer to Yossarian's question, but instead of relating it explains to the narrative audience why the question is so upsetting. But in doing so, the narrator also makes it part of another narrative, that of the Fall. "Group Headquarters was alarmed, for there was no telling what people might find out once they felt free to ask whatever questions they wanted to" (35). At this moment, the story is simultaneously proceeding on different narrative planes, its comedy, in part, stemming from the incongruity that results.[24] Heller's discourse takes Yossarian's question to a higher level where Group Headquarters' response echoes the fears of the God of Genesis, who worries that Adam and Eve, possessing the knowledge of good and evil, may now be tempted to eat from the tree of life. The mythic echoes refigure Yossarian's Avignon experience as fall, a point made more forcefully in the subsequent tree-of-life scene.

The reference to "the secret Snowden had spilled to Yossarian" exemplifies the synthetic narrative progression of *Catch-22*, the progression implied by the novel's language. The episode advances the plot: for Yossarian, being in the hospital is better than flying over Avignon with Snowden dying (165). As the narrator formulates the matter, it is not just because the hospital is safer, protecting Yossarian from war, but also because "They [people] couldn't dominate Death inside the hospital, but they certainly made her behave" (164). Death has become a character and its plot is the Eliza Doolittle story: "They had taught her manners. They couldn't keep Death out, but while she was in she had to act like a lady" (164). With this conception, Yossarian and the narrator seek to control death. Of course, their plotting undoes them. In Heller's mordant novel-long joke, death is no lady, though this metaphor does, for Heller, speak to its nature.[25] As with the many euphemisms for death, this reference makes death seem familiar, comfortable, and acceptable. As novelist, Heller knows better, representing death as violent, certain, and inevitable; and yet, he rages against its sway. In *Catch-22*, he finds a form to express his outrage, the novel's discourse being its expression, working to accomplish what Yossarian and the narrator cannot.

One of Heller's authorial idiosyncrasies bears on the issue of how to tell a story. For each of his novels, Heller has found it necessary to recount when and how the idea for the novel came to him. The pattern of these accounts is always the same. As he describes it, his imagination responds to a few genetic lines, the lines simultaneously spawning and shaping the conception of the novel that results. Of the genesis of *Catch-22*, he says:

> I was lying in bed in my four-room apartment on the West Side when suddenly this line came to me: "It was love at first sight. The first time he saw the chaplain, Someone fell in love with him." I didn't have the name Yossarian. The chaplain wasn't necessarily an army chaplain— he could have been a *prison* chaplain. But as soon as the opening sentence was available, the book began to evolve clearly in my mind —even most of the particulars . . . the tone, the form, many of the characters, including some I eventually couldn't use. All this took place within an hour and a half. It got me so excited that I did what the cliché says you're supposed to do: I jumped out of bed and paced the floor. That morning I went to my job at the advertising agency and wrote out the first chapter longhand.[26]

It does not matter if this account is accurate or not. In fact, given the similarities among the accounts for the beginnings of his novels, the chances are Heller is mythologizing the process. What is significant is the pattern that his explanations take—the sense that the story presents itself as embedded in the originary lines. His "imagination"—a key Heller term whenever he talks about his creative process—is the recipient of the story contained in the lines; it fleshes out possibilities that are already there. "The novel comes to me as it's written. I did not sit down to write a novel about World War II, and I didn't decide to put it in the third person rather than the first person. . . . The idea occurs to me as a novel, rather than as a subject, and the novel already encompasses a point of view, a tempo, a voice."[27] This explanation intimates that all his novels are twice-told—Heller's imagination responding to a story that already exists and then he, as novelist, incarnating it with his words and retelling it for his readers.

Catch-22 exhibits the artistic control that Heller gained over his inspiration (for an illustration of this control, see Heller's overview of the novel in Appendix B), and this is what I propose to trace in the rest of the chapter. In order to do so, I will unscramble the novel's chronology to reveal the nature of Yossarian's initiation and to explicate his war with mortality: Yossarian's vow "to live forever or die in the attempt" designates both the lesson to be learned and the nature of the campaign. To subject the novel's discourse to a similar examination is to learn that its author participates in Yossarian's campaign. Heller's stylistic, comic, and narrative methods defuse death with ridiculing laughter. Exploring these elements one discovers that the story of *Catch-22* is unfinished; Heller's essay, "'Catch-22' Revisited," confirms that it—what he calls "my war"—still strains toward completion. So does *Closing Time*, Heller's sequel to *Catch-22*. Characterizing the nature of literary texts, Edward Said puts the matter this way: "the text is a multidimensional structure extending from the beginning to the end of the writer's career. A text is the source and aim of a man's desire to be an author, it is the form of his attempts, it contains the elements of his coherence, and in a whole range of complex and differing ways it incarnates the pressures upon the writer of his psychology, his time, his society. The unity between career and text, then, is a unity between an intelligible pattern of events and for the most part their increasingly conscious transformation into writing."[28] *Catch-22* offers testimony to Heller's increasing consciousness.

■

Yossarian's Promethean Spirit and Heller's Initiation Story

Yossarian defines the meaning of his story when he vows "to live forever or die in the attempt" (29). Ironically, a copy editor wanted to excise the line, indicating that not all readers take Yossarian's intentions as seriously as Heller himself does.[29] At root *Catch-22* recounts Yossarian-cum-Heller's attempt to overcome death. Within the novel, death is a worthy opponent for it is omnipresent, and by novel's end most of its characters have died.[30] The proximate cause of the novel's extreme mortality rate is not so much the war as it is the Cathcarts, Milos, and Peckems of the world, who sacrifice others' lives to secure their own advancement. Another source of mortality concerns Yossarian and by extension Heller equally, but it lies within the self rather than without. Yossarian repeatedly experiences the immanence of death: "There were lymph glands that might do him in. There were kidneys, nerve sheaths and corpuscles. There were tumors of the brain" (171). To Yossarian's fertile imagination, sinister forces that could kill him abound, and "each day [becomes] another dangerous mission against mortality" (174). In this context, the use of the word "mission" resonates for it offers a counterbalance to the operative definition of the novel—combat bombing runs. Most simply, Yossarian's mission in *Catch-22* is to live.

Yossarian's vow "to live forever" calls attention to the mythic dimension of *Catch-22*, to the way in which Heller appropriates the story of the quest for eternal life. Yossarian's vow recalls quests for immortality as different as those of Gilgamesh, Christ, and most especially for the purposes of my argument, Prometheus. Yossarian echoes Prometheus's cry of defiance to Zeus: "my mind remains immortal and unsubdued."[31] By examining Prometheus's defiance more closely, I will illuminate the cast of mind that underlies Yossarian's and chart Heller's Promethean logic. Prometheus's cry proclaims human defiance of the omnipotent power of the universe. Chained to a rock and threatened with an eagle that "will fly to you every day and will tear the flesh of your body into rags, feasting on your liver and gnawing it black," Prometheus asserts that he possesses inner immortality—the power of the free mind to circumvent even its own death. As David Leeming argues in his interpretation of the myth, Prometheus's self-identification opens the way to immortality.[32] The Promethean hero must chart the inner terrain of the self, for the path to immortality resides within rather than without.

There are numerous Promethean echoes in *Catch-22*.[33] The most obvious are all the liver references and the connection the text makes between the liver and mortality, a connection linguistically reinforced by the organ's name. Obviously, there is Yossarian's recurring liver ailment or, more ominously, Kid Sampson's liver, which "might come washing right up" (332) after he was chopped into pieces by McWatt's plane. Similarly, Snowden's liver is the first organ that slides out when Yossarian exposes his wound, and the two doctors who want to do a liver operation on Yossarian want to "jab [their] thumbs down inside his wound and gouge it" (421). In a comic vein, there are Chief Halfoat's complaints that Doc Daneeka is insulting his liver and Captain Black's curse, "Eat your livers, you bastards" (110)—the latter a turn on Aeschylus's line about the eagle devouring Prometheus's liver until it turns black. By the novel's end, Yossarian's liver ailment has become a Promethean malady, which is appropriate because within the novel he causes a Promethean problem. As Colonel Korn tells Yossarian, referring to the way his refusal to fly has affected the other men in the squadron: "you've given them hope, and they're unhappy" (411). But of course, Zeus similarly accuses Prometheus of giving humans "blind hopefulness" with his gift of fire. And most tellingly, Prometheus's legacy is also Yossarian's—"I caused men no longer to foresee their death" (28).

Although the novel's scrambled chronology obscures the sequence of events in Yossarian's life, his story has the distinct pattern of an initiation story: pre-knowledge innocence, the acquisition of knowledge that destroys the innocence and psychically wounds the self, and the incorporation of knowledge that enables one to live.[34] In the novel, the pre-knowledge stage is represented by the training camp episodes and early missions before Colonel Cathcart assumes command. The acquisition stage occurs mainly in the five key bombing missions—Ferrara, Bologna, Avignon, Parma/Leghorn, and La Spezia. The incorporation stage begins with Yossarian's refusal to fly more missions (chapter 38) and continues to the end of the novel.[35] Appropriately, the crucial episode in Yossarian's initiation occurs in the underworld where, in the tradition of the mythic hero, he finds the secret to life/eternal life. Throughout his initiation, Yossarian reexamines himself, affirming a power of self that is anchored in the mind and positing an "eternal life," albeit one residing within the self.

By distorting the chronology of Yossarian's experience, Heller obscures, even seemingly undermines, the progress that an initiation story insists upon and casts its lessons into doubt. He has several reasons for this.[36] First, he wants to create for the authorial reader an experience analogous to that undergone by Yossarian, a progression from confusion and doubt to mature knowing. Second, having read and admired Céline's *Journey to the End of the Night*, he found a model for articulating his vision of war. Third, Heller prefers retrospective narration, in which events are not understood as experienced, but as remembered (a technique which I will examine in detail in connection with *God Knows*). Yossarian comes to terms with Snowden's death in this way and, thanks to Heller's chronological distortion, the reader does as well. I will say more about the authorial reader's experience later in this chapter, when I explore style and narrative sequence, but now I want to straighten out the novel's chronology to reveal the pattern of Yossarian's initiation.[37] Avignon, however, will be explored as the climax of Yossarian's experience, for its chronological displacement is the key to his initiation.

The pre-knowledge stage contains the motifs of the novel as a whole, though Heller handles these episodes with a much lighter comic touch than he uses in the later events. Appropriately, the earliest episode occurs in the hospital at Lowery Field where, thanks to a sympathetic doctor, Yossarian discovers the power of his liver ailment (chapter 18). Fondly remembering the "halcyon fourteen-day quarantine" (179), he will repeatedly return to the hospital to escape the war and recover the calm of his first visit. An artificial world, the hospital is largely removed from external reality. As the doctor who knows that Yossarian is faking his liver ailment tells him, "We're all in this business of illusion together" (181). Not that reality cannot intrude. Giuseppe, the soldier who saw everything twice, dies, and Yossarian experiences a vicarious death when he is forced to impersonate Giuseppe for his visiting parents. While the premise of Yossarian's playing the part of Giuseppe for his parents is absurd and the humor of the exchange of identity slapstick, Heller uses the episode to reinforce his theme.[38] " 'It's not Giuseppe, Ma. It's Yossarian.' 'What difference does it make?' the mother answered in the same mourning tone, without looking up. " *'He's dying'* " (184, emphasis added). Indeed, in the terms of the novel, all the characters, including Yossarian, are dying even before they go to war. Listening to Giuseppe's father, Yossarian gains his first lesson in mortality and gets his mission for the novel: "[T]ell Him it ain't right for people to die when they're young" (184). Like Prometheus, who defies Zeus to save humans "from total death," Yossarian must save humans from death by teaching them how to live.[39] Now that Yossarian has his antagonist, death, he is ready for the second stage of his initiation.

In the five missions that constitute the acquisition stage, Yossarian learns about himself, death, and the army that condemns men to die. Viewed chronologically, the five missions give Yossarian's career within the novel the shape of a parabola—an intensification of Yossarian's apprehension of death, heightened to a climax, followed by its diminution. Appropriately, the apex of the parabolic curve is Avignon, the mission on which Snowden is killed. In the novel's scrambled chronology, however, Avignon is also the last mission to be narrated. The delayed narration makes the center of the sequence and, for most of the novel, the center of experience seem empty. With the exception of La Spezia, which serves as a coda to the sequence, each episode follows a similar pattern. Each mission is marred by human error, usually by Aarfy getting lost, and results in someone being killed. Each time Yossarian is touched by the death until he comes to know its reality. Eventually, the knowledge of death convinces Yossarian that in order to live he must abandon public duty and dedicate himself to personal survival.

Ferrara, the first mission, sets up the workings of the sequence. The episode is simple. On the flight to Ferrara, Aarfy gets lost, which necessitates Yossarian's leading the planes on a second pass to bomb the bridge successfully. On the second pass, Kraft's plane is shot down. The effects the mission has on Yossarian, however, are complex. Kraft's death crystallizes Yossarian's awareness of the "vile, excruciating dilemma of duty and damnation" (136). Duty demanded that, as lead bombardier, Yossarian take the squadron on a second pass over the target, yet the result is private damnation, for he feels responsible for Kraft's death. Yossarian compounds his feelings of ambiguity when he suggests to Cathcart that he should get a medal for Ferrara so that Cathcart will not have his service record blackened by the lost plane. In his tangled reactions to the death, Yossarian sometimes acknowledges the guilt he feels and other times admits that he has forgotten the death entirely. Yossarian cannot forget, however, "the incessant *cachung! cachung! cachung!* of the flak" (135) or the metal fragments from Kraft's aircraft raining down on his own plane. Heller's charged prose reproduces the way the crash works in Yossarian's consciousness. Sometimes remembered, sometimes forgotten, Ferrara becomes a permanent locus of fear in Yossarian's consciousness.

Bologna, the second mission, provides an even more intense experience of mortality, as even before they fly the men expect to die there. From the beginning the mission has a surrealistic tone. The fear-charged atmosphere starts when Sergeant Knight goes to get an extra flak jacket. Again and again rain delays the mission, with Heller using the rain, much as Hemingway did in *A Farewell to Arms*, to symbolize the hopeless atmosphere of war. When the rain stops Yossarian arranges his own delays, first by having Corporal Snark put soap in the mashed potatoes, thereby giving all the flyers diarrhea, later by moving the bomb line on the unit map so that it looks like the Allies have captured Bologna. The latter ploy creates a series of episodes from General Peckem's getting a medal for capturing Bologna (but only after it is certain that it has not been captured) to Major ———— de Coverley's disappearance when, as always, he goes to have his picture taken with the liberating forces. When the mission is finally flown, Yossarian arranges a personal delay by pulling the intercom wires on the plane and persuading Kid Sampson to turn back because of the intercom malfunction. This mission turns out to be a milk run, and this, of course, is the prelude to the catastrophic second run to Bologna.

From the first reference to Bologna, Heller defines it as a mission into the land of death, as taking place in a time when "the moldy odor of mortality hung wet in the air" (107). Appropriately, just when Yossarian thinks that he has escaped the mission, he finds death, but in another form, in the mushrooms—those "lifeless stalks of flesh, sprouting in . . . necrotic profusion" (142). The mushroom scene represents the way in which death has become a part of Yossarian's mental landscape; his imagination and his guilt animate the mushrooms so that he expects to find them in "sightless pursuit" (142). Similarly, his haunted imagination colors his sensations over Bologna, transforming the flak into "mushrooming clusters" (145). Seeing the light from Aarfy's pipe, he thinks that the plane is on fire, and to him, Aarfy's bloated body seems to block the escape passage like one of those necrotic mushrooms. In what Yossarian calls a "waterlogged unreality" (149), the scene unfolds as in a surrealistic dream: shreds of Aarfy's maps whirl in the air after the plane is hit by flak. Aarfy responds to the confusion with lunatic happiness, and Yossarian suffers in actuality his nightmare version of the mission to Bologna.

Although Avignon is the center of Yossarian's experience and the approximate chronological center of the novel, it has an indefinite status in the narrative, knowable only by its effects until Heller finally describes Snowden's death at novel's end. Cryptic markers signal the importance of the mission: references to the mission on which "Yossarian lost his nerve" (229) and the refrain-like line, "Where are the Snowdens of yesteryear?" (35). Neither Yossarian nor a first-time reader understands the event. Even in recollection, Yossarian feels "inarticulate and enfeebled" (388) in response to Snowden's death. Both reactions are appropriate, because Yossarian misperceived the event from beginning to end. He confidently treated Snowden's leg wound, without realizing the mortal wound was in the chest; he heard Snowden's repeated cry, "I'm cold," without comprehending its significance; and he misapprehends the scene because he does not understand mortality—neither the dying Snowden's nor his own. To know the shape of mortality, Yossarian will first have to know himself. As is his method, Heller handles both Yossarian's acquisition of self-knowledge and the narration of the actual Avignon experience retrospectively. Taking a cue from Heller, I will return to consider what Yossarian learns from Avignon after looking at the missions that follow it.

As the center of Yossarian's experience, Avignon marks the turning point of the novel. Heller defines the nature of the turn in a parodic inversion of the Adam and Eve story in which Yossarian tries to return to the Garden of Eden.[40] Watching Snowden's funeral, Yossarian stands naked in a "tree of life . . . and of knowledge of good and evil" (257). Milo, who plays the part of the serpent, climbs the tree to entice Yossarian into eating his chocolate-covered Egyptian cotton and thus into joining the syndicate. Refusing to wear clothes, Yossarian insists upon his Adamic innocence. In his own imagination, he can even taste Milo's cotton without losing his virtue and certainly without becoming part of the syndicate. However, Yossarian pays a price for this belief in his innocence. He remains detached from Snowden's funeral, the very scene that he tries to observe and understand. While Yossarian thinks that he "can see everything" (256) from the tree of knowledge, he "sees" the funeral as only a "fustian charade" (258). The pun on fustian is Heller's, not Yossarian's; Yossarian can recognize the funeral bombast, but not the fabric that obscures his vision. It goes without saying that in the world of *Catch-22* one cannot return to the Garden. Removing his clothes neither cleanses Snowden's blood from Yossarian's consciousness nor allows him to retreat from the knowledge of death. As in all quest stories, the path of life leads through the land of death. So in returning to the tree of life, Yossarian has ironically gone the wrong way.

The next two missions, those to Leghorn and La Spezia, enable Yossarian to find his orientation. Unlike the earlier missions, Leghorn occurs in the narrative present. The pattern of the other missions still obtains, though: Aarfy has misnavigated again (the squadron is supposed to be on a milk run over Parma); in the confusion, Yossarian again misperceives the scene; and death again intrudes. What Yossarian misapprehends this time is his own wounding. At first, he thinks that his leg has fallen asleep, not that he has been hit by flak. Discovering the wound, he mislocates it, believing that he has been hit in the groin. For both Yossarian and Heller, the wound occasions an experiential awareness of personal mortality. Yossarian's belief that he has been wounded in the groin has symbolic resonance, signaling that his wound is in fact life-denying. Yossarian's assumption that "he [is] dying, and no one [takes] notice" (284) distracts him from what he should understand, just as he was earlier distracted by Snowden's leg wound. Of course, he is dying; Giuseppe's mother told him that long ago (and she took notice). But Yossarian's leg wound is neither cause nor symptom of his mortality. The intimations of mortality that it occasions, however, enable Yossarian to begin to find his orientation. This new sense of direction can be acted upon only when Yossarian learns how to decode the secret of the dying Snowden's entrails.

The last mission, the one to La Spezia, provides the impetus for Yossarian to act. The mission itself is described in a single paragraph. Dobbs, the chronically inept pilot, tries to take evasive action to avoid flak, but in doing so collides with Nately's plane, killing everyone on both aircraft. The spartan account of the mission is set in relief by the extended account of Milo's conversation with Cathcart about the number of missions he has flown (six if one counts Parma, which Milo's planes bomb for the Germans, and Orvieto, which he arranged but did not fly). In Heller's black comic method, what is not narrated in the scene is as important as what is narrated. Of Yossarian's role in the attack on the La Spezia we learn nothing. We see him only indirectly, through the chaplain's reactions to finding him alive. The chaplain's "immense joy" turns to "unbearable horror" when he notices "Yossarian's vivid, beaten, grimy look of deep, drugged despair" (371). Reading Yossarian's visage, the chaplain realizes that Nately is dead. The death has undone Yossarian as well as Nately. After La Spezia, Yossarian acts. Marching backwards with a gun at his hip, he refuses to fly any more missions. In this gesture of defiance, he begins to incorporate the knowledge he has acquired and in "reverse" begins to make the knowledge of death his own.

The incorporation stage of Yossarian's initiating journey takes him through "The Eternal City," his aborted deal with Cathcart and Korn, and his remembrance of Snowden's death. In this stage, Yossarian learns how to overcome death and therefore how to live. As Heller's oxymoronic image of Yossarian's marching backwards indicates, this stage is both progressive and regressive. Heller's shift to chronological narration and insistence that Yossarian is "running *to* [his responsibilities]" (440) emphasize the progressivity of Yossarian's experience—the maturation of Yossarian's understanding of death and of his ethical sensitivity. Simultaneously, the images of flight (to Rome and later Sweden), of return (to the whore's apartment), and of remembrance (of the many dead, but especially of Snowden) reveal the regressive character of Yossarian's experience. This dual directionality is appropriate because simple progression would propel Yossarian toward death and neither Yossarian nor Heller can accept that. But regression cannot of itself provide an escape from death either, as Yossarian's return to the tree of life demonstrated. In order to live, Yossarian must go in both directions—as does Heller's narrative, with its scrambled chronology and delayed decoding.

In his AWOL flight to Rome, the "Eternal City," Yossarian takes his first steps toward finding life. As Minna Doskow has shown, his journey works as a traditional night journey through the land of death.[41] It is a death journey in a number of senses: first, Yossarian remembers many of his dead compatriots; second, he learns about the death of the old man, the only natural death in the novel; third, he sees a whole series of dead and dying people, culminating in the maid whom Aarfy rapes and kills; and finally, he consciously explores his own mortality. As a critical moment in the chapter, the old man's death compels Yossarian to acknowledge death in a way that he never has before. By accepting the reality of the old man's death, Yossarian gains new insight—that "once again the old man had marched along with the majority" (399). Heller's turn on the marching image indicates that Yossarian's effort to escape death by marching backwards will necessarily fail. In dying, the old man—the Teiresias figure of *Catch-22*—holds a wisdom that Yossarian has refused to share.[42] Only after this death can Yossarian enter "the dark, tomblike street" (402) and traverse the Dantean landscape of the "Eternal City" chapter. There is no need to catalog all the deaths that Yossarian sees, nor to recount all the violence that he internalizes in his wanderings. In the novel's grim logic, the night journey inexorably propels Yossarian toward "Catch-22," the life-denying paradox that controls the world of the novel.

The "Catch-22" is that Yossarian can have what he wanted all along —to go home without flying any more missions—but not on the terms that he wants. To stop flying, he must agree to give his life for Colonels Cathcart and Korn. In this profane version of the religious paradox "by dying you shall live," Yossarian can save his life only by giving it up. To accept Cathcart and Korn's deal is to "[b]ecome one of the boys" (416). As Yossarian will later recognize, the demand means the extinction of the self, or in his words, "It's a way to lose myself" (437). In effect, Cathcart and Korn ask Yossarian to deny his identity, to deny who and what he is. Throughout the novel, Heller has insisted upon Yossarian's uniqueness— using, for instance, the pseudo-derivation of Yossarian's name (Assyrian). Momentarily, Yossarian accepts the offer, thereby earning the name Yo-Yo from Colonel Korn. The erratic trajectory of Yossarian's initiation journey continues. Momentarily triumphant, Yossarian believes that "his rebellion had succeeded" and that he has eluded death. Fortunately, the wound that Nately's knife-wielding whore inflicts on him reminds him otherwise.

In the hospital recovering from the wound, Yossarian realizes the implications of Cathcart and Korn's deal and meditates on Snowden's death. To discover how to live, Yossarian must first unravel the message of the strange man who keeps repeating, "We've got your pal, buddy. We've got your pal" (425). At this point in the novel, Colonel Korn, the chaplain, and Aarfy all fit the message: Korn because he knows what the deal demands, Aarfy because he has been the navigator on so many of Yossarian's "missions," and the chaplain because he has indeed been Yossarian's friend. Instinctively, Yossarian realizes that each of the obvious possibilities is wrong, and in "those sleepless, bedridden nights that would take an eternity to dissolve into dawn" (426), he resolves the riddle. In the perverse logic of riddles, Snowden "had never been his pal" but was "a vaguely familiar kid who was badly wounded and freezing to death" (426). If Snowden was only vaguely familiar in life, he will become, through the power of recollection, intimately known in death. In death, he is Yossarian's pal and the catalyst for his essential discovery of self.

In *Catch-22*, Heller expects the authorial audience to return to Avignon with Yossarian, demanding that they, together with him, inspect Snowden's exposed vital organs and understand their message. The passage and death scene are so frequently analyzed that they need little further examination here. I want, however, briefly to consider a passage from earlier in the novel that sets up this inspection. Its progression is reminiscent of Heller's own artistic journey toward Avignon: slow, hesitant, made in uncertain steps.

> And Yossarian crawled slowly out of the nose and up on top of the bomb bay and wriggled back into the rear section of the plane—passing the first-aid kit on the way that he had to return for—to treat Snowden for the wrong wound, the yawning, raw, melon-shaped hole as big as a football in the outside of his thigh, the unsevered, blood-soaked muscle fibers inside pulsating weirdly like blind things with lives of their own, the oval, naked wound that was almost a foot long and made Yossarian moan in shock and sympathy the instant he spied it and nearly made him vomit. And the small, slight tail gunner was lying on the floor beside Snowden in a dead faint, his face as white as a handkerchief, so that Yossarian sprang forward with revulsion to help him first. (325–26)

Yossarian crawls back through the plane, as if moving back in time as well as in space. He mislocates the wound and even then cannot immediately bring himself to treat it, choosing instead to aid the tail gunner. The essential story, human mortality, is reified in Snowden's flesh. In his revulsion, Yossarian can better deal with the gunner's "dead faint" than with Snowden's living wound. The simile, "like blind things with lives of their own," renders mortality as a mysterious otherness, not just Snowden's but also implicitly Yossarian's own.

Eventually, Yossarian traces the wound with his fingers, just as he did in the manuscript version, and when he does, he unwittingly begins to explore his own mortality. Yossarian finds "[t]he actual contact with the dead flesh . . . not nearly as repulsive as he had anticipated, and [makes an] excuse to caress the wound with his fingers again and again to convince himself of his own courage" (428). The reworking of these details from the manuscript version confirms their importance, but significantly shifts the emphasis and meaning of the scene. In the manuscript, Yossarian caresses the viscera, in the novel the fleshy leg wound. In the manuscript, Yossarian attempts to "impress" others with his actions, as if this will authenticate his courage, while in the novel he wants to ascertain his own courage. But in both cases he initially touches without understanding. In fact, after fingering and then treating Snowden's leg wound, Yossarian can assure him confidently, "You're going to be all right, kid. . . . Everything's under control" (429). Of course, it isn't. For Heller, the mystery of mortality lies in human embodiment, in the flesh not in the spirit. Life begins and ends with the body. With his hands inside Snowden's wound, Yossarian experiences this, feels what he does not yet understand. However, his physical grasp anticipates and makes possible apprehension of the message of Snowden's entrails.[43] In Yossarian's insight, Heller defines mortality as a fusion of mind and matter, Yossarian's conceptualization of man enduring even as Snowden's body dissolves into bloody inert matter.

Reflecting upon Snowden's death, Yossarian comes to understand his own mortality. As Denis de Rougement observes, "Suffering and understanding are deeply connected; death and self-awareness are in league."[44] Heller insists that Yossarian trace the contours of Snowden's and thus his own mortality: "liver, lungs, kidneys, ribs, stomach, and bits of the stewed tomatoes Snowden had eaten that day for lunch" (429). The prose is hard and violent, as hard and violent as Snowden's wounds; its violence partakes of the violence of Heller's experience of treating a wounded comrade. Humans' viscera ground them in the material world. They also take in the material world, digesting it like Snowden's stewed tomatoes. When the digestive process is viewed, as Snowden's is, it becomes ugly and repulsive. But Heller believes these entrails also allow the viewer, as prophets have long believed, to detect the secrets of human existence. "It was easy to read the message in his [Snowden's] entrails. Man was matter, that was Snowden's secret. Drop him out a window and he'll fall. Set fire to him and he'll burn. Bury him and he'll rot like other kinds of garbage. The spirit gone, man is garbage. That was Snowden's secret. Ripeness was all" (429–30). Finally, Yossarian deciphers the message that has been available to him all along (in a sense even Giuseppe's mother knew it). The message identifies the two components of humanity: the material, which inexorably leads to death, and the spiritual, which Heller leaves deliberately ambiguous. In formulating the spiritual element, Heller omits the verb, so that the statement reads "the spirit gone." This formulation neither affirms nor denies the existence of spirit; it simply announces the concept. Without predication, the concept cannot be completed or brought to fulfillment. As deconstructionists would argue, only its absence can be noted.

Having unraveled the secret of Snowden's entrails, Yossarian achieves the Promethean wisdom of being wise before the event. With his hard-won knowledge, Yossarian shifts his attention from death to life—as does the text itself. Yossarian rejects Cathcart and Korn's deal and vows to run *to* his responsibilities (440) by fleeing to Sweden and by taking Nately's whore's kid sister with him. Rejecting the deal also confirms Yossarian's individuality, that he will not become "one of the boys," and signifies what can be gained with his death-inspired self-awareness.[45] For Heller,

Sweden denominates a direction, not a place, for it is, as the text makes clear, a "geographical impossibility" (441).[46] In his former bunkmate Orr, Yossarian has a pilot who can help chart the course. And if we follow Yossarian, we achieve a Promethean legacy: "I caused men no longer to foresee their death." Paradoxically, this lack of foresight allows humans to live, and in Heller's more intractable paradox, this loss of foresight can come only after readers, like Yossarian himself, have seen death and thus understood their own mortality. Now indeed Yossarian can "live forever or die in the attempt." With the novel's discourse, Heller guides his audience to a similar point of view.

HELLER'S STYLE AND THE CATCH OF "CATCH-22"

With his language play, Heller insists that the authorial audience attend to his prose performance, as he will in each subsequent novel.[47] His exuberant style—his self-negating sentences, puns, and other language games—requires that the reader see the novel's words as words. Borrowing a term from the Prague school of linguists, Tony Tanner calls this kind of writing foregrounding, by which he means language that invites inspection of its workings rather than pointing to its referents. By way of definition and contrast, Tanner cites Jane Austen's prose as exemplifying "a minimum of foreground, the language inviting no lingering at the surface but directing us instantly back to its referents."[48] For Tanner, attention to foreground is one of the defining characteristics of contemporary American literature, and such attention marks a writer's heightened consciousness of "the strange relationship between the provinces of words and things, and the problematical position of man, who participates in both" (Tanner, *City of Words* 21).[49]

Specifically, Heller uses Catch-22, his title concept, to heighten his authorial audience's awareness of this problematical position. Catch-22 invites explanation and, in this way, becomes a narrative instability.[50] Yet when readers in their effort to understand the concept try to fix its meaning —as a good many critics have done—it usually catches them. A particular instance induces a general explanation, or the affirmation of one meaning neglects its equally valid opposite, or the label "absurd" purports to explicate the concept.[51] In each of these instances, readers find themselves in a position analogous to Yossarian's, trapped inside *Catch-22*. As Heller constructs Catch-22, it is a paradox, a conception not unlike Godel's Incompleteness Theorem or a quantum physicist's characterization of the nature of light. Even when understood, such paradoxes seem to defy explanation, their power as haunting as that of the frequently cited example of Epimenides' paradox: a Cretan said "All Cretans are liars." In such paradoxes, language confounds. But such paradoxes also educate. By making Catch-22 an element of the novel's discourse as well as a principle governing its world, Heller uses it to index his authorial audience's education.

For the authorial audience, Catch-22 necessitates attention to foreground. Its first appearance in the text is a case in point: "Catch-22 required that each censored letter bear the censoring officer's name" (8). The rule itself is clear and unambiguous; the problem is the way in which Yossarian performs as censor: "To break the monotony he invented games. Death to all modifiers, he declared one day, and out of every letter that passed through his hands went every adverb and every adjective. . . . He reached a much higher plane of creativity the following day when he blacked out everything in the letters but *a*, *an* and *the*. That erected more dynamic intralinear tensions, he felt, and in just about every case left a message far more universal" (8). As censor, Yossarian ignores meaning entirely, dealing only with language qua language. In his fondness for "dynamic intralinear tensions," Yossarian concerns himself with linguistic effects. Confirming this attitude toward language, Yossarian complies with Catch-22 by signing himself Washington Irving (or Irving Washington). The army does not understand Catch-22 in the way that Yossarian does and sends a literal-minded C.I.D. man to find out who Washington Irving is. For the narrative audience, Catch-22 will be equally problematic.

In *Catch-22*, the narrative audience is caught because they presume a relationship between word and thing that the text does not sustain. Systematically, from the first chapter on, Heller renders the relationship between word and referent problematic. Three early examples will illustrate this detachment:

> Yossarian had stopped playing chess with him [the artillery captain] because the games were so interesting they were foolish. (9)

> Dunbar was working so hard at increasing his life span that Yossarian thought he was dead. (9)

> The Texan turned out to be good-natured, generous and likable. In three days no one could stand him. (9)

By negating the meaning they advance, these statements close off possibility.[52] Their language effects are like the perceptual effects that Douglas

Hofstadter explores in his book *Godel, Escher, Bach*. In an illustration that he entitles "Smoke Signal," Hofstadter embeds a hidden message—*Ceci n'est pas un message*—inside a drawing of a pipe.[53] While the hidden message denies its own existence, the illustration's title, "Smoke Signal," proclaims the existence of a message, for as the title tells us, the illustration is about messages or, more accurately, meta-messages. If the message denies its own meaning, then the title makes meaning out of the act of denial. The illustration's signal is clearly about itself and its processes, or to paraphrase Wallace Stevens, the illustration is "the cry of its own occasion." So too are Heller's self-negating sentences, or so too is his style.

Catch-22 itself exemplifies the self-denying logic that Heller, like Hofstadter, wants to explore. In a well-known and much analyzed passage, Heller defines the concept and the workings of his fictional world.

> Yossarian looked at him soberly and tried another approach. "Is Orr crazy?"
> "He sure is," Doc Daneeka said.
> "Can you ground him?"
> "I sure can. But first he has to ask me to. That's part of the rule."
> "Then why doesn't he ask you to?"
> "Because he's crazy," Doc Daneeka said. "He has to be crazy to keep flying combat missions after all the close calls he's had. Sure, I can ground Orr. But first he has to ask me to."
> "That's all he has to do to be grounded?"
> "That's all. Let him ask me."
> "And then you can ground him?" Yossarian asked.
> "No. Then I can't ground him."
> "You mean there's a catch?"
> "Sure there's a catch," Doc Daneeka replied. "Catch-22. Anyone who wants to get out of combat duty isn't really crazy." (45)

This dialogue operates like a variant of Epimenides' paradox: "The following sentence is false. The preceding sentence is true." While each proposition holds the possibility for truth, the combination creates neither truth nor falsity, but paradox. The dangers of the paradox are apparent in Yossarian's dilemma. The sanity of recognizing the insanity of war subjects one to the very insanity that one recognizes, and insanity merely leads to unknowing cooperation in the war—and, within the novel, to almost certain death. The Catch-22 paradox holds dangers for Heller the author and his audience as well, because it disavows meaning and possibility.[54] Yet clearly Heller is as concerned about meaning—and meta-meaning—as Hofstadter is in "Smoke Signal." Heller's style, particularly his handling of Catch-22, provides guide and occasion to the meaning that he wants to explore.

The Catch-22 sequence quoted above also illustrates one of Heller's characteristic stylistic features, repetition.[55] A pattern of unfolding language and plot structures repeats itself with minor variations. The sequence makes sanity and insanity mean the same thing, because each calls up and resolves into the other. This textual oscillation yields no resolution, only unchanging expansion. Heller's early drafts of the sequence, which are approximately twice as long, convey this possibility of endless expansion even more forcefully.[56] The copy editor's pen heightens the impact of the paradox by compressing it, but also undercuts the effect of unlimited repetition. The sequence holds the possibility of narrative tedium—a story in which the same thing happens again and again. Early critics were on target when they focused on this kind of repetition as a defining characteristic of Heller's art.

Many of the novel's most memorable episodes operate in the same fashion as the Catch-22 scene.[57] Some of the more obvious examples include Clevinger's trial, the chaplain's internment, Captain Black's loyalty oath campaign, the Major Major sequences, and the soldier-who-saw-everything-twice scenes. For sheer comic exuberance, Clevinger's trial is particularly striking.

> "You're a windy son of a bitch, aren't you? Nobody asked you for clarification and you're giving me clarification. I was making a statement, not asking for clarification. You are a windy son of a bitch, aren't you?"
> "No, sir."
> "*No*, sir? Are you calling me a goddam liar?"
> "Oh, no, sir."
> "Then you're a windy son of a bitch, aren't you?"
> "No, sir."
> "Are you trying to pick a fight with me?"
> "No, sir."
> "Are you a windy son of a bitch?"
> "No, sir."
> "Goddammit, you *are* trying to pick a fight with me." (77)

This scene goes on for seven pages, with Heller pairing alternatives so as to make meaningful exchange impossible. The logic of the sequence is always that of Catch-22. Clevinger is guilty or he would not have been accused, but since "the only way to prove it [Clevinger's guilt] was to find him guilty, it was their patriotic duty to do so" (79). There is much of the Xerox machine to Heller's verbal art. Patterns of sentences and scenes— writ small or writ large, copied in one color or many—remain the same.

The comic effects of the repetition are obvious, but repetition is important to Heller in other ways as well. It is also a vehicle for meaning, as Heller's extension of the Catch-22 episode illustrates.

> He [Yossarian] had Orr's word to take for the flies in Appleby's eyes.
> "Oh, they're there, all right," Orr had assured him about the flies in Appleby's eyes . . . "although he probably doesn't even know it. That's why he can't see things as they really are."
> "How come he doesn't know it?" inquired Yossarian.
> "Because he's got flies in his eyes," Orr explained with exaggerated patience. "How can he see he's got flies in his eyes if he's got flies in his eyes?" (46)

Initially, the scene might be explained as a comic extension and inversion of the Catch-22 exchange, demonstrating that Orr is indeed insane. In the algebra of the novel, Heller has merely substituted values, an x for a y, as it were, with flies in the eyes taking the place of insanity. Yet in the transition between the Catch-22 and the flies-in-Appleby's-eyes sequences, Heller signals the authorial audience that the flies sequence has its own importance. "Yossarian wasn't quite sure that he saw it at all, just the way he was never quite sure about good modern art or about the flies Orr saw in Appleby's eyes" (46). The transition tells us the issue here is seeing, or more particularly, "[seeing] it at all."[58] And seeing it at all is also, as we will see, the trick of paradox. It is precisely the sequentiality of the propositions in the Catch-22 and flies-in-the-eyes sequences that entraps one. When Yossarian acknowledges either of Doc Daneeka's propositions, which he continually does in the novel, he activates the oscillation between the paired alternatives. Before exploring further Heller's way out of the Catch-22 paradox, I will examine another Heller stylistic feature that also illuminates the problem.

Heller's stylistic counterbalance to replication is transformation. If repetition emphasizes the sameness of apparently disparate situations, then the transformations unfold a world of constant variation.[59] In *Catch-22*, language has a talismanic quality, altering the identity of the things it represents. Examples of transformations abound in the novel, but for purposes of illustration two come to mind: Doc Daneeka's death and the chaplain's "hot tomato."[60] In the first case, words are more powerful than things, for Doc "dies" when his name is listed in the flight log of McWatt's plane, which has crashed killing all aboard. Doc is killed by the power of words, and all the characters abide by their force. Doc's assistants Gus and Wes solemnly advise him of his medical predicament: "You're dead, sir" (335); his wife ignores his letters and moves to Michigan to start a new life; and Sergeant Towser, even while talking to Doc, worries about the disposition of his remains. In Doc's death, linguistic reality supersedes actuality. Appropriately, the most powerful characters in this environment are those who can manipulate words, for instance, ex-P.F.C. Wintergreen, who is, arguably, the most powerful character in the novel because he runs the unit's ditto machine.

In the case of the "hot tomato," words are associational, generating a number of meanings. Like a kaleidoscope, they create variation after variation out of the same stuff, again with linguistic reality taking precedence over actuality. The chaplain's "hot tomato," an elaborate pun that Heller sustains for over two hundred pages, begins with Colonel Cathcart trying to interest the chaplain in plum tomatoes he has gotten from Milo.[61] The tomatoes are so "firm and ripe they are," Cathcart beguilingly says, "like a young girl's breasts" (189). According to the punning logic of *Catch-22*, Cathcart's tomatoes have indeed become hot tomatoes, and now that the chaplain has one, he has more than he bargained for. Seeing the chaplain's tomato, Sergeant Whitcomb, a more puritanical type than Colonel Cathcart, interprets it quite differently—as something the chaplain has stolen from Cathcart and consequently something that must be written up for the army investigative unit, the C.I.D. Sergeant Whitcomb's interpretation proves to be the more persuasive one, for in the internment scene the chaplain literally is questioned about his "hot tomato."

> "Why should a superior officer give you a plum tomato, Chaplain?"
> "Is that why you tried to give it to Sergeant Whitcomb, Chaplain? Because it was a hot tomato?"
> "No, no, no," the chaplain protested . . . "I offered it to Sergeant Whitcomb because I didn't want it."
> "Why'd you steal it from Colonel Cathcart if you didn't want it?"
> "I didn't steal it from Colonel Cathcart!"
> "Then why are you so guilty, if you didn't steal it?" (377)

As if contaminated by this tomato, the chaplain has indeed been acting guiltily (but what chaplain wouldn't who has a hot tomato in his possession?). Finally, in Heller's last turn on the pun, the chaplain ends up protesting feebly, "I give you my sacred word it was not a hot tomato" (377). In this transformational world, Cathcart's firm, ripe tomato has indeed produced the chaplain's "sacred word," the profane made sacred. Having heard the chaplain give his sacred word, the C.I.D. appropriately responds, "do you believe in God?" (377), thereby profaning the sacred.

Heller uses the transformational powers of language to explore the way in which reality can be reorganized, or even remade.[62] Perhaps the episode that best illustrates this form of stylistic play is the psychiatrist's scene, because its whole premise is transformation. The material base of the scene, Yossarian's leg wound, will be exorcised with the magic of language. In fact, by its end Yossarian's leg wound will be displaced, and he will be treated for insanity instead. The transformation begins with Dunbar "maintaining that he was not Dunbar but *a fortiori*" (285), a Latin phrase meaning with greater force or stronger reason. And in Heller's verbal edifice, "Dunbar was right: he was not Dunbar any more but Second Lieutenant Anthony F. Fortiori" (285). The change of identity insisted upon by this formulation is explainable on two levels, but the lexical is the more important. First, Dunbar became Lieutenant Fortiori by ejecting the lieutenant from his bed so that he could be near Yossarian. But linguistically Dunbar can assume a new identity merely by thinking in another language; saying it makes it so. By referring to Dunbar as A. Fortiori for the remainder of the scene, Heller gives his narrative authority to Dunbar's change of identity.

The center of the scene is Yossarian's fish dream, and the humor and *frisson* of the scene grow out of contrasting assumptions about the way in which language works. The psychiatrist Dr. Sanderson sees both dreams and language as referential. Questioning Yossarian about his dream, Sanderson repeatedly wants to know, "what does the fish remind you of," only to hear Yossarian's refrain-like answer, "other fish." If Sanderson wants dreams and words to refer to something outside themselves, then Yossarian exploits exactly the opposite principle of referentiality, one in which language refers to itself and its own categories. But Yossarian can also play the game of referentiality on Sanderson's terms.

> "I'd like to show you some ink blots now to find out what certain shapes and colors remind you of."
> "You can save yourself the trouble, Doctor. Everything reminds me of sex."
> "Does it?" cried Major Sanderson with delight. . . . "Now we're *really* getting somewhere! Do you ever have any good sex dreams?"
> "My fish dream is a sex dream."
> "No, I mean real sex dreams—the kind where you grab some naked bitch by the neck and pinch her and punch her in the face until she's all bloody and then throw yourself down to ravish her. . . ."
> Yossarian reflected a moment with a wise look. "That's a fish dream," he decided. (291)

In this transformational world of language, both of Yossarian's assumptions obtain: everything does remind him of sex, and he proves it ("My fish dream is a sex dream"). And, as Yossarian demonstrates, Sanderson's sex dream is a fish dream—an odd unlikeness to itself ("That's a fish dream"). For someone with Yossarian's verbal facility, difference—fish dreams/sex dreams—resolves into similarity. Linguistic categories are interchangeable.

In all these changes, Heller the author stands behind his prose like a magician who pulls a rabbit out of his hat, only to put it back and pull out a string of scarves instead. Heller, never content to wring one change of meaning when he can wring three, continues the scene with Yossarian and Sanderson talking more about sex:

> "Hasn't it ever occurred to you that in your promiscuous pursuit of women you are merely trying to assuage your subconscious fears of sexual impotence?"
> "Yes, sir, it has."
> "Then why do you do it?"
> "To assuage my fears of sexual impotence."
> "Why don't you get yourself a good hobby instead?" Major Sanderson inquired with friendly interest. "Like fishing. Do you really find Nurse Duckett so attractive? I should think she was rather bony. Rather bland and bony, you know. Like a fish." (293)

Naturally, talking about sex means talking about fish, even bland and bony ones like Nurse Duckett. The transformations are multiple: Nurse Duckett's "angular, ascetic New England features" (288) now become fishlike. And more sensitive to transformational possibilities than is Sanderson, Yossarian can awaken desire in Nurse Duckett and become her lover, thereby altering her ascetic character. Nothing remains as it seems in the psychiatrist's scene. Words change the real, which in turn changes words, and on and on.

If the transformational pyrotechnics of the psychiatrist would seem to offer liberation to someone with Yossarian's verbal facility, they do not. In fact, the wordplay here, as everyplace else in the novel, leads back to Catch-22. While Yossarian eventually succeeds in convincing Sanderson that he is crazy and should be sent home, he finds himself back in combat and someone else sent home in his place—who else but Lieutenant Fortiori. Obviously, Lieutenant Fortiori has the "stronger reason." In a conversation with Doc Daneeka, to whom he is pleading his case, Yossarian finds himself caught once more by Catch-22. Confident that the psychiatrist's verdict that he is insane will allow him to return home, Yossarian righteously proclaims, "They're not going to send a crazy man out to be killed, are they?" (299). Doc's laconic reply, "Who else will go?" (299), returns both Yossarian and the reader to the trap of Catch-22.

Although Catch-22 controls the novel, the question again arises: how can one escape its impossible choices? At first there seems no chance, for

Catch-22 has come to mean everything and anything: as when the officers who censor letters must initial the documents they censor (chapter 1), or when all officers who don't sign the Pritchard and Wren loyalty oath must starve (chapter 11). These occurrences and the transformational power they signal are all preliminary to chapter 39, "The Eternal City," in which Catch-22 gets its final definition. As so often in literature, the interpreter's key lies beyond human understanding. In this night world, Yossarian encounters Catch-22 in its most powerful form when the old woman explains to him why the whores have been driven from their apartment. According to the old woman, Catch-22 "says they have a right to do anything we can't stop them from doing" (398). She expands the concept, severing it from any specific referents. It no longer applies to military authority, but to that of all institutions; hence it no longer denotes a single rule, but a way of life. In the bureaucratic world of Pianosa, the individual is powerless because the force of others—the old woman's nameless "they"—is always greater than that of the individual.

This is not yet, however, Heller's final turn, for Yossarian and the authorial audience must be brought to one final discovery. "Yossarian left money in the old woman's lap . . . and strode out of the apartment, cursing Catch-22 vehemently as he descended the stairs, even though he knew there was no such thing. Catch-22 did not exist, he was positive of that, but it made no difference. What did matter was that everyone thought it existed, and that was much worse, for there was no object or text to ridicule or refute, to accuse, criticize, attack, amend, hate, revile, spit at, rip to shreds, trample upon or burn up" (400). Catch-22 exemplifies, to borrow William Blake's formulation, society's "mind-forged manacles." People's belief in it contains their subjectivity by shaping the way in which they think about everything, even themselves. Paradoxically, even when Yossarian recognizes that Catch-22 exists only as a concept, he cannot escape its hold: "Yossarian . . . curs[ed] Catch-22 vehemently . . . even though he knew there was no such thing." Here is another self-negating sentence, another sentence that swallows its own meaning. Yossarian's curse restores the existence of Catch-22, making it part of his subjectivity. Later in the novel the hold it has on him will be confirmed when Yossarian recognizes that his deal with Cathcart and Korn depends upon Catch-22—yet another meaning of the concept. For the reader observing the workings of Yossarian's consciousness, Catch-22 also exists. The title of the novel tells us that it exists both as object and text.

Again Heller brings the authorial audience to consider the problematic relationship between word and thing. Heller's *Catch-22*, like Hofstadter's "Smoke Signal," makes meaning out of the disavowal of meaning and possibility. Responding to the title and to Yossarian's flight to Sweden, the reader recognizes that Heller's novel is about the possibility for human action, just as the viewer of Hofstadter's drawing realizes the drawing is about signals or messages. In this moment of recognition, the reader as observer stands detached from the paradox, seeing it without being caught in its impossible choices. Achieving this moment of vision is what the novel is about, and style is Heller's vehicle for guiding authorial readers to this moment. The novel's discourse renders a solution to the existence of Catch-22 impossible. The reader can only see its paired alternatives, but can never restate them in a way that resolves them into unity.[63] Recognizing paradox and the constant alternation of its premises paves the way to understanding. Of such paradoxical understanding, it has been observed about the great physicist Niels Bohr's world view: "whenever any two such idealizations turn out to be incompatible, this can only mean that some mutual limitation is imposed on their validity."[64] Or, as Bohr himself says in this regard, "It is wrong . . . to think that the task of physics is to find out how nature *is*. Physics concerns what we can *say* about nature" (quoted in Rhodes 77). Heller's *Catch-22* is akin to physics in this respect; it is about what language can say about modern life.

■

HELLER'S COMITRAGIC BLEND: NARRATIVE SEQUENCE AS COMIC STRATEGY

Shortly before he began *Catch-22*, Heller said that he had conversations with two friends about their wartime experiences that influenced his conception of the novel. The first friend, who had been severely wounded, told marvelously funny war stories, but the second, who had also been wounded but only slightly, could neither tell funny stories, nor see anything funny about the war. When Heller tried to explain the point of view of the first friend to the second, the second friend could recognize "that traditionally there had been lots of graveyard humour, but he could not reconcile it with what he had seen of the war."[65] After these conversations, Heller claims that he got the idea for the opening of *Catch-22* and for many of its incidents. Heller's linking these conversations to the origin of *Catch-22* tells us much about the novel's humor. First, for Heller the humor grows out of the war itself—his own laughter and that he wants to provoke respond to the terrifying and the psychically wounding. Second, the novel blends the comic and the tragic in such a way that the horrific is viewed through the lense of the comic.[66] And third and most important, there is something explanatory about Heller's humor, as if he is still trying to explain the point of the first friend to the second. Many of the comic episodes have the effect of asking us: can't you see the humor here? Can't you see the comedy of the horrifying? Can't you see how death must spawn laughter? Throughout *Catch-22*, there is a self-reflexive and self-questioning quality to Heller's humor.

Heller's comic strategies are an extension of his stylistic strategies, in that he continually negates or reverses the expectations he sets up. Typically, Heller's scenes suddenly darken in mood, as he reveals that what the reader has just been laughing at begets violence, death, or the morally outrageous; or similarly, dark scenes beget comic ones, changing the character of the text as dramatically as the graveyard scene does in *Hamlet*.[67] His handling of the soldier-in-white episode illustrates the point—an episode which in typical fashion he tells twice. The first telling is essentially comic, detailing the grotesqueries of the soldier in white's predicament:

> The soldier in white was encased from head to toe in plaster and gauze. He had two useless legs and two useless arms . . . all four limbs pinioned strangely in air by lead weights suspended darkly above him that never moved. Sewn into the bandages over the insides of both elbows were zippered lips through which he was fed clear fluid from a clear jar. A silent zinc pipe rose from the cement on his groin and was coupled to a slim rubber hose that carried waste from his kidneys and dripped it efficiently into a clear, stoppered jar on the floor. When the jar on the floor was full, the jar feeding his elbow was empty, and the two were simply switched quickly so that stuff could drip back into him. (9–10)

The exchange of the drip and drain jars occasions the characteristic Heller moment of reversal—in this case rendering sustenance and waste interchangeable categories. The passage has the tone of black humor—the tone that Mathew Winston identifies as "simultaneously frightening and threatening and farcical or amusing."[68] Heller continues the scene in the same vein, describing the care the soldier receives, the other patients' reactions to him, and so on. Then he adds in what seems almost an afterthought to a paragraph: Nurse Cramer "read his thermometer and discovered that he was dead" (10). Death emerges here out of the comic ingredients of the scene, for the soldier in white must be dead if his waste is also his sustenance. Responding to the death, Yossarian and his pal Dunbar in antic fashion look for the killer and find him, they think, in the Texan who befriended the soldier. In the soldier-in-white scene, Heller's narrative sequence constructs a comic frame so that the soldier's death can be approached only through the dark humor of his predicament and absorbed through Yossarian's farcical search for the killer. This narrative frame conjoins the humorous and the horrifying as part of the same experience.[69]

In chapter 17, sixteen chapters later, Heller's retelling of the soldier-in-white episode confirms the inextricable connection of humor and death.[70] This time Heller places the scene in Yossarian's memory. While using many of the same ingredients—the elaborate descriptions of the soldier's predicament, the outrageous dialogue, the search for the killer, and so on—the scene has a different mood and feel. The authorial audience's knowledge—their power of memory—changes the comic effects, such that Heller's jokes ring differently now. "Why can't they hook the two jars up to each other and eliminate the middleman?" (168). Because the audience knows that the soldier in white is already dead, the joke becomes an explanation as well; by this medical treatment the middleman is indeed systematically eliminated. The comedy also works differently because the scene is encased in memory: *"Now that Yossarian looked back*, it seemed that Nurse Cramer, rather than the talkative Texan, had murdered the soldier in white; if she had not read the thermometer and reported what she found, the soldier in white might still be lying there alive" (166, emphasis added). Memory narrates (which has been overlooked by critics writing about this scene) and, as Yossarian tells the tale, to notice, in this instance, is to kill. Yossarian and Heller are not alone in this interpretation. The physics paradox of Schrödinger's Cat works in analogous fashion, the experimenter's observational choices determining whether a cat caged with radioactive material lives or dies. Such power of notice outrages Yossarian: "Lying there that way might not have been much of a life, but it was all the life he had" (166). For the authorial audience which has experienced the soldier-in-white scenes, life and death, the comic and the tragic, function both as figure and ground in much the way they do in an Escher drawing. They constitute a pattern in which the relationship between figure and ground constantly reverses itself, so that first one element then another assumes the foreground.[71] Heller's wrenching shifts of tone and mood and continual reversal of readerly expectation create a narrative texture that is both tragicomic and comitragic.

Chapters 12 through 15, Heller's account of the deadly mission to Bologna, afford the opportunity to explore the mechanics of his comitragic art in more detail. His narrative strategy might be called narrative by delay. Chapter 12, "Bologna," does not (as the chapter title would seem to promise) recount the deadly mission to Bologna, which Heller has already cued the narrative audience to anticipate. Instead it teasingly recounts all the delays in the mission by unfolding a loosely connected series of episodes which seem to retard rather than to advance the plot. Simultaneously, it describes the inexorable intensification of the men's fears and their certainty that they will have to fly the mission.[72] Recording the series of delays in flying the mission, the scenes in the chapter consistently lead away from Bologna and defuse the narrative audience's expectations that the mission is dangerous. In this method of narration, the scenes themselves become delays. For example, not content to tell us that Yossarian gets the mission canceled by moving the bomb line on the squadron's map, Heller pauses to tell us how General Peckem gets his medal for "capturing" the city and how ex-P.F.C. Wintergreen (now ex-Corporal, later ex-Sergeant Wintergreen) feels cheated because he did not get a medal. Later, Heller shifts from describing Hungry Joe's Bologna-caused nightmares to recount his fight with the cat—Hungry Joe wins and "swagger[s] away happily with the proud smile of a champion" (129). These narrative detours and deflections not only take us away from Bologna, but also from the sense of plot in which events succeed one another as the necessary or probable result of what has gone before. The realistic-minded reader might respond to this narrative technique in the way Clevinger responds to Yossarian's moving the bomb line: "It's a complete reversion to primitive superstition. [Yossarian is] confusing cause and effect. It makes as much sense as knocking on wood or crossing your fingers" (118). Indeed, Heller's narrative is unabashedly primitive and anti-realistic: "Yossarian knocked on wood, crossed his fingers, and . . . move[d] the bomb line up over Bologna" (118).

If for the narrative audience the sequence of scenes wanders to the humorously irrelevant, for the characters it relentlessly intensifies their fears. For them, the delays cannot change the character of the mission or the necessity of flying it; they are certain that they will fly the mission and Yossarian at least is certain that he will die there. As in the rain delays, "[the flyers'] only hope was that it would never stop raining, and they had no hope because they all knew it would" (117). Each of the delays, even those of their own devising, shares a similarly hopeless logic. Their mood darkens, and their plots for somehow escaping Bologna and the death it promises fail: "They [begin] to invent humorless, glum jokes of their own and disastrous rumors about the destruction awaiting them at Bologna" (123). Yossarian, for example, always the novel's master plotter, invents the three-hundred-and-forty-four-millimeter Lepage glue gun, a diabolical weapon which glues the planes together in midair. Then, forgetting his own authorship of the invention, he crumbles in terror when he hears someone else describe the gun. In Heller's narrative method, his characters become his authorial partners, adding to the narrative abundance with their ceaseless plotting. Yet they undermine the power of their own imaginations by terminating their plots with the closure of death.

Chapter 12 establishes a multidirectional narrative in the text that takes on the qualities of an Einsteinian space-time continuum. In such a continuum, any narrative direction is simultaneously moving toward and moving away from Bologna. Chapters 13 and 14 operate in similar fashion, apparently retarding the narrative thrust toward Bologna, yet in fact they propel both the characters and the narrative audience to encounter certain death there. Chapter 13 takes the reader to Rome to the apartments that Major —— de Coverley arranges for the unit's R & R; this backtracking is occasioned by Major —— de Coverley's disappearance in Bologna after Yossarian moves the bomb line. Since —— de Coverley's disappearance cannot be narrated (for like Clevinger's or Orr's it is a narrative non-event), the narrative reverses itself and proceeds in this-is-the-house-that-Jack-built fashion: the reader learns how Major —— de Coverley loses his eye when the old man hits him in the eye with a rose; how —— de Coverley's efforts to remain "binocular" lead to his conversation with Milo, as the result of which Milo becomes mess officer; and how Milo can buy eggs for seven cents and sell them for five and still make a profit. This backtracking also takes us on another mission, for in *Catch-22* death lies behind as well as in front. Chapter 13 describes the Ferrara mission on which Colonel Kraft is killed, and this description becomes a proleptic version of Bologna. Lest the authorial audience be seduced by the narrative digression, Heller flashes forward to the day after Bologna, when Yossarian makes love to the maid in the lime-colored panties in Snowden's room, thereby affirming the conjunction of love and death that Leslie Fiedler sees as defining the American novel.[73] The multidirectional narrative of chapters 12 and 13 weaves the comic and tragic inextricably together.

Chapter 14 might be described as the intrusion of the unconscious, yet another dimension of the narrative flow of experience. It describes the first mission to Bologna, the one that turns out to be a milk run. Thanks to a malfunctioning intercom which he himself causes, Yossarian escapes this bombing run when he persuades Kid Sampson to turn back. But unlike the men who bomb Bologna, Yossarian does not escape death—the real enemy. Instead he encounters it in the camp landscape, in the mushrooms that have the feel of death. What Yossarian does not realize is that his own haunted consciousness has created this land of death. As if to cleanse his consciousness Yossarian goes swimming, but his efforts at cleansing himself also fail. When the planes return unscathed in perfect formation, Yossarian misapprehends the significance, believing the mission had been canceled because of cloud cover over the target. Distracted by Heller's digressive embellishments, the first-time reader similarly misconstrues what will immediately follow in a chapter entitled "Piltchard & Wren."

After its description of the mild-mannered title characters, chapter 15 unfolds the details of the deadly Bologna mission with concentrated intensity. In part, the intensity is the result of Heller narrating the scene from Yossarian's point of view. Helpless with fear, Yossarian experiences the run in what Heller calls in his notes to the novel "a nightmarish unreality."[74] Locked in Yossarian's point of view, the narrative audience participates in his fear. Yossarian's directions to McWatt on how to evade the flak give the chapter the erratic trajectory of the previous chapters. *"Turn right hard!"* (145), *"Climb, you bastard! Climb, climb, climb, climb!"* (146), "Turn left! *Left*, you goddam dirty son of a bitch! Turn left *hard!"* (147). Yossarian's actions are similarly erratic. He begins hitting Aarfy, but that "was like sinking his fists into a limp sack of inflated rubber. There was no resistance, no response at all from the soft, insensitive mass" (148). Frustrated, Yossarian starts hitting himself in the forehead. In the confusion, the scene dissolves into noise: the roar of flak, McWatt's frantic shouts for direction, and Aarfy's burbling joy. The pandemonium yields the one constant in the novel, more death: "Behind [Yossarian], men were dying" (149).

Once away from the flak, Yossarian recovers himself, and with his recovery, the narrative rights itself as well. Having left death behind, Yossarian pauses to see if Orr, his roommate, is safe. With Yossarian's attention on Orr, Heller can reintroduce the joke of Orr crash-landing, safely as always. In the dark comedy of the crash landing, Heller sets up the pattern out of which the ending of the novel will come. Orr, Heller insists, knows the way out of the narrative, because he knows how to crash. Eventually Yossarian learns how to see and thus how to value and act on Orr's knowledge. This comic resolution of the Bologna sequence emerges maggot-like out of the mission's many deaths.

Chapters 35 and 36 provide another particularly clear example of Heller's narrative conjunction of the comic and tragic. Here the narrative pattern might be called the principle of misplaced proportion. Chapter 35, "Milo the Militant," has a short frame, an opening scene in which Yossarian pleads with Nately not to fly any more missions and a two-paragraph closing which describes the La Spezia mission and Nately's death. The extended middle in which Milo "pleads" with Colonel Cathcart to be allowed to fly more missions stands in comic contrast to the frame. Like many of the novel's episodes, the scene between is itself a plot, so complete that it could be excerpted and stand alone. It depends upon the reversal structure common to so many jokes: after successfully overcoming Cathcart's opposition to flying any more missions, Milo changes tactics to show why he cannot possibly fly any more missions. In the happily-ever-after solution, the other men will fly Milo's missions (and if necessary die on them) and Milo will get the credit, that is, the combat medals. Of course, Milo finds this capitalistic resolution eminently satisfying. The comic expansion of this miniplot threatens to overwhelm the framing episodes so that Nately's death will become only a background detail and thus easily forgotten. With this misplaced proportion, Heller works to achieve the opposite effect, the prominence of Nately's death.

The narrative impulse of the entire Milo/Cathcart sequence is comic expansion. For example, Milo increases the number of missions he has flown by "twenty per cent in just a couple of minutes" (364) when Colonel Cathcart insists that he count the Orvieto mission, which Milo had, in fact, arranged but not flown. But Milo, the businessman, knows that even a twenty percent increase will not solve his problem: "I want to get in there and fight like the rest of the fellows. That's what I'm here for. I want to win medals, too" (364). Medals and promotions are the real currency of the novel, and when Cathcart agrees to allow Milo to fly, Milo must work one more conversion so that he can earn his medals without the danger of death that flying would bring. Heller's shaggy dog story accomplishes Milo's goal and introduces into the episode the possibility of endless elaboration. The story hangs on how the syndicate will run with Milo absent. As Milo instructs Cathcart on its working, narrative details multiply logarithmically: galvanized zinc for delivery in Damascus, cedars from Lebanon for a sawmill in Oslo, a Messerschmitt full of hemp due in Belgrade, the Piltdown Man for the Smithsonian, coals for Newcastle, ad infinitum. As the syndicate spreads out to cover the globe, Heller's narrative embodies E. H. Gombrich's etc. principle, with its illusion of endless expansion.[75] The expansion becomes digression leading away from La Spezia and death, until Milo gets what he wants—others to fly his missions.

With Milo's goal accomplished, the narrative can proceed to La Spezia, the first mission that the other men fly for Milo. The run takes two paragraphs, its brevity making it a coda to Milo's expansive manipulations. The wrenching shift in proportions and tone replaces the excess of the conversations between Milo and Cathcart with unadorned prose: "It was over in a matter of seconds. There were no parachutes. And Nately, in the other plane, was killed too" (369). With these words the chapter ends. Milo's scheming and the expansive comic capital that Heller works out of these schemes collapse back in on themselves. After the chapter's humorous plenitude, the narrative dissolves into white space, silence, and death.

As Heller designs the chapter, the verbal comedy of the extended middle and the muted tragedy of Nately's death are not discrete elements, but aspects of the same story. The complication of each part stands as a variation of the same story. While Yossarian pleads with Nately not to fly any more missions, Milo pleads with Cathcart to be allowed to fly (which in self-negating fashion means that Milo does not want to fly at all). There are a number of other correspondences as well. For instance, Yossarian's concern for Nately's safety is mirrored in Milo's concern for Yossarian's safety. But what finally connects the two stories is Yossarian's role. When he goes to enlist Milo's help in Nately's predicament, he initiates a causal chain that leads to Nately's death. Yossarian's conversation with Milo prompts him to see Cathcart so that he can fly more missions. At a crucial moment in the conversation, Milo discloses Nately's willingness to fly, which allows Cathcart to raise the number of missions, which, in turn, leads to Nately's death. On the level of plot the chapter unfolds with episodes following as a necessary consequence of what has gone before, thereby making the comic and tragic aspects of La Spezia elements in the same story.

In another of the reversals of which Heller is so fond, chapter 36 reverses the pattern of chapter 35; the serious opening gives way to the extended comedy of the internment scene. In a brief introductory scene, the chaplain reads Yossarian's face and understands what happened over La Spezia. As he deciphers Yossarian's grief, death radiates outward. As the opening sentence tells us: "Nately's death almost killed the chaplain" (370). But there are more deaths as well: twelve men have died on the mission and the survivors have the shadow of death on them as well. The progression of death parallels the comic expansion of Milo's syndicate and Heller's narrative in the previous chapter. When the chaplain "started toward Yossarian on tiptoe to mourn beside him and share his wordless grief" (371), he is arrested, and the tragedy dissolves into comedy—narrative sequence serving Heller here in the same manner as the transformative power of language does. His arrest leads to the internment scene and the punning high jinks of the chaplain's hot tomato. In chapter 36 then, tragedy begets comedy, furnishing yet another illustration of the inextricable connection that Heller finds between the comic and the tragic.

Like his seriously wounded friend, Heller must laugh at the wounds of war. The proximity of death is bearable only when defused by the comic. Bakhtin's account of the comic necessity that underpins the novel as a genre also serves to describe Heller's method in *Catch-22*:

> Laughter has the remarkable power of making an object come up close, of drawing it into a zone of crude contact where one can finger it familiarly on all sides, turn it upside down, inside out, peer at it from above and below, break open its eternal shell, look into its center, doubt it, take it apart, dismember it, lay it bare and expose it, examine it freely and experiment with it. Laughter demolishes fear and piety before an object, before a world, making of it an object of familiar contact and thus clearing the ground for an absolutely free investi-

gation of it. Laughter is a vital factor in laying down that prerequisite for fearlessness without which it would be impossible to approach the world realistically.[76]

Death is the object that Heller wants to inspect. The dark comedy of the Bologna and La Spezia sequences accomplishes this inspection. Like the chaplain reading Yossarian's death-worn face, the authorial audience traces the shape of death, gaining the familiarity that makes its horrors endurable. In these sequences, this authorial reader stands in the chaplain's position, removed from death itself, for at Bologna and La Spezia, Heller announces the deaths, but does not describe them. At Avignon, Heller confronts death directly. What Bakhtin calls the "familiarization of the world through laughter" is a novel-long process before death itself; even death, reified in Snowden's vital organs, can be inspected.

"In this plane (the plane of laughter) one can disrespectfully walk around whole objects; therefore, the back and rear portion of an object (and also its innards, not normally accessible for viewing) assume special prominence" (Bakhtin, 23). Heller has taken his audience on this kind of narrative walk over Bologna and La Spezia, and the novel itself provides this peripatetic approach to Avignon. There is no need to describe Heller's approach to Avignon again, only to recall Yossarian's glimpse of mortality and death: "Here was God's plenty, all right . . . liver, lungs, kidneys, ribs, stomach and bits of the stewed tomatoes Snowden had eaten that day for lunch" (429). In this catalog, Yossarian and Heller act out the imperatives for Bakhtin's comic formula. Having already familiarized the reader with the elements of this catalog, especially the liver and the tomatoes, the beginning and ending of the catalog, Heller allows the reality of mortality to be known, familiarized in a laughter that ridicules. All those liver jokes and the punning comedy of the chaplain's hot tomato pay their dividends, so that even in the most serious moment of the novel—the death litany of Snowden's organs—comic elements are present, present in the reader's associations of liver and hot tomatoes. Death, as well as life, is stripped in Heller's catalog. Heller's comic dismemberment destroys the power that death had when it was unknown. Only on the plane of laughter can Yossarian (hero as jester) vow "to live forever or die in the attempt" or Heller (novelist as jester) vow to "be holding on to the bedposts" at the moment of his death.[77]

■

HELLER'S POSTSCRIPT: "'CATCH-22' REVISITED"

" 'Catch-22' Revisited," Heller's suave, chatty piece for *Holiday* magazine, contains the genotype for all Heller's narratives, the story of the dead child. Its patterns—simple, rich, formative, and identifying—reveal the distinctive cast of Joseph Heller's imagination. The article recounts Heller's trip with his family through the sites of his war experiences. On one level it is a family journal, sketching the features of traveling with a family—what the children will not eat or their impatience with yet another museum. On another level, it unfolds the ritualistic "tour of battlefields" (145) that many veterans make. Like other returnees, Heller finds a landscape in which the war remains only in monuments or in the eyes of the observers. As Heller remarks about his return, "[i]t brought me only to scenes of peace and to people untroubled by the threat of any new war" (145). Beneath these two levels, the article tells Heller's core story, that of the death of a child. As climax, this story provides the organizing principle of " 'Catch-22' Revisited."

Little attention need be given to the first narrative level, Heller's descriptions of his family. These accounts are handled with reticence typical of whenever Heller talks about family life. None of the family members is named; rather they are referred to as "my wife," "my daughter," "my son." The details of family travel are only slightly more individualized. For instance, Heller tells of his son's momentary interest in the trip when he wins $8 at a Florence racetrack. A trip to the opera the next night dampens his enthusiasm and returns him to boredom that is alleviated only when returning home is mentioned. Familial indifference becomes the backdrop for Heller's own memorial journey.

> "I'm thirsty," said my daughter.
> "It's hot," said my wife.
> "I want to go back," said my son. (53)

Such choral refrains punctuate the narrative, lending the authenticity of the ordinary to Heller's account. His family's indifference—their non-story—sets Heller's own interest in the war in relief.

As his title indicates, Heller's battlefield tour is literally an act of revisitation. The journey begins in Corsica (the Pianosa of the novel) and moves up the Italian peninsula, more or less approximating the spatial organization of *Catch-22*, which in turn reflects the sequence of combat missions Heller actually flew. As in the novel, Avignon is the last place visited. Heller's accounts of the journey stress its two levels: the prominent details of his 1944 memories and the present landscape, which has been metamorphosed by peace. "I was a man in search of a war, and I had come to the wrong place. My war was over and gone" (53). His tone betrays his disappointment that the world has not retained the features so prominent in his war memories. War's plenitude—all the richness of experience that provided the narrative impulse for *Catch-22*—is gone. The present journey pales in significance to the past bombing missions, its narrative of family travel merely a debased version of Yossarian's "epic" journeyings.

Heller recounts his adventures as tourist with the brash, streetwise voice of his heroes Bruce Gold and King David. This Heller knows enough not to believe a tour guide's story about Michelangelo hurling his ax at his statue of Moses in frustration that a statue so lifelike would not speak. "I know that if Michelangelo ever hurled an ax at it, Moses would have picked the ax up and hurled it right back" (60). Occasionally, Heller describes his own reactions to what he sees more personally. For instance, he is moved by Michelangelo's *Last Judgment*, "the perpetual movement in its violent rising and falling, and perpetual drama in its aging and wrath" (60). Given the transience of the Italy of Heller's experience, the attraction of experience rendered immutable is obvious, particularly when the rendition preserves the action and the turmoil. Then, in a characteristic shift of tone, Heller laments that he cannot see the painting whenever he wants; he would put the painting up in his apartment, "[b]ut my landlord won't let me" (60). Heller's readers have heard this voice before and know his penchant for closing an episode with a one-liner.

His accounts of the battlefield sites layer the past and the present, creating a textual palimpsest on which most of the past has been written over. At the airfield on Corsica, Heller finds that nothing remains from the war. "A lighthouse that had served as landmark for returning planes left no doubt we had the right place, but there was nothing there now but reeds and wild bushes. And standing among them in the blazing sunlight was no more meaningful, and no less eccentric, than standing reverently in a Canarsie lot" (53). Revisitation is always fraught with difficulty, in that what one hopes to find is often marked chiefly by its absence. For all Heller's or a reader's desires, Corsica or Pianosa or even *Catch-22* cannot be finally revisited. Thus at every stop on the tour, Heller notes differences: the new bridge at Poggibonsi (one of the few locations that did not figure prominently in the novel, but the target of Heller's first bombing mission); civilian Rome where Heller a la Yossarian took his R & R ("I don't think the Colosseum was there then, because no one ever mentioned it" [59]); or the tourist Avignon in which the Hellers' hotel abuts a bordello. Recounting such differences, Heller is genial and nostalgic, but ineffably sad that despite his memorial efforts the past recedes out of reach like Gatsby's Daisy.

At odd moments, Heller does find reminders of his war, and his narrative preserves them as oases in a peacetime world. The bridge at Poggibonsi has been replaced, but the hole in a nearby mountainside where the young Heller dropped his bombs too late to hit the target is still there. Heller's insistence on inserting the memory of this bombing run into the narrative becomes his own act of wartime preservation. His mistake remains —and thanks to his narrative—always will remain, more permanent than most of the landscapes of war. In Bologna, Heller also encounters the war in a woman's reminiscences. She was in the Bologna train station when it was decimated by American bombers. "She could not distinguish the rubble of the railroad station from the rubble of the other buildings that stood nearby. . . . And the thought that terrified her—she remembered this still— was that now she would miss her train" (56). The woman's memory—in the perverseness of human recollection—preserves the incidental detail, making it the focal point for the experience. The war itself stays at the remove of memory, "so far in the past" (56).

In "'Catch-22' Revisited," Avignon occasions the narrative anticlimax, the obverse of the climactic Avignon mission in *Catch-22*. Heller prepares the narrative audience for the approach to Avignon much as he does in the novel itself. He describes the details of the missions over Avignon: the first flight, when he saw his first plane shot down and the second, when the copilot "went a little berserk" (56). As in the novel, details come out intermittently. Prefatory to his actual entrance to Avignon, Heller relates his own experiences taking care of the wounded gunner in his plane —the seminal experience for the Snowden death scene. The episode is narrative by ellipsis, in which Heller leaves out all but a few cryptic comments about visiting the wounded gunner: "He looked fine. . . . But I was in terrible shape; and I had twenty-three more missions to fly" ("'Catch-22' Revisited" 142), another joke that deflects the terrifying into the humorous. As the joke confirms, however, Heller was himself wounded over Avignon, albeit psychically rather than physically. After the exuberance of his initial months of combat, the twenty-one-year-old Heller would take a first-aid kit on all his subsequent missions. In "'Catch-22' Revisited," Heller's statement that he is in terrible shape means more than it says. Revisitors to *Catch-22* already know this. Like Heller, they know "*There* was the war, in Avignon, not in Rome or Île Rousse or Poggibonsi or even Ferrara" (142). But that was then, in 1944. On his present journey, Heller finds no war there, nor anyone with whom to share his war. Only the hotel with the bordello behind it merits a place in the narrative now.

No Heller authorial reader will be surprised, though, when he does find the war. "[I]t was in neutral little Switzerland, after I had given up and almost lost interest, that I finally found, unexpectantly, my war" (145). As in Snowden's death, the wounds of war are never where they seem. In a chance meeting with a Frenchman who stops the Hellers from boarding the wrong train, Heller discovers his war. The man impulsively begins talking about his son, who has been seriously wounded in Indochina, but is overwhelmed with grief in the telling. The son was wounded in the head and now cannot take care of himself, nor go anywhere alone; his life has become a living death. In the son, Heller has indeed found his "war." His war is about children maimed or dying young. This war brings us to the third level of Heller's narrative.

Readers of *We Bombed in New Haven, Something Happened, God Knows*, and *Closing Time* will find Heller's choice in making the stranger's story the climax of "'Catch-22' Revisited" predictable. The story of a child dying young is Heller's story, the story that he must tell over and over again. It is as crucial to his imagination as tales of youthful aspirations are to Fitzgerald's or memories of the blacking factory are to Dickens's. Because this version contains the pattern that appears in his novels as well, it is worth quoting in its entirety.

> He began telling us about his son, and his large eyes turned shiny and filled with tears.
> His only boy, adopted, had been wounded in the head in the war in Indochina and would never be able to take care of himself. He could go nowhere alone. He was only thirty-four years old now and had lain in the hospital for seven years. "It is bad," the man said, referring to the wound, the world, the weather, the present, the future. Then, for some reason, he said to me, "You will find out, you will find out." His voice shook. The tears were starting to roll out now through the corners of his eyes, and he was deeply embarrassed. The boy was too young, he concluded lamely, by way of apologizing to us for the emotion he was showing, to have been hurt so badly for the rest of his life. (145)

The narrative focuses attention on the son, but his story is left curiously incomplete. Or rather, since the son's living death cannot provide further narrative complication, the story shifts to become that of those around him. The inconsolable grief and the tears are the Frenchman's, but in the retelling they become Heller's as well. Opened and closed by tears, the tale is one of grief.

Tears are also the figure for the story that Heller wants to tell, but can only announce, never bring to consummation. Telling this untold story would necessitate finding meaning in the death of a child. For Heller, the Frenchman's tale approximates the meaning of an untold story: "'It is bad,' the man said, referring to the wound, the world, the weather, the present, the future." When quotation gives way to interpretation, Heller transforms the man's tale. In Heller's interpretive transformation, the son participates in the realm of myth and stands between the temporal and quotidian, and the eternal and transcendent. In this mediating position of myth, the child story not only illuminates the ordinary—the world of weather and the future—but also holds the possibility of transcendent meaning. Repeating the man's words, "You will find out, you will find out," Heller signals his understanding of the story, even if he cannot incarnate it in his own words.

Telling is the crucial concern here, as it is in his novels. If the story could be told, it could gain the substantiality of the word.

> "Why was he crying?" asked my boy.
> "What did he say?" my daughter asked me.
> What can you tell your children today that will not leave them frightened and sad?
> "Nothing," I answered. (145)

As this conclusion demonstrates, Heller can and cannot relate the man's tale, can and cannot relate his own. The family again becomes the chorus, still outside Heller's story. Throughout the trip, Heller has wanted his family to share his Europe, his war, his memories and experience, and now he cannot tell them what they want to know or, paradoxically, what he wants to tell them. The curious penultimate line is deliberately left ambiguous: "What can you tell your children today"? Whose line, whose question, is it? No answer is given. The line's meaning, however, is not ambiguous, for it identifies the dangers of telling children what is in fact their own story. Heller's "nothing" speaks to these difficulties, but it also betokens a larger difficulty—that the child story is as untellable as it is tellable.

Heller himself is aware of the way in which the child story figures at the end of his narratives:

> Death is always present as a climactic event that never happens to the protagonist but affects him profoundly. I think I'm drawing unconsciously from experience for inspiration. The child, the dependent child or sacrificed child, is always there. I would think that the death of my father when I was about five years old had much to do with that. . . . But it leaves me very sensitive to the helplessness of children and the ease with which they can be destroyed or betrayed, deliberately or otherwise. In each of my books, when the key death takes place, there's a great deal of pain and tenderness involved.[78]

The resonance of this account makes one wish for a good biography of Heller. However, for now, one must be contented with the suggestiveness of this account with respect to Heller's fiction: the reversal in which a child rather than the father unexpectedly dies; the guilt, denial, and coming to terms that inevitably accompany the death; the death in which the protagonist immerses himself in the mortal blood as Yossarian does (or is covered with it as Slocum is or is figuratively tainted by it as David is by Bathsheba's menstrual blood); the approach of death as catalyst to narrative itself, both to story and discourse; and, finally—to appropriate Denis de Rougemont's formulation—"death as goad to sensuality" (Rougement, 53). This last element should be briefly explained. In a Heller novel, death activates passion, causing, for example, Yossarian to "thirst for life and reach out ravenously to grasp and hold" Luciana and Nurse Duckett and to try to rescue Nately's whore's kid sister (347). This topic invites much more explanation, and I will return to examine it in more detail in connection with *God Knows*.

The child story controls each succeeding narrative, just as it has controlled "'Catch-22' Revisited." In *We Bombed in New Haven*, Captain Starkey must tell and retell each newly named version of his son that he will die on the next bombing mission. But, of course, he does not really tell his son, or rather Starkey seeks to undercut the story that he has just told. Turning to the audience at play's end, he shouts, "There has never been a war. . . . Nobody has been killed here tonight. It's only . . . make-believe; it's a story . . . a show" (*We Bombed* 159–60). In the ending of *Something Happened*, Slocum finally calls back the details of the accident in which he killed his son, but concludes the recollection, like the accident itself, with the plea, "Don't tell my wife." In a reversal of the pattern, *Good as Gold* closes with Bruce Gold standing at his mother's grave hoping for a message which he cannot find. The death of another "child," his brother Sid, has brought him to the grave. *God Knows* concludes with King David yearning for a God who will understand and make understandable the grief he feels for his dead sons. "I feel nearer to God when I am deepest in anguish" (338). David's hope for the transcendent mirrors Heller's own. In *Picture This*, Heller revises one of history's most famous death scenes, that of Socrates (an innocent if not a child) so that he dies with retching and convulsions that injesting hemlock occasions. Finally, in *Closing Time*, Heller uses Kilroy's death to mourn the passing of the World War II generation, to parody the dead-child story, and to cast a retrospective light upon *Catch-22* in general and Snowden's death in particular.

There is no reason to think that future Heller novels will not continue to tell the dead child's story. And no reason to think that Heller will not continue to wrestle with the problem of "'Catch-22' Revisited," the story which moves him, which impels him to tell the story he cannot tell. It is after all a story of death, not life, and the death of a child—if not rendered in the transcendent myths of religion—ends without the consolation of the end. So Heller will continue to revisit *Catch-22*, the place of "[his] war," and to enact the ritual of telling, not telling, and suppressing the telling of the death of children.

3

SOMETHING HAPPENED

HELLER'S GREAT MONOLOGUE

> Wandering between two worlds, one dead,
> The other powerless to be born . . .
>
> MATTHEW ARNOLD, "Stanzas from the Grand Chartreuse"

CONFINED SPACE

After charting the surfaces of American life in *Catch-22*, Joseph Heller turns his concerns inward in *Something Happened* to explore the workings of a single consciousness.[1] Examining the psychic life of an ordinary American, Heller locates his novel entirely within the constricted consciousness of his Babbitt-like hero, Bob Slocum. For Heller, Slocum's anxieties exemplify the psychological disruptions of contemporary, middle-class life.[2] *Something Happened* tracks the restless circlings of Slocum's mind as he searches for the roots of his unhappiness. In his wanderings, Slocum looks for an event—the "something happened" that the title proclaims—that will illuminate his life. But, whether he sifts through the past or turns toward the future, he always sees the portents of catastrophe: "something *is* wrong. . . . Something bad is going to happen" (230). Such warnings occur with metronomic regularity. Caught between the traumas of the forgotten and the forecast, Slocum seeks an explanation for himself and his forebodings that he can never allow himself to find.[3]

Heller records the story of Slocum's search so that chunks of his memories and imaginings spill onto the page in what seems random order. As in *Catch-22*, the plot emerges in fragments; events are narrated in a chronologically and developmentally distorted order. Further, by confining the reader to Slocum's point of view, Heller makes any objective ordering of the events of Slocum's life impossible. The difficulties multiply when, in the later stages of the novel, Slocum verges on a nervous breakdown and his narrative collapses into virtually inchoate shards of memory and perception. As a result, *Something Happened* does not yield the clear, orderly plot summary that can usually be given for most novels, even modern ones.[4] There are, however, three tracks to Slocum's restless wanderings and thus to the novel itself, and these tracks help to orient the reader: Slocum's family life, his company fears and expectations, and his early memories, many of which are fixated on his teenage infatuation with Virginia (the girl who worked in the office in which Slocum was a file clerk). In the first track, Slocum's thoughts about his family inevitably turn on their unhappiness or on his dissatisfaction with them, while in the second track, Slocum has a single corporate aspiration, to give a three-minute speech at the company's annual convention (out of which Heller works as many variations as Charles Schulz does with Snoopy's authorial ambitions). In the third track, Slocum obsessively reminisces about Virginia, about their sexually flirtatious conversations and frantic supply-room gropings. In the novel's concluding pages, the three tracks of Slocum's experience converge and something does happen—his elder son dies, accidentally killed by Slocum, who suffocates him while trying to comfort the injured boy.

In *Something Happened*, Heller reconfigures the relationship among the concerns of his Avignon stories and *Catch-22*: guilt, secret knowledge, bad faith, and dead children. The principal change is assuming the father's point of view, for this perspective on mortality is Janus-faced, life-giver and -denier. The secret knowledge is Slocum's alone, signalled by the title of the novel's last chapter, "Nobody knows what I've done." However, the etiology for this escapes Slocum; celebrating his erotic drives, his many liaisons and imagined liaisons, he overlooks their Freudian complement, thanatos. As monologist, Slocum's chief tasks are to direct attention away from his son's death and to shield himself from responsibility for it, thus from guilt as well. In order to do so, he adopts two "authorial" strategies: he conceives a prelapsarian self, who though admittedly lost, is still him, and he refigures his experiences so that he is the injured innocent. He is, however, confined by the story that he—and Heller—have to tell, that of the dead child. With this story, Heller uses Slocum's monologue to accomplish the inspection that Slocum suppresses, his novel inexorably propelling the authorial audience toward this domestic Avignon, in which "streams of blood" spurt from the dying son (562). For Heller, the dead-child story resides not only within the self, but also within American culture.

Constructing *Something Happened* as an interior monologue, Heller uses Slocum's mental ramblings to reveal the conformity of corporate and suburban America. By reproducing Slocum's efforts to understand himself and his unhappiness, the monologue interiorizes the conformity of American life and dramatizes its awful costs.[5] Through the mechanics of the monologue, Slocum's experiences and memories themselves become Heller's statement about conformity. These experiences—Slocum's aspiration to give a three-minute speech or his sense that not even his name is his own—document his failure to establish a coherent sense of self. As represented in the novel, this failure is a process—not a state—in which Slocum gradually loses control over memories, desires, perceptions, and sensations until he can finally find nothing that he considers his own.[6] Yet, through the medium of the interior monologue, Slocum's inability to define his identity and thus to complete his story becomes Heller's completed novel. In *Something Happened*, the shape of Slocum's failure becomes the shape of the novel itself.

As critics have long noted, Heller also constructs the novel as an extended interior monologue so that he can involve the reader, his narrative audience, in Slocum's experience, or, as he puts it, "my objective is not merely to tell the reader a story but to make him a participant, to have him *experience* the book rather than simply to read it."[7] The monologue technique requires a reader to see Slocum's situation as he himself does and by doing so brings the reader into sympathetic identification with him. Locked in Slocum's point of view, the narrative audience shares Slocum's memories and sensations.[8] The sympathetic participation that results causes this reader temporarily to suspend judgment about the accuracy or the ethics of Slocum's concerns—an effect that Robert Langbaum sees as intrinsic to the monologue form.[9] Readerly suspension of judgment is important for Heller, because he does not want the audience to criticize or condemn Slocum as they read. Rather, he wants the narrative audience temporarily to internalize Slocum's concerns, for, as Thomas LeClair persuasively argues, "the reader must learn the nature of Slocum's failure by participating in it."[10] And Heller does not want to describe the alienation and conformity of contemporary American life, but to make them manifest.[11]

The monologue form allows Heller to make quite different, but essentially complementary, demands on the authorial audience. Heller uses the monologue to invite this audience to attend to the way in which Slocum tells his story and by extension to inspect the discourse of his novel. This is a daring invitation on Heller's part, for Slocum tells about his life with pretentious banality. As the example of T. S. Eliot's "The Love Song of J. Alfred Prufrock" illustrates, the choice of such a narrative voice is not without precedent—although Heller, unlike Eliot, suspends readers in his protagonist's claustrophobic consciousness for more than five hundred pages.[12] In the emptiness of Slocum's narrative, the process by which he tells about his life gradually takes precedence over the story he tells. As Slocum returns again and again to the same concerns and themes—as for example to his premonition that "something bad" will happen to him—the authorial audience begins to focus on Slocum's fixation itself, rather than simply on the fears that he relates.[13] In doing so, she notes the way "something bad" recurs in Slocum's thoughts and observes his pattern of mind. During such moments of awareness, the reader sees the shape of Slocum's memories and imaginings—in much the same way she, having heard a grandparent's stories many times, might discern his or her core patterns and thereby apprehend the grandparent's cast of mind.[14]

By asking the authorial audience to attend to the way in which Slocum narrates his experience, Heller proffers another kind of invitation as well. He asks this reader to observe and participate in the construction of the novel, for he wants the reader to share in the difficulties of his compositional tasks: to see the interest of a mind that trivializes its experience and to see order in the disorder of memory.[15] This requires more of the reader than the foregrounded language of *Catch-22* did. An example from "The Love Song of J. Alfred Prufrock" will illustrate how Eliot involves the reader in similar compositional difficulties as well as shed light on Heller's techniques. Consider the famous couplet: "I grow old . . . I grow old . . . / I shall wear the bottoms of my trousers rolled." These lines produce a moment of narrative tension for the authorial audience by counterposing the pathos of Prufrock's situation and the language play of the poem itself. The tension between Prufrock's self-absorption and Eliot's poetic wit dramatizes opposite tendencies: Prufrock's consistent use of details of little significance except to himself and Eliot's restoration of poetic significance to the same elements. For the authorial reader, the old-rolled rhyme is plangently playful and yet also yokes old age and rolled trousers, turning cuffs into a synecdochic evocation of old age. And in doing so the poem extends Prufrock's hyperbolic meditation on mortality and old age, distinguishing Prufrock's understanding of his situation ("Do I dare / Disturb the universe") from that of the authorial audience. As I have noted, Heller sets himself similar tasks: 1) he wants to use Slocum's self-absorption to tell the story of the mindless conformity of corporate and suburban America, and 2) he chooses the monologue form so that his audience can watch him accomplish this authorial task.

Having briefly sketched out Heller's choice of the interior monologue, we will look more closely at the workings of Slocum's mind—the ways in which he mythologizes his experience with his lost-child story and in which he envisions the self in time. To explore these elements is to learn how Heller implicates his readers in Slocum's concerns, staining them with his guilt much as the writers of Genesis do with the story of Adam and Eve or as Freud does with his reading of the Oedipus myth. Similarly, to investigate Heller's narrative strategies is to learn how Heller involves the authorial audience in the novel's construction and, therefore, how he achieves order out of emptiness. If Heller strains the limits of readers' patience with so extended an account of Slocum's ceaselessly trivializing mind, he also creates a startlingly inventive and darkly comic record of such a mind.[16] Like Eliot in "J. Alfred Prufrock" or Faulkner in the Benjy sections of *The Sound and the Fury*, Heller deliberately makes the limitations of his hero the grounds for his artistic endeavor.[17] And like them, he succeeds.

Slocum's Myths, Oedipal Echoes, and Heller's Novel

In a brilliant review of *Something Happened*, Kurt Vonnegut argues that Joseph Heller is a myth maker and that the novel constitutes his myth about contempory life, about

> the middle-class veterans who came home from that war to become heads of nuclear families. The proposed myth has it that those families were pathetically vulnerable and suffocating. It says that the heads of them commonly took jobs which were vaguely dishonorable or at least stultifying, in order to make as much money as they could for their little families, and they used the money in futile attempts to buy safety and happiness. The proposed myth says that they lost their dignity and their will to live in the process.
> It says they are hideously tired now.[18]

According to Vonnegut, this myth could become the explanatory fiction for post World War II America, or as he puts it, "an epitaph for our era in the shorthand of history" (2). Perhaps, but if so, it is difficult to imagine a more painful story for Americans to call their own.[19] Viewed as myth, the novel tells Americans that, while affirming family values and the sanctity of childhood, they have produced emotionally stunted lives, selves shrivelled by their concern with crabgrass, country club, and career. More insidiously, they have destroyed the children for whom they claimed to make their choices. For Americans who lived through Vietnam and Watergate, this myth holds the frightening possibility that Bob Slocum is their own darker self—their own Mr. Hyde—and that these events betoken an inner darkness rather than an external one.

Although Vonnegut's contention is richly suggestive, I want for now to pursue another aspect of Heller's myth-making. Within Slocum's monologue, Heller embeds the personal myths with which Slocum recasts his memories. Slocum's myths are explanatory reshapings of experience that account for feelings and desires he cannot otherwise explain. I use the word "myth" to characterize the way in which Slocum rearranges and transmutes his memories according to fictional patterns. By filling in the lapses of memory and giving experience narrative order, his myths supply what his memories and experience cannot themselves supply—meaning, order, and coherence.[20] Most simply, then, Slocum's myths are a way of making sense of things. They can explain both his fears that something catastrophic has happened to him and his premonition that something will happen again. Given a world made unstable by these fears and premonitions, Slocum's myths enable him to fix a sense of identity and to explain himself to himself.

Within the novel *Something Happened*, Heller uses Slocum's myths as narrative patterns, making the idiosyncrasies of his protagonist's mind the structural principles for his novel. The crucial correspondence between Slocum's mind and the construction of the novel—and the one I want to explore in detail—is that between Slocum's lost-child myth and the novel's climax. Unconsciously acting out the requirements of his story of destroyed innocence, Slocum accidently kills his son. Building the end of the novel out of the lost-child story, Heller sets up a complex relationship between the meaning Slocum sees in his life and the meaning the novel itself unfolds. Paradoxically, Slocum's myths, which fail as explanations even for himself, reveal the tenor of Heller's novel: its meaning dependent upon interplay between narrative levels as well as between story and discourse. This narrative complexity, in turn, enables Heller to probe more deeply into the dead-child story of "The Miracle of Danrossane," "Crippled Phoenix," *Catch-22,* and " 'Catch-22' Revisited."

Heller also places Slocum's lost-child myth in relation to pre-existing myths, especially the Oedipus story. Yet as Heller presents them, these longstanding myths have been deprived of their explanatory power. Like a dead god, they take much with them, for with their disappearance, the possibility for extra human meaning vanishes as well. J. Hillis Miller's characterization of the consequences of the disappearance of God can also describe a world in which myth has lost its efficacy: it "transforms every-thing for man, changing not only his experience of the world but also his experience of himself. It is associated with a situation in which human subjectivity seems to become the foundation of all things, the only source of meaning and value in the world."[21] Thus, when Slocum invokes the Oedipus story to explain his experience, he finds it a debased currency. Yet out of the incoherence of Slocum's experience and the shards of the Oedipus myth, Heller reconstitutes a mythic dilemma—fathers who kill their children—and thus affirms mythic meaning. In this invocation of the force of myth, *Something Happened* has affinities with Wallace Stevens's "Notes toward a Supreme Fiction": "There was a myth before the myth began, / Venerable and articulate and complete."[22]

Slocum's central myth—that he has within him a child who is alone and lonely, innocent and unchanging—enables him to believe that he has an identity distinct from the facts of his life. Continually, he probes his memories for signs of this child who he feels must be himself: "there must have been a time, I think I recall, when I was unable to believe I would ever be any different from the lonely, isolated little boy I was then" (260). Given Slocum's preoccupation with the isolated little boy, his memories hold a story distinct from the experiences they recall. The memories record the loss of the child-self: "He [the child-self] has never been found. . . . And I can't keep looking back for sight of him" (307). But Slocum's narrative does keep looking back, continually trying to recover a self he never had.

Slocum's lost-child myth describes both the self he thinks he has lost and that for which he longs. It memorializes a childhood self uncorrupted by the world, knowledge, and sexuality, a self not unlike that implied by the tree-of-life scene in *Catch-22*:

> hidden somewhere inside every bluff or quiet man and woman I know, I think, is the fully formed, but uncompleted, little boy or girl that once was and will always remain as it always has been, sus-pended lonesomely inside its own past, waiting hopefully, vainly, to resume, longing insatiably for company, pining desolately for that time to come when it will be safe and sane and possible to burst out-side exuberantly, stretch its arms, fill its lungs with invigorating air, without fear at last, and call:
> "Hey! Here I am. Couldn't you find me? Can't we be together now?"
> And hiding inside of me somewhere, I know (I feel him inside me. I feel it beyond all doubt), is a timid little boy just like my son who wants to be his best friend and wishes he could come outside and play. (231)

This passage unfolds the central features of the little-boy myth. Here the self exists alone, a monad of pure sensation, unchanging and unchanged. The child has preserved its exquisite innocence, and as the passage makes clear, the myth enshrines feelings of loneliness—feelings so striking and so present that they supply, when remembered, their own fulfillment. Yet the boy longs for material existence, "to burst outside exuberantly," and for friendship that will release him from his longings. He desires to make his identity known, for the little boy is always hidden inside, never seen by the world.[23] Parentless and alone, this child—like James Gatz's Jay Gatsby —springs from his own "Platonic conception of himself."

As Slocum imagines the little-boy story, it can never be completed. At root, the story is of loss. "Lost: one child, age unknown, goes by the name of me" (307). For Slocum, the child is the repository of some secret knowledge, and he wants to ask "where did you go and what did you mean" (307). This child exists as in a Golden Age, not remembered, but only glimpsed through earlier memories. The "original article" exists only in "some inaccessible black recess" (307). In this formulation, the little-boy story creates two orders of time, experience, and existence: the boy in the wish-memories on the borders of consciousness, and the man in the chronological tyranny of the present. Slocum's rhetoric and the orders of temporality that his imaginings posit detach him from his own fabrication.

Slocum persists, though, in seeing the mythic child as the locus of his own identity, for the child provides an unvarying self in the face of inevitable change and decay. According to Slocum's bonding, "He's me. But I'm not he" (398). In this bonding, Slocum insists upon their similarity, while acknowledging the space between the identity for which he yearns and "what [he] . . . has been forced to become" (307). The space between the two selves is crucial, for it enables Slocum to protect his essential self, which, ironically, he identifies as "all those truly important parts of my past that no longer exist in my memory" (134). It also allows him to disassociate himself from the tawdry stuff of day-to-day life. Thus, after listing such experiences as singing army marching songs, masturbating, eating baloney, egg, or canned salmon sandwiches and earning Boy Scout badges, Slocum can assert, "it [the set of memories] never happened—I do insist on that—not to me" (135). Shielded by the child myth, Slocum can assure the endurance of an essential self even when he is part of the "tired, hostile, grimy" world of "adults who glared, sighed, snored, and sweated" (135).

Slocum's persistence in seeing the child-self as the seed of his own identity undermines his own myth. Slocum glimpses but never understands the paradox embodied in the story. When he says of the child, "He's me. But I'm not he," he is indeed no longer seeing himself as the child; he is seeing difference. Perception and knowledge are the great enemies here, literally making Slocum other than the child or, as he would have it, other than himself. Moreover, when Slocum differentiates the child from himself, his fear-haunted mind makes the child a part of an alien world, a world of secrets, dangers, and threats. "I think he [the child] may be hiding inside my head with all the others I know are there and cannot find, playing evil tricks on my moods and heartbeat also. . . . I am infiltrated and besieged, the unprotected target of sneaky attacks from within" (398). This vision partakes of the "something happened" motif, rendering the child as another indication of imminent catastrophe. Unable to close the circles of myth and experience and of child and self-image, Slocum finds that the little-boy myth begins to unravel.

The unraveling of Slocum's myth becomes most noticeable when he applies its premises to the present. To Slocum's mind, seeing his present as if he were still a child-innocent returns him to the secure identity of his imagined past. For example, playing the part of the little boy during the critical moments of an argument with his wife and daughter, Slocum can sit back and enjoy his performance. "(I am enjoying my fit exquisitely. I am still a little boy. I am a deserted little boy I know who will never grow older and never change, who goes away and then comes back. . . . He is always nearby)" (158). As little boy again, Slocum can become victim, when in fact he has been the victimizer. His assumed innocence affords him the luxury of feeling helpless and abused in a low-life, domestic drama. Yet, as the passage reveals, Slocum's drama escapes his own imagining. "He [the child] is . . . out of my control. . . . Between us now there is a cavernous void" (158). Again Slocum becomes spectator to his own myth and isolated from the child he had hoped the myth would allow him to become. Recognizing the space between the little boy and himself, Slocum becomes aware of a "cavernous void." This void, however, does not protect the imagined essential self. Rather it calls attention to the differences between the two selves, thereby unmasking Slocum's motivations and assumptions. In this domestic drama, he is the petty belligerent, not the endangered innocent. When Slocum recasts actual events in the terms of his myth, it loses its crystalline purity.

While Slocum's handling of the child story has the effect of demystifying it, Heller infuses the present with the tenets of Slocum's imaginings. Heller wants the authorial audience to see what Slocum cannot: when Slocum reshapes his experience with personal myths, he constructs the patterns his present life will take. Thus, Slocum's myths contribute to the narrative design of Heller's novel. When Slocum leaves the quarrel with his wife savoring his feelings of being abused, he paradoxically brings the story of the innocent to life. Storming from the room, he accidentally steps on his son's foot, thereby acting out—albeit unconsciously—the premises of his own myth.[24] The innocent child materializes in the son's wail, still frightened, abused, and lonely. The features of the child story have come to shape Slocum's understanding of what happens to him. In the quarrel episode, then, the revitalized child-myth again appears phoenix-like at the very instant that Slocum has drained it of meaning.[25]

While Slocum cannot recover this self, he can project its patterns upon his sons, seeing each as a lonely, injured innocent. Slocum's elder son embodies the myth in its most hopeful formulation. His is an Adamic story of prelapsarian goodness: "He is a good little boy and always has been . . . almost too good to be true" (230).[26] Punctuated by such lines, each account of the son becomes an exemplum of pristine innocence and its dangers. For example, the son allows his fat, wheezy opponent to catch him in a race while he collapses in wholly enjoyed laughter, which prompts teammates and counselors to descend on him, pushing and abusing. Or the son defuses his father's anger at him for always giving away his things with a triumphant shout, "Daddy, I love you!" (304). As Slocum recounts these occurrences, he begins to make them his own, projecting his own emotions into what happens to his son. Thus, Slocum says of his son's refusal to participate in Forgione's gym class (one of the many situations from which Slocum feels that he must rescue his son): "I am more tense than my boy because I can objectify anxieties he does not even know he suffers from yet" (249). More accurately, Slocum sees the son as repeating the experiences he imagines he had as a child. Then Slocum reverses the process. Recognizing his son's feelings, especially his son's suffering, he comes to share these feelings. In this way, Slocum sees himself repeating his son's experience. Given this two-way identification, Slocum means more than he knows when he says, "I identify with him [the son] too closely" (338).

By contrast, Derek, Slocum's mentally retarded son, embodies an anxiety-darkened version of innocence. Slocum's picture of Derek parodically inverts the principle of unchanging innocence. Thus, Slocum repeatedly imagines his son's manhood as disintegration. His formulation is always the same: "He'll be balding. His suit won't fit. No one will groom him. His dandruff falls like fish scales" (453). Repulsive physical details dominate Slocum's descriptions of Derek, calling attention to human decay in the absence of enlivening powers of mind. But even Derek repeats Slocum's self-story. He will have a "resemblance to a secret me I know I have inside me and want nobody else to discover, an inner visage" (391).[27] In Slocum's formulation, the fears of a secret resemblance signal a larger pattern of replication. Derek is a nightmare copy of the self that he fears he is becoming: "My memory's failing, my bladder is weak, my arches are falling, my tonsils and adenoids are gone, and my jawbone is rotting" (561). Both visions are stories of flesh, the matter of *Catch-22*. For Heller,

SOMETHING HAPPENED ■ 95

material innocence is sinister, for matter holds mortality, the secret danger to existence.

In projecting his child-myth upon his sons, Slocum constrains the way in which he experiences his life, although he does not recognize this. Heller uses three successive episodes—the first two set at summer camp and the last at Atlantic City—to show how Slocum externalizes his lost-child myth and, by doing so, is bound by its requirements. The three episodes refigure ordinary childhood events. In the first, Slocum's son arouses his teammates' ire by allowing his opponent to catch up with him in a medicine ball race; in the second, the son cries helplessly when his parents are late to pick him up; and in the third, the boy gets lost on the Boardwalk in Atlantic City. As transformed in Slocum's mind, each episode becomes a "bad dream" in which he plays all the parts: first, identifying with his son, then hating his son's innocence; second, wanting as father to protect his son, then wanting to kill him. Slocum's "dream" foretells his actions, although he, of course, does not know this.

The first camp episode establishes the way in which Slocum's myth informs his perceptions of day-to-day experience. Recounting his son's helplessness when attacked by a teammate, Slocum activates his helpless child story. It is a parallel drama: what happens to his son and what goes through Slocum's mind.

> My boy fell back a few steps (his knees were buckling again), turned white as a sheet (Oh, God, I thought—he's going to vomit, or faint. Or cry. And make me ashamed), and waited limply. He did nothing else. He stood there. He did not speak or protest, or cast his eyes about. . . . (I shuddered and thought that I might puke.) The other boy rushed forward again and slammed my boy in the chest with his open hands. . . . For a fleeting instant, I was enthralled by the dignity and courage I sensed he was showing just by holding his ground and waiting for the next battering charge. He would not move to save himself. (I do not move to save myself.) For a second, I could actually make myself feel proud. But that wasn't enough. I wanted him to have more guts. (I wish I had more guts.) I heard myself rooting for him to strike back. (315)

The narrative strands here create a series of mirror images: the son looks as though he will vomit, Slocum wants to puke; the son's seeming paralysis, Slocum's own paralyzed response to his son's helplessness; the son's inability to save himself from his assailant, Slocum's inability to save himself from the humiliation he feels at the scene. The mirroring affirms the incomplete identity he posited in the myth of the child-self: "He's me. But I'm not he." Watching the fight, Slocum takes over the son's sensations, making them his own, telling of the fight as if he were the helpless victim. But Slocum is not his son. His shame keeps him outside the scene, an onlooker who can only mumble: "Move, you dope" (315).

Even while responding to his son's predicament, Slocum realizes that he is conceiving his son's sensations in the terms of his own imaginings and fears. As he says of the scene, his son could not "release himself from that lifelong, terrifying nightmare of mine" (316). This nightmare renders the child-innocent as mute and immobile in a terror-charged world, creating an ever-unvoiced cry for help, a cry that must be answered. "(I am there, and someone can get me—I am dead already because I cannot free my feet or yell for help—I am speechless too)" (316). In this formulation, Slocum imagines existence as the infant Oedipus might have experienced it on the mountainside, abandoned, his feet pierced and bound. This nightmare vision creates fear which cannot be resolved, only heightened to a crescendo: "Here was that bad dream of mine coming to life. Here was onrushing death and degradation bearing down upon him once more in the senseless, stupid action of a little, slightly sturdier boy" (315–16). The nightmare has its own imperatives, transforming Slocum's fears and desires until they are outside of his control. It is also a vision of loss of control, a recurrent motif in the novel. In the vision, muteness begets violence —just as it did in Melville's *Billy Budd*. As Slocum acknowledges: "I would have murdered my boy" (316). The violence destroys what Slocum most wants to protect, his son—thereby hinting at a dark truth: it is ineffectual innocence that Slocum cannot endure. Continually confronted by such innocence, Slocum will eventually destroy its embodiment.

The second day-camp episode—when the son cries desolately because he thinks his parents have abandoned him—provides a counterpoint to the first. The premises of the two scenes are inverted: a cry for help rather than silence at the center of the scene; the decisiveness of Slocum's response to his son's helplessness, in contrast to his own earlier helplessness; the emphasis on Slocum as parent-protector, rather than on his inability to protect. But the core of the scene is the same, the son's defenseless innocence and Slocum's ambivalent reaction to it. "We were late coming for him that day, and we saw him, half a block from the play area, standing alone on the sidewalk in his bare feet and bawling loudly, helplessly" (318). The son's defenselessness infuriates Slocum, and the awful responsibility of having to safeguard his son grates on him. In his frustration, Slocum, even while rushing toward his son, responds to his son's predicament by conceiving his son's death. "[T]here was a small boy standing in one place on the sidewalk who had been crying there all day and night and was in danger of dying from starvation, fright, or loneliness" (320). This is not the son murdered, but the son abandoned. Nevertheless, however Slocum imagines the story, it always ends with the son's death.

If in the first day-camp episode Slocum senses that he is part of a story already told, in the second episode Heller shows that it has been told by Sophocles. Ironically, Slocum, who lards his monologue with references to Oedipus, cannot see that the patterns of the Oedipus myth inform his own experience. "He remained stationary on the pavement in that single spot on his tiny bare feet as though every bone in his ankles had already been crushed (I noticed then, I think, for the first time, how his feet pronate, how his arches are almost flat, and how large and sharp and close to the ground his ankle bones are) and even to continue standing there was excruciating and unendurable" (319–20). While Slocum's attention is riveted on the scarred ankles, he does not see their significance, but the authorial audience can remember that Oedipus's name means swollen-footed. In Slocum's and Heller's Oedipal account, childhood innocence threatens the father and so the child must die.[28] For Slocum—as for the Heller who plots *Catch-22*, "'Catch-22' Revisted," *We Bombed in New Haven*, *Something Happened*, and *God Knows*—the death of the child provides the crucial moment of narrative clarification. The son must die. Like a string of DNA molecules, the day-camp episodes disclose the design of the novel as a whole. At this moment the end of the novel is already in sight, the blood already on the sidewalk, and Slocum's story of the destruction of childhood has already been told.

As the third of the lost-son episodes demonstrates, Slocum resists the knowledge that is available to him and refuses to acknowledge the parallels with Oedipus that he himself invokes. Amidst "the familiar signs and structures" (336) of the Boardwalk, Slocum's son loses his way, uncertain, as he subsequently tells his father, even if he is lost. The son's helplessness causes Slocum to lose his way as well in "a terrible rush of ungovernable, dissonant emotions in which landmarks made no sense to me" (337):

> I wanted to kill him. I was enraged and disgusted with him for his helplessness and incompetence (standing there like that on the sidewalk in town that day as though all the bones in his ankles were broken. I was ashamed of him and wanted to disown him. I was sorry he was mine), then I wanted to clasp him to me lovingly and protectively and shed tears of misery and deepest compassion over him (because I had wanted to kill him. Imagine having a father that wanted to kill you. That's that part they all leave out of the Oedipus story. Poor Oedipus has been much maligned. He didn't want to kill his father. His father wanted to kill *him*). (336)

Retrospectively, Slocum glimpses the way in which he has imposed the Oedipus story on his son's losing his way returning home from summer camp. Having activated this association, however, he casts the Atlantic

City experience as another Oedipal drama, perversely taking the part of
the injured innocent. As always, he turns away from the illumination the
comparison with Oedipus affords. As helpless child, Slocum can forget
the originating impulse of this episode—"I wanted to kill him [his son]"
(336).

In his recollection of the Oedipus story, Slocum can assume the
perspective of the child whom Laius wanted to kill, but not that of the
adult Oedipus who has killed. Confronted with the plague on Thebes that
cannot be ended until Laius's killer is found, Oedipus seeks to unravel the
mystery, even when it is clear that this mystery is bound up with himself.
Despite being warned by Teiresias and Jocasta of the dangers of knowledge, Oedipus pursues the truth of who he is and what he has done. In so
doing, he achieves the strength necessary to accept and endure his actions:
"The horror is mine," he says, "and none but I am *strong* enough to endure
it."[29] Not so Slocum. He consistently displaces his responsibility for his
actions; readers will recall, for example, that he announces his son's death
by saying, "[m]y boy has stopped talking to me" (549). Confounded by an
emotional landscape "that made no sense," Slocum retreats into the lost-
child story, a narrative he already knows. This is easier than making manifest the territory that is unknown to him, the emotions of a father who
wills the death of his son.

In the way Heller embeds the Oedipus myth in *Something Happened*,
he is not invoking its explanatory power, at least not in the usual ways. As
James Mellard argues, the novel resists Freudian readings.[30] And Heller
does not build a systematic set of associations between his novel and the
myth, in the ways that Joyce does between *Ulysses* and *The Odyssey* or
that Faulkner does between *The Sound and the Fury* and the passion story.
Rather Heller invokes the Oedipus myth in a way analogous to the way
linguists talk of the meaning of words—as deriving from the play of differences between one sound and another as they are juxtaposed. Similarly,
Heller juxtaposes narratives: Slocum's lost-child myth, his sons' experience (which Slocum sees as replicating the child myth), Slocum's actual
experience, and the echoes of the Oedipus story. The result is in accord
with what J. Hillis Miller calls the Quaker Oats box effect: "When a novel
presents a fiction within a fiction within a fiction, the reality at the beginning and ending of this series tends to be assimilated into and to appear as
itself a fiction. . . . A real Quaker Oats box is fictionalized when it bears a
picture of a Quaker Oats box which in turn bears a picture of a Quaker
Oats box, and so on indefinitely, in an endless play of imagination and
reality."[31] The picture on Heller's Quaker Oats box is the death of the
child; no matter what narrative level the reader attends to in *Something
Happened*, the child always dies. The meaning of this death, however, remains elusive, existing in the interplay of the embedded narratives.

According to Joseph Campbell, myths invite an inward turn for, like the Oedipus story, they enact journeys into the self.[32] Slocum fails as myth maker precisely because he resists such a turn. In his review, Kurt Vonnegut recounts the internal journey that reading the novel occasioned for him, a journey into "the cage of those experiences" of "clever white people" of his generation (2). If Vonnegut's journey foretells that of other readers, then *Something Happened* will indeed have occasioned "the birth of a new myth" (2), although the stuff of this myth—the death of children —is as old as myth itself and the dread that it occasions as primordial. Certainly, Heller constructs his novel as an interior monologue in order to invite his authorial audience to make this inward turn. To move inside his story or to see this story inside oneself is to enter the realm of narrative itself. Great readers inevitably do this. Kierkegaard did so when reading the story of Abraham's sacrifice and, with his retellings, he shared the plenitude that he found there:

Abraham's eyes were darkened, and he knew joy no more

or

[H]e threw himself upon his face, he prayed God to forgive him his sin, that he had been willing to offer Isaac, that the father had forgotten his duty toward the son

or

He seized Isaac by the throat, threw him to the ground, and said, "Stupid boy, dost thou then suppose I am thy father? I am an idolater. Dost thou suppose that this is God's bidding? No, it is my desire."

or

Then they returned home, and Sarah hasteneth to meet them, but Isaac had lost his faith. No word of this had ever been spoken in the world.[33]

Myths beget possibility, compounding meaning rather than restricting it, even as they reveal the destructive compulsions to which we readers as well as Slocum are party.

▓

TIME AND THE SELF

The undoing of Slocum's myth-making is time, for the shape of Slocum's temporal vision entraps him.[34] In *We Bombed in New Haven*, a character says of the play: "It's about time," but the play does not fulfill the promise of this line. *Something Happened* does. Slocum conceives temporality as inextricably linked to biological degeneration and decay, to "life turn[ing] old, threadbare (teeth come out, toes abrade, arches begin to ache and spinal columns too, and shoes no longer fit), dry, and sour" (206). This sense of the life cycle partakes of the riddle of the Sphinx (what goes on four legs in the morning, on two at noon, and on three in the evening?). But Slocum always fixes on the end of life, not the noon. If Slocum can reshape the beginnings of life with his lost-child myth, he cannot do so with old age. In old age, he sees a single possibility—senility—and senility embodies the entropic principle that locks energy in matter, thereby increasing disorder. As in *Catch-22*, the thrust of Heller's temporality is death, but in *Something Happened*, the boundaries blur between death and life as death penetrates life. Pictures of living death abound in the novel: Slocum's mother's senility, Derek's idiocy, the whole series of mental breakdowns, most notably Martha's (the secretary whose breakdown Slocum handles at the end of the novel). It is as if Slocum and, by extension, Heller, see Alzheimer's disease as endemic to humanity.

In *Catch-22* (as well as in *We Bombed in New Haven*), time is chiefly an external construct, represented in the novel by the bombing missions. They are the clock to which the novel beats and by which it unfolds; their chronology—not the calendar—provides its time line, enabling readers to orient themselves. In *Something Happened*, time is inseparable from Slocum's consciousness, and like this consciousness, it is a multivalent reality: biological, psychological, social, as well as chronological. The ever-increasing missions of *Catch-22* designate a temporal destiny that, as the ending illustrates, can be evaded. By contrast, *Something Happened* depicts a destiny that cannot be avoided and whose progression is entirely relative. Events—and not all of them at that—can be designated only as before or after, nothing more. By confining the reader in Slocum's consciousness, Heller renders time as a continuous flow, retrospection merging into anticipation, the already joined to the not yet. *Something Happened* is about time, which, in this instance also means that it is about consciousness.

Slocum's sense of his own identity participates in the disorder that he sees in time.[35] The series of "I feel afloat" descriptions Slocum gives in answer to the question "Who am I?" depict a self adrift in time. "I float like algae in a colony of green scum, while my wife and I grow old, my daughter grows older and more dissatisfied with herself and with me" (306–7). "I feel afloat (legless). Legless, I walk around with headaches that do not seem to be mine (on feet that do. Arches ache and seem to be crumbling, I have a spur on one heel, middle toes are hammered, others are gnarled and require Band-Aids or corn plasters." (304–5). Unlike the myth of the child-self, this self-image provides no promise of stability or fixity. Rather the self is carried along, the only certainty in its drift the certainty of old age. In Slocum's dark joke, "I have exchanged the position of the fetus for the position of the corpse" (340). In these images, the self partakes of its fluidic surroundings, its form indefinite, its identity uncertain. Again and again, Slocum will wonder who and what he is. His self exists as a series of loosely connected moments of consciousness, propelled by forces outside its control. Slocum cannot even be assured of the continuity of its experiencing: "The cable of continuity is not unbroken . . . it wavers and fades, wears away in places to slender, frayed strands, breaks. . . . Mountainous segments of history appear to be missing. There are yawning gulfs into which large chunks of me may have fallen" (505). No wonder Slocum cannot tell his story with the Aristotelian neatness of an orderly beginning, middle, and end.[36] Time does not provide the comfort of a clearly differentiated chronology, rather it erodes one's sense of identity.

Adrift in time, Slocum narrates his life as if he stands apart from it. For example, in describing the self who watched his parents in bed together, he says, "I don't know where he [himself as a boy] came from; I don't know where I went; I don't know all that's happened to me since. I miss him" (206). The space between the boy observer and himself signals Slocum's divided sense of self. In fact, Slocum describes himself as having a series of selves which embody different aspects of his experience. There is the self who fills in for "things of which I did not wish to become part"; the self who judges "everything, even me"; and the self of whom he is aware but knows nothing (135). This fragmented sense of his own identity is symptomatic of Slocum's alienation, as is his inability to identify himself. "Nameless I came and nameless I go. I am not Bob Slocum just because my parents decided to call me that. If there is such a person, I don't know who he is. . . . I don't even know who I'm not" (490). Time and experience exist on different planes, such that the experience of the self does not provide knowledge or illumination. Rather, the sensations of the self in time become a source of alienation, for Slocum always feels other than his experience and, paradoxically, other than himself.

To Slocum's mind, his mother, daughter, and wife exemplify different aspects of the self in time. Their stories provide the counterbalance to his lost-child myth and to the way in which his sons embodied this myth. If the myth opened the world of fictional possibility, Slocum's accounts of mother, daughter, and wife bring him back to the day-to-day world. Their lives speak for the reality principle: his mother's for old age, his daughter's for puberty, and his wife's for middle age. The common denominator in each moment is the dissolution of the self.

Slocum's image of his mother conveys the message that in our origins lie our ends. In thinking about her, Slocum returns again and again to her last days: "she was bedridden with arthritis and painful, cramping limbs and joints and stricken speechless by her brain spasms . . . and in the end, ha, ha, she died, crying for her mother, moaning 'Ma! Ma! Ma!' in a drone that was clear and loud" (325–26). This is not so much the end as a process of irreversible degeneration and decay. Senility robs life of a sense of finality, its death cry, returning life to where it came. But the closing circle of origins and ends negates possible meaning. As the doctor says in explaining the mother's final moments: "she . . . did not know *what was happening*" (emphasis added, 326). Slocum himself defines the meaning of his mother's death when he looks back to the days which preceded it. "Now you're just hanging around, ruining my weekends and costing me money, splotching my moods and splattering my future" (326).

Slocum's memories of his mother's death shape his sense of how his own life will end. "I'll have bladder and prostate trouble—that's if I'm lucky and don't have a coronary occlusion or stroke first. . . . But I know I'll probably want to hang around as long as I can too, pain, pity, self-revulsion and all, clinging with weakening fingers to vaporous mirages above the bedsheets and muttering 'Ma! Ma! Ma! Ma!' . . . instead of 'ha, ha, ha'" (327). In this formulation, life is a process of degeneration leading to an almost insensate end, and death is a sinister form of repetition. Darkly ironic, Slocum's imagined final cry repeats the cry of a mother to whom he was indifferent. As if signalling a sequence that will repeat itself generation after generation, he does add one more "Ma" to his death cry. Death is a cry in a void, a last desire for union with one's mother and the simultaneous denial that motherhood is anything but a biological relationship. The conclusion of Slocum's anti-apocalyptic portrait of the end is being filed under dead records and thus into oblivion.

Slocum portrays his daughter's life as perpetual pubescence, a contrast to his tendency to fix his sons in eternal childhood. Envisioning her life as constant change, he sees all the dangers his child myth exorcises: lost innocence and the knowledge it brings, unceasing wants and dissatisfactions, and sexuality reduced to a biological drive. While Slocum can recall moments in his daughter's childhood in terms strikingly similar to the child myth, his monologue always places such moments in an unrecoverable past. The few occasions when such memories intrude prompt

Slocum, who is obsessed with his daughter's rebelliousness, merely to ask what has happened. The unvoiced answer—the answer woven into every memory—is change. His daughter is a teenager, her story is one of meta-morphosis. But Slocum has a Kafkaesque sense of the results of metamor-phosis: "I find myself grieving silently alongside her, as though at an open coffin or grave in which her future is lying dead already. (She is not yet sweet sixteen . . .)" (166). For Slocum, visions of life inevitably resolve in visions of death.

In contrast to his child myth, which insists, paradoxically, upon the particularity and the uniqueness of experience, Slocum's accounts of his daughter are generalized. Her story as teenager is inextricably linked with American teenage life. "She wants to become a part too, I guess, of what she sees is her environment, and she is, I fear, already merging with, dis-solving into, her surroundings right before my eyes" (74). This model for change is becoming what you are not, losing your identity by turning into an American stereotype. His daughter's metamorphosis follows a generic pattern. Hence Slocum's descriptions of her recount typical behaviors: her foul language, smoking, complaints, and announcements of unhappiness. Such descriptions always shift emphasis from what his daughter is to what she is becoming. Most simply, "[s]he is going to become a lonely, ner-vous, contemporary, female human being" (180), and for Slocum the cru-cible for this change is American culture.

Slocum's vision of what his daughter is becoming partakes of Heller's satirical view of what America is:

I know where my daughter is heading from the girls I know who have already been there. . . . She will drink whiskey for a while . . . then stop; then start in again after she's been married several years and drink whiskey regularly from then on, like my wife. She will have two children or three and be divorced (unlike my wife), and she will marry a second time if she and the children are still young when the first marriage breaks up. She will smoke marijuana. . . . She will get laid. (There is just no other way to deal with that fact; and the best one can wish for her in this area is that she enjoy it wholesomely from the start. . . .) She will go wild for a while (and think she is free), have all-night revels and bull sessions, complain about her teachers and curriculum requirements, have no interest in any of her academic sub-jects but get passing grades in all with very little work, if she doesn't drop out altogether because of sheer dejection and torpor (which she will eulogize into something mystic and exalted, like superior intelli-gence). She will experiment with pep pills (ups), barbiturates (downs), mescaline, and LSD, if LSD remains in vogue; she will have group sex (at least once), homosexual sex (at least once, and at least once more with a male present as a spectator and participant), be friendly with fags, poets, snobs, nihilists, and megalomaniacs, dress like other girls, have abortions (at least one, or lie and say she did . . .)." (181–82)

The profusion of details recapitulates the rhythms of American life and the way Americans look at themselves—the America viewed in movies or on TV. Amid the seeming variety, there is an unchanging cycle, first voiced by Ecclesiastes: "What has been is what will be and what has been done will be done; and there is nothing new under the sun." This vision often informs the satirist's art—think, for instance, of Thackeray's *Vanity Fair* —and its mechanics are always the same: the vanity of human aspirations, the sterility of social life, the unchanging changeability of fashion and manners, and the ceaselessness of human longings and dissatisfactions.[37]

When Slocum describes what his daughter is becoming, he recounts a way of life that he has already entered and announces a self that he has already become. "I know this bumpy terrain too well, and I know she is already bouncing and tumbling through it downhill, with a will and momentum that cannot be stayed and which is not really entirely of her own choosing. . . . She is skidding and falling ahead resolutely out of control" (182–83). The vision elaborates the disintegration of personality, of values, and finally of the self. Continuing in this manner, Heller piles verb upon verb—a stylistic strategy that is highly unusual for him. The verbs render experience as process and change as deterioration. The location of change shifts in the passage from the outside world to the inside. What is being lost is identity, so that death of the self precedes material decay—a much darker social vision than that of *Catch-22* and one anticipating those of *Good as Gold*, *Picture This*, and *Closing Time*. According to Slocum, his daughter is dying, but so is the mind that conceives her experience in these terms.

Slocum associates his wife with the present. His descriptions of her have a restlessness about them. Thinking about her, Slocum cannot dwell either in the present or in the past. In the present, he sees a wife who drinks too much and the effects alcohol has on her personality and appearance. Like a fastidious person entering an untidy apartment, Slocum notices the disorderly details: the girdle she does not wear, the slight slurring of speech, and the heaviness of manner. To turn to the past only reminds Slocum what time has done to her. "It is painful for me to recall how my wife was, to know the kind of person she used to be and would have liked to remain" (103). For Slocum, his wife's story is easily plotted. As Slocum says: "My wife is unhappy. She is one of those married women who are very, very bored, and lonely, and I don't know what I can make myself do about it" (71).

Slocum's account of sexual intercourse with his wife epitomizes his view of her and their common present. "And she swarms all over me irrepressibly, her arms and legs and mouth opening and entwining. . . . And I am the one now who wiggles free . . . to close and lock the door and extinguish the overhead light" (125–26). There is a base of physical satisfaction to this sexual coupling, but underneath is a deeper longing. In such moments Slocum does not find the fulfillment of which he dreams or that he experiences in his memories of fondling the satin coolness of Virginia's lingerie. Moreover, Slocum's prose suggests the embarrassment he feels in his wife's drink-quickened desire (although, of course, he feels no embarrassment in his masturbatory desire for Virginia). There is an unspoken nostalgia for the reticent wife of the past who would dress and undress in the closet. In his account, Slocum seems to want "to wiggle free" of the experience. In this moment of physical intimacy emotional distances yawn.

Something Happened is about the dissolution of the self in time. In *Catch-22* and *We Bombed in New Haven*, time is chiefly an external construct, determined by society's needs. But in *Something Happened*, it has a biological, psychological, and social dimension, as well as a chronological one. Unlike the temporal destiny of *Catch-22*, which can be evaded, this temporality designates an unavoidable destination—inevitable senility and death. Lying within Slocum, the biological and psychological realities of time make the dissolution of the self an ineluctable process. Similarly, as Slocum's daughter shows, the erosion of the self in time occurs as a virtually inevitable social phenomenon—a contemporary American myth as Vonnegut would say—which dissolves individual identity into cultural types. *Something Happened* is about time, and, for Heller as well as Slocum, time spins out the single, unending tale of the breakdown of the self.

▦

THE LOGIC OF EMPTINESS: FORM IN *SOMETHING HAPPENED*

Novelist William Kennedy's description of *Something Happened* as "devoid of story, structure, tidy continuity and other accoutrements of the conventional novel" sounds a critical note that reappears in appraisals of all Heller's novels.[38] Reviewers and critics, even those praising Heller's achievement, often present him as a novelist who has never quite mastered the formal requirements of his craft.[39] Or critics take a different tack and argue that apparent "defects" in structure are vehicles for Heller's absurdist vision—a defense resting upon the assumption that a disorderly structure is necessary to represent the absurdity of modern life.[40] Neither position is adequate, for Heller's novels are, in fact, elaborately structured. *Something Happened* has story, structure, and even remarkable, if unconventional, continuity.

The novel's second chapter, "The office in which I work," affords a typical example of the structural principles of Heller's fiction. As the title implies, Heller intends the chapter as a description of Slocum's workplace and by extension as a satiric view of corporate America. In terms of the plot, the chapter introduces the complication of Slocum's replacing Kagle as head of sales, and it is most important in iterating the tone of the novel. The chapter also contains the lines that gave Heller the idea for the novel and was originally designed to be the opening chapter.[41]

The chapter does not disclose its unity of design on first reading.[42] Its narrative progression is diffuse, since the chapter's seventeen sections move in different directions—some relate memories, others language games, still others meditations or imaginings. The details are frequently confounding. There is, for example, the first reference to Virginia, identified only as the "witty older girl . . . [who] sat under a big Western Union clock" (14). At this point, such details occupy narrative space but have no significance. Similarly, Heller's depiction of Slocum's company, populated by Browns, Greens, and Whites, is as amorphous as a Dickensian cabinet with Boodles, Coodles, and Foodles. When first read, then, the chapter seems to exemplify the lack of formal unity for which Heller has been criticized. In fact, however, the chapter is organized around a single idea, the dynamics of fear. Slocum's mental wanderings portray a satiric view of a company organized by fear and represent the workings of a mind that participates in this fear. Slocum's words—"I've got anxiety; I suppress hysteria" (67)—might serve as a description of the chapter's method, the alternate dramatization and suppression of fear. The chapter also illustrates the lessons that Heller learned about discourse in *Catch-22*, that is, discourse is essential to the story as well as the means of its transmission.

The first section strikes the key note, as the fear that Slocum describes radiates outward, then collapses back in on itself.

In the office in which I work there are five people of whom I am afraid. Each of these five people is afraid of four people (excluding overlaps), for a total of twenty, and each of these twenty people is afraid of six people, making a total of one hundred and twenty people who are feared by at least one person. Each of these one hundred and twenty people is afraid of the other one hundred and nineteen, and all of these one hundred and forty-five people are afraid of the twelve men at the top who helped found and build the company and now own and direct it.

All these twelve men are elderly now and drained by time and success of energy and ambition. . . . They seem friendly, slow, and content when I come upon them in the halls (they seem dead). (13)

The first paragraph makes fear a multiplicative progression with an ever-widening network of relationships, but the second paragraph shrinks the fear rapidly, until it is as diminished as the company's twelve founders. Simultaneously, the two paragraphs introduce the corporate structure that underpins the novel. The twelve dessicated apostles of the company provide the novel's empty center; they are also the nexus of the novel's web of fear. The directors exemplify the paradoxical reality of fear generated by emptiness. At first Slocum can detach himself from this fear by saying, "Since I have little contact with these twelve men at the top and see them so seldom, I am not really afraid of them" (14). Slocum's brave formulation undoes him, for before the chapter is over Slocum will have had his meeting with Arthur Baron, who will tell him that he is to replace Kagle as head of sales. After the meeting, Slocum will close himself in his office and announce laconically, "I've got anxiety" (67). The narrative rhythm of expansion and contraction, the pulsations of fear, has been set.

The opening section also establishes the associational workings of Slocum's monologue, which conflates past and present as if they exist on the same temporal plane. "Just about everybody in the company is afraid of somebody else in the company, and I sometimes think I am a cowering boy back in the automobile casualty insurance company for which I used to work very long ago, sorting and filing automobile accident reports after Mrs. Yerger was placed in charge of the file room and kept threatening daily to fire us all. . . . A witty older girl named Virginia . . . traded dirty jokes with me" (14). Fear is the connective here. The cowering boy of the little-boy myth is brought into the present, so that momentarily Slocum is a little boy again. But Slocum is also looking backward to a primary source of boyhood dread, Mrs. Yerger, the predecessor of the twelve founders. And turning back, Slocum cannot think of Mrs. Yerger without thinking about Virginia, who provides the most cherished of his past memories. Temporarily, the fear is displaced—but not gone. Slocum himself cannot entirely suppress the fear. "(Virginia herself had told me that one of the married claims adjusters had taken her out in his car one night, turned insistent, and threatened to rape her or put her out near a cemetery, until she pretended to start to cry.) I was afraid to open doors in that company too" (14). The parenthesis signals the way in which the half-remembered apprehension intrudes on Slocum himself, as well as upon the narrative. Also, the authorial audience recognizes the dread embedded in the Virginia memory when they come upon Slocum's reference to being afraid to open doors. That reference recalls the first sentence of Slocum's monologue: "I get the willies when I see closed doors" (3). Finally, readers who look back on these pages after reading the novel recognize the anxiety at the core of the memory. These readers remember that Virginia and Slocum never had intercourse because she always fled his clutching embraces, imagining someone would discover them, and because Slocum, not knowing how to get a hotel room, was afraid to accept her invitation for a liaison. The associations of Slocum's monologue reveal an order of which he is not aware and dramatize fear where he sees none.

In the sections that follow, Heller—much like a jazz pianist—works variations on a theme: section 2 demonstrates the symbiosis of fear; section 3 locates fear in Slocum's department; and section 4 introduces the source of universal fear, Martha the typist who is going crazy. The first sentence of each section is suggestive of the workings of the sequence.

> In the normal course of a business day, I fear Green and Green fears me. (16)

> In my department, there are six people who are afraid of me, and one small secretary who is afraid of all of us. (17)

> The thought occurs to me often that there must be mail clerks, office boys and girls, stock boys, messengers, and assistants of all kinds and ages who are afraid of *everyone* in the company; and there is one typist in our department who is going crazy slowly and has all of *us* afraid of *her*. (17)

In section 2, fear is a diurnal emotion, the basis for business relationships. By making fear so commonplace and easily explained, Slocum drains it of its terror. Most simply, Slocum fears Green because Green is his boss, and Green fears Slocum because he is popular and has associations with a more powerful department than Green's. Section 3 works a similar reversal in the Hellerian joke that the one person in the office Slocum wants to fire cannot be fired because Slocum is afraid of him. If sections 2 and 3 have the effect of making fear rational, ordinary, and finally trivial, section 4 makes it irrational and threatening. Initially, Heller again reduces the fear with a joke: people are afraid of Martha because they think that she will go crazy during work hours and someone will have to take responsibility for her. But Slocum's description tells us more about the hidden terrors that reside in his own consciousness than it does about Martha's becoming insane: "that last, decisive second in which she finally does go insane—shrieking or numb, clawing wildly or serene, comprehending intelligently that she has now gone mad . . . or terrified, ignorant, and confused" (18). The alternatives that Slocum balances speak about his own anxiety. At first his language helps to contain and control his unease, as he supplies a calm alternative for each dreaded one. But then the pattern reverses itself, as calm begets dread. When Slocum thinks about Martha's irrationality, his prose partakes of the insanity that it is trying to represent, becoming "terrified, ignorant, and confused" (18). Together, these sections establish the Heller rhythm: the reduction of mystery followed by its powerful magnification.

While repeating the same rhythms, Heller uses section 5 to make Slocum's company a metaphor for contemporary life. The use of the company as symbol recalls Dickens's technique in using institutions like Chancery or the Marshalsea as metaphors for society. The opening sentence—"The company is benevolent" (18)—serves to frame the section. The symbol of the company's benevolence is its paycheck, "patterned precisely with neat, rectangular holes and words of formal, official warning in small, black, block letters that the checks must not be spindled, torn, defaced, stapled, or mutilated in any other way" (19). Its benevolence is orderly, systematic, and cannot be resisted. As Slocum realizes when contemplating rebellion against the system by defacing the checks, "I know what would happen: nothing. . . . My act of rebellion would be absorbed like rain on an ocean and leave no trace" (19). The company structures its employees' lives in the same way it stamps out their paychecks. "They [the file folders containing people's records] were dead. . . . What impressed me most was the sheer immensity of all those dead records, the abounding quantity of all those drab old sagging cardboard file cabinets rising like joined, ageless towers from the floor almost to the ceiling, that vast, unending sequence of unconnected accidents" (20–21). Humans have been replaced by their records. Martha's fate demonstrates the brutality of this equation: "she'll be filed away" when she goes crazy (19). In recording the transactions of life, the company drains the life-blood. Human lives become file folders, their story finally contained in a green cabinet for dead records (20).

Section 5 tells another story as well, that of mental breakdowns. Like the file folders, they accumulate: Martha's, the nameless girl's, and the "middle-minor executive's." No wonder Slocum concludes the section with the understated generalization: "I think that maybe in every company today there is always at least one person who is going crazy slowly" (21). What bothers Slocum is not only the breakdowns but also their disorder and uncertainty. Unlike the file folders, which stand for the rational, orderly structures of life, the breakdowns point to what cannot be known or controlled. As Slocum will observe in section 6, "who knows with certainty when a person is breaking down?" (22). The breakdowns intrude the irrational into the highly sanitized rationality of the company. Section 5 tells a two-part story, then, that of the orderly, oppressive, and finally life-denying benevolence of the company and that of the breakdown of individuals within the company. Slocum, however, does not see the connection between the two parts.

In subsequent sections, Heller repeats the same rhythms, gradually widening and deepening the fear-produced connections and associations. For example, sections 9 and 10 show the relationship between fear and belief. The opening sentence to section 9 identifies this relationship. "The people in the company who are least afraid are the few in our small Market Research Department, who believe in nothing and are concerned with collecting, organizing, interpreting, and reorganizing statistical information about the public, the market, the country, and the world" (28). Fear is directly related to belief, and for Slocum, the only protection from fear is to divorce action from belief. In Slocum's words, we are in the business of "converting whole truths into half truths and half truths into whole ones. I am very good with these techniques of deception" (29). This is the alchemy of advertising. The whole trick is not to fall victim to one's own propaganda. Holloway, a salesman in Slocum's department, looks for truth in this world of deception, and, therefore, Holloway is going crazy (also, of course, he loses his effectiveness in the company). Slocum does not make this mistake, although he has his own private demons: "Really, I ask myself every now and then . . . is this *all* there is for me to do? Is this really the *most* I can get from the few years left in this one life of mine?" (30–31). Slocum answers both questions affirmatively. Having drained the world of truth, he has also severed action from meaning. Within the world of corporate life, actions cannot mean, they can only be. There is nothing else. The bitter parenthesis at the end of the section confirms and extends this truth. "(I have dreams, unpleasant dreams, that relate, I think, to my wanting to speak at a company convention, and they are always dreams that involve bitter frustration and humiliation)" (31). Truth, personal action, and now dreams exist only in relation to the company, and the company denies the importance of any of these things.

In voicing Slocum's own stance within the world of the company, section 10 provides the climax of this vision of corporate fear. "So I scare Green, and Green scares White, and White scares Black, and Black scares Brown and Green, and Brown scares me. . . . I know it's true, because I worked this whole color wheel out one dull, wet afternoon" (32). This is business according to the rhetoric of fancy, and Slocum is as comically inventive as the Heller who keeps spinning out the variants of Catch-22. In

addition to their fears, Slocum also charts people according to the occupa-
tion signified by their names (Millers, Bakers, etc.) and according to their
emotions: "envy, hope, fear, ambition, frustration, rivalry, hatred, or disappointment" (34). To Slocum's fertile imagination, there is no end to
possible schemes for organization and classification. Designed to alleviate
boredom and melancholia, such exercises help to "pass the time," another
of the chapter's motifs. They also control Slocum's uneasiness, giving his
emotions, especially his anxiety, the familiar regularity of the organization
chart. In his mania for organization, Slocum shares much more of the corporate mentality than he recognizes.

These charts are not merely static structures, for within them Slocum
plots yet another version of his story.

> I put these people [for whom the company is only a place to work] at
> the top because if you asked any one of them if he would choose to
> spend the rest of his life working for the company, he would give you
> a resounding *No!*, regardless of what inducements were offered. I was
> that high once. If you asked me that same question today, I would
> also give you a resounding *No!* and add:
> "I think I'd rather die now."
> But I am making no plans to leave.
> I have the feeling now that there is no place left for me to go. (34)

In vignette form, this contains the plot of *Something Happened*. Slocum
imagines, or more accurately fails to imagine, life within the company.
Unable to conceive an alternative to the company and to the American
myth of getting ahead, he chooses death, the death of the freely acting self.
By agreeing to conform to company policy, he destroys himself—just as
he destroyed the little boy of the lost-child myth and just as he will later
destroy his son. While Slocum has sprinkled his monologue with allusions
to Freud, his company story embodies a Freudian principle to which he
does not refer—that of the death wish.[43]

After a series of sections that fill out the relationship between Slocum
and Green, the closing sections of the chapter introduce the complication
of Slocum's being asked to replace Kagle and the choice this request imposes on him. The chapter's conclusion indicates what Slocum's life in the
company story has already shown: he will choose company advancement
and agree to have his life shaped by company policies. His joke—"The
company has a policy about getting laid. It's okay"—defines his own
choices. His formulation is muted, the chapter's ending understated: "And
I find I am being groomed for a better job. And I find—God help me—that
I want it" (67). Despite the intrusion of the "God help me," there is no pathos here, only self-lacerating irony. Slocum has fallen victim to decep-

tions he has helped to design. Unable to imagine alternatives to corporate life, he says in effect what he said earlier: "I think I'd rather die now" (34). In a further irony, Slocum desires what he fears, the death of the self that exists apart from the company. Even at its end the chapter is about fear, but Slocum does not realize this.

The concluding section extends Heller's vision of fear, conjoining the vision of America as a place to be feared with the workings of Slocum's own mind. "I've got politics on my mind, summer race riots, drugs, violence, and teen-age sex. There are perverts and deviates everywhere who might corrupt or strangle any one of my children. I've got crime in my streets. I've got old age to face. My boy, though only nine, is already worried because he does not know what he wants to be when he grows up. My daughter tells lies. I've got the decline of American civilization and the guilt and ineptitude of the whole government of the United States to carry around on these poor shoulders of mine" (67). In responding to such passages, critics have tended to look at the critique of America without paying equal attention to the vehicle, Slocum's consciousness. Slocum's meditation is less about the fragmentation and decay of American life than about his desire for Kagle's job. Slocum has indeed "got anxiety" about American life, but he has necessarily had to "suppress [the] hysteria" that is embedded in his desire for a promotion. The story of fear in the chapter "The office in which I work" is that of coming to know about fear as well as coming to know, paradoxically, why one cannot really know about that fear. Slocum can know the mechanics of corporate fear, but not why he values the company so greatly. To know that, Slocum would have to know himself—to be able to explain why he wants what he dreads. This problem is not Slocum's alone. Rather, Heller insists that it is a thoroughly American preoccupation as well as the basis for the myth which, according to Kurt Vonnegut, undergirds *Something Happened*.

The proliferation of details in Slocum's monologue and their banality can tax the reader's patience and lead to charges of looseness of form. In the second chapter as in the novel as a whole, Heller sets himself the task of generating interest in a mind that trivializes. If we return to the matter of the Western Union clock under which Virginia sits, we see a characteristic Heller solution to this dilemma as the intricacy of his fictional form. When Virginia reappears in the third chapter (still identified as the girl sitting beneath the clock), all of Slocum's thoughts and memories of her have a temporal cast—for instance, "Now I *would* know what to do with her" (86), or "But the memory lives (but not for long. Ha, ha)" (89). Such lines produce moments of narrative tension counterpoising the restless flitting of a mind which continually returns to maudlin memories and Heller's playful discourse which builds into each Virginia reference another image of time. For the reader, the temporal references gloss the meaning of the Virginia memories, unfolding a kind of negative version of *carpe diem* in which Slocum has failed to live for the moment. The tension between the banality of Slocum's mind and the wit of Heller's dramatizes opposite tendencies. Slocum consistently empties details of significance other than to himself, and Heller restores meaning to these same details by demanding that the authorial audience attend to them. In the context of the novel, the Western Union clock signifies, providing a synecdochic representation of Slocum and his quality of mind. In such details, Heller generates interest out of Slocum's mental wanderings, thereby building order out of emptiness and narrative amplitude out of the same old story.

THE RESOLUTION OF *SOMETHING HAPPENED*: IMAGES OF OPENNESS AND CLOSURE

When Slocum announces in the first sentence of *Something Happened* that he gets the "willies" when he sees closed doors, he introduces the novel's central narrative pattern: the opening up and closing off of experience. This is also, as we have seen, the pattern of the Catch-22 paradox. Slocum begins his narrative by recalling what he has seen behind the doors he has opened in the past: his father and mother in bed together on a day he has come home unexpectedly from school; his sister standing nude on a white-tile floor; and most importantly his brother and Billy Foster's skinny sister entwined on the coal shed floor. By reopening these doors, albeit in memory, Slocum attempts to understand what he could not when he first opened each door and encountered the secret knowledge behind. But in reopening the doors, Slocum looks for something more important than knowledge hidden outside the self; he searches for what happened inside the self. He is convinced that he has been irremediably changed by what he has seen, for he experiences a dread for which he cannot account and which he feels must be the result of some past trauma. "Even at work, where I am doing so well now, the sight of a closed door is sometimes enough to make me dread that something horrible is happening behind it, something that is going to affect me adversely" (3). At such moments, perspiring freely, voice quavering, Slocum voices his repeated question, "I wonder why" (3).

Heller makes clear from the outset that Slocum will never find the answer to his question. The last doors that Slocum opens in the first chapter, those to cupboards in which he is checking mousetraps, show us why. The core of the memory is again fear and revulsion, recollections of the nausea he felt and the certainty that something behind the doors would affect him. As Slocum confides to himself, it is not the mouse that he fears, but the possibility that "I would have to do something about it" (10). In this recognition, Slocum turns from the memory—just as, we will later learn, he turned from the cupboard doors originally, leaving his wife to handle the problem. If Slocum began this chapter by asking what has happened to him and reopening the core memories of fear, confusion, and dread, Slocum closes the doors he has just opened. "Today, there are so many things I *don't* want to find out" (6). *Something Happened* is a novel about Slocum's quest for something that he will not allow himself to find.

As his account of his brother and Billy Foster's kid sister in the coal shed demonstrates, Slocum also does not know how to look for an answer. There are two perspectives built into the memory. The first is that of the child-Slocum who, seeing his brother's coupling, felt safe the moment that he recognized his brother, only to be shocked when his brother threw a lump of coal at him and drove him from the shed. The second is that of the Slocum of the present, who "fantasize[s] and dwell[s] upon that episode": on "the many wet, scratchy, intense, intimate things that probably *had* happened on the floor of that coal shed that day" (5). In looking for what happened to him that day, Slocum stands in the second position, as chronologically he must. But he does so without self-reflection and, therefore, does not realize that the second perspective has considerably reshaped the experience, supplying the wet, scratchy, intimate center to the memory. He persists in locating the something that happened in the event, the image of his brother and the girl entwined, rather than in his experience of that event. The skinny sister episode is a figure for the action of *Something Happened:* looking for something that happened that has changed him, Slocum cannot see the happening, either in the past or the present.

Heller's mind works differently from Slocum's, for he builds the novel to fulfill the promise of the title.[44] For Heller, the end of the novel clarifies, just as Snowden's death did in *Catch-22*. Actually, there is a series of happenings at the end of the novel, one at the end of each of the last three chapters. In the first of these chapters, Slocum recalls his mother's dying words to him: "you're no good. . . . You're just no good" (545); in the second, he tells how, cradling his injured son, he has accidentally suffocated him; and, in the third, he explains how he took charge when Martha went crazy. But while Slocum opens up each of these happenings by recounting them, he resists the knowledge they hold. Moreover, in each case, he acts so as to displace the truth continually available to him: what and who he is. Much has happened at the end of *Something Happened*, only Slocum cannot understand what it is.

In his mother's death, Slocum believes that the lesson to be learned from her dying words does not reside in the words themselves, but in his mistake in telling them to his wife. Brutally acknowledging this mistake, he says, "I should never have told the bitch. The bitches remember things like that" (545). Slocum regrets his momentary indiscretion, because his wife has repeated the mother's judgment during an argument about Slocum's firing Kagle. Even Slocum knows that he should lose, but he will not allow himself to. The bitter irony underlying the argument is Slocum's justification for his actions: his concern for his two children. As his wife reminds him, Slocum has forgotten Derek, whom he earlier identified as the person he was protecting by firing Kagle. Stung by his wife's words, Slocum crushes her insubordination by reminding her that she is afraid of him—at least when she is sober. The very mechanism of Slocum's victory undoes him, though, and, after the argument, he feels only weary and empty. In reminding his wife of the patterns of behavior that entrap her, he repeats the patterns in which he himself is trapped.

Even in the moment of emptiness after the argument, Slocum resists the call for self-examination that his wife's and mother's words hold. Instead of facing his mother's evaluation or acknowledging his wife's position, Slocum retreats into his little-boy myth: "Those are some last words for a dying mother to tell a child, aren't they?" (545). In the myth, Slocum recovers his childhood innocence, the innocence that made him the victim of adult knowledge. Launched into his myth-memories, he simply repeats the same story of the sadness of the world and the sensitivity of the child to this sadness. "The world was a rusty tin can. We used to curl ourselves up inside discarded old automobile tires and try to roll down slanting streets. We never could. We made pushmobile scooters out of ball-bearing roller skates. It was easier to walk. Mommy caught me when I fell, kissed the place to make it well" (545). With imagined memories, he can supply the mother's kiss as the natural resolution of childhood hurt—an end shockingly different from her dying words and from their actual relationship. As the creation of desire, the child story insulates the self from the shocks of experience: his mother's last words, his wife's repetition of them, and Arthur Baron's order that he fire Kagle.

Slocum's coda to the memory of his mother's dying words shows how the child story, now the child/mother story, has become a structure embedded in Slocum's own consciousness. "(The linings of my brain, they give me such a pain.) The linings of my brain are three in number and called collectively the *meninges*. They surround it on the outside. The innermost is called the pia mater" (546), and pia mater, as Slocum reminds us, can be translated as tender mother. For Slocum, the pain that comes from the pia mater and, by extension, from the memory of his actual mother is built into the self, and the pressure—the physical analogue of the dread that Slocum feels—is literally a part of self-consciousness. Of course, the lost-child story must have as its central component a tender mother, although the mother is outside of all but memory. Yet the absent mother becomes a presence in the story, as she also does in the fairy tale "Snow White" or the story of the Dickens orphan, *Oliver Twist*. In Slocum's darkly ironic formulation, the mother and source of pain is the biological center of consciousness.

The son's death provides the novel's climax, fulfilling the promise of Heller's title. In fact, the phrase "something happened" is used to announce the accident.[45] Yet Slocum refuses the death this status, because he cannot acknowledge or confront his role in it. As he says, "Don't tell my wife" (562). Having learned that knowledge revealed can hurt him, Slocum will keep the knowledge that he has accidentally killed his son to himself. In doing so, he cannot look at the patterns of experience and memory that have led to the event.

> A crowd is collecting at the shopping center. A car has gone out of control and mounted the sidewalk. A plate glass window has been smashed. My boy is lying on the ground. (He has not been decapitated.) He is screaming in agony and horror, with legs and arms twisted brokenly and streams of blood spurting from holes in his face and head and pouring down over one hand from inside a sleeve. He spies me with a start and extends an arm. He is panic-stricken. So am I.
>
> "Daddy!"
>
> He is dying. A terror, a pallid, pathetic shock more dreadful than any I have ever been able to imagine, has leaped into his face. I can't stand it. He can't stand it. He hugs me. He looks beggingly at me for help. His screams are piercing. I can't bear to see him suffering such agony and fright. I have to do something. I hug his face deeper into the crook of my shoulder. I hug him tightly with both my arms. I squeeze. (561–62)

The story has the same shape as the Forgione and summer camp episodes —Slocum's coming to the rescue of his endangered son. Yet, in coming to save his son, he, as always, hurts him: "I hug his face deeper into the crook of my shoulder. I hug him tightly with both my arms. I squeeze" (562). The fate at work is Slocum's unchanging pattern of mind, but Slocum cannot look at this pattern of mind and experience.[46] He is afraid. Slocum's plaintive cry after learning how his son has died—"I am afraid to be alone"—can be extended to include—I am afraid to look at what I have done, I am afraid to look at myself.

In moving the narrative audience toward the climax of the son's death, Heller carefully frames the death by pointing to the breakdown of Slocum's consciousness. Before the compressed account of the accident, the mode of the chapter is memory, but memories out of control. "My memory does get faulty of late, merges indistinguishably with imagination, and I must make efforts to shake them apart. I remember waking up as a child, howling from a dream my bed was crawling with roaches" (550). The narrative circles back to past days, to the days of closed doors and mice. But, as his wife reminds him about his fear of mice in the cupboard, it was not mice but cockroaches, and it was not Slocum who killed them but his wife. Awake in the present, Slocum is no more comfortable: "I feel locked inside a hopeless struggle. Forecasts are coming true" (552). Memory, the past, the family, the self have all become uncomfortable for Slocum. He can no longer control his anxiety by draining it into fear tables and happiness charts. So he closes the door on memories of fear and disruption, not realizing that he will soon act out the patterns of memory in his son's death. In killing his son, Slocum has acted out the shape of his deepest fear.[47]

Laying his son to rest, Slocum extinguishes consciousness, the complementary counterpart to the accident of killing his son. As the title to the last chapter tells us, "Nobody knows what I've done" (565). Ironically, this applies to Slocum as well, for he has closed off the experience, turning instead to putting his affairs in order: "I have told my wife I love her. We have decided to keep Derek longer (he may get better). . . . I have given my daughter a car of her own. . . . I have retired Ed Phelps and fired Red Parker" (566). The style affirms the new order that Slocum imposes on his life. The doubts, fears, and prevarications are displaced—now seen only obliquely in Slocum's allowing himself false hope about Derek or in firing Red Parker without telling him. He has accepted the world of the corporate and suburban present. Hence, for the first time in the novel, he can identify himself directly. With a rambunctious laugh he introduces himself on the golf course: "Slocum's the name. Bob Slocum" (568). This affirmation of his identity ironically memorializes the irrevocable loss of the knowledge that he sought. There has been no epiphany to force Slocum to revise his earlier lament: "I don't even feel my name is mine, let alone my handwriting" (490). Instead he joins the country club, playing a game he hates. Slocum has joined his identity to that of the company, fulfilling the American destiny that he foresaw for his daughter. He has become what he feared and what he desired; unlike Yossarian, he has chosen to become "one of the boys."

For Slocum, the story of his handling of Martha's breakdown culminates his efforts to put his affairs in order and to close his monologue: "I miss my boy. Martha the typist went crazy for me finally at just the right time in a way I was able to handle suavely. I took charge like a ballet master" (568). His account of the episode is the triumph of personal action and responsibility—of the ripeness of time. Even while juxtaposing his feelings of loss for his son and of exhilaration for handling Martha, he does not comprehend what the connection signifies for his manner of dealing with death. He does not realize that he has displaced his fear, guilt, and uncertainty about his son's death and has conceived instead a fairy tale-like resolution of his fortunes. Although Slocum has not been able to face mice or for that matter cockroaches, he can handle insanity, while congratulating himself for the way he has taken charge. Of course, the company approves of his handling as well and no doubt congratulates itself on its wisdom in promoting him.

Having filed Martha away, Slocum can suppress the dark underside of corporate life, the whole pattern of insanity and death for which Virginia, Holloway, and now Martha are the figures. He confirms an identity that is not his own; he has indeed become Bob Slocum. His latest color wheel provides a gloss on the change: "A man named Gray has joined the company from a high government post and will fit right in between Black and White" (567). Slocum cannot know what he has become, though, cannot recognize that Gray's story is his own.[48] To do so would be to wonder why: about his mother's dying words, about his son's death and his own role in it, and about Martha's breakdown and his taking charge. The answer in each case would be bound up with himself. It is easier to think as Slocum does, "Everyone seems pleased with the way I've taken charge," thereby converting whole truths into half ones.[49] It is easier to extinguish consciousness (except as it is imposed on him by his recurrent dreams) than to probe its sources. It is easier to have looked for what happened than to look at what is happening (as Bruce Gold will also discover).

4

GOOD AS GOLD

"WRITING IS REALLY PERFORMING FOR PEOPLE"

Then ideas . . . came to me because I was a Jew.
They were a trust to fulfil, because I was a Jew.
GEORGE ELIOT, *Daniel Deronda*

CLOSE TO HOME

Distinguishing his achievement in his first two novels, Joseph Heller spoke of putting everything he knew about the external world into *Catch-22* and everything he knew about the interior into *Something Happened*.[1] By extension *Good as Gold* could be called Heller's mediational novel, an attempt to mediate between the outside public world and the inside private one. Indeed, the novel divides into two halves—half its action set in the public Washington political world and half in the private world of the Jewish family.[2] Bruce Gold, the novel's professor hero, shuttles between the two realms. Aspiring to political success, Gold discovers that such success demands the annihilation of the private self. If Gold fails to bring the two worlds into accord in this sense, he succeeds in another. He must write a book about the Jewish experience in America, but a book written from the perspective of "some unique and significant personal elements" (156). To write the book, Gold's private life must become public autobiography. Reading the novel, the authorial reader realizes that *Good as Gold* is the book that Gold will eventually write. Thus, public and private worlds come into alignment, as Gold's experience provides the basis for Heller's public statement about Jewish life.[3]

In the device of a book about a man writing a book, Heller's technique is also mediational. The novel is about the transformation of experience into art. For now, a single example will illustrate the process. In chapter V, Gold tells Pomoroy, the editor for his Jewish book, how tedious his life has become: his complaining father, his jealous older brother, the birthday party for his sister Rose. Hearing these details, the reader experiences a moment of deja vu; the most prominent scene in chapter IV is the birthday party scene in which everything Gold complains about is rendered for the reader. Listening to his complaints, Pomoroy suggests to Gold an approach for his book: "I'm suggesting a work from your own vantage point. I like the idea of Luna Park, and Steeplechase, tailor shops, and beach peddlers" (156). For the reader, Gold-cum-Heller is at this moment writing such a book and in this scene Heller provides self-conscious commentary on his approach to his principal theme, Jewish life in America.[4]

Good as Gold might be called Heller's mediational effort in another sense as well. In trying to write his book about "The Jewish Experience" (the title to chapter I), Heller, like Gold, discovers the difficulty of disentangling the subject of Jewish life from his private experience of it. Also, I suspect that Heller's joke about Gold's writing about Jewish experience, "when [he doesn't] even know what it is" (11), is grounded in personal truth—at least in the sense that Heller like Gold comes to reflect most fully on his life as a Jew retrospectively.[5] Growing up in the essentially Jewish Coney Island environs of the 1930s, Heller only later comes to confront the distinctiveness of his Jewish identity. The novel's first paragraph dramatizes Heller's mediational effort, for it almost exactly parallels his explanation of the seminal moment of *Good as Gold*.

> Gold had been asked many times to write about the Jewish experience in America. This was not strictly true. He'd been asked only twice, most recently by a woman in Wilmington, Delaware, where he had gone to read, for a fee, from his essays and books, and, when requested, from his poems and short stories. (11)

> With *Good as Gold*, I was giving a reading in Wilmington, Delaware, and a woman asked me why I'd never written about the American Jewish experience. I told her it had taken me 18 years just to write two novels and I'd never really thought of it before. . . . Anyway, I had a three-hour train ride back from Wilmington with nothing to do. I took out a pencil and some cards and that's how it started.[6]

The similarity between the two accounts suggests that *Good as Gold* conveys Heller's (as well as Gold's) "abstract autobiography" (313). Certainly, there are striking correspondences between Gold and Heller: both were dissatisfied professors seeking public acclaim and financial success; both grew up on Coney Island and have Luna Park and Steeplechase as the focal points of their childhood memories; both saw their war experiences as a break from the limited Coney Island world, propelling them to college and fueling their aspirations for public success.[7] Additionally, Heller endows Gold with some of his own memories and associations. For example, Gold's memory of the murder of Raymie Rubin's mother is based upon an actual incident that occurred in Heller's neighborhood.[8] In these and other correspondences, *Good as Gold* is intermediary between Heller's private experience and his fictional dramatization of Gold's experiences, between his private sense of himself as a Jewish author and his public proclamation of this fact with *Good as Gold*. And, as *God Knows* demonstrates, Heller becomes increasingly interested in the personal dimensions of Jewish identity.

From his earliest stories, Jews and the meaning of Jewish experience have been a concern to Heller, although it sounded like background chord to a melody in the fiction we have so far examined. Together with "Castle of Snow," the unpublished stories "The Man Who Came Looking for Moses Richmond" and "A Scientific Fact" provide the earliest examples of the way in which Jews figure as subjects in Heller's imagination.[9] In "Moses Richmond," the Ku Klux Klan drives Moses Richmond from a small town and the town is educated to its anti-Semitism by a mysterious stranger (with bloodspots that appear on his hands at a crucial moment in the story). Sensitizing the townspeople to Jewish history, the stranger says, "They [Jews] have undergone centuries of pain and torture and slaughter, they have experienced every form of deprivation and suffering, they have endured all abuse because they would not forsake their belief in God. What other race, I ask you, has ever suffered so much for their religion?" The baldness and stridency of this vision will disappear in later work, but not Heller's association of Jewish life and moral value.

A richer and more suggestive story, "A Scientific Fact" has affinities with Elie Wiesel's *Dawn*, though it presents a British rather than Jewish point of view on an execution. Harry Gordon, a young lieutenant in the British Army, will be one of the executioners of five Jews in Haifa, Palestine. Like Eliezer, Wiesel's protagonist, Gordon is disquieted by fear and guilt (and like Slocum he dreams). To set the meaning of Gordon's eventual choices, Heller includes an early episode, in which a doctor is summoned to a ship of Jewish refugees who are being turned away from Palestine. The pregnant Jewish woman, whom the doctor has been sent to help, refuses his assistance, in fact, dies in intense pain because she will not let her child be born. Alluding to a line by Oscar Wilde ("the death was but a scientific fact"), the doctor reports the death and advises Gordon about how to handle his own assignment. While Gordon wants to know what the woman's death means, the doctor refuses to think about it and mocks Gordon: "You figure it out, Harry, but don't tell me. I don't want to know." Like Eliezer, Harry Gordon chooses duty and acts as executioner but, unlike him, does so with stoic composure and with his guilty feelings under tight rein. Heller contrasts Gordon's stoicism with the shattered nerves and ethical questioning of Cole, another executioner. Previously, Cole, a hard-drinking cynic, had seemed impervious to the ethical and human dilemmas of occupied Palestine. But Heller gives him the key question at story's end: what differentiates the British political executions from those conducted by the Jewish freedom fighters?

Like Wiesel's *Dawn*, "A Scientific Fact" plumbs the moral ambiguities of British-occupied Palestine. Heller dramatizes this ambiguity by juxtaposing radically different points of view: the doctor's "scientific" objectivity; Gordon's fear and guilt combined with his curiosity; Cole's cynicism and troubled questioning; and finally the viewpoint of the Jews themselves. The doctor's unwillingness to consider the ethical and personal issues discredits his point of view. While Heller renders Harry's perspective more sympathetically, particularly his curiosity about the Jews, he also shows its limitations. Gordon can track down the source of their Zionist anthem to Smetana's "Die Moldau," but remains oblivious to the aspirations and fear behind the anthem. Similarly, Heller approves Cole's questions, but not his shattered nerves. Heller does not provide the Jews with a spokesman as he does in "Moses Richmond," but rather represents their point of view by their Zionist anthem, which serves as a refrain to the key events in the story, and by their actions, most notably the pregnant woman's. This viewpoint, as figured by the pregnant woman's death, is also problematic. The Jewish characters exhibit extraordinary courage, yet it is a courage whose choices seem leavened with fanaticism. In rendering the complexity of the Jewish experience, "A Scientific Fact" anticipates *Good as Gold*.[10]

Although Jewish references do not figure prominently in either *Catch-22* or *Something Happened*, there are indications in Heller's notecards and in his interviews that the possibilities of Jewish dimensions to each novel were much on his mind.[11] The most suggestive references occur in two notecards to *Catch-22*, which sketch plot possibilities. One card, which has the notations "hospital" and "Hemingway," reads as follows:

> B Perfect plot idea This time they had close to a perfect unit. Even the Jew was almost exceptable [sic]. His one weakness was that he was stronger than the anti-Semite, who was afraid to pick on him, which

left the Jew a static character. So if that weren't enough, he didn't wear glasses. Furthermore he had never been to City College and had never been interested in socialism. Karl Marx was the kid brother of a girl he'd almost been forced to marry when he was sixteen because she couldn't subtract 7 from thirty-one and add enough to get twenty-eight. Karl, who was only six at the time and wondering why his sister wrestled with him so much when all he wanted was to pick his nose, wasn't even concerned.[12]

The label "perfect plot" signals Heller's self-consciousness about the imaginative possibilities of his Jewish character. As possibility, the Jew provides the vehicle for Heller jokes—like the Karl Marx line—and for Heller to revenge himself on Hemingway for his portrait of Cohn in *The Sun Also Rises*. Yet there is also something constraining about the plot that Heller imagines, for the Jew is a "static character." The companion card sounds a similar note of constraint: "There was nothing in the world you could do with a Jew like that." Such comments point to an ambiguity in the way that Heller conceives Jews as fictional subjects. At the very minute he plays with Jewish plot possibilities, he finds limitations in his plots. Although Jews as fictional subjects offer imaginative release and creativity, they occasion plots that are not without restrictions.

Heller's explanations about why he chose not to make Yossarian and Slocum Jewish further illuminate the limitations that he sees in Jews as protagonists.[13] Heller explained his choice concerning Yossarian, "I didn't want to have a Jewish name . . . an Irish name, I didn't want to symbolize the white Protestant—but somebody who was almost a *new* man."[14] By making his hero the descendant of an extinct culture, Heller believed he had created someone capable "of ultimately divorcing himself completely from all emotional and psychological ties" (quoted in Krassner, 22). By extension, Heller's reasoning conveys his sense of Jewish ethnic identity. To be Jewish is to have a unique emotional and psychological character and to be context bound—bound by Jewish tradition itself as well as bound within gentile American society. Heller's conception of the emotional and psychological dimensions of Jewishness becomes more clear in his account of how Slocum would have changed if he had been Jewish: "he would have had to dwell an enormous amount of time on the sense of his own Jewishness and to what extent that affected his marriage and his job, and I didn't want it to be a book about that."[15] This explanation conveys two salient aspects of Heller's conceptions of Jews as fictional subjects: 1) the Jewish concerns of the protagonist would predominate in a novel, redefining in *Something Happened*, for example, Slocum's understanding of his job and marriage; and 2) the Jewish hero would be self-conscious about his own Jewishness. Both of these elements hold true for *Good as Gold* and *God Knows*.

When Heller comes to write *Good as Gold*, he commits himself to the plot possibilities of Jewish life for the first time since he wrote "The Man Who Came Looking for Moses Richmond," "A Scientific Fact," and "Castle of Snow." But he does so in a special sense. He does not simply write about Jewish experience, rather he writes about writing about Jewish experience. And it is not primarily Jewish life that concerns Heller, but rather looking for the ways that Jews make sense of their lives. To express these elements, Heller places the compositional process itself in the foreground of *Good as Gold*, using the device of a man writing about writing a book. Yet Heller conceives his subjects with the same dividedness that he displayed in the *Catch-22* notecards. On the one hand, Gold as purported author rejoices about the ease and the rewards of writing about Jews. "Jews were a cinch. It [the Jewish book] was good as gold" (16). On the other hand, Gold wonders, "How can I write about the Jewish experience . . . when I don't even know what it is?" (11). The novel *Good as Gold* embodies both attitudes, the imaginative plenitude of plotting Jewish life and the limitations that a Jewish plot inevitably holds, as does *God Knows*.

To explore Heller's use of the device of a book about a man writing a book is to witness the evolution of his conception of the compositional process, and it is to this that I will now turn. Heller's self-conscious use of this device enables him to dramatize his particular understanding of Jewish life and to synthesize the tensions he associates with it. Following Heller's focus, this chapter will center on Heller's portrait of Jewish life, both within the world of the family and in the world of politics. The family half of the novel talks about learning to accept what one is by learning to accept where one comes from. The political half depicts a world in which Jews are given a role that denies their individuality, as are Blacks, women, and other minorities. Together the halves offer contrapuntal variations on Heller's theme—learning to see oneself as Jew and then confronting the more difficult task of learning to act as oneself.

JOSEPH HELLER AND THE PERFORMING SELF

As we have seen, Heller's prose in *Catch-22* and *Something Happened* has a self-dramatic quality, but in *Good as Gold* he extends the performance to his own role as author. "Writing," Heller has said, "is really performing for people," but he defines this performance and its audience in surprising terms: "unconsciously I must have an audience I'm writing for—someone who is really me, I suppose, with my degree of sensibility, my level of education, my interest in literature."[16] While the compositional solipsism of this formulation is striking, more striking yet is the doubleness of the authorial self. Heller first writes and then as audience watches himself write. For this reason, the much used device of a book about an author writing a book serves Heller well.[17] Using the figure of Bruce Gold composing his experience, Heller projects the rituals of self-performance, simultaneously participating in and observing the writing of the novel.

In dramatizing the authorial process, Heller wants his authorial audience to attend to the way that he constructs the novel, although in a way different from the attention he required in *Something Happened*.[18] He wants his audience to see the tools of his satire, rather than simply to focus on its targets—the self-deceptions and moral corruptions of Washington politics. The presidential commission scene provides a typical example of the self-reflexive impulses in Heller's narrative. When the governor lectures Gold on the way that the commission works, he simultaneously supplies a description of the way that Heller has designed the scene. "Now, Gold. Everybody here is a somebody, and I don't know why you're being so captious about who it is you are. He is the Spade, she is the Widow, I am the Governor, and you're the —" (197). Indeed the commission scene works stereotypically, as Heller plays character types off one another—the Spade, for instance, acting like a "darkie" in a thirties film comedy. Heller wishes the reader not only to laugh, but to see the mechanisms that provoke the laughter.

Heller's self-reflexiveness becomes self-questioning, inquiring into as well as displaying the authorial role and its construction of the novel. As he tells interviewer Charles Reilly, he wants the text to be identified with himself: "From the start I planned injecting the first-person into the novel fairly regularly, and doing so in a way that would incline the reader to infer that the first-person voice belonged to me, Joseph Heller. I wanted very much to have some kind of sustained, perhaps disconcerting, reminder to the reader that this is only a story, that it shouldn't be taken too seriously."[19] While Heller revised his plan frequently to interject his own authorial voice into the novel, he does not change the self-dramatic quality. The authorial intrusions undercut the power of the story, revealing it for what it is—a contrived verbal artifact—but they also magnify the power of the discourse, reminding readers that they have succumbed to a fabrication and are attending to the representation rather than to its author. Lest the authorial audience miss the point, Heller mentions himself by name in the text by incorporating a *New York Times* story that lists clients of the "powerful literary agency" International Creative Management (together with Steve McQueen, Peter Benchley, Arthur Miller, Barbra Streisand, Tennessee Williams, and Henry Kissinger, among others; 331). Readers familiar with Heller's interviews and journalistic pieces will also recognize his presence in the text, for the same opinions are expressed.[20]

With these authorial intrusions, Heller constructs the implied author of *Good as Gold* as well as reflects back on that of *Catch-22* and *Something Happened*.[21] This author knows the literary tradition and places himself within it both seriously and parodically. With his allusions and borrowed techniques, he makes himself the descendent of and heir to a comic tradition that began with Sterne and continues through Dickens and Waugh. As implied by the novel, the connecting threads of this tradition are satiric humor, authorial self-consciousness, and a critical perspective on the values of its author's time. This author also rebuts criticisms of Heller's previous novels and the ones expected of this one by building them into the text: the novel is too long and has too many characters and improbable events.[22] Such criticisms, he pointedly reminds the authorial audience, can also be leveled at Dickens. Albeit with good humor, the implied author asserts his power.

But there is also an element of anxiety in this, just as there was in Heller's short stories about authors and as there will be in *God Knows*, *Picture This*, and *Closing Time*. In the stories, the implied author accomplishes what his writer-protagonists cannot, writing seriously undistracted by the world or commercial success. However, when the viewpoint is changed and one looks from the representation of writing and authorship to the actual author, the implication changes: an aspiring novice displaces his own concerns onto his characters—finding subject, maintaining the discipline necessary to write, keeping "art" rather than financial success the goal. In Heller's intrusiveness in *Good as Gold*, there is a related kind of anxiety. Entering the text as narrator/author, Heller can construct a portrait of the implied author, but he cannot determine how this portrait will be viewed. Nor can Heller, or any actor, fully control his own performance. These tensions may be illustrated in Heller's reference to himself in the *Times* story about International Creative Management. Gold and by extension Heller include this story as part of a satiric critique of Henry Kissinger's cynical self-promotion: "To enhance the *value* of his memoirs in the marketplace, Secretary of State Kissinger has retained a powerful literary agency to represent him" (emphasis added) (331). By incorporating this line from the *Times* as well as the list of clients, Heller can pun on the concept of value, play its mercantile and financial connotations off against its associations with literary merit and enduring achievement (and thereby excoriate Kissinger's venal motives and pretentiousness). In the terms of the list, the pun turns on the difference between Peter Benchley and Arthur Miller (or Tennessee Williams). This raises the question: where does Heller himself stand? For *Good as Gold*, he has negotiated a highly lucrative contract, one befitting a best-selling author (but not one that Miller or Williams would have received). And he signed the contract in order "to dash off a short, frivolous book" (Reilly interview, 26).[23] But as a novelist Heller has always aspired to something more, something befitting the descendent of Laurence Sterne. The two dimensions of art—as emblem of high culture and as commercial entity—disquiet Heller, and the tension between them informs *Good as Gold* as well as each subsequent novel.

The most overt self-reflexive intrusion that is self-questioning occurs in the opening to the fourth section of chapter VII, "Invite a Jew to the White House (and You Make Him Your Slave)." Heller begins the section so as to jar the reader, to create a moment of dissonance much like that which Stravinsky uses in his music. But since readers, like listeners, prefer consonance and repress the dissonance they hear, the narrative intrusion tends to go unnoticed, particularly on first reading.[24] "Once again Gold found himself preparing to lunch with someone—Spotty Weinrock—and the thought arose that he was spending an awful lot of time in this book eating and talking" (308). Thought arose for whom? Book, what book? After beginning the sentence in Gold's point of view, readers find themselves sharing another point of view, at this moment an unfamiliar, even alien, one. The passage continues:

> There was not much else to be done with him. I *was* putting him into bed a lot with Andrea and keeping his wife and children conveniently in the background. For Acapulco, I contemplated fabricating a hectic mixup which would include a sensual Mexican television actress and a daring attempt to escape in the nude through a stuck second-story bedroom window, while a jealous lover crazed on American drugs was beating down the door with his fists and Belle or packs of barking wild dogs were waiting below. Certainly he would soon meet a schoolteacher with four children with whom he would fall madly in love, and I would shortly hold out to him the tantalizing promise of becoming the country's first Jewish Secretary of State, a promise I did not intend to keep. He would see Andrea's father, Pugh Biddle Conover, one more time before his tale was concluded, and Harris Rosenblatt twice. (308)

This passage summarizes the novel's remaining action, but simply to say this obviously sidesteps the specific questions raised by the intrusion.

For the authorial audience, the intrusion displays the making of Gold's story and the conditions for this making. Some of these conditions are set by the nature of the story that Heller narrates and by the character of its hero—"There was not much else to be done with him." The story of an ambitious English teacher hardly affords many possibilities for action. There are also the conditions of the mind of the maker—"I *was* putting him into bed a lot with Andrea." The "I *was*," particularly the italicized *was*, shows an authorial mind thinking about its own authorship.[25] While the passage displays the operations of the narrative mind, the audience observes this authorial contemplation with incomplete knowledge, seeing a mind which talks of its concerns without explaining them. We might question the narrator, why are you putting Gold in bed with Andrea—to titillate the audience? to advance the plot? The answers are not clear, for, as the passage tells us, the activities of the making are not fixed. They grow out of the act of amusement. The Heller persona plays over the upcoming Acapulco scene, imagining different comic climaxes.[26]

Amidst the details of what might happen, the narrative mind is continually present, alerting the reader to its concern with how to tell Gold's story. The narrator's "certainly" when he plots the Linda-Gold affair deflects attention from the affair to himself. For the narrator, the Linda Book story already exists, but not yet in the text. In fact, the story seems to have a double existence: as construct in the authorial imagination, but as construct that has its own separate existence as well. Heller's rhetoric—the formulation "he would soon meet"—distinguishes the separate modes of existence. Heller's formulation recalls the accounts of the creative process that he gives in interviews—what he calls "doing a story."[27] For the narrator, Gold's story already exists as idea and is already complete. Gold will not become secretary of state, but will see Harris Rosenblatt twice "before his [Gold's] tale [is] concluded." This account destroys the illusion that novels traditionally create for their readers, that the characters' futures exist as potentiality and that this potentiality is determined by the characters themselves—by their actions, choices, and desires. Gold exists as a figure of Heller's narrative imagination; his story and his future are both contained by this imagination. And Heller's mind—as the passage tells us—is concerned with what is to "be done" with the story.

Throughout *Good as Gold*, Heller makes Gold the agent for self-conscious commentary on his own novel and his methods. For example, when Gold stops for a moment to consider a Dickens simile he has used, he simultaneously furnishes a description of the scene in which he is an actor: "'solitary as an oyster,' in that unique simile of Charles Dickens, a long winded novelist, in Gold's estimation, whose ponderous works were always too long and always flawed by a procession of eccentric, one-sided characters too large in number to keep track of, and an excessive abundance of extravagant coincidences" (378).[28] The critique of Dickens— his eccentric, one-sided characters, coincidences, and unlikely events—

describes the action of the novel at this moment. For instance, Gold's contemplation of Dickens's faults is interrupted by "the longest shadow in the universe" (378) announcing the arrival of Harris Rosenblatt. Rosenblatt, who once had an appearance to match his Jewish name, now fits his WASPish job of secretary of the Treasury—"the tallest, straightest, strictest human being walking the face of the earth" (378). Before the Dickens simile came to mind, Gold had just come from visiting the brazenly anti-Semitic Pugh Biddle Conover who had been telling him of the love of his life, Gussie Goldsmith—now Gold's stepmother. And the whole Conover scene is handled with extravagant black humor, as for instance the accounts of Conover's favorite activity, gelding colts. Heller writes his Dickensian scene so as to invite the reader to applaud his Dickensian performance.

Heller has thematic reasons for dramatizing his Dickensian and other similarly appropriated strategies. In interviews, Heller recounts reading Dickens and other English comic writers as a way of thinking about his own novel: "I was looking for certain kinds of 'literary cliché,' and I needed to find the right kind of language . . . and pacing for my book."[29] In one sense the scenes with Conover and Rosenblatt are indeed simply clichés, particularly the extraordinary coincidence of Conover's great, unrequited love being Gussie, Gold's loony stepmother. But in using the clichés, Heller adopts Dickens's satiric strategy of deliberate exaggeration to identify the inhumanity of the evil he attacks. When trying to expose the evils of the Court of Chancery or the Marshalsea and a government indifferent to these evils, Dickens continually resorts to hyperbolic descriptions. To represent this kind of evil realistically would be to dignify what should outrage. Heller adopts a similar tack in *Good as Gold*, using comic hyperbole to render the Washington characters as stereotypes and the political episodes as tired literary plots. Through this device, Heller wants to shock the authorial audience into an awareness of the moral corruption of Washington politics by having us view the WASP politicians in the same way they have seen minorities.[30]

Heller's chapter titles, many of which are titles of articles that Gold has written, also serve as self-conscious commentary on his novel.[31] This correspondence asks the authorial audience to re-see such chapters as "Every Change Is for the Worse" and "Nothing Succeeds as Planned." For example, the chapter "Every Change Is for the Worse," which tells of Gold's being invited to Washington, renders the whole Washington half of the novel ironic before it has really begun, because the reader realizes Gold's article could be used as a gloss on his political experience. From this second perspective, Gold's observations become self-reflexive, describing the inevitable result of his Washington aspirations. "Certainly, nothing proceeded according to desire. In the long run, failure was the

only thing that worked predictably. All else was accidental" (73). This
kind of statement resonates in another sense, for Gold's article becomes
Heller's device for commenting upon the design of his chapter. The
chapter juxtaposes a series of episodes about intentions miscarrying—a
design scheme reminiscent of the second chapter of *Something Happened*
with its variations on the mechanics of fear. The chapter title "The Jewish
Experience," while not a Gold article, works in this double sense as well.
The chapter relates how Gold got the idea for his book on the Jewish
experience, but because this is the first chapter of Heller's novel, the title
shifts emphasis from the Jewish life as subject written about to the act of
writing about this subject. In the terms of the novel, the Jewish experience
does not yet exist; Gold, the purported author, remarks that he doesn't
even know what it is. Through the artifice of the chapter titles, Heller
makes the authorial reader a sharer in the composition of the novel.

Heller's extensive literary allusions, especially to self-conscious texts,
illuminate his authorial concerns as well. For example, Gold's Tristram
Shandyean view of life becomes a commentary on authorial self-
consciousness in *Good as Gold* .[32] "Should I try to keep count of the plots
that are thickening, Gold marveled to himself as he drove toward
Brooklyn with Belle, I surely must fail, for their sum increases even while
I am busy totaling them. Like the President endeavoring to chronicle
events of his office that unfold more swiftly than he is able to describe
them, or like Tristram Shandy relating the helter-skelter circumstances of
his birth and his life" (160). As Gold talks about the complexities of his
life, Heller describes his method of self-conscious fiction, which is indeed
analogous to Sterne's. Like Sterne, Heller writes a book about a man
whose central problem is how to begin writing a book: Tristram's problem
of how to begin the story of his life and opinions informs Gold's unsolved
problem of how to begin his book about the Jewish experience. In this
sense, both books are failures or, rather, are about the limits of novels.
Tristram falls farther and farther behind in his effort to record his life; he
is not even born until volume IV. Gold never actually begins his book on
Jewish life, although he realizes that he must do so in the last sentence of
the novel. Gold's Shandyean reverie does, however, shed light on the
novel's actual beginning. "Gold had been asked many times to write about
the Jewish experience in America. . . . most recently by a woman in
Wilmington, Delaware" (11). With its reference to the Wilmington train
ride, this opening partakes of the genesis of Heller's novel. By his
reference to the actual beginning of *Good as Gold*, Heller requires the
authorial audience to attend to the writing of the novel; for in one sense
one cannot write about the Jewish experience, but only write about writing
about the Jewish experience.

In reflecting on the process by which *Good as Gold* comes to be written, Heller resolves the problem that he finds with Jews as fictional subjects by making himself the subject, although not in the usual autobiographical sense. The novel is fundamentally about how Joseph Heller wrote about the Jewish experience. In the novel's discourse, Heller shares and resolves the compositional difficulties that writing a "Jewish novel" pose for him: 1) "Gold does dwell an enormous amount of time on the sense of his Jewishness and to what it extent it affects his job and marriage"; 2) this Jewish plot, which Heller has previously seen as constraining, can be liberating when the focus is on writing it, rather than living it; and 3) plotting a Jewish life means just that—to chart how Jews look at themselves as well as how gentiles view their lives and to make of this a source of authorial possibility and imaginative hopefulness. The reader who watches Joseph Heller writing about the Jewish experience in this is the reader who responds to the drama of his authorial performance, the reader for Heller who is so much like himself.

■

"A Study of the Contemporary Jewish Experience in America"

Joseph Heller has said that he cannot write description and could not write "a good descriptive metaphor if [his] life depended on it."[33] While true for *Catch-22*, *Something Happened*, and for most of *Good as Gold*, this is not true of the latter novel's ending, which closes with two images that become metaphors: Gold visiting his mother's grave and watching some *yeshiva* students play baseball. Compressing Gold's experience, both scenes render it as visual perception. They recall Ernst Cassirer's account of the making of metaphor: perceptual "excitement caused by some object in the outer world furnishes both the occasion and the means of its denomination."[34] After the extravagance of the Washington political scenes and the comic pyrotechnics of the Mexican trip, the scenic resolution is muted, even anticlimactic. As Gold turns from what he has observed and wonders where to begin his Jewish book, the novel circles back to its opening, with Gold still uncertain how to write about Jewish America. In the graveyard and at the *yeshiva* on Coney Island Avenue, Gold has begun his book, although he does not yet realize this, and in constructing the images, Heller has metaphorically delineated the Jewish experience in America and identified Gold's relationship to this experience.

In the graveyard scene, Heller locates Gold in his personal past and shows how he both shares and stands apart from his familial heritage. At first, the choice of placing Gold at his mother's grave seems an odd one. The mother died when Gold was in high school, and she appears in the novel only indirectly, chiefly in the memories of early family life. She has been an absence in the novel, not a presence, her place usurped by Gussie, Gold's stepmother, and by the attention that Heller lavishes on Gussie's eccentricities.[35] In Gold's spare memories, he recalls that her English was so poor that she could not understand her children's talk with each other and recollects the bandages that hid the goiters on her neck and his embarrassment at being seen with her. Seamstress, mother, Jewish immigrant, she lived beneath American society. Her story—her Jewish experience—is untold and largely unremembered even in the Gold family.[36]

In constructing the scene, then, Heller does not focus on the mother or on Gold's memories of her, but rather on what Gold himself sees and feels. In Gold's perceptions, we observe the making of metaphor. "Gold felt like a big *schmuck* when he finally found his mother's grave after the final prayers on the last day and saw that every character on the headstone was in Hebrew. He recognized not a one. The earth had no message for him. He put his arm around the weatherbeaten stone monument for a moment in a strange kind of hug and that felt a little bit closer and warmer. He left a pebble on her grave" (446). A stranger to the gravesite, Gold cannot be sure where it lies. He does not remember the inscription, either, and finding it written in Hebrew cannot read its words. His mother was a part of a Jewish and American past which he no longer shares and which even returning to the grave he cannot recover. The distances widen between life and death, mother and son, Jewish past and Jewish present. The unread Hebrew symbolizes a communal heritage and family connections that are no longer shared.

Gold's return does lessen the distance between his mother and himself and does signal the continuity of Jewish life in America. The warmth that Gold feels when he hugs the gravestone comes from himself, not from the stone, for it is winter. When Gold says that he feels like a *schmuck*, it is one of the few times in the novel he criticizes himself, voicing humiliation which he himself has caused. He also acknowledges his Jewishness and defines his feelings in terms of Jewish values. While Yiddish appears throughout the novel, Gold himself only uses it in the novel's later stages on occasions when he thinks of himself as Jewish. Finally, there is the stone that Gold places on the grave, his participation in the rituals of the past, although for Gold the act is carried out without full understanding. If belief in Judaism as a religious system is gone for Gold, its rituals can still be connectives, joining those who participate in them, and its practices can, as Wayne C. Miller observes, "serve as moral sources of strength and continuity."[37] The stone, the memorial to his mother, tells us that Gold has become, at this moment, his mother's son.

In the baseball scene, Heller portrays the way in which Gold tries to decipher the Jewish present.[38] Heller equally emphasizes the scene and the way that Gold decodes it.

> Athletes in skullcaps? The school was a religious one, a *yeshiva*. Some of the teen-agers had sidelocks, and some of the sidelocks were blond. Gold smiled. God was right—a stiff-necked, contrary people. *Moisheh Kapoyer*, here it was winter and they were playing baseball, while everyone else played football and basketball.
>
> And a stubborn dispute was in progress. The boy at first base had his back to the others, in a pose of limp exasperation. The pitcher was sulking and refused to throw the ball. The batter was waiting in a squat with his elbows on his knees, his head resting with disinterest on one hand. As Gold watched, the catcher, a muscular, redheaded youth with freckles and sidelocks and a face as Irish or Scottish or Polish as any Gold had ever laid eyes upon. . . .
>
> "*Varf!*" shouted the catcher. "*Varf* it, already! *Varf* the fucking ball!" (447)

Gold observes the scene with a visual particularity that Heller seldom uses in *Catch-22* and *Something Happened*. The details ground the scene, rendering it with photographic specificity: the first baseman with his back turned, the sulking pitcher, the blond sidelocks, and the red-haired catcher. Each detail also signifies, either describing the game that is being played or identifying the Jewishness of its participants. In the catcher's "*Varf* it already!" the details assume a mosaic-like harmony—baseball, the American game, and the Jewish players as part of the same pattern. Like Gold, we see in this moment the Jewish experience in America. The particularity of the Coney Island Avenue scene establishes its authenticity; the attention that Gold gives to the particularized details makes it emblematic of contemporary Jewish experience.

Gold the observer decodes the emblem. His generalization—"God was right—a stiff-necked, contrary people"—shifts attention from the scene to its meaning. Becoming an interpreter, Gold explains the life of the Jewish people. The stuff of his interpretation, however, is traditional, formulated first in the Exodus account of God's contrary people. The boys are playing baseball in the wrong season, and the game itself is stopped by an argument. Gold's observation, however, also attends to the American context. It is a baseball game, a uniquely American game that Gold watches, and it was the game itself that prompted Gold to stop his car. Gold's pause brings the reader as well as Gold himself to see the game as a symbol of American life. Through the mechanism of Gold's perceptions, the scene has become a visual metaphor of contemporary Jewish life in America.[39]

In the images, Heller completes Gold's task for him, representing the contemporary Jewish culture. The images tell a double story, isolating the unique character of Jewish experience and rendering it inextricable from its American context. The sidelocks and yarmulkes identify and differentiate, while the baseball game shows a process of cultural assimilation. The images tell a double story in another sense as well, dramatizing both the changes and the continuity in the Jewish heritage. The grave image evokes the changes, the sense of loss of language and of experience no longer shared. But the same image also demonstrates continuity as the stone ritual becomes a connective, signalling a heritage transmitted, one whose vitality informs the present. And finally there is a third doubleness, as Gold both feels that he shares and is separated from his Jewish heritage. At the grave and on Coney Island Avenue, Gold appreciatively recognizes the distinctive features of Jewish life even while standing outside what he observes. In the images, then, Heller gives the novel's Jewish theme graphic representation: "What it's been like for people like you and me, our parents, wives, and children, to grow up and live here now" (15).

Heller's pictorial method in the grave and baseball scenes marks a radical shift in technique from the anti-realism of *Catch-22* and from the sustained monologue of *Something Happened*. Here he uses the methods of realism. His language is referential, creating visual correspondences between the scenes and the outside world. In these scenes, there is none of the language play that Heller foregrounds in the Major Major sequences or in Slocum's happiness charts—although this kind of playfulness occurs in other sections of the novel. The view of life is rooted in the circumstantial, fixed in space and time and framed by the consciousness of an observer.[40] With their photographic details, the scenes have a rare verisimilitude for the contemporary novel. The realistic method provides the illusion that Gold is indeed writing the autobiography that he said he would write. The shift in technique reinforces the Jewish theme in the novel, joining the book that Gold wants to write to the novel that Heller actually composes.

To set up the pictorial conclusion and to bring Gold to accept his Jewish ancestry, Heller uses the traditional comic pattern of the hero's education. In this sense, Heller's plot has an elegant simplicity: the hero, Gold, initially stands outside the community, the Jewish family, and in order to join it he must become educated to its ways and values.[41] Gold's education involves learning to see and to know his family and by so doing to accept them. This education is also required for Gold to write his autobiographical book. The novel's family scenes tell a two-part story, then—the story of Gold's education and the story that Gold must write, that of Jewish experience in America.

To dramatize Gold's education, Heller uses a series of family scenes that he works out in essentially similar fashion.[42] Each scene contrasts Gold's desires and point of view with those of the rest of the family. For Gold, whose point of view the narrative audience shares, the gatherings are chiefly occasions for goading and baiting him. For other family members, they are occasions for affirming familial relationships, occasions of community. The chief action of the scenes is conversation, and the conversation takes three forms: memories of the familial past, schemes for moving Julius and Gussie to Florida for the winter, and, most importantly, exchanges between Gold and his father and brother. The exchanges, so humiliating for Gold, provide Heller with the occasion for writing humorous dialogue as well as for portraying Gold's education. As Julius and Sid succeed in making Gold's pretensions and insecurities public, Gold comes to perceive himself and the family in new ways and in doing so to recognize enduring Jewish values.

The surprise party for Rose at Gold's house can serve to illustrate the use Heller makes of the family gatherings and the way he portrays Gold's ethical initiation. In the birthday party, Heller sets up the structure of the family—its roles, rules, and rituals—using food to dramatize the workings of this structure.[43]

> Harriet excelled at baking and was forever miffed upon arriving with two or three of her cheesecakes, moist chocolate cakes, or coffeecakes to find a deep-dish fruit pie, cookies, and a high whipped cream or chocolate layer cake already purchased. . . . Esther specialized in stuffed derma and noodle puddings; living alone now, she was expanding into potato and cheese blintzes and experimenting with dishes other than derma, unaware that with chopped liver and stuffed cabbage she was encroaching upon Ida's traditional territories and that with chopped herring she was transgressing against Rose, who was unmatched in the family with all edible things from the sea, as well as with soups, matzoh balls, and other varieties of dumplings. (98–99)

Heller continues in this fashion for more than a page and by the time he finishes the characters of the family members are established and the rules of family life are clear.[44] In the description Heller brings the narrative audience into the scene so that they look at the family as the family members look at themselves. "There was unofficial agreement in the family that Rose was the best-natured, Esther the slowest-minded, Harriet the least sociable now, Ida the pickiest, Belle the most dependable, and Muriel the most selfish" (99–100). In such paragraphs, Heller seats the audience at the dining table, making them sharers of family assumptions and lore. Like the family, they will type Muriel as the *farbisseneh* sister, recoiling as they do from her ketchup-laced corned beef hash. In this scene the Gold family has become an environment enclosing the action of the party.

The birthday party scene illuminates the way in which the family's present is formed by its past. Rose, the self-sacrificing oldest sister, voices the significance of this past. For her, the central experience of her life has been her search for her first job. "Every morning . . . the four of us [Rose and her friends] . . . would have to go to the agencies mainly, because they were the ones who had jobs to give, and they took a nice percentage of the pay. It was not an easy time for Jews, what with first the Depression and then Hitler and all those anti-Semites here" (111–12). Built into the memory is her feeling of being a Jewish immigrant and hence an outsider— something that Gold in his pursuit of a Washington appointment refuses to acknowledge. The anti-Semitism lives on in memory, still occasioning anxiety. No wonder Rose has kept the same job for forty-two years, even now earning only slightly more than the newest teenage newcomer. A sense of family and a gentle regard for its frailties acts upon her memories as well. She pauses for a minute in talking about the awful corned beef hash lunches to assure Muriel that her hash is better. Rose's tears of happiness on learning the party is for her—the emotional center of the chapter —are set in relief by her story. Her job search frames the present, molding what her life has become. But Gold perceives and values none of this.

Through the party conversation, Heller simultaneously exercises his talent for comic repartee and dramatizes Gold's initiation. In the party, Heller, with Sid as his mouthpiece, works variations on a single joke: "Isn't it lucky . . . that we found ourselves on a planet where there's water? . . . Otherwise . . . we would all be very thirsty" (95–96). Almost all of Sid's jokes work in this fashion, reversing the usual premises with which we explain the world. But Heller uses Sid's absurdities for more than entertainment; the establishment of the preposterous becomes part of Gold's education. With his professorial certainty about the ways of the world, the illogic of Sid's jokes infuriates Gold. By the time Sid has led a family chorus exhausting all the variations of our watery world, Gold's pride is so piqued that he responds to Sid's absurdities and Sid literally turns the *world* upside down.

> "But turn the *world* upside down," suggested Sid with an air of craftiness in the intimidated lull that ensued, "and then see what would happen."
> "Nothing!" roared Gold.
> "Nothing?" said Sid.

"The North Pole would be the South Pole," said Muriel.
"The Big Dipper would spill."
"We'd go south to get cold."
"Niagara Falls would fall up."
"And he calls that nothing." (107)

This reversal unmasks Gold's intellectual arrogance, not Sid's ignorance.[45] He mistakenly perceives Sid's foolery as an attack on his knowledge.

Unlike the others, Gold cannot laugh and so must be taught. Heller uses the family's discussion of Gold's latest article, "Nothing Succeeds as Planned," to teach him. For Gold, talk about his article provides the occasion to assume the "plush conversational robes of the pedagogue-prophet" (102), which he does with zest, arguing that money always is spent in ways other than intended. But he does not realize that his article proves true in ways he has not planned. In the article as in his life, Gold wants adulation for his intellectual superiority. However, he does not realize that the discussion of his article celebrates his achievements, but not as he would like. "The ovation, to the extent that one occurred, was a standing ovation only because Esther was standing while she clapped her hands. Her mouth was trembling with an uncommon palsy that seemed to shake her lower jaw now and again" (100). In receiving his sister's applause, Gold attends to the wrong things, noting the signs of her aging, not her sisterly affection. Gold's critical vision detaches him from the very context in which his ideas can be explored. In writing "Nothing Succeeds as Planned," Gold has exempted himself and his ambitions from his thesis, while the party demonstrates that his insight applies especially to himself. What does not go as planned is what Gold wants to happen at the party, to his article, and finally to his conception of the Jewish experience.

Heller further dramatizes Gold's inability to see and appreciate his family with a textual joke, a joke that also alerts the reader to Gold's own capacity for misperception.

"What was it Sid used to tease him about?" asked Emma Bovary.
"Go out for the fencing team," said Echo. "He was so skinny they'd never be able to hit him."
"Remember the time they wouldn't let him sing in school and he came home crying?" asked Natasha Karilova. (109)

Reading these lines, the authorial audience stops short, for they strike a discordant note in the realistic account of the party. Only after a few lines does Heller disclose that the lines are really an integral part of the scene: "Gold returned from his daze and realized he'd been giving the names

Emma Bovary, Echo, Natasha Karilova, and Aurora to his sisters Muriel, Ida, Rose, and Esther. There were just too fucking many of them" (109). Gold's explanation reveals that he does not really see his sisters or recognize their individuality. For him they are only voices in an all too familiar family scene. The lines are also educative for the audience, particularly for its academic members. The reader who recognizes the allusion to *Madame Bovary* and stops to ponder the seeming break in the realistic texture of the text is unmasked as a pedant. The details reveal the point of view of someone, either character or reader, who detaches himself from what he observes.

Gold's blindness to his family signifies his larger ethical blindness. Heller has talked about the essentially traditional moral pattern that underpins *Catch-22*, and much the same kind of pattern holds in *Good as Gold*. When the water/world turned upside-down joke is interrupted by Ralph Newsome's call from Washington, Gold immediately imagines how Ralph and Washington officialdom would react to the party: "The delusion possessed him that Ralph and rulers in all the capital cities of the world had been witness to the disgraceful scene just completed. Television cameras had recorded it. Woodward and Bernstein would write a book. He was ruined" (107). In his Washington view of the family dinner, another example of his capacity for misperceiving, Gold focuses upon the family's eccentricities, the many marks of its Jewishness, and feels embarrassed. This kind of discomfiture will later prompt Gold's hallucinatory dream that he is not a Jew—not his father's son. With his Washington aspirations, the ethically blind Gold does not recognize the communal values of his family.

Celebrating the connective values of the Jewish family, the party scene points the direction for Gold's ethical regeneration, that is, when he can come to acknowledge and accept his familial, and by extension his Jewish, past. Gold's emotions offer the possibility for moral regeneration. He feels like crying when he sees Rose's happiness at the lighting of the birthday candles and the family gather about her. Although his tears discomfit him, making Gold fear that he might run from the room, he has joined the emotional community of the moment. The values become visible in the lighted birthday candles and Rose's reaction to them. The story of her job search, one of the few times she speaks in the novel, can be told, noticed, and valued only within the context of the family. The darker side of Rose's story, its memories of anti-Semitism, sets in relief the decision that Gold must make in accepting Ralph Newsome's offer of a Washington position—to betray or deny his Jewishness in order to gain recognition in a gentile world, or to acknowledge his Jewish ancestry and become the inevitable victim of anti-Semitism. These are the choices of the novel's other half, the Washington half, but they are illuminated by Rose's birthday candles.

Heller portrays the culmination of Gold's education in Sid's death. It precipitates Gold's rejection of Ralph Newsome's latest Washington offer and prompts Gold's active participation in family affairs. Heller marks the change by shrewd description. "Mourners connected most closely by blood to one of the two contending families divided themselves into separate camps. Gold was a reluctant link between. . . . The burdens of responsibility for the numerous roles to be filled fell increasingly upon Gold. . . . Harriet sent word now that she wanted just Gold to walk with her to the farthest wall of the room for another look at Sid in his coffin" (434–36). As these lines emphasize, Gold has replaced Sid as de facto family leader and problem-solver. Gold's ascendance as oldest son occurs naturally as family members and Gold unthinkingly assume that he should take Sid's place. He simply fills the demands of the role, demands necessitated by the peculiarities of the Gold family and by Jewish life. Gold's new involvement does not signal the complete cessation of his dissatisfactions or even a religious awakening. When Gold intones the *Yiskadal v' yiskadish*, he reads phonetically from the English text, and even while handling family problems he still thinks of Washington.

Always, death provides the concluding moment of narrative clarity in a Heller novel. The death rituals—sitting *shivah* for Sid and visiting his mother's grave—reestablish Gold's connections with his past and confront him with his Jewish identity. While reciting Kaddish for Sid, Gold has the shock of recognizing himself as Jew. Seeing Greenspan, the Jewish F.B.I. agent, unshaven, he feels embarrassed, realizing that he himself had violated the ban against shaving during the seven-day period of mourning. Yet he also becomes angry at Greenspan, who keeps trying to insinuate himself into the Gold family mourning activities, and calls him a *shonda*, a disgrace. Greenspan violates the death rites in quite a different way, for he joins them chiefly to share in the food. In these moments Gold examines himself and his beliefs. He acknowledges his Jewishness but in familial and cultural terms, not in religious ones. He also confronts his mortality, for in reciting Kaddish to mourn Sid's mortality, Gold experiences his own.

As delineated in the novel's last chapter, Gold's education involves acceptance of the ordinary, the quotidian demands of Jewish family life. Gold attends to Rose in her worries about a biopsy for a lump on her breast and talks to Joannie about the concerns of her upcoming divorce. With Sid's death, Gold becomes a son, brother, and father; he begins to live a Jewish life that Heller's pictorial conclusion dramatizes. The concluding sequence of scenes from Sid's *shivah* to the *yeshiva* baseball game provides, to borrow Frank Kermode's formulation, a sense of an ending.

As the grave and baseball scenes demonstrate, Heller's two-part story—of the Jewish experience in America and writing about this experience—are really threads of a single narrative. Both are stories of seeing, of looking at the world through the eyes of a Jew, and at the grave and at the *yeshiva* Heller dramatizes Gold's moment of vision and shows the authorial audience how to achieve this quality of sight.

■

"If You Ever Forget You're a Jew, a Gentile Will Remind You"

As this epigraph from Bernard Malamud indicates, the Washington half of *Good as Gold* is about Gold being reminded that he is Jewish. It also examines the society that does the reminding, completing Heller's exploration of the Jewish experience by looking at what it means to be Jewish in contemporary America. This symbiotic story tells about Jews, or rather about Gold, Henry Kissinger, and Harris Rosenblatt alternately, effacing and trading upon their Jewishness in order to join the WASPish political establishment and about the establishment's bringing Jews into government in such a way that they remain outsiders—"Jews" in a gentile world. In particular, Heller's chronicle of Kissinger's political rise, which he weaves into the novel through a series of newspaper clippings, symbolizes the symbiotic relationship. Gold's attempt to follow Kissinger's path in becoming secretary of state teaches him the meaning of being Jewish in Washington. The governor defines Gold's role most succinctly: "Gold, every Jew should have a big gentile for a friend, and every successful American should own a Jew. I'm big, Gold, and I'm willing to be your friend" (431).

In the political half of the novel, Gold is taught his Washington role in the constant reminders that he is Jewish. Ralph Newsome, Pugh Biddle Conover, and the governor all allude to Gold's being Jewish in the first moments of their conversation: Ralph remarks to Gold about "your kind" of people; Conover punctuates his conversation with Gold with variations of his name, "Goldberg," "Goldsmith"; and the governor observes, "Gold, you a Jew, ain't you?" (196). Like the governor, Heller hammers the point home: in Washington, gentiles remind Jews of their background. The label defines their place in society: "[T]his is a social world, Bruce, where competence doesn't count. . . . Try to remember who you are. Let's face it, Bruce—Jews don't really make it in America. They never did" (424). Although hyperbolic, Ralph's words convey Washington's attitude toward Jews and the inevitability of their being viewed as outsiders.

In his pursuit of becoming secretary of state, Gold willingly accepts the role offered him. Gold himself recognizes that he is being subservient even in his first visit to Ralph's office, that "[h]e'd been fawning" in his talk with Ralph (124). Gold tries to please Newsome in the same conversation in which Ralph tells him about his proposal to "build some death camps" (122). Similarly, Gold launches his pursuit of Andrea because Ralph has told him a tall wife will add to Gold's professional stature, and also because marrying her would bring him closer to the moneyed society he so desperately wants to join. Finally, Gold responds to the governor's offer, "I will support you, Governor . . . in any cause to which you choose to commit yourself" (431). Accepting his role in an institutionally anti-Semitic society, Gold becomes a Washington Jew.

Heller's portrait of Gold's political aspirations also depicts the society in which they occur. In general terms his social vision is akin to that of *Something Happened*, a social breakdown which is figured in urban decay:

> There was no longer a movie house operating in Coney Island: drugs, violence, and vandalism had closed both garish, overtowering theaters years before. The brick apartment house in which he had spent his whole childhood and nearly all his adolescence had been razed; on the site stood something newer and uglier that did not seem a nourishing improvement for the Puerto Rican families there now. . . .
> Every good place has always been deteriorating, and everything bad was getting worse. Neighborhoods, parks, beaches, streets, schools were falling deeper into ruin and whole cities sinking into rot. . . . It was the Shoot the Chutes into darkness and dissolution, the plunging roller coaster into disintegration and squalor. Someone should do something. Nobody could. No society worth its salt would watch. (323–26)[46]

But Heller's view of the hopelessness of this decay has changed. He stands with Gold when he voices the futility of action, either governmental or individual: "Gold knew something no one else did, but was not going to reveal it: he knew there was no longer anything legal to be done under the American system of government to discourage crime, decrease poverty, improve the economy or nullify the influences of neglect, and when he got to Washington he would not even try" (325).[47] The New York landscapes are the legacy of a society whose energies are spent. South Brooklyn, Joseph Heller asserts, inevitably follows from Washington's vision of a great society.

In his satiric examination of Washington politics, Heller insists that the social malaise originates in Washington. As in *Catch-22*, Heller piles instance upon instance of official irresponsibility, indifference, and abuse of power. The breakdown begins in the White House, with the president, who likes Gold's article, "Every Change Is for the Worse," because it justifies his inaction, and who begins each workday with two sleeping pills so that he can go back to sleep.[48] His presidential commission functions in similar fashion, adjourning immediately after convening and congratulating itself for having done nothing in record time (195). The White House briefing session is the "frankest and most informative" in memory because the president's press secretary admits that he does not know the implications of administration policy (204). In Heller's Washington, advancement is directly inverse to achievement. Harris Rosenblatt succeeds as secretary of the Treasury because he has a single idea, upon which neither he nor the government wants to act. And Gold's biggest Washington accomplishment is not writing the presidential commission's report, which wins the acclaim of Ralph, Andrea, and the governor for the brilliance of Gold's writing and insight.

For Heller as for George Orwell, the decline of politics is accompanied by the decline of language.[49] Ralph's self-negating sentences exemplify what Heller sees as the failure of language in the contemporary world. You can do "[a]nything you want, as long as it's everything we tell you to say and do in support of our policies, whether you agree with them or not. You'll have complete freedom" (52). Or, "[we]'ll want to move ahead with this as speedily as possible, although we'll have to go slowly. . . . We'll want to build this up into an important public announcement, although we'll have to be completely secret" (53). By negating the meaning that they advance, these statements close off possibility. Like a TV camera pointing at a TV screen, they are self-engulfing, holding the illusion of meaning while simultaneously canceling the very possibility.[50] When Gold calls Ralph's attention to his language, Ralph acknowledges his contradictions unabashedly: "Maybe I do seem a bit oxymoronic at times. I think everyone here talks that way. Maybe we're all oxymoronic" (122). Ralph's explanation serves as vehicle for Heller's attack on Washington rhetoric and his own language play, the pun on oxymoronic emphasizing the moronic root of Ralph's linguistic strategies. For Heller the writer, the failure of language betokens a greater failure of will and spirit.

In the Kissinger sections, Heller attacks Washington values and the debasement of language most directly. Buttressing the claim with a variety of press clippings from the Kissinger years, Gold-cum-Heller advances the thesis that Kissinger is not a Jew. Heller's point draws upon his thematic linkage between Jewish and communal values in the family section of the novel. He uses the clippings, particularly excerpts from the notorious

Oriana Fallaci interview, to unmask Kissinger's pretensions and to expose the vanity behind Kissinger's aspiration of becoming a twentieth-century Metternich. For Heller, the most revealing evidence of Kissinger's betrayal of his Jewish heritage lies in his famous cowboy comparison: "I've always acted alone. Americans admire that enormously. Americans admire the cowboy leading the caravan alone" (335). Again and again Heller has characters refer to the lone cowboy comparison, always to the point that Jews do not speak of themselves in this way. In terms of the novel's thematic values, Kissinger has betrayed his Jewishness and abandoned its ethical precepts.

According to Heller, Kissinger's own language damns him, for he like Ralph Newsome uses language to disassociate himself from his own actions. To prove his case, Heller juxtaposes Kissinger's inconsistencies. "I have always considered the U.S. involvement in Indochina to have been a disaster." "No, I have never been against the war in Vietnam" (354). Or he quotes Kissinger's equivocating response to a question about whether Kissinger had not privately tried to disassociate himself from President Nixon's bombing policy: "I was in favor of attacking the North. It was an agony for me" (354). Kissinger's formulations always qualify and contradict, continually shifting responsibility for his actions outside himself. In the clippings, boundaries between the fictional world and the real world blur, as Kissinger's rhetoric parallels Ralph's. Heller includes Kissinger in the novel not only to exemplify the self-serving political behavior that he satirizes, but also to prove that the seeming unrealism of the Washington sections is no more unreal than Kissinger's actual Washington doings.[51] Heller sides with Gold when he concludes a Kissinger section with the summary generalization: "The transition from Kissinger to blight, rubbish, rot, and moral defilement was a natural one" (336). For Heller, Kissinger personifies the blight afflicting American society, and for him, urban landscapes like South Brooklyn embody the true legacy of the Kissinger years.

Although their function is clear, the Kissinger sections weaken the novel. The attack on Kissinger is carried by statement—by the clippings and Gold's accompanying meditations. Heller does not use the scenic method that renders his concerns dramatically as he does in the family half of the novel. Without the scenic animation, the Kissinger material is flat, even dull; and it will be even duller for future readers who are no longer familiar with Kissinger. Heller's technique of embedding nonfictional material proves problematic. Although Heller directs the authorial audience to see Gold's transition from decrying the decay of South Brooklyn to thinking about Kissinger as a "natural one," the novel does not sustain the connection. When Heller places the Kissinger material next to events like the murder of Raymie Rubin's mother, the connection unravels. The Kissinger references take their meaning from the reader's familiarity with actual events, especially those of the Vietnam War. By contrast, the murder and similar events take their meaning from the fictional world which the novel posits. The Kissinger references work centrifugally, the murder and similar episodes centripetally. Heller wants the murder to outrage (presumably because the crime upon which it is based appalled him), but it does not carry such emotional weight. The death of Raymie Rubin's mother and the Kissinger-Fallaci interviews exist as part of different orders of reality.

The troublesome ambiguity of the Gold/Kissinger parallel also weakens the novel. Given the similarities in the two men's careers, such Gold lines as "[e]ven that fat little fuck Henry Kissinger was writing a book" cut two ways, castigating Kissinger and revealing Gold's splenetic envy (330). Such lines raise the larger question of where the authorial reader is to stand with respect to the Gold/Kissinger parallel. Should the reader disregard Kissinger's vanity because it is viewed through the lens of Gold's own vanity? Clearly not. Or to reverse the relationship, should the reader condemn Gold for his Kissingeresque ambitions? Yes, but that is not quite right, either. Heller bids the reader to sympathize with Gold, even when he is acting disreputably, in a way he never allows sympathy for Kissinger. Heller designs the Washington scenes so that the reader responds emotionally to Washington's anti-Semitism—specifically, so that the reader shares Gold's humiliation in being labelled a "Jew." The Gold/Kissinger parallelism tilts to one side: Heller allows no sympathy for Kissinger while inviting it for Gold.

The imbalance would work if Gold underwent an initiation in Washington comparable to that of the family section of the novel. The learning process would create grounds for the reader's sympathy, but Heller does not dramatize Gold's education—his learning to see the similarity between his aspirations and Kissinger's and his moral culpability in assenting to be the governor's friend.[52] Heller depicts Gold's education with a single choice, his rejection of Ralph's offer to become secretary of state. There are some preparatory signs of Gold's change of heart—his boredom with Andrea and his disaffection with Ralph, who says that he would not hide Gold if there were a second holocaust. But Gold maintains his Washington ambitions virtually to the end of the novel, agreeing to be the governor's Jew on the same night that Sid dies. Only Sid's death and the necessity that Gold replace Sid bring about the real choice. Heller tells us of Gold's choice, but does not show us.

Gold's Washington career is defined by his context, by a gentile society which systematically excludes Jews, Blacks, and other minorities. This anti-Semitism is repulsive not only for the ugliness of the prejudice itself, but also because Washington society, like Ralph, congratulates itself because anti-Semitism no longer exists. In Washington, when the governor says, "Gold, you a Jew, ain't you," the word *Jew* resonates, conveying a central feature of the Jewish experience, the sensation of being the victim of bigotry. The line also conveys Heller's satiric critique of the ethical emptiness of Washington. The symptoms of the corruption reside in the attitudes of Kissinger, Newsome, Conover, and the governor; the effects appear in the blighted urban landscapes. Given the wasteland that politics has created, the only possibility for corrective action lies in retreat from society into the family, where individual actions still have controllable effects. Familial action, of course, is Sid's story and in a larger sense that of the novel itself.

In his much-praised critique of contemporary life, *The Culture of Narcissism*, Christopher Lasch draws extensively upon *Something Happened* for illustration. He might just have easily cited *Good as Gold*, for Gold is a narcissist, albeit one who eventually confronts his self-absorption. In fact, Gold matches the clinical criteria for the narcissistic personality: his grandiose self-importance; his preoccupation with unlimited power and success; his exhibitionism; his responding to criticism with marked feelings of inferiority, shame, and humiliation; and his disturbed interpersonal relationships.[53] For Heller, his protagonist must have occasioned a measure of anxiety, especially about the potentially narcissistic self-absorption of the writer.[54] As we have seen in such stories as "Girl from Greenwich," "Young Girl on a Train," "World Full of Great Cities," and "Early Frost," Heller's writers have always been cut off from the world by their self-involvement and by their desire to appropriate it for their own artistic ends. In a novel about Gold's self-conscious authorship, Heller probably could not help but reflect upon himself as writer and artist, something to which *God Knows*, *Picture This*, and *Closing Time* further testify. In these novels, Heller turns to explore the destructive potential for narcissism of the writer or artist. In David, Aristotle, Rembrandt, Singer, and Yossarian, Heller subjects the artist's self-preoccupation to relentless scrutiny. The novels are not psychological case studies. However, they examine the complexity of artistic creativity in a way that strips away the romantic myth of the artist who heroically creates. His artists are flawed mortals.

5

GOD KNOWS
POSSIBILITY AND CONSTRAINT

> the king is but a man . . . all his senses have but
> human conditions: his ceremonies laid by, in his
> nakedness he appears but a man
>
> WILLIAM SHAKESPEARE, *Henry V*

"THE REVOLUTION OF THE TIMES"

King David, the protagonist of *God Knows*, is no hero whose feats remove him from the world of mortals. Rather he shares our vanities and perversities, our hopes and fears. Heller locates the novel so that David's human frailties are most visible both to himself and to us, his readers. David lies on his deathbed remembering the events of his life. The shadowy imminence of death chills his body and spirit, so that even Abishag, the virgin who sleeps with him, cannot warm him. With weakened bowels and palsied hands, David cannot escape the mortal grounding of his being: "They have perfumed my bed with aloes, cinnamon, and myrrh, but I still smell me. I stink of mortality and reek of mankind" (107). Facing death, he can only remember and, through memory, trace the contours of a life. Yet, in the remembering, possibilities open up, if only those embedded in the life that he has lived and the stories that it holds: "I don't like to boast . . . but I honestly think I've got the best story

146

in the Bible. Where's the competition?" (5). In this, the genetic narrative moment of *God Knows*, David—poised between what has been and what must be—purportedly begins to conceive the novel that we read.[1]

In the novel, humanity and human mortality are the essential subjects. For Heller, as for Shakespeare, the enduring story of kingship concerns the man who is king.[2] But Shakespeare's method and Heller's are quite different. Shakespeare reworks Holinshed's *Chronicles of English History* to show that what one is as man determines what one is as king. In the plays of the Henry IV–Henry V cycle, Shakespeare chronicles ideal kingship, dramatizing that Hal succeeds as king precisely because he has previously succeeded as man. He tells an initiation story in which Prince Hal discovers his identity. Later, when he becomes king, Hal must act upon this self-knowledge or, as he says, "again . . . be himself." Heller's method is exactly the opposite. Beginning with the record of kingship that the Bible supplies, he imagines what the man must be like who has done such deeds.[3] In exploring the personal consciousness behind kingship, Heller finds David a powerfully attractive figure—the man who has wooed Bathsheba, only to have their child die as a consequence; the man whose cry of grief for his son Absalom still inspires and moves. Heller wants to know: how would it feel to have slain Goliath? To have slept with Bathsheba? To have one's mentor, Saul, tormented by fits of melancholy and envy? And above all, how would it feel to have one's beloved son Absalom rebel and die? The common ground between Shakespeare's and Heller's accounts lies in their heroes' humanity.

For Shakespeare, the king's humanity exists as potential, possibility figured in the ideal of kingship itself. Describing this potentiality, D. A. Traversi says of kingship: "It demands, in the first place, an absolute measure of self-domination. Called upon to exercise justice and shape policies for the common good, the king can allow no trace of selfishness or frailty to affect his decisions. He must continually examine his motives, subdue them in the light of reason."[4] And, indeed, the plays of the Henry cycle are largely about the process by which Prince Hal learns self-control. He needs to control his passions, which he does, in events as different as his dealings with Falstaff and his preparations for Agincourt. As Hal's triumphant reign as Henry V demonstrates, self-control realizes and expresses his potential. It is not that such control does not have its costs, costs demonstrated in Hal's insensitive dismissal of Falstaff. Although politically successful, Hal is less humane than he was in his youthful days as Falstaff's friend.

For Heller, a king's humanity resides primarily in his physical embodiment, and so, while Shakespeare emphasizes possibility, Heller calls attention to limitation. David experiences this when, lying in bed, he smells the "stink of mortality and reek of mankind" (107). The stench, of course, is that of matter, first experienced by Yossarian when attending the dying Snowden. Yossarian, Slocum, and Gold fear old age; David lives it. From the perspective of old age, self-control and self-realization as Shakespeare dealt with them are largely irrelevant. Not that David's exercising restraint with Bathsheba would not have changed his kingship, but neither David nor Heller is interested in restraint. Like his hero, breathing his own mortality, he decries human limitations.

While Shakespeare and Heller construe a king's humanity differently, their accounts of kingship share a common trajectory and evoke a similar sense of mutability. Shakespeare's Henry IV voices this vision of a king's life:

> O God! that one might read the book of fate,
> And see the revolution of the times . . .
> O, if this were seen,
> The happiest youth, viewing his progress through,
> What perils past, what crosses to ensue,
> Would shut the book and sit him down and die.
>
> (*Henry IV, Part II*, III, i)

From this perspective, life assumes the moods of tragedy, not comedy. Both Shakespeare's Henry plays and Heller's novel follow the implications of this change in point of view: the comic high jinks of the Falstaff scenes of *Henry IV, Part I* disappear from the later plays, and David and Bathsheba's battles of wit early in the novel are replaced by the successive death watches of its end. Ahead of Shakespeare lie the great tragic figures —Macbeth, Othello, Lear—whose view of the world partakes of Henry's somber vision. While the world of the tragedies is not without possibility, it is anchored in mortality, in the old age which Lear and Shakespeare know. To suggest that Heller's career will follow Shakespeare's would be foolish, as foolish as it would be to imply that he will take on Shakespeare's tragic vision. But Heller is clearly writing out of a recognition of "the revolution of the times" that he shares with Henry IV and Shakespeare.

Of this revolutionary outlook, Heller observes, "[w]hat there is in all my books, part of the central consciousness, is a philosophical despair on the inevitability of age, of aging, and dying."[5] Heller's philosophical despair does not despair in *God Knows* any more than it did in *Catch-22* or *Good as Gold*. Rather, Heller assumes the outlook of the man whose life is recorded in the Bible and construes this life as a text, a tale whose telling (and retelling) embodies more narrative complexity, drama, and passion than any other one in the Bible. As David argues, buttressing his claim to have the best story in the Bible: "Where's the competition? Job? Forget him. Genesis? The cosmology is for kids, an old-wives' tale, a fey fantasy spun by a nodding grandmother already dozing off into satisfied boredom. Old Sarah's fun—she laughed and lied to God, and I still get a big treat out of that" (5). As this suggests, David's history possesses the imaginative plenitude that Heller associates with Jewish life—as Bruce Gold might say, it is as good as gold. In this vein, David continues, "Moses has the Ten Commandments, it's true, but I've got much better lines. I've got the poetry and passion, savage violence and plain raw civilizing grief of human heartbreak" (5). Such a text allows one to live, a point that David-cum-Heller underscores with the punning joke (lifted, perhaps, from "Shall I compare thee to a summer's day?") about the elegy for Jonathan: "I could live forever on my famous elegy alone, if I wasn't already dying of old age" (5–6). The elegy enables David as well as his subject Jonathan to gain immortality. By such authorial efforts death can be transcended.

As biblical character and compositional subject, David may be able to transcend death, but as the purported author of *God Knows*, he cannot when he is "already dying of old age." The proximity of death renders his story, his text, as a "book of fate," one in which the life spirit drains from him as inevitably as it has from Snowden. David's cry—"I hate God and I hate life. And the closer I come to death, the more I hate life"—is more piercing than Snowden's, "I'm cold," but its meaning is the same: he is dying. His chill, that which Abishag cannot warm, informs every page of the novel. The act of authorship itself expends his life energy, rekindles regrets and dissatisfactions, and propels him toward his death. Walter Benjamin's description of the storyteller applies to David and, of course, to Heller as well: "he is the man who could let the wick of his life be consumed completely by the gentle flame of his story."[6]

Heller's own circumstances both influenced and were affected by this vision of mortality and authorship. Two hundred and twenty-five pages into the manuscript of *God Knows* and recently separated from his wife of thirty-eight years, he fell victim to Guillain-Barré syndrome, a rare and sometimes fatal form of paralysis. When David's deathbed infirmities became his own lot in the intensive care unit of Mount Sinai Hospital, he must have had an uncanny feeling of déjà vu. As he later recognized, the hospital ICU became a mirror to his own mortality, just as in the novel Abishag was the inescapable reminder of David's impending death.[7] Heller himself frequently jokes about the correspondences he sees between the novel and his life. As he told *New York Times* reporter Walter Goodman, "I did draw on my experiences as a bombardier in *Catch-22* and my experience working for *Time* in *Something Happened*, but . . . [t]his time I was a prophet."[8] In this way, his biblical subject had an unforeseen hold on his life: David's lonely, debilitating old age incarnated in the terrors and indignities of his own paralysis.[9] For the novel, Heller drew upon these experiences and sensations, in details such as David's trembling fingers, sleepless nights, and nagging dread.[10] While *God Knows* takes its departure point from the Bible, it forecasts and assumes the sensibility of a man who has suffered Guillain-Barré syndrome.

With this in mind, I turn now to explore in more detail Heller's treatment of humanity and human mortality, his presentation of the human condition as an unceasing interchange between possibility—or freedom—and constraint. In order to do so, I will look at Heller's self-consciously retrospective narration; his open-ended portrait of David's identity; his treatment of women, love, and desire; and his use of the Bible as a source. In these topics we will see that physically embodied, David as desiring subject finds that possibility exists only within the boundaries of limitation. In this, *God Knows* demonstrates that Heller's imagination is similarly constrained; Catch-22, the intractable paradox at the center of Heller's famous masterpiece, unleashed his novelistic imagination, yet still confines his imaginings.[11]

■

HELLER'S RETROSPECTIVE METHOD

According to William Wordsworth, poetry "takes its origin from emotion recollected in tranquillity" (Preface to *Lyrical Ballads*). This formulation holds that poetry begins with acts of memory that preserve and display not only the emotion and the thing remembered, but also the process of remembering itself. Heller's fiction, like many Romantic lyrics, works as emotion recollected. In his novels, emotion-charged events such as Snowden's death or the death of Slocum's son are not presented directly to the reader, but occur as memories recalled. As Heller explains his method: "I have a preference for dealing with the more dramatic scenes in retrospect, after they've taken place, rather than telling a straightforward narrative and building to a climax to keep the reader in suspense. . . . I have a preference for that which I cannot justify except with the feeling that, the way I work, the way I write, *the way I perceive*, it would be better done that way than to have the actions proceed chronologically" (emphasis added).[12] Heller constructs his novels to display the way he perceives key narrative events and to invite the reader to share his perception.

Heller's handling of Snowden's death offers an introduction to his retrospective method. Although referred to throughout the novel, the death becomes comprehensible only at novel's end, when Yossarian meditates on the remembered images of Snowden's viscera. For Yossarian, recollection brings his crucial insight about human mortality and about himself, voiced in the famous "man is matter" speech. For the authorial audience, Heller's retrospective presentation of the death pulls the novel's fragmented episodes into mosaic-like harmony, allowing the story to be seen as a whole and connected. Earlier events like the tree-of-life episode, in which Yossarian, naked, stands in a tree watching Snowden's funeral, can be re-seen and re-understood. Having inspected the dying Snowden's entrails along with Yossarian, the authorial reader apprehends the knowledge of good and evil that he acquires and more fully appreciates the symbolic resonance of his stand in the tree of life. For both character and reader, memory holds the material and becomes the catalyst for understanding. All Heller's fiction affirms the value of recollection, of sifting through and pulling together, for he, like Wordsworth, believes that the re-creative powers of memory clarify and illuminate.

Heller believes that memory enhances narrative progression, supplying a developmental logic and the meaning that chronology does not. Tracking the story, the narrative consciousness in his novels shuttles back and forth in time. The narrative vantage point is never fixed, shifting back and forth between the time of the action and the time of the narration. As a result of this, the meaning of events is fluid during the course of the novel, changing according to the vantage point, the narrative context (the particular sequence of episodes), or the nature of perceiver (as, for instance, Slocum's loss of control in *Something Happened* as he verges on nervous breakdown). In the process of remembering, the narrative consciousness detects a structure in experience, preeminently in such crises as Snowden's death, crises that signify the existence of a story and that must be narrated. Contemplating such critical moments, memory intuits how they came about and what followed from them. In these moments, the meaning of a Heller novel emerges, whether it lies in Yossarian's insight about the nature of mortality or in Slocum's suppression of the facts of his son's death.

While all of Heller's novels work retrospectively, none does so as insistently and self-consciously as *God Knows*. Both its subject and method are retrospective in that the novel portrays David lying on his deathbed reviewing the events of his life. Heller uses the convention of deathbed remembrance that makes memory the vehicle for grasping the meaning of one's life. He would agree with Walter Benjamin that the pressure of death gives shape to both one's life and the story of one's life: "It is, however, characteristic that not only a man's knowledge or wisdom, but above all his real life—and this is the stuff that stories are made of—first assume transmissable form at the moment of death."[13] On his deathbed, Heller's David indeed transmits his life—his impending death authorizing the story that he wants to tell.

Heller simultaneously parodies the convention of deathbed remembrance, for David already knows the biblical account of his life and assumes his audience does as well. As parodist, he scoffs at the Bible's pale rendition, especially the sanitized version of the Book of Chronicles. Like a reporter writing an exposé, David takes his reader into his confidence, purporting to give the behind-the-scenes facts. In describing his battle with Goliath, for instance, David tells us, "[i]f you want to believe what you've heard, I halted along the way to choose five smooth stones out of the brook. That was just for show. Any slinger worth his salt always carries his stones with him" (71).[14] Or David will confide, "killing Goliath was just about the biggest goddamn mistake I ever made" (15). This cocksure David does not search for illumination. Even with death imminent, he simply wants to "screw" Bathsheba one more time. There is a doubleness to the retrospection, then, as David tries to confront death so as to decipher his life and to deny that either death or life itself has any intrinsic importance. Such doubleness is not, as we have seen, unusual for Heller, for whom the comic and the serious are different sides of the same coin.

The deaths of David's sons—those of his infant son by Bathsheba and of Absalom—provide the climax of *God Knows*, controlling the novel as Snowden's death does *Catch-22* and Slocum's son did *Something Happened*.[15] Relentlessly, David's deathbed recollections propel him to re-experience the pain and loss of their deaths. These deaths, rather than the imminence of David's, dominate the novel. A father who has outlived his children, Heller's David finds that his grief- and anger-laden memories retain the immediacy of the emotion. This is the source of the poetry of *God Knows*. As always, Heller's novelistic imagination is engaged by a child's death, prompting him to refigure the biblical accounts of these deaths so as to place David's emotional anguish at the narrative center. Even twenty years after his sons' deaths, David wants to know why: why would God kill an infant in retribution for David's adultery with Bathsheba? Memory does not bring resolution to such questions; grief always wonders why.

Neither David's memory nor his narrative approaches his sons' deaths directly. Like his creator counterpart, Joseph Heller, David meets death by deflecting it into jokes. He is a hip, brash New Yorker, whose vulgarity protects him from death's brutal reality. As he says in his first allusion to his infant son's death: "Fucking Bathsheba, then fucking her again, then again and again and again . . . could have been my second biggest mistake. Nathan really got on my ass about that one, and the next thing I knew there was a dead baby. Love is potent stuff, isn't it?" (15). In memory,

David gets waylaid again by Bathsheba and pauses to savor their illicit passion. Much of the novel recapitulates the implications of this tarrying, as David repeatedly dwells on his relationship with Bathsheba, especially on their lusty couplings. In this first reference to the dead infant, David's mordant witticism about the potency of love keeps the child a detail in the luxuriant tale of sexual passion and its results. For David as well as for Heller, humor distances and controls the emotional desolation that re-experiencing the death will bring. When he turns later to meditate on his son's dying days, anguish replaces laughter.

"I will never excuse Him," David says, "for killing the baby in retribution. That was an act of God that was warped and inhuman" (285). For David, the meaning of his child's death is unambiguous for, as he argues, God has violated the human norms of justice, and David values justice. He would have died himself in contrition for having had Uriah killed. In his own eyes, he follows Job's example in calling upon God to explain his ways—a parallel that Heller enforces by larding the scene with passages from the Book of Job. In his imaginary dialogue with God (for God never answers his prayers or complaints), David supplies God with the Book of Job's voice-out-of-the-whirlwind speech. The might and majesty of His words ring out again: "'Who is this that darkeneth counsel by words without knowledge? Gird up now thy loins like a man'" (289). Unlike Job, however, David is unsubdued and unrepentant; he imagines a triumphant reply that dismisses God's assertion of omnipotent knowledge with a sarcastic "[t]hat no longer matters" (289). From the perspective of personal grief, God's speech to Job evades the issue. God speaks about the ways of the universe; David only wants his son to live. Grief finds any God irrelevant who does not respond to the loneliness and pain of the human heart.

Remembrance sharpens the loss of the infant's death for David and his readers. Its spare details preserve in the manner of poetry his emotional desolation: "I lay on the earth a few minutes longer, weeping in silence into the dirt, then surrendered all hope and began pulling myself together" (287). In such memories, neither sorrow nor hope ends. On a deathbed so cold that Abishag's virginal warmth cannot touch him, David can only recollect: "I could not make sense of the quiet in the universe. I wanted the entire world to be heartbroken, to be choked with sorrow and outrage at so heartless an event" (287). Nothing has changed, David is still outraged. His pain chokes him. David, the psalm writer and soother of Saul's moody passions, cannot assuage his own affliction. His grief is swallowed up by the quiet of the universe, such that his words, like those of T. S. Eliot, "reach into silence." So do his memories.

In retrospect, David discerns the patterns of behavior that have controlled his life and that of his family. While he sees the hand of God in the infant's death, he discovers his own in Absalom's. He intuits that his desire for Bathsheba recurs in his son Amnon's lust for his sister, Tamar, and that his challenge to Saul's kingship is repeated in Absalom's challenge to his throne. The pattern is not of fate, but of character. As David says, "each of us—Amnon, Absalom, and I—was aggressive contributor to the brutal climaxes betiding us" (295). Uncovering his authorship of his own suffering, David relives the turmoil of Absalom's rebellion and maps the shape of the self.

David's memory refigures his life as a text that can best be understood in its re-reading. As he remembers the events that lead to Absalom's death, he apprehends what he could not recognize at the time.[16] His ineffectual reaction to Amnon's rape of Tamar and to Absalom's demand that Amnon be punished has been the catalyst for the insurrection. His self-indulgent love of his children initiates the sequence of events that leads to Absalom's death. Only through hindsight does he comprehend Absalom's rage over his sister's defilement and his hatred for David as father and king. He saw none of this at the time—just as he had earlier been blinded by his love for Bathsheba. Now David discerns what he should have said and done: that he should have awakened Amnon to his crime and the biblical precedents that he could have used to do so, that he should not have brought Absalom back from exile and should have responded to Absalom's growing popularity.

While remembrance makes clear his overindulgent love for Absalom, this realization does not change his affection for his dead son or alleviate the pain of his loss. When Absalom died, grief consumed David. Looking back, David says, "*I heard myself wailing*, 'O my son Absalom, my son, my son!'" (emphasis added, 327). The beautifully balanced elegiac rhythms render the feeling unforgettable. Repeated in David's memory, as they are in the Bible (2 Samuel 18–19), these lines become woven in the texture of the events themselves. They take on a mnemonic function such that, when David recalls his famous lament, he simultaneously calls up his grief and the images of those desolate hours. In the past, sorrow incapacitated him such that it "felt so much easier to continue weeping than even to think about ever, ever doing anything else" (327). In the present, David finds himself similarly debilitated, bereavement still crippling him. Responding to Absalom in death as he did in life, David makes him the object of a father's idolatry.

Absalom's death shatters David's emotional life and prefigures his own death for, as he says:

> I have really not felt much of anything since my wife Abigail died and my son Absalom betrayed me and was killed. I still do not know which of these two facts about Absalom has been more unhappy for me. I know I didn't feel like a victor when I started back from Maha-

naim after that distressing triumph. I felt instead like a fugitive, and I feel like one now, a fugitive long pursued by invisible demons that can no longer be held at bay. In my intervals of broken sleep I feel like exhausted prey at the end of a fatal chase. . . . Defeating my son in battle was much more important to me, for that kind of victory is a loss, and I feel it still. (337–38)

David's narrative darkens, as he wrestles with a life that turns into loss. He cannot supply the elegaic wholeness that makes death the completion of life. His image of himself as a "fugitive long pursued by invisible demons" transforms his own memories into furies. Even though the triumph over Absalom signifies the fulfillment of God's promise to Abraham that the Israelites would conquer Canaan, it brings him emotional defeat and emptiness. "I feel," observes David about the death of his son, "nearer to God when I am deepest in anguish . . . and I yearn to call out to Him . . . with those words of Ahab to Elijah in the vineyard of Naboth, 'Hast thou found me, O mine enemy?'" (338). This call resounds only in his mind and memory and is followed by silence. Silence turns him back into the self. "The fault, I know, was not in my stars but in myself. I've learned so many things that have not been much use to me" (338). The darkly comic allusion to *Julius Caesar* affords neither insight nor consolation. In the absence of God, there is only the self, nothing else. And as David finds in reexamining his emotional wounds, the self cannot illuminate its own recesses. Its only healing comes in resignation, but how, David asks along with Heller, can one be reconciled to the death of children?

Heller intends that David's act of recollection prompt the authorial reader's own textual retrospection. Absalom's death, like those of Snowden and of Slocum's son, forces the reader to re-see the narrative and to reassess the relationship of its parts. For example, the reader can now understand why David says that killing Goliath was his biggest mistake. When David first says this, the line pricks readerly attention, but gets lost in David's rambunctious recounting of his life. The zest with which David describes his naked dance before the Ark of the Covenant or his escape from Saul by climbing out Michal's window takes precedence over any expressions of regret. Even when David later explains the reason that he regrets killing Goliath, we readers note his explanation and let it pass into the edges of consciousness. "If I'd known in my youth how I'd feel in old age, I think I might have given the Philistine champion Goliath a very wide berth that day, instead of killing the big bastard and embarking so airily on the high road to success that has carried me in the end to this low state of mind in which I find myself today" (56). Reading this originally, we readers stand in the position of the young David, inexperienced in the lonely pains and physical debilitation of old age. After experiencing with David the deaths of his sons, we understand: killing Goliath led inexorably to David's ravaged old age. Through remembrance we bring David's regret over killing Goliath and his anguished cries for Absalom—"O my son, my son, Absalom!"—into conjunction, and we understand, memory serving us as it serves David.

With the crisis of memory past, Heller drops the retrospective mode and moves the novel toward completion, just as he did in *Catch-22* and *Something Happened*. The novel's brief concluding chapters, almost a coda to what has gone before, take up the matter of succession. The details follow the account of Kings I, with Adonijah trying to usurp David's throne and David responding by passing over Adonijah to pick the younger Solomon. Heller's method is comic, as it is in any scene involving Solomon, for Heller finds that it is never too late for another dumb Solomon joke. David's elaborate instructions fall on deaf ears with Solomon. Having heard David say, "I want you to kill Joab. Don't you understand? Blow the bastard away," Solomon assures his mother that he is pretty sure he understands what his father wants him to do (351). Succession accomplished, so is David's life. The novel ends with David about to sleep, a sleep that prefigures death.

In the twilight moments between wakefulness and sleep, David has a final vision, itself a retrospective image of himself as a youth. In a bleak present, memory reaches back.

> I see an eager, bright-eyed youth there on a low wooden stool; then one bare knee of his is bent to the ground, and he is holding in his lap a lyre with eight strings. The apparition has come to play for me. He is ruddy, and withal of a goodly countenance, and very pleasant to look at. His neck is as a tower of ivory. His locks are bushy, and black as a raven, and his head is as most fine gold. . . . He starts with a song I used to know, in a clear, pure voice too sweet for a girl's and too young for a man's. His music is soothing, almost divine. I have never been so happy as when I hear him begin. (352–53)

Memory reconstitutes David as he was before Saul, confident that his song could soothe and heal a damaged human heart. As if calling upon his youthful self, David seeks the consolation for which he desperately yearns, but finds nothing soothing about the remembrance. Like Saul before him, David reaches for a "javelin to hurl at his head" (353). As so often in his life, triumph dissolves into pain. His memory has an obsessiveness to it, as the patterns of the past contain the present, just as they did in *Something Happened*. In *Light in August*, William Faulkner put it this way: "Memory believes before knowing remembers."

Vision banished, David must face the night. Even Abishag's coming to comfort him cannot satisfy his unremitting longings. "I want my God back; and they send me a girl" (353). In these, the novel's final words, Heller jabs his authorial audience with the recognition of earthbound mortality. David's final plea for God wrenches memory from the earth, mixing hope and despair. With its voicing, *God Knows* moves in the fashion of serious novels to question the meaning of life. David's plea provides the potential for our epiphany. For the authorial reader aware of mortality, Walter Benjamin's remark about the nature of the novel obtains: "What draws the reader to the novel is the hope of warming his shivering life with a death he reads about" (101).

■

DAVID'S PROTEAN IDENTITY: UNLOCKING THE POSSIBLE

Heller depicts King David's identity as open rather than closed, his self offering entrance into what might be as well as what is or has been. Each of David's experiences offers him—what it did not offer Yossarian, Slocum, or Gold—the opportunity to reinterpret the self or to assert a new aspect of himself. Unlike his protagonist predecessors, David has a multiple identity: king and rebel, warrior and coward, womanizer and lover, believer and agnostic, writer and plagiarist. Such multiplicity signifies a plastic self, capable of being molded and remolded by external circumstance and inner drives. In social psychology, the idea of multiple identity is not new, but it is for a Heller hero.[17] The contrast between conceptions is clear if one remembers the deal that Yossarian is offered at the end of *Catch-22*. Yossarian understands that the deal with Cathcart and Korn is a way to "lose [him]self," that is, to destroy who he is. In a similar situation, David would not face the same choice, for he does not have Yossarian's coherent sense of self.[18]

Previous to *God Knows*, Heller's presentation of the self is most fully represented by *Something Happened*. In this novel, identity resides in a core self and is pre-existing. It gains expression in Slocum's narrative voice. Even when Slocum postulates multiple selves—the self who fills in for "things of which I did not wish to become part" (123), and so on—the text undermines his view. The reader recognizes the same Slocum s/he has seen all along. There are threats to identity in *Something Happened*, of course, just as there are in *Catch-22*, and in one sense the novel is about these threats. American culture can destroy the self, as Slocum believes it is destroying his daughter. Or one can destroy the self by cooperating with the system, as Slocum himself does when he fires his best friend Kagle and takes over his job. Or more insidiously, time itself can erode both the self and self-consciousness, which is Slocum's abiding fear. With all these dangers, there is a sense of nostalgia to Heller's presentation of the self. Slocum yearns for communication with his lost child-self, which he sees as the repository of his identity. But the core self—either as mythologized by Slocum or as conceptualized by Heller—remains inaccessible to present knowing, located in the Golden Age of a pre-conscious past. Given this mode of existence and the persistent threats of the self's annihilation, it is not surprising that Heller's presentation of the self and its identity changes.

In *God Knows*, Heller makes identity a dialectic between role and inner self, thereby construing it as multiple and potential rather than as unified and completed. As figured in the novel, David's identity is continually affirmed and transformed by the interactive relationship between role and inner self. This dialectic does not, however, resolve into the frequently cited formula thesis-antithesis-synthesis, which, as Northrop Frye demonstrates, oversimplifies Hegel's conception.[19] Rather, to adapt Frye's formulation of the dialectic and apply it to identity, this process combines the self with the otherness of role "in a way that negates itself and yet passes through that negation into a new state, preserving its essence in a broader context, and abandoning the one just completed like the chrysalis of a butterfly" (Frye, 222). Such a conception of identity expresses the paradoxes of unity and multiplicity, constancy and change, that Heller comes to believe are embodied in the self. Heller's David can be both believer and agnostic, king and rebel, and if confronted with such contradictions might respond with Walt Whitman, "Very well then, I contradict myself. (I am large. I contain multitudes.)" (*Leaves of Grass*).

To appropriate a literary metaphor, the identity formed by the dialectic between David's inner self and his role can be called character.[20] The "character" David is the verbal artifact about which David as purported author of *God Knows* writes. Drawing on the research of the third-phase psychologists, Norman Holland uses the phrase "theme with variations" to conceptualize the mixture of sameness and difference that results from such an interactive sense of identity.[21] Applied to *God Knows*, variations on a theme would be a better formulation, for as David says in his Whitmanesque braggadocio about himself and his story, "I've got wars and ecstatic religious experiences, obscene dances, ghosts, murders, hair-raising escapes, and exciting chase scenes" (6). *God Knows* simply fills out the implications of this narrative sense of life. David must construct an account of himself that lives up to the billing of "best story" in the Bible. As protagonist of his own life, he has lived this best story, in fact, he has been its hero; now, as purported author of *God Knows*, he must compose the character that matches the life.

Much of *God Knows* concerns the roles that David adopts, for his life consists of a succession of performances, often contradictory ones.[22] As "hunted criminal," he "stole, plundered, or extorted, with Judeans or Israelites as the victims" (8). As beloved king, David unites the feuding Judeans and Israelites in a Jewish kingdom. David learns to play such antipodal roles with verve, insight, and enjoyment. Conceiving his life as drama, he self-consciously performs for the audience, calculating the effects he seeks. "I knew the impression I hoped to make, the kind of comment I wanted to incite," David says preparatory to his being designated as antagonist for Goliath. "I wanted to startle, gall, and taunt, and to set people buzzing about me" (66). Through their performance, David's roles become himself. Forged by his choices and circumstances, what David is partakes of the variousness of his roles.[23]

Much of David's success lies in his ability to adopt masks appropriate to the situation. Whether driven from his capital by Absalom's rebellion or accorded a hero's welcome for his victories over the Philistines, he is the consummate showman. On his return to Jerusalem after putting down Absalom's insurrection, David generously plays the part of the forgiving king with Shimei in order to consolidate his power, but in a Machiavellian transformation has him quietly assassinated. Similarly, after his infant child by Bathsheba is killed by God, David immediately goes to the temple to worship, although he confides to the reader, "you can guess how reverent and forgiving I really was in my heart" (288). Publicly, his show of reverence succeeds, or as David immodestly assesses his work, "The behavior I displayed has now become the substance of legend" (288). The multicolored tapestry of the Book of Kings provides David a script equal to his dramatic talents.

Many of David's roles are not spontaneous creations, but rather are dictated by circumstance. Saul's efforts to assassinate him, for instance, turn him into the hunted criminal, who flees through the hills of Judah and allies himself with the Philistine king Achish—not that David cannot play the part of outlaw with relish. He steals, plunders, and extorts Judeans and Israelites with no pangs of conscience. Similarly, Samuel's secret anointing makes him adopt the role of king, albeit a king without a people when he is first chosen. In Heller's joke, David even assumes the part of Bathsheba's lover as the result of happenstance: "the devil made me do it." So David, as though he were familiar with American television, plays the temptation scene as comedian Flip Wilson would, with the devil leading him into temptation. Circumstance embodies the principle of necessity in David's life, shaping his identity.[24]

As a result of the variety of roles available to him, David has a fluidic sense of his own identity. Unlike Yossarian, Slocum, or Gold, he has the capacity both to define himself and to change his definition. He need not worry about how he can be a hunted criminal when he is really the king. Rather, he believes that he, as well as all others, "are complete, and . . . capable of everything" (7). Everything is a matter of choices and options, even stealing from his own people, and if one is unburdened by the need for consistency, these options open up a virtually endless variety of selves. This ability to define and redefine oneself offers a remedy to the strictures of a univocal self, allowing for regeneration as well as destruction. Crucially to Heller, the resulting elastic sense of identity is less susceptible to the destruction of time and thus provides a partial solution to Slocum's dilemmas.

As long as David can see possibility, his identity—his story—is not complete. The critical instance of David's open-ended sense of self occurs in his vow to make love to Bathsheba "at least one more time before I give up the ghost and bring my fantastic story to an end" (12). Throughout the novel, he plots to realize his vow and thus to renew himself. Even temporarily, making love to Bathsheba would allow him to revive the role of lusty lover and thus to circumvent the degeneration of old age. In his effort to seduce her, his last act in the novel, David renews himself—something that Slocum could never accomplish. The role of lover has an element of immortality to it that is ever expressive of possibility. Additionally, David's ability to conceive new parts or new ways to play old parts keeps his identity open.

In Heller's dialectical conception of his protagonist's identity, the counter-principle to role is inner self, which chiefly manifests itself in the novel in David's narrative voice. Or rather it manifests itself in the consciousness behind the narrative voice, behind the narrative "I."[25] The narrative voice itself is, of course, another construct, for as David frequently reminds us, he is an author. And arguably, authorship is his favorite role. An example from early in the novel will illustrate the ways the inner self appears in the novel: "I've led a full, long life, haven't I?" (4). The second "I" points to the inner self, to the voice of consciousness. It is aware of its own existence, aware, as it tells us, that "I[t] ha[s] led a full, long life." In fact, it needs to call attention to its existence with the self-dramatizing second "I." Such a doubleness carries on throughout the novel. The continuation of the "I've led" passage further illustrates this duality:

God knows I fucked and fought plenty and had a rousing good time doing both. . . .

And God certainly knows I was always a vigorous, courageous, and enterprising soul, overflowing with all the lusty emotions and desires of life until the day I waxed faint in warfare on the field at Gob. . . . Between sunrise and sunset, I had aged forty years. In the morning I was feeling like an indestructible young man, and in the afternoon I knew I was an elderly one. (4–5)

The expression "God knows"—the first appearance of the title phrase in the text of the novel—signals and stands for the inner self. Unable to assert its existence directly even when it proclaims "I fucked and fought," for this formulation collapses back into David's roles—David the womanizer, David the warrior—it asserts its existence through artifice. The pun "God knows" substitutes for self-consciousness, signifying, in effect, "*I know that* I fucked and fought." The passage, especially the second part, reflects the way in which the self can think about itself and the way it has changed. The "I knew I was an elderly [man]" makes clear that David thinks about himself in different ways, not only in the past on the battlefield but also in the present. It knows that it has the capacity for change and being changed. Behind the calculated narrative "I," the inner self remains distinguishable.

David's inner self is also manifested in his self-consciousness about his roles. When he incessantly interrupts his performances to comment and criticize, he raises not only dramaturgic issues, but also issues of "self-consciousness"—that is, questions about the inner self. In this respect, when he assesses his final charges as "marvelous, witty, dramatic, climactic" (11), he speaks about his values, the values that have shaped his performance as king, as well as about the theater of his final charges. Similarly, when he critiques the drama of his harp performance for the melancholy Saul or when he shares his performance strategy for getting Saul to pick him to fight Goliath, his comments point inward as well as outward, providing a glimpse at the self behind the role as well as at the way in which he performed the role. And obviously such assessments as "What a splendid and inspiring picture I must have made!" (120–21) tell us more about David's way of thinking about himself than they do about any picture he made.

Although David's inner self gets voiced through the narrative, it can be expressed only in the most generalized and distant terms. Narration approximates the self in much the same way images of an electron microscope approximate atoms—only as pale, indistinct simulacra. Just as the wavelength of visible light is too great to represent the existence of atoms accurately, so too the generality of words is too great adequately to express the inner self. While David wants to relate the story of the self, he finds himself telling that of David the king, David the slayer of Goliath,

David the wooer of Bathsheba, and so on. When he tries to articulate the sensations behind these roles, language fails him. For example, on the death of his sons, core events that his entire narrative struggles to convey, David can finally only say, "Rachel weeping for her children was as apathy itself compared to the misery I suffered at the death of these two of mine, for Rachel weeping for her children was but a figure of speech" (288). David finds that emotion cannot be spoken of directly, but only related to something outside the self. But even the comparison does not get at the thing itself, for as Heller's punning joke on "figure of speech" indicates, emotion voiced resolves into words.

Paradoxically, David—and Heller—can most successfully articulate the sensations of the inner self in language that is most stylized and in prose that aspires to poetry. David's elegaic lament on Absalom's death best illustrates this: "O my son Absalom, my son, my son Absalom! Would God I had died for thee, O Absalom, my son, my son!" (327). In *God Knows*, as in the Bible, this famous lament rings out, communicating the inexpressible desolation of a parent who would give up his life for his dead child. Lest the reader miss the significance of the lament, David (really Heller) introduces and frames it with the comment: "I heard myself weeping" (327). This observation authenticates the emotion by indicating that the anguish springs from beneath consciousness itself. Grief begins in the inner self. Similarly, as we have seen at his infant son's death, David turns to literary prose to express his deepest sensations, appropriating passages from the Book of Job. Only the poetry of Yahweh's anger can represent David's emotion at his son's death. Emotion can be quoted, but not directly written. And Heller's strategy for signalling this is the whole variety of quotations and allusions that he weaves into the novel, particularly at moments of intimate feeling. As plagiarist, not as writer, David most successfully represents the inner self.

As bridge between inner self and his role, David asserts the character of David the king. With this character, he can compose the story of his life and proclaim his identity. Assertions of character punctuate the text: "I am David, not Oedipus" (18); "I am David the king, not Oscar Wilde" (26); or "Imagine me doing things like that [gnashing his teeth and weeping], me, David, the warrior king, the sweet psalmist of Israel" (221). "David" as voiced in these passages is a construction, a fiction for maintaining commerce between mind and world, self and role. This character provides the master plot that conjoins the scenes of his life: the astonishingly beautiful cry of bereavement at Absalom's death; the aged, shivering David's loneliness even with Abishag; his innocence when he meets Samuel coming toward him with a red heifer.

As a construction, David's character is a fiction, a mask expressive of the identity that he believes he has. For example, when David asserts that he is David, not Oedipus, he does so to isolate his deepest attitudes about his self and the world. Similarly, he wants to identify the kind of story, the nature of its plot. Thus he continues saying, "I would have broken destiny to bits. To save my children then, I would have drawn thunder from the sky" (18). The evils of David's life—the death of his children—are not the result of fate, even though both were prophesied in advance by Nathan. Rather, David's own nature betrays him in that he did not listen while "Nathan rambled on with so much Delphic obscurity" (although "God was canny in selecting an addlepate like Nathan. He knew I'd be listening with one deaf ear; otherwise I might have averted it all" [18]). He believes that the character of David the king controls his own life, his own destiny. This David loves his children above all else. To himself, this David is the architect of his own destiny and the maker of himself. Yet he realizes this aspect of his identity is an illusion, for as he observes, "This danger in being a king is that after a while you begin to believe you really are one" (183).

Through his narrative, David explains himself to himself, so that everything fits and creates the coherence of character. But he confronts one critical inconsistency in his story. Because his sons' deaths were prophesied in advance, he ought to have been able to save them, if one is to believe that he would have done anything rather than let them die. As memoir, *God Knows* is in part about this inconsistency. As David composes his autobiography, he constructs a text filled with intermediary verbal formulas that make the inconsistency disappear—at least to his own eyes.[26] If one sets enough straight lines angled ever so slightly against each other, a circle is formed; so too if David fills in enough statements to round off the differences, he can have it both ways: 1) he would do anything to save his children; but 2) as a result of his adulterous liaison, his infant son died. By the end of *God Knows*, David works the narrative magic that eliminates this apparent inconsistency of character.

Although David is its architect, his character has limits. David the king becomes a construct that he must fulfill. Or, put another way, he must be himself, although not in the same way as Shakespeare's Prince Hal. Joab exploits this aspect of David's situation when he insists that David mask his grief for Absalom and celebrate the victory over the rebels with his troops. Here as elsewhere Joab insists that David act consistently the character of the king. Joab's principle of consistency is that of the world, and he wants David to fulfill his function and to deny any distinction between a unique self with unique feelings and his role. It is not simply, however, the role of king that Joab requires David to fulfill, although he does that as well when he shows him the soldiers are "ashamed, ashamed of themselves and of you" (328), or when he asks sarcastically, "When will you learn to be a king?" (329). Joab also gets David to recognize that his inordinate grief is destructive of character as well as role.

"For this day I perceive that if Absalom had lived and all of us had died this day, then it had pleased thee more. You would not have carried on for any or all of us as you do for him, would you?"

In craven admission I answered him weepily. "No."

"Let's keep that our secret," said Joab, speaking in a more moderate voice. (328)

Joab has the crucial insight into David's character to be able to locate the vital interstice between public and private, between role and self. Joab takes advantage of his insight to get David to realize that now when he wants to act other than his character he cannot. The character that David has constructed has come to contain his self.

As memoir, *God Knows* recounts the making of character. When David announces that he has the "best story in the Bible" (5), he celebrates the nature of the life he has lived and commences the authorship of the hero of *God Knows*. The dual process of character formation develops throughout the novel, as representation of lived life and as construction of its literary artifice. It proceeds self-consciously, and in this spirit David observes, "Of the making of books there is no end and the longer I reflect on this tale of mine, the stronger grows my conviction that killing Goliath was just about the biggest goddamn mistake I ever made" (15). The two processes are mutually informing. Making his book, David comes to a new realization of who he is. But in writing his life, he continues to live as well as to make and remake his character—to multiply his identities. And so it goes.

In this duality of character, David has the multiple identity that no other Heller protagonist possesses. King and rebel, writer and plagiarist, he embodies and will embody multitudes. In conceiving David in these terms, Heller has significantly shifted his understanding of identity. At the conclusion of *Catch-22*, *Something Happened*, and *Good as Gold*, the Heller protagonist confronts, although in different forms, the choice between being himself or becoming "one of the boys." What changes in these situations is how these protagonists conceive of themselves. This change is most apparent in *Good as Gold* for, by rejecting the offer of a Washington political appointment, Gold does not confirm his identity, but only begins the process of finding it. That identity will emerge through writing his book on Jewish life—only Gold does not know this at novel's end. In Gold's authorship, Heller refigures the possibilities of character, opens up identity as potential rather than as something unified and complete—which returns us to *God Knows*.

If protean and possible, David's self remains human. Because of its humanity, his identity has another aspect that cannot be remade—only lived. It is his physical embodiment that frames the novel *God Knows* and circumscribes the narrative present, the "stink of mortality and reek of mankind" (107). Restated subjectively, this is the message embodied in Snowden's entrails. Mortality limits, its materialization reeks, its end is final. Yet on his deathbed, authoring his life, David dreams, "watch[ing] a vision slowly take shape. I see an eager, bright-eyed youth there on a low wooden stool . . . he is holding in his lap a lyre with eight strings" (352). Even amidst the stench of mortality character is reborn and possibilities repeated. The character "starts with a song I used to know" (353), and in the telling the constraints of mortality recede—momentarily. "I want my God back; and they send me a girl" (353). In this, "they"—David's court —perceive him too narrowly. They do not see the inner self, the David who wants passionate involvement with Bathsheba and God. Nevertheless, in David's desire for restoration of his relationship with God, his story—his character—begins again, even as it ends for the reader.

■

WOMEN, LOVE, DESIRE, AND DEATH: JOSEPH HELLER'S OTHER PLOT

While Joseph Heller's fiction is propelled by his dead-child story, this plot has a counterpart in which a woman rather than a child holds the key. The narrative structure of the female plot is just as certain as the dead-child story (with its constellation of guilt, secret knowledge, bad faith, and death), consisting of desire in which love is either absent or driven into sensuality. In either case, the passion activated by desire leads via twists, turns, and detours to death. Like the dead-child story, this plot holds Heller's essential thematic dichotomy between matter and spirit, but has thus far eluded scholarly attention. This is not, however, surprising, for as feminist scholars have taught us, women's stories—or, in this case, the roles women play in men's stories—tend to go unnoticed and unvalued in fiction, just as they do in history. Yet, when they are observed as they easily can be in *God Knows*, they prismatically reveal the myriad colors of experience, colors whose shadings imperceptibly pass from one into another.

Like many male authors, Heller places women characters at the cross-roads of quest plots, where they become symbols of the protagonist's choices. Thus located, women are not so much characters as they are figures of desire.[27] They appear most frequently as occasions of male arousal; they are lovers, virgins, mistresses, or wives.[28] As receptors of desire, women have no subjectivity, Heller never allowing them their own mental life, aspirations, or identity. In *Good as Gold*, for example, Andrea represents Washington power and WASPish values—the things to which Bruce Gold aspires—while his wife Belle embodies middle-class Jewish life—the heritage that he should embrace. Her hearty rye bread nourishes, but for most of the novel Gold finds Andrea's frozen dinners more enticing. As this dichotomy suggests, Heller's female plot turns upon the constancy of the hero's desire and the inconstancy of his love. However, desire itself is unstable, always propelling the Heller protagonist other than where he intends, and the women who are the object of this desire hold a dark truth, that of mortality. By succumbing to passion, the physical manifestation of desire, the protagonist opens up a narrative path along which he will inevitably find death. This depiction of the hidden linkage between desire and death is in accordance with Denis de Rougement's argument about the destructive nature of romantic love: "*But myth* (of Tristan) *is needed to express the dark and unmentionable fact that passion is linked with death*, and involves the destruction of any one yielding himself up to it with all his strength."[29]

Catch-22 introduces the pattern for Heller's presentation of the instabilities of desire and the dynamics of his female plot. In the beach scene in which Yossarian fondles Nurse Duckett while playing cards with Hungry Joe and the other squadron members, Heller takes a seemingly stable situation of desire and its fulfillment and shatters it. Nurse Duckett obligingly arouses Yossarian without demanding anything in return. Heller renders desire as touch, the erotic counterpart to Yossarian massaging Snowden's wounded leg: "[Yossarian] had a craving to touch her always, to remain always in physical communication. He liked to encircle her ankle loosely with his fingers as he played cards . . . to lightly and lovingly caress the downy skin of her fair, smooth thigh . . . [to] slide his proprietary, respectful hand . . . beneath the elastic strap of the top of the two-piece bathing suit she always wore to contain and cover her tiny, long-nippled breasts" (328–29). However, Yossarian's desire seeks something beyond the flesh, something that he does not as yet fully understand; "[h]e thirsted for life and reached out ravenously to grasp and hold Nurse Duckett's flesh" (331).[30] While Yossarian searches for security in the novel's deadly world, his clutching, grasping, and groping for Nurse Duckett do not afford this, initiating instead, although indirectly so, an inexorable slide from desire to arousal to passion—and thence to death. When McWatt flies too low and hits Kid Sampson, death intrudes in the scene, the oceans turning red with blood and organs and severed limbs. This depiction of the hidden linkage

G O D   K N O W S   ■   167

between desire and death is in accordance with Denis de Rougement's argument about the destructive nature of romantic love.

Also in *Catch-22*, Heller unfolds in the Luciana episode another version of the instabilities of desire and depicts its opacity to those who desire. As with the Snowden death scene, the scene with Luciana has its origin in Heller's actual experience. As he presents her, Luciana teasingly arouses Yossarian by insisting that she will not let him sleep with her, although she eventually does, on terms that she dictates. In this configuration of desire, she, not he, makes the critical choices, and she realizes what he does not, that physical desire may activate love, but may never consummate it. Her attractiveness—she is pretty, earthy, buxom, exuberant, flirtatious—conceals something that has an even greater hold on Yossarian: "He wondered about the pink chemise that she would not remove. It was cut like a man's undershirt, with narrow shoulder straps, and concealed the invisible scar on her back she refused to let him see after he had made her tell him it was there" (157).[31] The scar, the result of wounds from an air raid, symbolizes her wisdom as well as her suffering. Despite Yossarian's protestations of love, Luciana knows that he cannot love her because she is not a virgin and that, although she freely offers herself to him, he will tear up the paper with her address and thus will never find her again. When he does tear up her address, Yossarian's desire is forever stirred, and his frantic search takes him other than where he intends: into dreams in which he again dodges flak over Bologna and into Snowden's room, who is still alive then but not there (168). The reader knows the meaning of such details; Yossarian does not. In his memory, Luciana remains ever alluring, signifying the truth about desire that Yossarian never glimpses. Again to draw upon and, in this instance, to adapt Denis de Rougement's argument: "The essential happiness of this love is that what [he] desires [he] has not yet had—this is Death—and that what [he] had is now being lost—the enjoyment of life" (*Love in the Western World* 53).

In *God Knows*, Heller transforms these female subplots—which had previously controlled scenes or, at most, critical choices that the protagonist makes—into organizing principles for the novel. The women of the novel mark the way in which David as author and man plots his life, by which he orients his possibilities, scans the present, and numbers his losses. The women are presented more as types than as individuals, the description of each denominating the sexual and emotional relationship she shares with David: Bathsheba is the femme fatale, whose sexuality occasions some of David's crucial choices and arouses him even on his deathbed; Abigail is the wife, whose love for David is enduring and self-effacing; Michal is portrayed as the first Jewish American Princess and the bane of David's domestic life; and Abishag is the virginal innocent, uncorrupted by sexuality and experience, who reawakens David to his need for love.[32]

As this suggests, *God Knows* is Heller's first love story, something that Heller says he realized retrospectively.[33] In his relationships with Bathsheba, Abigail, Michal, and Abishag, David struggles to find what love is, then to find love itself. His effort recapitulates love as a theme in Heller's fiction. *Catch-22* begins with the sentences: "It was love at first sight. The first time Yossarian saw the chaplain he fell madly in love with him" (7).[34] But love is absent in the novel, except in its sexual manifestation: Yossarian's rendezvous with Nurse Duckett, the maid in the lime-green panties, and Luciana. In *Something Happened*, there is family life, but again no love except in Slocum's sexual desires. He and his wife share a loveless present—sex with her yields satiety rather than satisfaction. Loneliness and desire impel Slocum to return ceaselessly to his Virginia memories, memories which, like Virginia herself, titillate but do not quench. And they prompt his afternoon liaisons with Penny, though these bring only momentary sexual gratification. *Good as Gold* has the same split between a mistress who stimulates desire and a wife who deadens it, but Heller gives the motif much more attention. Gold discovers that while the luscious Andrea inflames him, sex with her does not appease his longings or alleviate his loneliness. Gold's choice to return to his wife Belle announces a partial renunciation of desire and the beginning of love that involves more than sexual gratification.

In contrast to the earlier novels, *God Knows* might be described as contrapuntal variations of a love story in that David experiences different aspects of love with each—Bathsheba, Abigail, Michal, and Abishag. In his relationships with these women, David begins to discover what love is —something that no other Heller protagonist has learned. He also limns the boundaries and connections between love and desire. Thanks to Bathsheba, Abigail, and Abishag, David learns how to love. He does not learn, however, how to bring a love story to completion. Rather, his relationship with each woman constitutes a different kind of story, although one with an underlying constant—"the person who wants love cannot be satisfied with love" (79–80). This formulation becomes another Catch-22, because Heller protagonists want love. As an account of love, *God Knows* has the instability of an unbalanced chemical compound: driven by desire, David seeks sex and love, but neither brings him emotional fulfillment or rest.

The most fully drawn of Heller's women, Bathsheba is frankly sexual and entirely self-absorbed; she has an intoxicating physical presence, which she understands and flaunts. In this, Bathsheba is subversive counterweight to God. Her knowledge, gained from her harlot friends, occasions the moral tests that David fails (but also without which there would be precious little novel). In Heller's reworking of the biblical story, Bathsheba herself has precipitated her affair with the king by bathing in the nude where she knows he will see her. As descendant of Nurse Duckett, Bathsheba kindles desire while being largely unaffected by it. As sexual come-ons, she, among other things, paints her toes, streaks her hair ash blonde (knowing that turning "herself into a WASP" [265] will excite David's Jewish manhood), and is partial to loud colors. To entice David, she also invents underwear, which predictably leads to one of Heller's many jokes involving her.

> "What are they for?"
> "To make me sexier, to make women more attractive to men. I have these smaller ones with lace that I call panties. And these I call bikinis. Do they work?"
> "How should I know if they work? Pull them down and let me get at you."
> "They work." (274)

Perpetually inventive of such enticements, Bathsheba holds sexual sway over David, confident that she will realize her only ambition of getting him to name Solomon as successor. She tells David why he will eventually capitulate to her demands and name Solomon as successor: because "I suck your cock. . . . And I'm giving you the greatest fucking you ever had" (294). As this raunchy joke indicates, Bathsheba celebrates her ability to stimulate desire, and in her mind, by controlling David's desire, she will also control the outcome of his kingship.

Bathsheba comes as close as any woman that Heller draws to having a life of her own. In fact, as if commenting on his previous portraits of women, Heller writes Bathsheba's aspirations for independence into the text. Throughout her relationship with David, Bathsheba insists upon having a private life. She demands and gets time and space of her own, including a workshop where she can weave, paint, and write. As a prototype for a twentieth-century woman, Bathsheba succeeds to a certain extent in living her own life, most tellingly as an author. In fact, in Heller's joke Bathsheba rather than David has conceived the metaphor "The Lord is my shepherd." David finds it farfetched, but nevertheless appropriates it for his Twenty-third Psalm, by his own assessment one of his most famous, but not one of his best, psalms. Heller's joke cuts both ways. As author, Bathsheba tries to establish what is allowed Slocum, Gold, and David— the right to tell their own stories and by doing so to authorize and authenticate their own lives. But David's put-down and Heller's joke of making Bathsheba the inspiration for the Twenty-third Psalm undercut Bathsheba's authority. Heller does not permit her to compose the story of the self; nor has he yet given a female character authorial power that compares to that of his male characters (with the partial exception of Claire Rabinowitz in *Closing Time*).

In David's responses to Bathsheba, Heller stresses that she occasions a kind of profane conversion, awakening him to sexual love and to the physical and emotional happiness that accompanies such love. David recalls their life together in terms of contemporary sex manuals—good sex leads to good love. "I did want to see her every day once I knew I was in love with her and once I had found out from her what great fucking was. I did not want to be without it" (271). The duality of this formulation, love and sex, quickly becomes one: "I did not want to be without it"—the most elemental statement of eros. David's affair with Bathsheba originated in desire, of course, albeit one that seeks its own satisfaction rather than her. Having seen David expose himself while dancing before the Ark of the Covenant, Bathsheba concocts her scheme of bathing in the nude where he will see her. As this indicates and as the novel subsequently demonstrates, her desire is for power. Their mutual lust fuels their adulterous liaison, "those first happy days of sinful, thrusting frenzy" (277). Adulterous pleasures, David argues, are always the most compelling.[35] The attraction remains vital as long as Bathsheba continues to invent more illicit pleasures: making love while she is menstruating, titillating David with the possibility of sodomy, and demanding multiple orgasms (a term that David learns from Bathsheba). Transgression renews desire.[36]

For David, sex with Bathsheba begets love. It is love discovered, or as David describes his feelings for Bathsheba: "So surprising a thing it is for a man who doesn't believe in love to find himself so deeply in it" (259). While a product of desire, love becomes distinct from it. And if David himself does not know what love is, Bathsheba can help him learn. As relational instructress, Bathsheba coaxes David into expressing his feelings and into becoming proficient in the mechanics of making love. Only with Bathsheba can David voice a simple "'I love you' . . . "without faltering with embarrassment, fright, humiliation, or shame" (46). For David and Heller, such instruction has its value. If David comes to call his relationship to Bathsheba a mistake, he continues to celebrate the emotion that she awakens in him. Purporting to explicate the biblical line, "Give not your heart to women," David says, "If the chance ever comes to you again to fall in love, grab it, every time. You might always live to regret it, but you won't find anything to beat it" (243).

However, like Yossarian before him, David finds desire and love have taken him other than where he intended or than he fully comprehends; it leads to the death of his infant son by Bathsheba. As Heller reconstructs this famous biblical episode, the pregnancy results from having sex while Bathsheba was menstruating.[37] She herself overcomes his reticence to have intercourse during her period, his reluctance to violate biblical law and to be contaminated by the menstrual blood. The transgressive passion inflames, even in memory: "I . . . exulted so greatly in the mere knowledge of what I was doing" (278). Even as the menstrual blood excites—as did Snowden's blood in the manuscript version of the death scene—it announces death. Hearing the words, "I'm with child," David imagines the possibilities—abortion (like the novel's other anachronisms, it occasions a joke), Bathsheba's death by stoning (Bathsheba responds in kind by telling David that by Jewish law the adulter as well as the adultress is stoned), and Uriah's untimely death. Violating chronology, his text at this moment intermixes what might have been with what would be: "my newborn baby was sick and doomed to early death because of me. So said Nathan. The poor little thing was burning with fever and perishing of thirst and starvation" (279). David, as we have seen, resists this interpretation, blaming God for the child's death. However, as Denis de Rougement observes, "Suffering and understanding are deeply connected; death and self-awareness are in league" (51). The suffering occasioned by this death as well as Absalom's later death eventually prompts David's realization that his own actions—like those of Amnon and Absalom—contributed to "the brutal climaxes betiding us" (295).

David's realizations extend to his love for Bathsheba. At the end, he confirms this love by acceding to Bathsheba's wishes in choosing Solomon as successor. In his words, "I decided for Bathsheba, because once, for a few years of my life, she had made me happy" (345). Although David can affirm love as a principle for action, he cannot imagine its complementarity. As David summarizes their relationship: "I love Bathsheba and she does not love me" (191). More darkly, David comes to believe that Bathsheba never loved him, that "she was more in love with the idea of being in love, and especially, of course, with the idea of being in love with David the king" (45). In David's version of this love story then, Bathsheba has awakened desire and through desire love, but now neither concerns her. This story remains open and unbalanced, its proportions of desire and love never capable of finding resolution.

Abigail is Heller's chaste contrast to Bathsheba, and her relationship to David the pale complement to the affair with Bathsheba. David's first reference to her sounds the keynote for Heller's presentation: "my elegant lady of quality and refinement who fed me the best lentil soup, barley bread, and leeks I ever ate in my whole life" (11). Obviously, Abigail is the consummate housewife. Even when David flees Saul through the hills of Judah, Abigail manages tablecloths and candlelight dinners. Michal interprets Abigail and her remarkable domesticity less charitably: "provincial, barren, and middle class" (266). And with her usual insight, Bathsheba plots Abigail's career: "Abigail was the dumb one who just kept working. She aged overnight, practically, and her hair turned ugly gray" (83). While David may object to these characterizations, his own depiction serves to confirm them. In David's memories of her, she is a housewife.

As exemplary wife, Abigail makes a desirable companion, but does not generate the narratable, except as love spurned. Unlike Bathsheba, the reticent Abigail has no wish to tell about herself, and David is too self-absorbed or too busy pursuing Bathsheba to know her other than in terms of the categorical label "wife." Rhetorically, she exists as the occasion for David's prose rhapsodies: "A virtuous woman like Abigail is a crown to her husband" (80) or "[h]er price is far above rubies" (208). But she provides no narrative complexity or richness—at least not to David or Heller. In *God Knows*, lentil soup provides less enticing satisfactions than good sex. David's recollections of Abigail almost always deflect to Bathsheba, or they recall how he turned from Abigail's durable love in his pursuit of Bathsheba.

While Bathsheba feeds David's sexual appetites, Abigail nourishes his emotions. As wife-mother, she comforts him with her unwavering love, continually assuring David that as his wife she has everything she desires. Even as part of David's harem and as second fiddle to Bathsheba, Abigail remains satisfied and uncomplaining, the most loyal of David's wives. Only after she dies does David fully appreciate the way in which she sensed and ministered to his needs. "Abigail would have been distraught to know how poorly I sleep and how isolated I feel. She would seek some way to relieve that wordless melancholy with which I am afflicted" (47). Like Bathsheba, she has become a part of David's consciousness, but unlike Bathsheba, she is also part of his sensibility. Thus, while David was hiding his grief over Absalom's death, he imagines that "Abigail would have seen into the window of my soul and known the truth" (331). In David's thoughts, Abigail registers the authentic and the caring, and David values her precisely because he is the chief object of her concern.

Like Bathsheba, Abigail fulfills the traditional novelistic role of instructress to the hero. She teaches David about unselfish love and the enduring satisfactions of life. In fact, Heller gives Abigail the epigraph he uses for the novel (actually a passage from Ecclesiastes): "If two lie together . . . then they have heat. But how can one be warm alone?" (209). But like her life, Abigail's authorship is anonymous (not that David fails to appreciate her way with words, for he borrows the line to try to seduce Bathsheba). Only the reader who recognizes that Heller's epigraph comes from Abigail's line will realize that she as well as David and Bathsheba is an author. Her goodness gives her insight into the emotional heart of experience. While she is alive, David believes her goodness and insight protect him. But "when Abigail died I was lonely, and I have been lonely ever since" (104). In this loneliness—the loneliness of *God Knows*—David turns to Abigail's memory for warmth and guidance. He finds solace meditating on the constancy of her affection and love for him and gains comfort from the realization that she would understand his deepest feelings. Abigail's wisdom, exemplified in Heller's epigraph, infuses David's consciousness and thus his memoirs. However, when that wisdom could have affected their life together or his crucial choices, David could not apprehend it; in this, the limit on David's possibilities has been the quality of his own consciousness.

For David, Abigail becomes an ideal, a bloodless abstraction rather than an actual woman. David's tendency toward idealization appears whenever he is in his self-consciously authorial mode: "if you find a woman as virtuous as Abigail, let her be as the loving kind pleasant roe, let her breasts satisfy thou at all times, and be thou ravished always with her love" (227). In this paean to Abigail, David renders the tale of their relationship as a moral exemplum, because he has already turned from her. In fact, even this flourish of praise gives way to the story that still shapes David's consciousness, the language of love precipitating that of passion, that language of extremity, blood, and eventually death. "Unhappily for Abigail, the heart of man being fickle, it was with Bathsheba's love that I was ravished always" (227). Herein lies another variant of David's and Heller's love story. "Abigail was the one woman in my life who really did love me" (47), but in his prose as in his life, David turns from this love—much as Bathsheba spurns David's love now. In Heller's formulation, love is triangular, much the way desire is mediated for René Girard.[38] Abigail's love cannot satisfy David's desire—neither in the past nor in the memories of the past. Rather, this love, especially in memory, kindles David's desire for Bathsheba.

Michal, who is according to Heller the first Jewish American Princess, is an authorial vehicle for endless jokes, but she, unlike Bathsheba and Abigail, is not allowed a story of her own. Cut from quite different cloth than Bathsheba and Abigail, Michal has no appetites and no intention of ministering to David's. Before she and David begin their hymenal festivities, she sets the rules of their relationship: "Go take a bath. . . . Wash under your arms. Make sure you comb your hair after you've dried it, the back of your head too. Rinse your teeth with a mouthwash. Use a perfume on your face" (139). Obviously, from David's point of view, Michal is sexually frigid. She puts up with David's advances once a month in hopes of conceiving an heir. Additionally, she scolds David for his sexuality and spontaneity, most notably on their wedding night and on the night David exposes himself while dancing before the Ark of the Covenant—an obvious contrast to Bathsheba's reaction.

In her own fashion, Michal does love David and acts upon her feelings to the extent of helping David escape Saul when she learns about her father's plot to kill David. But to her, marriage constitutes a politically expedient alliance, not a relationship. Michal can never respond to David the man; her consciousness of class can never set aside the social inferiority of a husband who is the son of a shepherd. In these and other details, Heller's portrait of Michal allows no sympathy (and one suspects that Heller could never have any authorial sympathy for someone with Michal's attitudes toward sex). Heller harshens the biblical characterization of Michal. In his depiction, her shrewishness acquires an animalistic ferocity. He describes, for example, Michal's "feral" response to David's dancing naked before the Covenant (263) and notes the "whited, sepulchral face solidified like stone into an expression of violent hatred and misanthropy" (264). Michal's misanthropy seems to partake of Heller's authorial misogyny. Heller's J.A.P. references make Michal the parodic inversion of Abigail and Bathsheba. Heller's humor, like the humor associated with many shrewish wife stories, mocks the idealization of love and inverts the expected results of desire.

A virginal innocent, Abishag combines Bathsheba's beauty with Abigail's unselfish love. Heller takes the character of Abishag from the Book of Kings, in which David's advisors send for a virgin to warm the king since he cannot warm himself. But Heller's presentation changes the biblical story by making Abishag the creation of David's desire. Before Abishag is born, David "dream[s] of someone as caring and as tender to me as Abishag the Shunammite" (143). Heller fractures the novel's chronology in this way to indicate that Abishag is not so much woman as ideal, literally the girl of David's dreams. Thus, David never tires of describing Abishag's phenomenal beauty in prose that lingers over the curves of her breasts, buttocks, and loins. Also, Abishag embodies solicitous love, maternal in its constancy yet the incarnation of the paradox of chaste sexuality. Such physical and emotional perfection renders David rather emotionless; in his descriptions of her, the right words are there but they are passionless. It is as if Heller is still confined by the Luciana story: perfection is sullied by an actual relationship.

David himself recognizes Abishag as the creature—and perhaps creation—of desire.[39] Gazing at her, David continually finds himself wondering: "Do I imagine Abishag the Shunammite, construct her out of wishes?" (107). Even while cataloguing all the signs of her materiality— the taste of her kisses, the smell of the myrrh which she rubs on her breasts, the fragrance of mountain grapes from her hair—David can never entirely acknowledge that Abishag exists apart from his fantasies. He does, however, realize the effect she has on his life: "I now know about myself . . . that all my life I have wanted to be in love" (109). Here, desire leads back to the self, for Abishag is the catalyst for the interiority of memory. These memories, in turn, prompt David's new self-knowledge. If his desire begot Abishag, then her materialization begets his knowledge of self.

Desire for Abishag propels another tale of the unbalanced proportions of love. Abishag thinks that she is falling in love with David; he, having learned its ways, knows that she is not. He wonders if he is "falling in love with Abishag" (26), but recognizes that he is not. In Heller's parable about love, David turns from Abishag, as he earlier turned from Abigail. David himself recognizes that he wants to make love with Bathsheba, not Abishag, one last time. More importantly, although flawless, Abishag cannot still the dissatisfactions of David's heart or warm his death-chilled consciousness. In bed with Abishag as the novel ends, David still complains, unsatisfied even by her flawless presence. The materialization of David's desires cannot quiet his yearning, nor can Abishag's unremitting solicitude end the pains of his loneliness.

The aches of the loneliness awakened by Abishag redirect David's thoughts toward God in a gesture of spiritual and existential desire. Following David's thoughts, Heller's concluding pages plot an ultimate love story. Its grounding again is the virginal flesh which David never tires of describing.

> Abishag the Shunammite washes and dries herself when she has finished with me and begins to annoint and perfume herself as she makes ready to join me. My lamps are lit. Her lips drip as the honeycomb, and I know that the smell of her nose is like apples. Honey and milk are under her tongue, and the roof of her mouth is like wine. . . . Abishag the Shunammite sits without comment on the indigo folds of her robe, which has slipped from her shoulders and settled in lush and gleaming ripples about her waist and thighs. She reaches out her arms to lave them in liquid myrrh and then applies the unguent lotion to her chest as well and to her purple-nippled breasts. (352)

But David seeks beyond the material, finding little satisfaction in Abishag's beauty. The moment of peace stimulates his memories, memories of God and Saul. Looking into a mirror that Abishag holds before him, David realizes that he has "never [seen] a sadder face on a human being" (352). Inspired when the incarnation of his physical desires is available to him, David's overwhelming unhappiness begets new desire and illuminates old dissatisfactions. David calls out for God, a new call for love.[40] But in Heller's reformulation of the Bible, the call must go unanswered. In *God Knows*, love can be felt, can be affirmed, but can never be completed either on earth or in heaven.

In the last analysis, Heller's portraits of Bathsheba, Abigail, Michal, and Abishag tell us more about David than they do about these women themselves. Each recounts David's loneliness and his yearning for a relationship that will extricate him from this loneliness. He imagines his life as incomplete—incomplete in much the way Slocum's lost-child myth is incomplete in *Something Happened*. It can become complete only through union with another, but the sense of completion David finds with each woman is at best temporary and partial and always located in a non-recoverable past.[41] Through Bathsheba, David learned about the explosiveness of eros and, through its aching pangs, about love. But now that David loves her, Bathsheba does not love him. Union with Abigail is impossible because she died long ago, and when her selfless love was available, David turned from it. Through Abishag, the materialization of his desires, David rediscovers the potency of love, an unrealizable love, because, while activated by Abishag, it seeks Bathsheba. And while David is physically aroused by Abishag herself, he finds himself too old to act on his concupiscence. So at novel's end, David is in bed with Abishag to warm him, yet, nevertheless, alone and lonely. "I want my God back; and they send me a girl" (353). His desire is transcendental, always seeking beyond itself. So is love, and for David and Heller it can never realize what it seeks.

As love story, *God Knows* is incomplete, affirming love but not its consummation. Desire is constant in the novel, as it always is in Heller's fiction, and while the novel aspires toward love, it resolves back into desire. In Heller's fictional universe, this is inevitable, for love is of the mind and spirit. Abigail offers David such love; she is his 'soul mate. But he cannot gain this lasting love, because of the desire for Bathsheba, who is his body mate.[42] This physical desire has produced love: "I think I may have been the first grown man in the world to fall truly, passionately, sexually, romantically, and sentimentally in love" (9). However, the love produced by the body ends with the body, and the body ends impotent and cold, these physical manifestations presaging death itself. In this way, *God Knows* begins and ends with Heller reprising the Snowden death scene, albeit with David taking the parts of both Snowden and Yossarian. Together with Freud, Heller would say that *"the aim of all life is death,"* though unlike Freud, Heller resists rather than embraces this truth.[43]

And so David cries out for God at novel's end; so does Heller, though not in the traditionally religious sense. Rather, as author Heller voices the hope for something that will quell the loneliness of the self, something that will assure that there is meaning in individual experience. His references to Ecclesiastes throughout *God Knows* insist upon the vanity of human endeavor and lend the novel the cadences of the preacher Coheleth (the speaker in Ecclesiastes). Like Ecclesiastes, *God Knows* raises the possibility that experience is as ephemeral as dust swirling in the wind. In a moment of particular darkness, David says, "I hate God and I hate life. And the closer I come to death, the more I hate life" (9). But of course, he does not entirely hate life. His accounts of Bathsheba, Abigail, and Abishag tell us otherwise. So he cries out to God, a cry hungering after love. Although David and Heller cannot supply its answer or completion, its voicing concludes *God Knows*. As novel, *God Knows* is its consummation. Ultimately, it is a story of love (which inevitably means a story of desire, which itself relates another story, one which must end in death).[44]

THE BIBLE AS HELLER'S PRE-TEXT

When Heller conceived the idea of appropriating the biblical story of King David, he must have felt relieved and elated. The story was all there—guilt, secret knowledge, bad faith, and dead children. All he had to do was to reconstitute it into his kind of novel, one (to appropriate Heller's own formulation) "deal[ing] with the imminence and inevitability of death, the possibility of disease, the fact of cruelty, social neglect."[45] The pressure to find a new fictional subject—and the means to still interviewers' unceasing questions about what he is working on and whether it will be like *Catch-22*—vanished, for Heller had everything he needed in the Bible. Most importantly, Heller found a protagonist capable of expressing Yossarian's outrage at the limits of mortality, but without the cloying self-pity and ethical myopia of Slocum and Gold. After conceiving Slocum, whom he viewed as "contemptible," and Gold, whom he found "morally . . . ignominious," Heller was ready to use a narrator-hero whose intelligence and wit were equal to his own.[46] In Samuel I and II and the opening to Kings I, Heller found the blueprint from which he could construct a novel.[47]

The Bible has provided Heller with inspiration before, although chiefly as a source of allusion. The unpublished story "Jephthah's Daughter" illustrates the use he makes of the Bible.[48] The title is an allusion to the Book of Judges' account of Jephthah's sacrifice of his virgin daughter in thanksgiving for a victory, and this allusion provides the interpretive key for Heller's story of a man who betrays his daughter's trust. He has promised to defend her wishes for a small family wedding against his wife's insistence that she have a large, socially prominent wedding. Rather than let his wife expose his bookmaking, the man agrees to her demands for the society wedding. Heller's allusive title heightens the implications of this realistic, slice-of-life tale, inviting a comparison of the protagonists' willingness to sacrifice their daughter's wishes to further their own aims and protect their own reputations. Biblical allusions similarly inform episodes in *Catch-22*, *Something Happened*, and *Good as Gold*, providing as they do in "Jephthah's Daughter" a moral cipher against which the protagonists' choices are measured.

As the first Heller novel to be fabricated from an existing story, *God Knows* illuminates Heller's authorial concerns: how he goes about making a story. In the main, the picture of composition that emerges is a familiar one: sculpting scenes for comedic and language effects; his consciously retrospective narrative method; the conjunction of moods, particularly comic and tragic; his extensive reliance on repetition; and his unremitting fascination with mortality. Similarly, Heller's compositional process has changed little since he wrote *Catch-22*, as he moves from idea to notecards, pre-writing characters, scenes, and dialogue. And yet the picture of composition emerges in a new light, changed like a room illuminated with an ultraviolet lamp. The room stays the same yet becomes strangely unfamiliar, cast in violet hues and shadows. So too readers, encountering a David story of which most already know the main points, have the opportunity to observe what Heller makes out of his version and thus to gain a new view of what makes a novel. And because Heller makes David the nominal author, the reader gains a new perspective on Heller's own conception of authorship.

Using the chronology and events from the Bible, sketching character portraits that fill out biblical ones, and borrowing Old Testament language, Heller places his novel in surprisingly close alignment with the Bible. The novel works as Heller's reinterpretation of the David story as he himself must have experienced it, albeit a David who has a comic imagination and twentieth-century knowledge and sensibility. Yet Heller's language—its street-wise New York idiom and its vulgarity—distance the novel from the biblical original. As novel, *God Knows* is both faithful (albeit updated) copy and ironic distortion.[49]

Apart from the fact that Heller recounts the David story in retrospect, *God Knows* follows its chronology from his victory over Goliath to the struggle over succession between Adonijah and Solomon. Heller does, however, alter the narrative proportions, expanding, for example, Bathsheba's and David's encounters into a series of comic set pieces. The Bathsheba episodes become the comic prelude for the deaths and rebellion that follow, and thus Heller retains the biblical rhythms of the rise and fall of David's fortunes. Placing David on his deathbed only heightens the impact of the decline, because his rise occurs in a flashback. David's manner of commenting on his memories also prepares the reader for what is to come: "There was nowhere to go but down" (256).

Heller's character portraits—with a few notable exceptions such as Solomon's near-moronic lack of intelligence—are rooted in the Bible. This is particularly true for minor characters like Barzillai the Gileadite, Shimei, and Benaiah. Barzillai's steadfast loyalty to David and his peaceful old age ring as clearly in the novel as they do in the Bible. Even characters who are comic foils are built out of biblical portraits, although in exaggerated form. For instance, Michal as the first J.A.P. has her origin in Heller's reaction to her disapproval over David's spontaneous exuberance in dancing before the Ark of the Covenant: "What a glorious day for the king of Israel, when he exposed his person in the sight of his servants' slave-girls like any empty-headed fool!" (2 Samuel 6:20). Heller also expands biblical presentation, as he does in the case of Joab. As David's alter-ego, Joab knows that David would rather his loyal soldiers die than the rebellious Absalom. Joab's psychological insight into David's character represents a plausible interpretation of the famous relationship between the two biblical heroes. As a result of Heller's adaptation of biblical chronology and characterization, a reader who turns or returns to the books of Samuel and Kings after reading *God Knows* will traverse familiar ground —as if repeating a journey.

Although Heller borrows extensively from the prose of the King James version of the story of David, he forms the novel in the idiom of a street-wise resident of the twentieth century, and thus in his biblical language *God Knows* departs from the Bible.[50] Encountering biblical passages in the novel has an effect similar to viewing medieval stained-glass windows rehung in a contemporary church. Although magnificently illuminated, the windows become artifacts, preserving the past while testifying to a culture that has changed. So too the biblical language of *God Knows*:

> "She feedeth among the lilies. . . . My beloved is mine, and I am hers. Your breasts are like two young roes that are twins. Your hair is like a flock of goats, your teeth like sheep that are even shorn. Thou art fair, my love, behold thou art fair. . . ." All I did was let myself speak the truth. (47)

> There are only four basic plots in life anyway, and nine in literature, and everything else is but variation, vanity, and vexation of spirit. . . . Such is the vanity of human wishes that in no time at all I was able to trick myself into believing he [Saul] now approved of me. All is vanity, you know, *all*, all in the long run is but vanity and vexation of spirit. (129)

In the context of the novel, each passage reveals more about Heller and his attitude toward the Bible than it recapitulates biblical rhythms and meanings. Often, Heller's borrowings function parodistically, as when David "quotes" the Bible when trying to seduce Bathsheba. The erotic laughter that Heller generates with his appropriation of the Song of Solomon has a point, however, as David's laconic remark—"All I did was speak the truth"—indicates. Indeed, there are multiple truths in David's words (and Heller's joke): the truth of quotation of the orginal source; the truth of recapitulation of the erotic nature of the Song of Solomon; the truth that this speech act is, as John Searle would say, illocutionary—that is, a product of intentionality whose meaning may not be literal and depends upon the manner and the context in which it is performed.[51] Heller also uses the Bible's language to give currency to its vision. The borrowings from Ecclesiastes, together with David's emendations, work this way. Like the preacher Koheleth, Heller wants to illuminate the vanity of human endeavor. And, as we have already seen, David's quotations bear witness to his deepest feelings of grief and anger.

Another sign of the way in which Heller wants to depart from the Bible lies in his extensive use of anachronism. The anachronism injects an ironic distance between his David and the Bible's. Anachronism has been a favorite Heller stylistic strategy, most notably in *Catch-22* where it serves to locate the text in the America of the 1950s rather than in World War II Europe. References to Xerox machines, attitudes of the McCarthy era, and familar maxims like "what's good for M & M Enterprises is good for the country" situate the novel in an implied present, inviting readers to see Catch-22 as a phenomenon of peace as well of war and to recognize in its characters the mind-set of the military-industrial complex that is America. But in *God Knows* anachronism has less to do with an exterior correspondence between Heller's fictional Israel and contemporary America than with an interior correspondence between his protagonist's authorial concerns and those of contemporary writers, including Heller. In *God Knows* anachronism makes manifest the self as artist.

Most instances of anachronism are comic, and like sight gags in film, they are calculated to provoke immediate laughter. Bathsheba's magenta, cerise, and scarlet toenail polish or her enthusiasm for ceramics and cloisonne work in this way. So too do linguistic anachronisms, such as "They say he [Amnon] is coming. . . . So is Christmas" (336), although, obviously, the quality of the laughter is that of a groan. Heller's predilection for bad jokes and clichéd humor remains a touchstone in his novels—one that makes him an easy target for hostile critics and reviewers.[52] But anachronism serves to create the comitragic narrative method. For example, he introduces the events of Absalom's insurrection with a series of comic anachronisms: the cheerleaders who celebrate the palace takeover ("Let's give him an *A*" [320]) or Bathsheba's threat to stick an Amnon doll with pins and thereby eliminate him from standing between Solomon and the throne. Yet such farcical comedy gives way to the tragedy of David's grief. Bathsheba's voodoo threat is a case in point, for it is immediately followed by a markedly different narrative mood: when David admits that he, Amnon, and Absalom were responsible for their falls from grace. Like his creator, the aging David can only approach his sons' deaths with humor, temporarily postponing their finality with ridiculing laughter.

David's authorship, another focus for Heller's anachronism, becomes self-conscious commentary on the writing process. Again, most instances are comic, often provoking the same groaning laughter of the Bathsheba jokes. David's claims to having composed Bach's B minor Mass, Mozart's *Requiem*, and Handel's *Messiah* function this way, as do his critiques of Milton ("Milton was a man of considerable ability. Who knows—who can say for certain that his works will not last as long as mine have" [30]) or Shakespeare ("that *gonoph* William Shakespeare, who pilfered from Plutarch too, as well as from Saul and me. A bard of Avon they called him yet" [146]. But in a manner similar to the self-conscious commentary in *Good as Gold*, other anachronisms lampoon reviewers and literary critics, as David discourses on poetry's capacity for catharsis or when he labels himself an able realist. The Heller who tells of Major Major being warned "never to trust a man who said he'd finished a book by Henry James" is still in evidence.[53]

For all his jokes about David's authorship, Heller wants the reader to explore the authorial process and the status of its artifacts. While there are many instances of this, one of the most extensive and interesting is Heller's handling of David's famous elegy for Saul and Jonathan:

> I was truly inspired when I wrote:
>> The beauty of Israel is slain upon thy high places: how are the mighty fallen!
>> Tell it not in Gath, publish it not in the streets of Askelon; lest the daughters of the Philistines rejoice, lest the daughters of the uncircumcised triumph. . . .
>> I am distressed for thee, my brother Jonathan: very pleasant hast thou been unto me: thy love to me was wonderful, passing the love of women.
> You see? I do call him a brother, don't I?
>> How are the mighty fallen, and the weapons of war perished!
> . . . Only a very sordid nature could find in those lines of platonic praise of Jonathan even a hint of any allusion to that reprehensible love that dare not speak its name. (216–17)

Framing and interrupting the elegy with David's entirely mundane and somewhat vulgar consciousness, Heller places the biblical text and his prose in paratactic relation to each other. Speaking as himself, David comes across like the Wizard of Oz after his curtains are pulled back. He is self-absorbed, small-minded, and painfully ordinary. He seems incapable of understanding the emotional nuances that his elegy conveys, let alone of composing it. But if he did write it, then its overpowering lament seems inauthentic, its effect cheapened because David does not really grieve for Saul or Jonathan. In the conjunction of elegy and implied author, the artistry of the famous elegy is demystified—at least in terms of the illusion that this King David is its author, as *God Knows* maintains. In *Picture This*, Heller will use different techniques with the same end, in order to demystify Rembrandt's artistry.

The relationship between the elegy as authored by David and found in the Bible can be understood in the terms of John Barth's influential essay on the postmodern situation, "The Literature of Exhaustion."[54] Barth observes that "Beethoven's Sixth Symphony or the Chartres Cathedral if executed today would be merely embarrassing" (30); though he later qualifies his point, "but clearly it wouldn't be necessarily, if done with ironic intent by a composer quite aware of where we've been and where we are" (31). Ironic awareness provides the pivot shifting a work from a merely embarrassing reproduction of the past to statement about the contemporary condition, and given this formulation, it comes as no surprise that Barth cites Jorge Luis Borges as the great postmodern master, praising stories like "Pierre Menard, the Author of the *Quixote*" in which Menard successfully re-creates *Don Quixote*. Heller's appropriation of David's elegy conforms with Borges's playful imitation and exemplifies Barth's "literature of exhaustion."

While obviously parodic, Heller's quotation of the elegy and the accompanying commentary function as a *mise en abîme*, directing the reader to think about Heller as implied author—an effect much like that of the authorial intrusion in *Good as Gold* on what to do with an English teacher-hero. This becomes most evident when David talks about the elegy. "Once again, the creative act had a salutary effect upon me, for I was drained of grief when I finished and of all pity and fear. My beautiful and famous elegy was a catharsis. I must admit I soon grew more absorbed in the writing of it than in the fact of the deaths of Saul and his sons and the total victory of the Philistines. Poetry works like that" (217). Again, David's comments jar the narrative audience, for he seems to mouth empty phrases. How can he talk about catharsis when he feels so little grief over Saul's and Jonathan's deaths? As implied author, this David de-illusions his readers when he admits, in effect, that he counterfeits emotion. And if the internal implied author is faking it, then what about Heller himself?

Why does he interrupt the elegy's extraordinary beauty for yet another joke about David's homosexual love, and what does he intend when he has David talk about the "salutary effect" of composition? There are partial answers to such questions: clearly, the passage satirizes the language and methods of critics and reviewers; it directs readers, as I have noted, to consider the relationship between text and author—which is Heller's point. To borrow John Barth's argument (who likewise appropriates it from Borges), the passage disturbs readers "metaphysically: when the characters in a work of fiction become . . . authors of the fiction they're in" (Barth 33). It also reminds them, as Barth further notes, of the fictional aspects of their own existence. Finally, the passage destabilizes the biblical text, reminding readers, as biblical scholars tell us, that no one really knows who wrote the elegy. And who is to say that Heller's portrait of its author does not correspond to its actual writer? Heller takes a similar tack in *Picture This*, when he follows the lead revisionist art historians, who undermine the Romantic myth of the artist by revealing the commercial circumstances that determined Rembrandt's art.

Heller's handling of the elegy brings it and the biblical original into ironic alignment. An amanuensis and revisionist, Heller's David fills in biblical omissions by sharing his intentions or private feelings. David's commentary serves to recopy the biblical story so as to get it right. As we have seen, he does this when he divulges how his premeditated theatrics got Saul to pick him to oppose Goliath or when he reveals that it was Bathsheba who seduced him. The nature and tone of such revelations are those of the contemporary exposé. Yet Heller's pseudo-exposé gets at a deeper truth: behind the pieties of the David myth lies a man whose "senses do have but a human condition." The Bible purports to be sacred history; Heller wants to evoke the human actuality behind its history. He will use a similar strategy in *Picture This* to different effects, when he debunks Plato's account of the death of Socrates by describing what follows from ingesting hemlock.

As purported author, David is the fulcrum between the Bible and Heller's novel, but he is also the hinge that connects Heller to the Bible as well. And it is clear that in language, sensibility, and view of the Bible, David is particularly close to his author. The affinity between author and character comes across in the ways that Heller talks about *God Knows*. For example, he tells Cathleen Medwick, "David has a phrase—or is it mine? It's hard to distinguish now which are the Bible's . . . 'the trouble with the loneliness I feel is that the company of others is no cure for it.' That is something I recognize in myself. There's a difference between solitude and loneliness."[55] Heller's inability to distinguish David's phrase from his own testifies to his engagement with his protagonist. His comment also reveals the way in which he uses his own sensations—his estrangement from his wife or the lonely terrors of his time in the intensive care unit of Mount Sinai Hospital—as gloss for biblical accounts of David's life. The relationship between author and character can be envisioned as two-way interaction: Heller finding in the biblical hero correspondences to his own situation and building David as character through the lens of his own personal sensations. Jan Wojcik has written of the way in which "the psychological realism" of the David story invites each generation to interpret it as a mirror of its own concerns; certainly, this happens for Heller.[56] The loneliness that Heller felt, separated from his wife of thirty-eight years, living alone in a Manhattan apartment, gets written into his David story.[57] But so too is David a construct, an evocation of fictional possibility. When Heller conceived the genetic lines for *God Knows*—"I really think I've got the best story in the Bible"—he simultaneously created the necessity for a character who could say this and say it in the right way. This character—David—evolved to fulfill the narrative potential of this first line. As a character close in sensibility and intelligence to Heller's own and as a character that Heller inherited from the Bible, David offers an unusual vehicle for gaining more understanding of Heller's creative process.[58]

Heller's ending to *God Knows* provides the perepeteia of this double-sided response to the Bible, which simultaneously seeks to create a faithful copy and an ironic distortion. The final vision scene of the "eager, bright-eyed youth" recapitulates the earlier scene of David's soothing music and Saul's jealous rage. By locating this reconstituted past in David's deathbed consciousness, Heller changes it, and, as denouement of the novel, the scene is in accord with the now familiar trajectory of his narrative imagination. Another story of the death of youth—or in this formulation the attempted death of youth—the ingredients have shifted: Yossarian ministers to the dying Snowden; Slocum accidently kills his beloved son; Gold mourns the death of his brother; after recollecting the death of his sons, David experiences—in fact initiates—the attempted murder of another youthful innocent—himself. "I have never been so happy as when I hear him begin [to play]. And then I look around me for a javelin to hurl at his head" (353). This parataxis—its wrenching juxtaposition of narrative events—signals the dark truth hinted at in all Heller's novels: these children who have died young are not simply casualties of the world, victims of war like the Frenchman's son in " 'Catch-22' Revisited." They reside within the self as well as outside, and so do the threats to their existence. Heller hinted at this truth earlier, with Slocum's lost-child myth and his accidental killing of his son. *God Knows* makes it explicit; the protagonists who mourn the innocent children also participate in their death and sometimes in their killing. David assumes the guilt for this as his own, while this guilt was variously displaced in *Catch-22*, *Something Happened*, and *Good as Gold*.

In *God Knows*, Heller discloses the hidden truth of all his novels, that the protagonist who desperately tilts at death's inevitability also wants to die. David—not Saul—throws the last spear at himself, and unlike Saul, his jealous rage is not directed outward at some external manifestation, but at an inward vision of himself. A novel about the myriad forms of eros, *God Knows* is equally about the inner compulsions of thanatos. Paradoxically, the drive toward the quiescence of death is most strongly evoked in the rage against death itself and, thus, most authentically voiced when David hovers near death at novel's end. "The approach of death acts as a goad to sensuality," inspiring David's last, lingering account of Abishag's beauties; "[i]n the full sense of the verb it aggravates desire."[59] It is exactly when caught most directly between eros and thanatos that David cries out for God—as does the novel itself. This aching desire for God originates in the Bible—in the David legend, in which an actively intervening God gradually disappears, as well as in Heller's own authorial response to this myth.

In this sense, like the novel itself, the ending of *God Knows*, while being an ironic distortion of the Bible, is born out of authorial reverence. Albeit in the way Cervantes venerates his chivalric sources or in the way Nabokov pays parodic homage to his Russian predecessors, Heller reveres the Bible; for all its bawdy humor and time-worn jokes, *God Knows* testifies to this reverence.[60] Like the biblical authors themselves, Heller revises the story so as to get it right. He rejects the implicit wisdom of the Bible, the soothing music by which its heroes live "full of years and full of days."[61] In the Bible, he finds only a man, one who "has discovered, on his deathbed, that life is a ruthless joke—which is not to say that it isn't funny. King David is, in short, a modern man" (Medwick 702). But then, again, he isn't. He shares the sensibility of Shakespeare's Henry V, that perceives man "in his nakedness." His sensibility is born in the Bible itself, in which the aging David cannot stay warm and is refined by Heller's own experience in the intensive care unit of Mount Sinai Hospital. Heller's portrait of old age—the loneliness for which the company of others is no help—is akin to Shakespeare's. As the ending to *God Knows* makes clear, the cries that result from such loneliness go unanswered.

6

PICTURE THIS

ANALOGICAL RELATIONSHIPS AND
COMPLEMENTARY TRUTHS

> Last scene of all,
> That ends this strange eventful history,
> Is second childishness and mere oblivion,
> Sans teeth, sans eyes, sans taste, sans everything.
> WILLIAM SHAKESPEARE, *As You Like It*

WESTERN CIV

Gary Michael Dault rightly contends that *Picture This*, like *Something Happened*, proceeds by accumulation, with Heller marshaling detail after detail until the reader is numbed by them.[1] The principles of accumulation in the two novels are different, though. While Heller fills *Something Happened* with the minutiae of Slocum's mind, he loads *Picture This* with the facts of Western history. Particulars multiply exponentially, as the narrator continually wanders from his ostensible subject, Rembrandt's *Aristotle Contemplating the Bust of Homer*, to recount such diverse events as the disastrous Athenian expedition to Syracuse and the trial of Socrates. In Heller's *Poetics* (the original title for the novel), the world is more various and elusive than any principle, and, in this sense, the novel is more threatening than *Something Happened*, bleaker in vision and more ominous in its humor.[2] While the threats that Slocum faces are largely self-generated, those of *Picture This* are ineluctably woven into the fabric of human experience and confirmed by the cycle of Western histo-

186

ry, in which the same errors are repeated with catastrophic results. Heller represents humanity with a Swiftian cast: Plato the philosopher, who is history's first fascist; Solon the lawmaker, who invents the self-serving law; Socrates the zealot, who brings martyrdom upon himself; and Rembrandt the self-absorbed artist, whose avarice ruins his family and economic life.

In Shakespeare's *Julius Caesar*, Cassius observes, "The fault, dear Brutus, is not in our stars, / But in ourselves"; in *Picture This*, Heller extends the message, insisting that the fault always lies in ourselves and allowing none of Cassius's hope for revolutionary change. "In what I hope is an amusing way," he tells interviewer Bill Moyers, "it's really an extremely pessimistic book."[3] The source of Heller's pessimism is human nature, for he believes that human beings are, at root, talented self-deceivers. More insidiously, they mythologize their history in a way that perpetuates their deceptions. Heller conceives his novelistic task as deconstructing these myths: the Golden Age of Pericles was really the time of the Peloponnesian War, which resulted in Athens' "total defeat, unconditional surrender, and loss of power and empire" (22); similarly, Holland of *The Embarrassment of Riches* (to appropriate Simon Schama's title) continually warred with Spain, England, or France. Both eras, Heller insists, bear an analogical relationship to our own.[4] In *Something Happened*, readers can detach themselves from Slocum's anxieties, even while recognizing the extent to which his fears are products of American culture, but they cannot disassociate themselves from Western history. Heller would say that it is human history, and, as he further argues, "men don't make history; history makes personalities" (quoted in Moyers 30).[5] Heller directs his readers' attention to the history that has made them, defining history both as the legacy of the past and as an individual's social and economic circumstances.[6]

By making Western history his subject, Heller shifts novelistic directions, turning from the character studies that were central to *Something Happened*, *Good as Gold*, and *God Knows*. In one sense, he abandons characterization itself. The narrative voice of *Picture This* is impersonal—aside from its telling relationship to the opinions of Joseph Heller. It resembles the narrating voice of a documentary film. While explicating such events as the trial of Socrates, it remains aloof and detached, an overlay to the images and events that it recounts. Even when Heller makes Aristotle's consciousness the narrative voice, he presents it as disembodied, speaking as if Rembrandt's painting were articulating itself. In the novel, Aristotle is an essentially two-dimensional, albeit intensely human, presence, just as he is in the painting. Heller transports the speaking voice of the *Ethics*, *Politics*, and *Poetics* to his novel, along with the necessary Heller additive, the one-liner. This is quite different from his three previous novels, in which Slocum, Gold, and David incarnate their existence with their words, as if their voices were the Word of John's gospel.

Heller is no more concerned with the three-dimensionality of the novel's other characters. Consider, for example, his treatment of his protagonist, Rembrandt. Heller dates the key events of his life, such as his marriage and bankruptcy, quotes his letters in detail, and has him banter with Jan Six (his patron), but does not do so in a way that individuates him.[7] In fact, he caricatures him, handling him in the manner of Major Major, Ralph Newsome, or Solomon. Heller's Rembrandt has no individualized psychology, no sense of himself or his identity. He has less insight about his life than Bob Slocum has. By contrast, as documented by his self-portraits, Rembrandt comes across as remarkably self-reflective and self-conscious about himself as artist. The self-portraits create a dramatic sense of self: playful, brooding, distant, calculating, but above all concerned with his identity as artist and man. And, according to George Steiner, "[t]ogether with the essays of Montaigne and the quartets of Shostakovich, the sequence of Rembrandt's self-portraits constitutes what may well be the preeminent discipline of introspection—of controlled descent into the creative self—in Western psychology."[8] With his characterization of David, Heller exploits this kind of record of the self; here he presents it as an irony of history and art—the artist whose creations embody a richer sense of self than he himself possesses.

One would like to be able to account for such a significant shift in method, but in the absence of Heller's notecards and other planning materials, explanations must necessarily be speculative. In one sense, *Picture This* represents an artistic return to the technique of *Catch-22*, which also uses an impersonal narrative voice and two-dimensional characters. In both novels, characters are, typically, ideas given flesh; for instance Milo exemplifies the capitalist imperative of unceasing expansion and Plato embodies a fascist's mentality. Also like *Catch-22*, *Picture This* presents a vision of the past, which, in actuality, comments on the present. But in other respects, *Picture This* marks a change. The novel is pictorial, providing a panoramic view of Western history. Its scenes are taken from Western Civ texts, each rendered as a tableau: the trial of Socrates, the English blockade of Holland, the revolt of Mytilene against Athens, and so on. As in the cinematographic technique of montage, the "story" emerges in the rapid flow of static images; in the flow, change is pictorial, not psychological, time is flux, not *duree*. And as in films using montage, the flow of static images creates as well as depicts a world, in the process constructing its own version of history.

Heller's darkening vision itself necessitates the changes in his narrative techniques. In different ways, each of his previous novels is about possibility. In each, Heller resists necessity, whether it is exemplified in the paradoxical logic of Catch-22 or by David's mortality. There is always a Sweden in his novels, if only one constructed out of memory and desire. Not in *Picture This*. The novel confines the individual in Western history, in much the same way that Oedipus is confined by his destiny. It is not that his characters lack choices, nor even that they are without hopes. Rather, like Oedipus, they find that their free choices lead them back into stories that have already been told and toward truths that they have consistently resisted. Unlike Oedipus, however, Heller's characters do not achieve knowledge of themselves and their situation; they act out their lives as if they were moths flapping against a lamp.

While Heller's fictional strategies change, his view of art does not. Art evokes emotions for him, sensations which are themselves ineffable. This has been the case from his earliest stories on. For example, the plot of his unpublished story, "Room for Renoir," turns on the failure of the protagonist's wife and boss to experience the emotion that he feels about a Renoir nude.[9] In its use of Michelangelo's art, "'Catch-22' Revisited" more directly anticipates *Picture This*. Of the *Last Judgment*, "the most powerful painting" he knows, Heller says, "There is perpetual movement in its violent rising and falling, and perpetual drama in its agony and wrath. To be with Michelangelo's *Last Judgment* is to be with Oedipus and King Lear" (60). The allusions are telling, referring as they do to tragic heroes whose stature, in part, comes from their ability to confront and to articulate their desolation: Oedipus—"You need not fear to touch me. Of all men, I alone can bear this guilt"; or Lear—"Howl, howl, howl, howl! O, you are men of stones: / Had I your tongues and eyes, I'ld use them so / That heaven's vault should crack. She's gone for ever!" (V.iii). Michelangelo's Moses provokes a similar response, which, preditably, Heller renders with a joke: "I know that if Michelangelo ever hurled an ax at it, [cry(ing) 'Speak! Why won't you speak?'], Moses would have picked up the ax and hurled it right back" (59). As author responding to Rembrandt's paintings, Heller still stands in much the same position— John Barth would say that all postmodern writers do. Although he can glimpse the deepest and most fundamental emotions of such artistic masterpieces, he cannot articulate them except by allusions and jokes; *Picture This* records the efforts that their author knows will finally fail.

Heller changes artistic priorities in *Picture This*, but not, as reviewers have agreed, successfully.[10] It is an intriguing but deeply flawed novel, and one might say of it what Heller says of *Good as Gold*, "It is not a book with that much depth."[11] Thematically, it can be described in a few pages, as Heller himself does in his interview with Bill Moyers. Yet its shifts in technique and its buffoonish Rembrandt raise unsettling questions about Heller's conception of artists and their art, and it is on these artistic/ novelistic issues that I want to focus: on the dialogical opposition of the novel's key premises, on Heller's change of temporal (narrative) emphasis to give priority to synchronic relationships over diachronic ones, and, finally, on the catachrestic nature of his art. To explore these elements is to learn that Heller's development, like that of any serious novelist, cannot be easily plotted, rendered into predictable patterns. Such novelists' stories occasion and anticipate our apprehension.

ANTINOMIES

Picture This has the most insistently antithetical vision and structure of any Heller novel. Heller has always been fond of paradoxical oppositions, as the Catch-22 sequences of *Catch-22* demonstrate. But in his earlier novels, he displaces the antitheses; Yossarian, for example, escapes the equally hopeless alternatives of Catch-22 by fleeing to Sweden. In *Picture This*, Heller pairs contradictory alternatives—about history, philosophy, and art—without picking between them or resolving them into synthesis. Even at its ending, the novel affirms that the oscillation of its competing premises cannot be terminated. Rather like the physicists who describe the dual nature of light as particle and wave, Heller relies upon complementarity as a structural principle. For him, as for quantum physicists, reality—or rather what we can say about reality—is inherently paradoxical. In the notionally real world of his novels, humans are confined by their material existence as well as by their social and economic circumstances. Together these factors create the inevitability of cause and effect, that narrative track whose destination is death. On the other hand, there is an element of Platonism in Heller's fictional world in that ideas precede existence. With Conrad's Marlow, Heller might say, "What redeems . . . is the idea only" (*Heart of Darkness*). In such things, there is possibility—that embodied by mind and spirit, which Heller affirms in Yossarian's memorial meditation on the dying Snowden or in David's deathbed memoirs.

In constructing his history-laden novel, Heller sets forth exactly opposite propositions—history illuminates, history reveals nothing. Given the abundance of historical material in the novel, this antithesis would seem resolvable—confirming, modifying, or denying one or the other of the competing propositions. It is not resolved, however, for depending upon which textual moment one examines, the value of history is either announced or denied. Early reviewers and critics have divided accordingly. For instance, the *Booklist* reviewer sees the novel as a "historical narration" of facts about the painting *Aristotle Contemplating the Bust of Homer* and about the life and times of Rembrandt and Aristotle; and, writing for the *New York Times*, Walter Goodman adds that the factual material is used to make the point that "all history is a compound of greed and violence."[12] By contrast, Gary Michael Dault argues that Heller's novel demonstrates the spuriousness of history. *Picture This* sustains both points of view, sometimes affirming and other times undercutting the value of history and historical explanation.

Heller sets up the novel in a way that underscores its historicity. His series of epigraphs—from Aristotle's *Poetics*, a Rembrandt letter, and Samuel Pepys's diary—culminate with Henry Ford's observation: "History is bunk, says Henry Ford, the American industrial genius, who knew almost none" (11). Framing this line that will appear again in the novel's last chapter undercuts Ford's view. Similarly, Heller's acknowledgments recognize the help that he has received from historians, art historians, and classicists, and portray himself as an author who is concerned with factual accuracy and who affirms the validity of historical interpretation.

Heller's attention to historical facts and details proclaims the historicity of his text. His depiction of Athens draws upon the writings of Xenophon, Thucydides, and Plutarch, as well as upon Plato's dialogues.[13] His portraits of Alcibiades, Nicias, Solon, and Pericles are based upon Plutarch's *Lives*: even personal traits, such as Alcibiades's lisp and sexual attractiveness, and such episodes as the medal that Alcibiades receives for Socrates's act of bravery (an episode, predictably, played by Heller for its humor). Similarly, his Amsterdam is indebted to Simon Schama's *The Embarrassment of Riches* and Paul Zumthor's *Daily Life in Rembrandt's Holland,* and his Rembrandt to Gary Schwartz's *Rembrandt: His Life, His Paintings.* Heller's handling of *Aristotle Contemplating the Bust of Homer* also indicates his interest in historical detail; he describes how the painting came to be done and Rembrandt's deteriorating financial situation at the time and lists all its title changes as well as all of its known owners. Amidst these myriad factual details, the reader may feel inundated—that Heller collects facts the same way Bob Slocum savors his fears.

Out of the mass of details and Heller's use of them emerges his point: history illuminates. His view of history is materialist, that is, social and economic conditions shape humans and their affairs, most notably Rembrandt and his art, not vice versa.[14] Section VI, "The Herring in History," explicitly presents this vision; it begins: "It was a ship's captain from Zeeland who, in 1385, perfected a process for curing herring at sea, thereby creating a fishing and shipbuilding industry and the vast international trade in herring that would grow into the largest commerical empire the world had seen and the mightiest naval power" (109). After this sentence the Zeeland captain is forgotten, just as the captain's agency is grammatically subordinated in Heller's sentence construction. In the rest of section VI, the narrator concisely recounts the expansion of Dutch mercantile power —to the East Indies, China, India, Japan, and finally, at section's end, to Manhattan. In Heller's metonymic method, the Dutch commercial empire together with the series of wars associated with its expansion and maintenance are Rembrandt's context. In this, Heller follows Gary Schwartz's argument that Rembrandt and his art were deeply affected by the history and politics of his time.[15]

The section that follows, "Biography," confirms the principle: Rembrandt's life and art become intelligible through the history of his times. "Biography" renders Rembrandt's life inseparable from its economic context. Again, Heller's opening sentence announces his design: "The Dutch East India Company was four years old when Rembrandt was born in Leiden in 1606" (115). While the section provides many biographical facts about Rembrandt, these facts are consistently subordinated to commercial realities. Because of its brevity, Heller's account of Spinoza's life can serve to illustrate his procedure:

> To a country whose economic health depended on sea voyages, the telescope, like cartography and all other navigational devices, was of primary importance, and even a man of great mind like the Dutch Jew Spinoza earned a respectable living grinding lenses. The philosopher Spinoza was another seeking coherent intelligibility in a universe that had none, and he was excommunicated from his Sephardic congregation for supplying his own when he could not find any. . . .
>
> Spinoza died at forty-four, from lungs ruined, it is conjectured, by particles of glass inhaled in the performance of his honest duties as a lens grinder. (116)

(As an aside, it bears notice that Spinoza's death is inherently related to Snowden's; in each the facts of material existence are the essential determinant.) Dutch mercantilism similarly determines the shape of Rembrandt's life. For example, in Heller's paratactic prose: "the potato was transported back across the Atlantic for cultivation in North America and Rembrandt was shipped to Amsterdam to train with an artist of better standing, Pieter Lastman" (120). According to Heller, Rembrandt's life— not just his art—is an economic commodity. Or, in the narrator's acidic formulation: "Nowhere in history is this assumption that human life has a value borne out by human events" (120). Consistent with this conception, Heller's "Biography" attends to the fluctuating economic worth of Rembrandt's art—notes the $10.3 million paid for a Rembrandt painting in 1986, his declining commissions when his former students Ferdinand Bol and Govert Flinck appropriate his style, the devaluation of the portrait of his mother owned by Queen Elizabeth II of England when it turns out not to be done by Rembrandt at all, and so on. Predictably, Rembrandt, the subject of "Biography," is displaced, and, at chapter's end, with Holland under blockade by England, he has not been seen for several pages.

"History is bunk," says Henry Ford, and so, at times, does *Picture This*. When Heller quotes Ford in the novel's brief concluding chapter, he does so in a way that aligns the narrative view with that of Ford. As the narrator observes, "You will learn nothing from history that can be applied" (350). The narrator provides three illustrations in support of this assertion, illustrations that recapitulate the crucial narrative motifs of the novel. First, Plato could not have been present at the banquet that he reports in the *Symposium* to hear the eloquent encomiums of Alcibiades to Socrates. Second, Socrates's death could not have occurred as reported in the *Phaedo* and mythologized in Western history, for death by hemlock is violent and painful. (With its affinities to the Snowden death scene, this description also documents the consistency of Heller's vision of mortality.) Third: "The Rembrandt painting of Aristotle contemplating the bust of Homer may not be by Rembrandt but by a pupil so divinely gifted in learning the lessons of his master that he was never able to accomplish anything more and whose name, as a consequence, has been lost in obscurity. The bust of Homer that Aristotle is shown contemplating is not of Homer. The man is not Aristotle" (351). With this third revelation, the historical account of the painting implodes. Heller's authority with respect to Rembrandt and his painting is rendered as questionable (albeit in a different way) as Plato's is with respect to Socrates and Socratic idealism.

While there are myriad historical facts, as the countless particulars about Rembrandt's painting demonstrate, these facts do not finally clarify or answer; rather, they confront humans with their blindness. It is not simply that there may or may not have been a historical Homer, or that Plato undoubtedly invented the Socrates known in Western philosophy, or even that Rembrandt's paintings cannot be authenticated as his own works or those of his talented students and imitators. It is that human life—the stuff of history—is constrained by unknowables or obscured by the human propensity for self-deception and that the most fundamental of human questions—the kind that propel *Picture This*—cannot be answered. As figured by Heller's own account of the Rembrandt behind the Aristotle, explanations of human behavior narrate the pre-existing. In particular, historical narratives are as distant from what they purport to explain as physicists are from their quarks and leptons. Particularly, when they attempt to explain motivations, hopes, and desires—those human elements which interest

Heller—they are as constructionist as Plato's dialogues. They replace actual events with idealized stories, transmuting the convulsions of death by hemlock into the splendid Socratic irony, "Crito, we ought to offer a cock to Asclepius." For Heller, history inevitably involves such a projection of ideology upon the past, and whether the ideology is personal, philosophical, or political, it supplies an intelligibility to events after they can be known. Such accounts necessarily misrepresent or deceive.

If the narrator concludes *Picture This* with so consistent a demystification of history and historical explanation, it would seem that he is endorsing the claim that "you will learn nothing from history that can be applied" (350). But clearly, Heller does not privilege this premise over its dialogical opposite. First, as I have already argued, *Picture This* does affirm the utility of historical explanation, especially in the way that it presents Rembrandt as inseparable from his social and economic context. Second, Heller paradoxically uses historical research to establish the premise that nothing can be learned from history, to reveal the fabrications so often taken as truths. Also, even the claim that nothing can be learned itself yields applicable knowledge, if only that he cannot apply the knowledge that he has just gained. But then the counter-claim is affirmed, history does illuminate. No (and yes), because as the last chapter demonstrates, historical constructs are a particular kind of fiction that are not historical at all. Rather like the bust of Homer that Rembrandt uses, they are latter-day interpretations of what might have been. The Catch-22s that intrigue Heller do not end when Yossarian reaches Sweden.

Heller builds a similar set of philosophic oppositions into the text, exemplified by the differences between Plato's and Aristotle's points of view. Antitheses, the ideas of each philosopher are defined by opposition to the other and, in being defined in this way, call the other's ideas simultaneously into existence and into question. An example from early in the novel illustrates the use Heller makes of the differences between Platonic and Aristotelian thought:

> Plato had his head in the clouds and his thoughts in the heavens and seemed to be preaching that the only things capable of being looked into were those about which nothing more could be found out.
> Aristotle had his feet on the ground and his eyes everywhere. He wanted to know more about all he observed.
> Plato rejected appearance: knowledge was obtainable only through things that were eternal, and nothing on earth was. He stressed geometry. . . .
> Aristotle craved definition, explanation, systematic investigation, and proof, even in geometry. . . .

"I have this beetle here in one hand," he [Aristotle] proclaimed one day, "with a single oval shell and eight jointed legs, and I have here in my other hand this second beetle of lighter hue which has twelve legs and a shell that is longer and segmented. Can you explain the difference?"

"Yes," said Plato. "There is no such thing as a beetle, in either of your hands. There is no such thing as your hand. What you think of as a beetle and a hand are merely reflections of your recognition of the idea of a beetle and a hand. . . ."

Aristotle did not inquire then whether the idea of the beetle to which Plato referred was of one with eight legs or twelve. (30–32)

This exposition of philosophic differences, Heller's version of Philosophy 101, elucidates the contrast between idealist and empiricist modes of explanation. The idealist Plato consistently transfigures experience to show that "[i]deas alone are worth contemplating" (31). The Platonic masterpieces *The Apology*, *Crito*, and *Phaedo*, excerpts from which Heller weaves liberally into the text, testify to the power of such idealism. They depict the death of Socrates as philosophic drama, rendering it as transcendent as that of Christ. With extensive quotations from these dialogues, Heller reproduces the force of Socratic thought, much as he conveys the tenor of the David story with quotation in *God Knows*. Yet, as in the passages above, the Aristotelian counterbalance to Platonic idealism is always present in the novel, as it is in the philosophic tradition. Analyzing, classifying, defining, Heller's Aristotle thrusts the world, like an eight-legged beetle, into Plato's ideas. No ideas but in things, this voice insists.

Plato's and Aristotle's voices enact a novel-long textual dialogue, without Heller prioritizing, mediating, or resolving their competing claims. Of the many examples that could be given, one moment from chapter 31, in which Aristotle questions Plato about the leadership of his *Republic*, illustrates the point. Aristotle convinces the reader, if not Plato himself, of the impracticality of his scheme; he raises such objections as who will compel the leader of the Republic to act virtuously and not to abuse his power. Finally, in frustration at Plato's refusal to join the issues in the debate, Aristotle asks, "why are you bothering? Why are we talking? Why did you write your *Republic*?" only to receive the bedimmed response, "Let me think about that. Because I wanted to" (291). As Aristotle walks off to study the legs of another beetle, the narrator takes up the argumentative cudgel on Plato's behalf, subjecting Aristotle's ideas to the kind of scrutiny that he has given to Plato's. Of course, Aristotle's contain similar unexamined propositions and contradictions; in the narrator's joke, "In a community that had the happiness of all members as a goal, even Aristotle's slaves would have to have slaves" (292). This sequence emphasizes the radical and irresolvable differences between the two perspectives, in which neither yields more nor less enlightenment than the other.

Such dialogues present Plato and Aristotle as bearing a symbiotic relationship to one another, in which each thinker establishes the necessary conditions for the other's ideas. In Heller's handling of the connection between the two, Plato's work furnishes the essential subject for Aristotelian analysis. "How ironic," the narrator notes, "that Aristotle, who had always stressed a methodology of observation and verification, should find himself the arbiter of where the thinking of Socrates left off and that of Plato began" (36). If Plato had not written his Socratic dialogues, Aristotle would have had no subject. Yet Aristotelian philosophic analysis—as Heller shows with another joke—ensures the enduring appeal of Platonic thinking. "Aristotle has been called the father of logic, psychology, political science, literary criticism, physics, physiology, biology and other natural sciences, aesthetics, epistemology, cosmology, metaphysics, and the scientific study of language. . . . It stands to reason Plato would have wider appeal" (261–62). As Heller conceives the relationship between Platonic and Aristotelian thought, Plato's ideas provide the source and stimulus for Aristotelian analysis, and Aristotelian analysis creates the inextinguishable longing for Platonic idealism.

Heller's presentation of the value of art constitutes another antithesis: artistic value as intrinsic (or immanent) and as extrinsic. The case for intrinsic value rests upon the assumption that value is dependent upon the qualities of the work itself rather than upon such external variables as the reputation of the producer or changing audience tastes. Heller buttresses this position with the examples of Homer and Shakespeare, reminding readers that there may or may not have been a Homer (or Homers) who may or may not have written *The Iliad* and *The Odyssey*. Or similarly, while there was a Shakespeare, there is no certainty that he wrote the works attributed to him. Therefore, the greatness of Homeric and Shakespearean art depends upon the works themselves, not on the reputation of their producers, and by extension, their value—unlike the fluctuating values of paintings by Botticelli or Van Gogh—can withstand the vicissitudes of time. By depicting Rembrandt as an artist who possesses no consciousness of what he is producing, Heller also privileges the work of art over its producer. His Rembrandt is a technician following procedures rather than an artist who knowingly creates, and, thus, the achievement of his paintings resides not in the producer but in the product.

Yet if the text sustains the intrinsic worth of a work of art, it also undermines it, revealing its problematic status in much the same way that Socrates demonstrated the difficulty of defining the nature of piety in the *Euthyphro*. After leading Euthyphro to accede to an intrinsic definition of piety ("what is pious is loved because it is pious, and not pious because it loved"), Socrates undermines it with a series of inquiries demonstrating that Euthyphro cannot distinguish the attributes of piety from its essential characteristics, nor the ends of piety from its means. In his befuddlement, Euthyphro retreats to the position that piety consists of what is loved by the gods—a position that Socrates has already discredited. In *Picture This*, Heller performs similar narrative maneuvers to call into question the intrinsic nature of art. One of the most simple and direct of these is his account of the plummeting worth of *The Man with the Golden Helmet* and a portrait of his mother once it was revealed that they were not painted by Rembrandt. Heller's unstated question is: why should a painting so long considered great have its worth so dependent on the reputation of the producer? Would the greatness of *Hamlet* be diminished if it could be proved it was not written by Shakespeare? The Govert Flinck jokes work in complementary fashion. Flinck, a former student of Rembrandt, gets more money for his Rembrandt imitations than Rembrandt himself gets for his originals. Or as Socrates might put the perverse conundrum conveyed by these examples, a Rembrandt painting—whether authentic or inauthentic —is valuable because it is valued, rather than valued because it embodies value.

For Heller, these fluctuating economic values call into question the intrinsic value of art in much more fundamental ways and argue for the extrinsic value of art. The reassessment of paintings like *The Golden Helmet* and the more economically valuable Govert Flinck imitations bring in extrinsic factors: in the first case, Rembrandt's reputation and in the second, the commercial demand for a piece of art. Heller's presentation of the production of Rembrandt's paintings, particularly *Aristotle Contemplating the Bust of Homer*, extends these lines of thought by showing the way the paintings themselves were determined by external factors, chiefly financial ones. In this Heller follows Gary Schwartz's thesis that Rembrandt's art is shaped by his relationship to his patrons. Predictably, Heller makes this relationship a source of humor, as when Rembrandt contemplates signing Flinck's name to his portraits so that they will be worth more money. Lest the reader too easily dismiss this presentation of Rembrandt as the product of his fertile, comic imagination, Heller uses the artist's letters as evidence for the centrality of Rembrandt's economic motivation. The letters function the way the excerpts of Henry Kissinger's Oriana Fallaci interview do in *Good as Gold*: they unmask, revealing to Heller's mind what is the essence of character.[16] For Heller, Rembrandt is at root a commerical artist, whose ends in painting are financial. The value of his art—like all else in *Picture This*—is determined by the commercial circumstances in which it was produced.

Given this presentation of Rembrandt's art, the value of art must be extrinsic. Yes, it is, as I have demonstrated in the course of showing the way Heller calls into question the intrinsic nature of artistic value. But Heller discredits this claim as well. Obviously, it is subverted by his examples of Homeric and Shakespearean art. But more importantly, it is undermined by Heller's presentation of Aristotle as a narrative consciousness who is activated by Rembrandt's painting. "To Aristotle by now the painting of which he and Homer were part was much more than an imitation. It had a character uniquely its own, with no prior being, not even in Plato's realm of ideas" (44). This passage—reinforced by Heller's pun on the concept of character—designates the painting as an entity unto itself, one whose essence depends neither on its creator, its relationship to the world, nor its audience. Its character is constituted only by its own existence, depending upon its own internal logic. Constituted in this way, the painting endures, its value resisting even Heller's final narrative thrust, "The bust of Homer that Aristotle is shown contemplating is not Homer. The man is not Aristotle" (351).

By making the key propositions of *Picture This* antithetical, Heller creates a novel in the manner of quantum physics, subject to the principle of complementarity. Its central terms—about history, philosophy, art— work dialogically, and, as in the principle of complementarity, to affirm one premise is to displace its counterpart. For example, when Gary Michael Dault argues that Heller agrees with Henry Ford that "history is bunk," he fails to account for the extraordinary number of historical details or the way these details are used to elucidate Rembrandt's life and art. Not that Dault is wrong in what he argues, for he, like all readers of *Picture This*, stands in the position of the observer in the well-known vase/ two faces perception test. This observer can alternately see a vase or two faces but never the two simultaneously. Moreover, this observer—like the reader of *Picture This* or the physicist investigating the duality of light— determines what he will see. Attending to Heller's indictment of the utility of history, Dault has necessarily restricted the information that he received from its equally valid alternative. Heller himself insists upon preserving the paradoxes involved in the principle of complementarity.[17]

In this, Heller adopts a stance not unlike that of the great physicist Werner Heisenberg. Heisenberg's Uncertainty Principle—which holds that knowledge of events occurring within the inner world of the atom is necessarily limited—resulted from his failure to resolve the wave/particle duality. During a time of frustration, Heisenberg remembered a paradoxical observation that Einstein had once made to him, which sparked the insight for his Uncertainty Principle: "It is theory which decides what we can observe."[18] Such is also the case of Heller's antithetical propositions. However, like Heisenberg, Heller affirms the paradoxical implication of this: human insight is, by necessity, limited no matter what propositional stance one assumes, in fact it is limited precisely because one assumes such a stance. As artistic representation and as commentary upon Rembrandt's representation in *Aristotle Contemplating the Bust of Homer*, *Picture This* makes this insight manifest, and it is to this that I will now turn.

▧

ART AS CATACHRESIS: NECESSARY MISREPRESENTATION

When Heller portrays art most comically, he is also the most serious—and perhaps the most worried. In *Picture This*, he depicts the artist-protagonist Rembrandt as if he were the hero of a farce, as buffoonish, conniving, petty, and greedy. Scenes involving him become comic set pieces, just as scenes involving Scheisskopf, Orr, Ralph Newsome, or Solomon do in Heller's earlier novels. Heller's Rembrandt has his students practice realist techniques by painting coins on the floor, only to be deceived into trying to pick them up. As driven by financial gain as Milo Minderbinder, he is too cheap to buy new canvas for his Alexander and writes a will for his son Titus in which he makes himself the universal heir (and which excludes his wife's relatives, from whom Titus received the money). Of his shrewdness in the matter of the will, Rembrandt brags to Aristotle in the slangy cadences of a Jewish New York street merchant: "Eh? You see, Mr. Philosopher? You're not the only smart fellow in this house, are you?" (69). Yet this callow Rembrandt paints such artistic masterpieces as *Aristotle Contemplating the Bust of Homer*. Whenever Heller describes Rembrandt's paintings themselves, his tone changes. His text becomes an art gallery, whose paintings inspire and move, evoke silence or muted tones. At its center, *Picture This* explores this paradox, an artist whose work produces emotion which he is incapable of experiencing or appreciating.[19]

In this paradox, Heller's novel functions in the manner of the rhetorical figure catachresis, which misuses language to make sense. It uses the figurative to evoke the actual.[20] Catachresis—such usages as blind mouths—performs linguistic alchemy, making rarer sense from base elements. Redirecting familiar words to unheard of meanings, it, as J. Hillis Miller points out, "brings something altogether new into the world, something not explainable by its causes" (*Ethics of Reading* 74). For Heller, Rembrandt's art operates in similar fashion. Rembrandt uses a model, not the bust of Aristotle that he owns, to paint the figure of Aristotle. Moreover, his model has nothing philosophical about him, but as he tells the worried model: "I'll make changes in you" (190). His paint is itself catachrestic: he "manufacture[s] gold" by laying a glaze of yellows, browns, and blacks on top of a white base (191). He reproduces the atmosphere of ancient Greece by cloaking Aristotle in the garb of a Renaissance nobleman. In Heller's joke, Rembrandt so successfully produces these clothes that his patron Jan Six wishes his laundress could do his collars and turned-up sleeves as well. In fact, his magisterial portrait of Six comes about catachrestically; it can be, as Rembrandt tells Six, a "copy by me of the imitation by [Govert Flinck] of the portrait of you by me" (195). Heller repeatedly exposes the bewitching fakery of Rembrandt's art, while lauding its inexpressible beauty.

Heller's portrayal of Rembrandt works by narrative catachresis, as he systematically empties Rembrandt of human complexity. His depiction deliberately departs from, even distorts, its sources, including his principal source, Gary Schwartz's *Rembrandt: His Life, His Paintings*. The episode in which Rembrandt stoops to gather up the painted coins illustrates how Heller's caricature works as well as the differences between his technique and that of biographers and art historians. For Heller, the episode provides the opportunity for a comic set piece of the kind he so enjoys; it is related to such episodes as the authorial and political credit that Gold accrues for the report that he did not write and the bedimmed Uriah's refusal to sleep with Bathsheba.

> Without a word [Rembrandt] was off like a shot. He lurched to his left and went lumbering across the loft to a corner near the door, casting a hurried look over his shoulder. When he stopped, he bent to reach down to the floor. Then he halted halfway. He plodded back slowly with an abstracted look of disappointment, puffing, growling curses underneath his breath.
>
> Someone had painted another coin on the floor.
>
> "And it was only a stuiver," Aristotle could almost swear he heard him mutter. (135)

With energetic prose filled with verbs and participles, Heller plays the painted coin joke for all its worth. Even Aristotle gets into the act when he repeats Rembrandt's mutterings. By contrast, Schwartz handles the story about the painted coins quite differently, including indicating its source, Houbraken's biography of Rembrandt. With the judiciousness of a careful biographer, Schwartz dismisses it, concluding "there is abundant evidence that Rembrandt was overly attached to his money, so that we may take Houbraken's story as an accurate reflection of what his pupils thought of him" (365). A judicious interpretation, but not one that lurches, lumbers, puffs, and growls as Heller's does—and all this for small change.

Heller's caricature of Rembrandt is part of a pattern throughout his fiction. Never heroes, his artists are usually driven by money and frequently use their talents for ignoble ends. In his short stories, writers come off most favorably, falling into two types, young writers struggling to find a subject and older writers who have prostituted their talents. Heller's younger writers, his most sympathetically rendered artists, are naive and uninitiated, and his plots turn on misassumptions and the resulting education. Duke, the morally earnest protagonist of several of these stories, gets an urban and artistic education in "Girl from Greenwich" or finds the world more inventive than his own imagination in the unpublished "Girl on a Train."[21] In the novels, Slocum (advertising man as artist manqué), Bruce Gold, and King David are Rembrandt's predecessors. Both Slocum and Gold write for hire, with no interest in factuality or truth. Crucially, however, Gold is redeemed by narrating his own story, as his purportedly coming to compose the novel *Good as Gold* signifies. As author, David can be as venal as Slocum or Gold, penning such raunchy aphorisms as "Like cunnilingus, tending sheep is dark and lonely work" or interrupting his famous elegy for Jonathan with his crass commentary. While David composes arrestingly beautiful prose and poetry, he fakes the emotion that his compositions celebrate or disassociates his authentic emotion from the works commemorating its occasion. Like Gold, though, he achieves personal and artistic authenticity in the process of recollecting his life.[22]

Rembrandt is as unscrupulous in his artistic motivations as Slocum and Gold but, unlike Gold and David, never achieves self-awareness or, by extension, artistic authenticity. Yet his art, in Heller's paradox, is authentic, in fact more authentic than Heller's own because it is not mediated by language. According to Heller, the more personal the art the more Rembrandt fakes it. Thus, his *Self-Portrait of the Artist Laughing*, which provokes "more pathos than [the] heart can bear," is his most fradulent work, for Rembrandt is incapable of experiencing the emotion the painting memorializes (303). In Heller's pointed irony, Rembrandt "express[es] himself with . . . true feeling" only twice in his life (234): in his factual inscription on the drawing commemorating his engagement to his wife, and in his last words—"I have to draw on the savings of Cornelia [his granddaughter] to cover our living expenses" (253). (Given the tone of the novel, it is surprising that Heller does not credit these final words with more honesty than those of Socrates.) As evocations of his inner life, Rembrandt's self-portraits are exploitive forgeries, which counterfeit emotional value. Yet Heller maintains that the self-portraits are authentic, although their authenticity depends upon the character they construct, not upon representational faithfulness. In feigning even his own representation, Rembrandt is, simultaneously, the greatest artistic charlatan and the most credible artist.

To see the authentic, I want to return to Rembrandt's *Aristotle*. As we have seen, Heller presents the painting as an entity "uniquely its own, with no prior being, not even in Plato's realm of ideas" (44). Surprisingly, like J. Hillis Miller's account of catachresis, this characterization describes a making which brings something into the world that is not explicable by its causes. Drawing upon investigations of art historians, including the X rays of the sketches beneath the finished picture, Heller recounts the process by which painting emerges on the canvas and the life that results. "Adding charcoal browns to his cream colors, Rembrandt bestowed for Aristotle an illusion . . . to grow warm with immortal life beneath Aristotle's hand" (45). As Heller's repeated puns on "immortal" and "life" tell us, the bust of Homer, like the figure of Aristotle, lives; it is created by Rembrandt's art, yet independent from his creator.

Heller insists on the character-creating nature of art by making Rembrandt the "author" of the novel's Aristotle—a choice ridiculed by most of the novel's reviewers.[23] As a character in the novel, Aristotle comes into existence as his figure emerges on Rembrandt's canvas. His presence exemplifies Heller's claims about the reality of art, that art has its own life and logic. Yet, as Heller represents it, the mode of Aristotle's existence is complicated, depending upon Rembrandt's compositional choices and painting techniques; the historical Aristotle's cast of mind; and Aristotle's own consciousness as well as his ability to employ this consciousness on himself, Rembrandt, Holland of the Golden Age, and all of Western history. This complexity is embedded into each scene in which Aristotle is involved. For example:

> [Aristotle] hoped fervently that others would not remember, while he tried grimly to forget, that the august creator of his *Ethics* and *Metaphysics* was not in his *Rhetoric* above teaching others to employ tricks to win arguments fallaciously through the artful use of words. . . .
>   Was that ethical?
>   Aristotle grew darker and darker in aspect as the painting of him by Rembrandt progressed. The misty gray European weather complemented his mood. When the fog was low, the sodden atmosphere of the city was rank with the smell of herring, beer, and tobacco. (187–188)

Heller's novel-long series of puns on Aristotle's darkening aspect emphasize his character's duality: a character whose existence depends upon the colors and palette strokes that Rembrandt employs and one who controls his own moods and choices. In this second aspect, Aristotle exists as human being. And for Heller, as we have seen, humanity is always anchored in mortality—something that art historians x-raying the painting discover when they find tumors on Aristotle's liver and bowels. As the narrator puts the matter, "Immortal Aristotle was only human" (329).

In fact, as Heller represents him, Aristotle is the most human of the novel's characters, a descendant in the line of characters from Yossarian to David. Aristotle has the complexity of motivation and the interiority that one would expect Rembrandt to have. These inner dimensions of character come across most clearly in the "Aristotle contemplating" passages with which Heller lards the novel:[24] "Aristotle contemplating Rembrandt contemplating Aristotle often imagined, when Rembrandt's face fell into a moody look of downcast introspection, similar in feeling and somber hue to the one Rembrandt was painting on him, that Rembrandt contemplating Aristotle contemplating the bust of Homer might also be contemplating in lamentation his years with Saskia. The death of a happy marriage, Aristotle knew from experience, is no small thing, nor is the death of three children" (19). As the reader already knows, Rembrandt is not contemplating the deaths of either his wife or children, but only concocting another scheme to extricate himself from his financial difficulties. Death is Aristotle's preoccupation, as it was David's and Yossarian's before him. Predictably, Aristotle's last thought in the novel involves death. In his grim speculation about Socrates's famous consolation to his grieving friends, "that nothing bad can happen to a good man, either in life or death," Aristotle wonders, "[w]ould it follow . . . that nothing bad could happen to a bad man either, since the same things happened to all?" (329). In such observations, Aristotle possesses his own character, although his sensibility owes much to Heller.

Aristotle's status as character serves as a reminder about the catachrestic nature of Rembrandt's and Heller's art. Rembrandt has refigured reality in order to educe it: a non-philosophic model providing the stimulus for Aristotle's contemplative visage, and so on. Yet precisely because of these distortions, Rembrandt's painting constitutes a plausible, even compelling version of reality. Similarly, Heller presents Aristotle as disembodied in order to portray his mortality, makes him Rembrandt's creation in order to give him his freedom. The beguiling recognizability of these Aristotles, begotten of artistic fakery, unsettles. But, if the seeming substantiality of these illusions appears to privilege the realm of art over the putative real world, it does not. As the narrator pointedly advises the reader, "Keep in mind that when we talk of a great painting we are not talking about anything great. We are talking of only a painting" (251). Obviously, the line deflates artistic pretensions, but it also self-consciously and ironically comments upon Heller's novelistic endeavor—writing a novel about Rembrandt's great painting.

In his series of commentaries on Rembrandt's painting, Heller explores the complex nature of artistic representation, his own as well as Rembrandt's. He is particularly intrigued by the relationship between the represented world and the world outside it. In his analysis of *The Syndics of the Clothmakers' Guild*, Heller stresses the way in which the painting's viewers are participants in its composition[25]: "In Rembrandt's great painting *The Syndics of the Clothmakers' Guild*, the ingenious composition is made complete only by eye contact with the staring spectator, at whom the unsmiling officials in the painting stare right back. We have interrupted them. They do not like us and want us to go. Try to imagine these officials unobserved in the Rijksmuseum and it is hard to imagine them doing anything but their work" (251). With the narrator's "we," Heller places his readers in the same position as visitors to the Rijksmuseum viewing the painting. Like the spectator, the reader becomes essential to the composition of a work of art, necessary to its completion. And like the spectator, the reader intrudes, as disturbing to the novel's characters as the spectator is to the Syndics. As Heller delineates the relationship between the painting and its audience and his novel and its readers, the boundary between the two realms is as permeable as "the silver screen" in Woody Allen's *The Purple Rose of Cairo*, in which a star-struck film viewer can climb into the glittering world of the screen and its characters can climb out into the notionally real world. Yet, if permeable, this boundary differentiates worlds operating by dissimilar principles—just as it did in Allen's film. Like Allen, Heller finds the differences crucial.

In his commentary on Rembrandt's *The Jewish Bride*, Heller probes the separation between the realms of art and life, the gap that makes residents of either alien in the other. It is a painting, as Heller tells us, in which "everything seems wrong in a picture that is absolutely right" (251). What is wrong is that the painting resists understanding, at least in the terms of the outer world—the narrator's, Heller's, ours. Heller directs the reader's attention to the painting's mysteries. In the painting, the couple's posture conveys a moment of emotional intimacy—the man's left hand embraces the woman's shoulder and his right rests upon her breast; the woman lightly touches the hand on her breast. And yet, as the narrator points out, the man and woman "are lost in thought worlds apart" (251). The painting's distant intimacy renders its viewers as voyeurs, transfixed by a human conjunction that they cannot understand. "No interpretation yet advanced of this enigmatic monument in pictorial art makes sense," the narrator observes (251–52). Its otherness cannot be familiarized, for no one knows who the couple are or what they are supposed to be doing; in Heller's joke, "we don't even know that they are married, and neither the man nor the woman looks any more Jewish than you or I" (252). What the narrator can know, thanks to the work of art critics and historians, are the particularities of the painting's composition, its lines, tones, and brush strokes. As J. Hillis Miller might say of the painting, Rembrandt has brought "something new into the world not explainable by its causes" (*Ethics of Reading* 74). Its interpreters will always be frustrated, for they —to draw again upon Miller's account of catachresis—use "terms borrowed from another realm to name what has no literal language of its own" (73). Interpreters use the language of their experience attempting to make known a world that has no language, that place of umbers, ochres, and shades.

As Heller demonstrates, the readers and interpreters of *Picture This* can come no closer to its world. His cartoon-like Rembrandt is as strange and foreign as the couple of *The Jewish Bride*; that this Rembrandt could have produced the paintings by which he is known defies explanation. Heller's caricature of the artist cannot be familiarized without distorting Heller's character Rembrandt. To comprehend the Rembrandt who stoops after painted stuivers is to assimilate him into the quotidian. Schwartz does this to the actual Rembrandt with his rendition of the painted coins story; he accommodates him to the expectations of late twentieth-century readers, to our sense of the plausible. Rather, with his insistence upon the implausibilities of Rembrandt's character and the complexities of Aristotle's, Heller invites readers to attend to and delight in the mysteries of artistic representation. Its portraiture, Rembrandt's and Heller's, operates by catachresis—with a buffoonish Rembrandt or an Aristotle in Renaissance garb. It must work this way, for catachresis functions "as like this or like that, since it cannot literally be described in itself" (J. Hillis Miller, *Ethics of Reading* 73). In making manifest the language-less world of Rembrandt's art, Heller has lured the reader into the realm of his fiction, which also cannot describe itself.

▨

THE CONJUNCTIONS OF THE TEXT: HISTORY AS REPETITION AND FICTION AS FALSIFICATION

In handling time and narrative sequence in *Picture This*, Heller departs from the diachronic principle of successiveness that characterized his earlier fiction.[26] Previously, his plots—the narrative sequence of episodes—proceeded teleologically, with the story progressing through time toward its fulfillment: Yossarian's flight to Sweden, Slocum's turn away from his son's death to pursue the empty life of corporate politics, Gold's taking up the pen to write his Jewish book, and David's memorial confrontation with his youthful self. In each case, both on the level of plot and character, Heller makes chronology the basis of explanation and fashions his fiction with the logic of a causal chain.[27] In *Picture This*, Heller is a constructionist, building a plot which unlocks narrative possibilities and which challenges the linear image of time presented by traditional narratives and by history. He explicitly denies readers a plot which begins from a readily determinable point and proceeds in a straight line. This difference is figured by the novel's Aristotle, who resides in ancient Greece, in Rembrandt's studio, and in the present.

In *Picture This*, Heller shifts temporal axes, giving priority to the synchronic.[28] While Heller uses the chronology of Western history from Periclean Athens to the present, his plot develops across time rather than through it, privileging rhetorical and logical relationships over developmental ones. This procedure emphasizes Heller's belief that Western history is neither progressive nor evolutionary, or as he describes his idea about the novel: "The idea was of making money and conquest and commerce as being the constants in human history" (quoted in Moyers 32). These terms supply the coordinates for arranging the narrative sequence, just as the bombing missions did in *Catch-22* and the events of the biblical David's life did in *God Knows*. The novel—like Billy Pilgrim's life in *Slaughterhouse-Five*—comes unstuck in time, moving across the events of Western history as if they were part of a simultaneous present. For example, section V, "Rise of the Dutch Republic," does not, as its title would seem to indicate, tell a developmental story of the Dutch revolt against Spanish dominance, but rather an analogical one. Heller juxtaposes the symbiotic national antagonisms of the United States and Russia, Athens and Sparta, and the Netherlands and Spain to show "the chaos that would result . . . from a sudden outbreak of peace. Peace on earth would mean the end of civilization as we know it" (100). As Heller represents them, these national antagonisms have an interpersonal corollary in the relationship between Rembrandt and his patron Constantijn Huygens. In these instances, as in the novel as a whole, money, commerce, conquest, and power are the great explainers, and they furnish the principles for narrative coherence and intelligibility.

In its synchronic impulse, *Picture This* plots interrelationships. Its events can be charted, much the way curves are on an x-y graph; they constitute a set of relationships, relationships obscured in traditional historical narratives. As David Seed demonstrates, Heller uses Aristotle to instruct the reader on how to perceive "the required connections" (206). "Aristotle, in whom the propensity for observing, classifying, correlating, and inferring had remained immutable, could spy the parallel in Socrates approaching his execution and Rembrandt approaching bankruptcy" (42). The novel enacts these Aristotelian impulses, highlighting the parallel and diverging trajectories of its characters' lives and national histories.

As Heller shifts away from the primacy of diachronic sequentiality, he alters the kind of clarification his narrative, especially his conclusion, affords. Previously, his fiction proceeded toward a revelatory moment. In his novels, this moment most frequently occurs in the penultimate chapter or section, as when Yossarian discerns the secret of Snowden's entrails or Slocum recollects his son's death. These moments, like Wordsworthian spots of time, illuminate, disclosing meaning in what has seemed a scarcely differentiated flow of experience. With the concluding moments of clarification, Heller bestows his endings with the apocalyptic satisfactions that Frank Kermode describes.[29] But *Picture This* works in the manner of a geometric proof, with Heller setting forth his conclusion at the outset ("Crito, I owe a cock to Asclepius" [13]), then showing the process by which this conclusion is reached. However, unlike a geometric proof, Heller's conclusion occasions negative rather than positive illumination. It demonstrates its own falsity and calls into question the kind of apocalyptic revelations that his previous endings have afforded.

To explore how Heller arrives at and invalidates his conclusion, I will focus on a single section, "The Last Laugh." Its opening paragraphs illustrate its own workings as well as the movement of the novel as a whole.

> It was the fortune of Rembrandt's Aristotle to begin his travels with a journey from Amsterdam to Sicily in 1654 and to conclude them in America in 1961 with a triumphant debut at the Metropolitan Museum of Art on Fifth Avenue in New York, three centuries short six years after the island of Manhattan was ceded to the English, the Dutch deciding they would not fight to hold what they could not keep and administer.
>
> In actuality, the painting had crossed the Atlantic soon after the turn of the century, in time to avoid the dangers of the First World War and the perils of crossing the Atlantic at any time. On the night of April 14 in 1912, the unsinkable British ocean liner the *Titanic* sank after colliding with an iceberg, with a loss of lives of over fifteen hundred of the twenty-two hundred people aboard, the same year U.S. troops occupied Tientsin, China, to protect American interests there, U.S. Marines landed in Cuba to protect American interests there, and U.S. Marines were landed in Nicaragua to protect American interests there too after rebels had massacred Nicaraguan soldiers, and the First Balkan War broke out. (297)

These two opening paragraphs interweave diachronic and synchronic sequences. The first paragraph identifies the primary chronology the chapter traces, that of the painting's movement from 1654 until the present. As usual, though, Heller moves the reader back and forth along this time line, as when he recounts the Dutch ceding New York to the English. More significantly, this detail works digressively, taking the reader away from the apparent subject of the paragraph (and chapter), the painting's journey. Other than the simultaneity between the Dutch ceding control of New York and Aristotle's trip to Sicily, the two occurrences have nothing to connect them. With such a conjunction of details, Heller's interest appears to be arrested by the arelevant.

The second paragraph gives priority to the synchronic movement, diverging even further from the subject, Rembrandt's painting. It substitutes associations for the developmental logic of diachronic sequencing. Specifically, Heller digresses from *Aristotle's* crossing the Atlantic, to the wartime dangers of such crossings (danger), to the sinking of the *Titanic* (a particular instance of danger occurring in 1912), to the U.S. occupations of Tientsin, Cuba, and Nicaragua (other dangerous, but also exploitive, events of 1912), to the First Balkan War (another event of 1912 and a specific war). While seeming to wander to the irrelevant, this kind of associative sequencing follows a path of contiguous relationships, propelling a plot in which every detail can be related to every other detail. In the logic of the paragraph, Rembrandt's painting is related to the sinking of the *Titanic*, even though "in actuality" it was in America at the time, as well as to the First Balkan War. In this detail the passage enacts a process that Heller describes as the composition of the novel as following: "and almost in spite of myself, it's [*Picture This* is] becoming a book about money and war."[30] Indeed, war and Rembrandt's painting are inextricably related in Heller's imagination. The chapter confirms this conjunction when the narrator lists, among other things, the twenty-nine wars Rembrandt's painting survived between 1651 and 1815, the year in which the painting was publicly displayed in London. In the terms of "The Last Laugh," *Aristotle's* journey is a martial one—as, to Heller's mind, is human history.

Continuing, Heller repeatedly digresses from and returns to the painting's journey and in doing so broadens the narrative context.

On May 7, 1915, the British liner *Lusitania* was sunk by a German submarine, with a loss of eleven hundred ninety-five, of whom one hundred twenty-eight were American citizens. Two years later, following a narrow presidential election, the U.S. entered World War I under Woodrow Wilson, who is still remembered as an idealist, a reformer, and an intellectual.

By then the Rembrandt painting was safely across the Atlantic, having traveled to New York in 1907 from the dealer Duveen to the American purchaser and collector Mrs. Collis P. Huntington. . . .

Nobody knows how many Rembrandts perished in the First World War because nobody knows how many Rembrandts were painted by Rembrandt, his collaborators, and his counterfeiters.

It was the fate of the *Homer*, scorched, repainted, and reduced by fire to almost half the original size, to make its way to the museum of the Mauritshuis in The Hague, where, presumably, like the *Aristotle* at the Metropolitan, it will stay forever, until the end of time. (298)

Heller's narrative works in the manner of the children's memory game, Johnny Has a String in His Pocket, a game in which players add to the list of items which Johnny has in his pocket. Now the context encompasses the *Lusitania* (another sinking), President Wilson (the president under whom the U.S. entered World War I), *Homer* and *Alexander* (the other Rembrandt paintings commissioned by Don Ruffo), and authentic and counterfeit Rembrandts (one of many anticipations of the novel's last paragraph). This narrative method might be called contextual integration, as Heller adds, combines, and juxtaposes elements, such that *Aristotle* becomes part of an ever-expanding network of relationships.[31] Among numerous other things, this network includes: other years (the events of 1936, for instance, among which are the publication of *Gone with the Wind* and the Italian invasion of Ethiopia), the other paintings that surround *Aristotle* at the Metropolitan (those by Titian, Goya, Velazquez, El Greco, and Holbein), record prices for works of art, and financial maneuvers in the 1961 bidding for *Aristotle*. The time line for the chapter runs from 1490 B.C., the date for the Sphinx of Queen Hatshepsut, another work of art near the *Aristotle*, to 1987, the date when Japanese bidders paid a record price for a Van Gogh painting. But along this time line, Heller opens up rather than closes off relationships. Like the game Johnny Has a String in His Pocket, "Last Laugh" is path and gateway to new possibilities and combinations.[32]

As even this brief description indicates, it is virtually impossible to note all the associations that Heller establishes in the chapter—nor is it necessary. But it is worth tracking Heller's use of the title concept, "The Last Laugh," for it sets up the conclusion of the novel, "Last Words." His method is associational and related to the way in which he uses fear in the second chapter of *Something Happened*. There are two references to laughter in the section, the first in the title of the Rembrandt painting *Self-Portrait of the Artist Laughing* and the second to Aristotle's snort of derision at the Metropolitan Museum's defense of the exorbitant amount of money spent to acquire *Aristotle* ("Money is only a medium of exchange"

[317]). In the first laugh, Heller works a typical ironic reversal, deriving the serious from the comic: "Put the *Homer* and the *Self-Portrait of the Artist Laughing* together, and you might find more pathos than your heart can bear" (303). Here the principles of adjacency and context reveal a core Heller truth—the pain of the comic. Aristotle's snorting laughter—and one suspects Heller's—is darker and more despairing. First, it signifies Aristotle's coming to doubt one of his own philosophic positions ("that money had no value and was useful only as a medium of exchange" [311]). Second, it imparts the pessimism and cynicism that he has previously criticized in Plato. But, as Heller acknowledges, *Picture This* "[i]s an extremely pessimistic" book. This laughter anticipates and prepares the way for the novel's de-illusioning "Last Words."

The "Last Words" referred to are, of course, Socrates's request that Crito pay the debt to Asclepius. In the *Phaedo*, the line holds a superb irony, testifying to Socrates's resolve to extend his way of life into death. The debt-offering to Asclepius, the god of healing, signifies that for Socrates his death can provide the remedy for the injuries of life. This moment of Socratic wit extends the philosophic argument of the *Phaedo* with its adumbrations of immortality as well as completes the circuit of life and death set up in the *The Apology* and *Crito*, making death the completion—not the termination—of life. In Heller's re-creation of Socrates's death, occurring crucially in his penultimate chapter, the novel's "sense of an ending" is subdued, yet suggestive that Heller's mortal enemy has been vanquished through force of intellect and wit. This outlook aligns the novel's vision with those as different as Shakespeare's sonnets, Donne's *Holy Sonnets*, and Milton's "Lycidas." At last, in Socrates's Asclepian cock, Heller seems to find the revelation for which he has searched through five novels. But as already noted, Socrates's death offers no such illumination. Socrates probably did not speak these "last words"; rather they were invented by Plato, who was not there. If he did speak them, he was deceived, for death by hemlock causes "retching, slurring of speech, [and] convulsions" (350). With this assertion, Heller's own narrative convulses; this is the death that Slocum figures for his retarded son, Derek. The death that Heller fears.[33]

Convinced of the falsity of Plato's interpretation of Socrates's death, Heller invents his own Asclepius, a leather merchant who will be sentenced to die for complicity in Socrates's treacheries after Socrates's disciples deliver the cock. This parodic inversion of Socrates's joke inverts its humor as well. In Heller's version, the death of Socrates is not cure, but plague; it does not evoke transcendence, but mortality. Socrates's "last words" are the poison that kills the innocent Asclepius; his joke initiates the sequence of events by which the intractable hold of the state is confirmed. Socrates's dying has more sinister parallels as well. Heller has earlier likened the defense of his life that Socrates offers in *The Apology* ("It seems to me that God has attached me to this city to perform the office of some stinging fly") to the justification offered by the schoolteacher who hacked up *The Nightwatch* with a serrated knife ("The attacker told bystanders he had been sent by the Lord" [23]). For Heller, this similarity signifies that Plato's fabrications are no less delusional and dangerous than those of the Dutch schoolteacher.

This ending is not, however, a complete change of authorial spots, for it embodies Heller's core pattern—a death that clarifies.[34] But the illustration afforded by the death of Socrates is deconstructive. As the narrator assesses its import, "There are outrages and there are outrages, and some are more outrageous than others. Mankind is resilient: the atrocities that horrified us a week ago become acceptable tomorrow" (350). This outlook makes the death of Socrates an aspect of the larger category, outrageous deaths, which, for Heller, is virtually all-inclusive. In this, it also argues against death's intrinsic significance; according to Heller, Socrates's death cannot be profitably differentiated from the innumerable outrages of which human history is constructed. Similarly, Heller deconstructs his own plot. His Asclepius story not only discredits Plato's account of the death of Socrates, but also itself, for as Heller acknowledges in the first chapter, it is his own contrivance. Even at the outset, he encourages disbelief, rather than its willing suspension. More tellingly, Heller uses the revelation that "the Rembrandt painting of Aristotle contemplating the bust of Homer may not be done by Rembrandt" to cast into doubt his own narrative. Like a Rembrandt painting whose Homer is not Homer and whose Aristotle is not Aristotle, it is not what it purports to be at all. It is a falsification, but in this the only pathway that Heller can affirm to what can be known, felt, and understood. This is because for him, as for Wallace Stevens, "we live in a place / That is not our own, and, much more, not ourselves / And hard it is in spite of blazoned days" ("Notes toward a Supreme Fiction"). And yet Heller believes that we must pretend that it is our place and that we must speak about its existence if we are to exist.[35] His novel as cock-and-bull story provides the necessary pretense.

CLOSING TIME

SEQUEL AND PERSONAL REFLECTION

> Harlequin without his mask is known to present
> a very sober countenance, and was himself, the
> story goes, the melancholy patient whom the
> Doctor advised to go and see Harlequin—a man
> full of cares and perplexities like the rest of us,
> whose Self must always be serious to him, un-
> der whatever mask or disguise or uniform he
> presents to the public.
>
> WILLIAM THACKERAY, "Swift," *The English Humorists of the Eighteenth Century*

SNOWDEN'S WOUND AND HELLER'S STORY

Joseph Heller opens *Closing Time* by taking readers behind his mask as harlequin and addressing them as if they were his contemporaries. The cares and perplexities revealed there are those of a generation about to pass away. Speaking for Heller, narrator Sammy Singer observes, "People I know are already dying and others I've known are already dead" (13). For the World War II generation, most of whom are well into old age, memory fails, flesh sags, aches are unremitting, careers are over. It is closing time, and little remains but to wait for the end, even to embrace its coming. This opening will be disquieting to readers who expect a reprise of *Catch-22*. At the outset, there is none of the rambunctious humor of the original, no Yossarian censoring letters by removing everything but the modifiers, no soldier in white with the interchangeable drip and excretion bottles, no Dunbar working so hard at living that Yossarian thinks he may be dying. In chapter 1 of *Closing Time*, death looms, presses in just as it does in a nursing home. The world behind harlequin's mask is an uncomfortable one; yet it is precisely there that Heller's comedy originates.

In bringing Yossarian and his supporting cast on stage in subsequent chapters, Heller reassumes his mask as harlequin. "In the middle of his second week in the hospital, Yossarian dreamed of his mother, and he knew again he was going to die. The doctors were upset when he gave them the news" (19). Worried by Yossarian's diagnosis, the medical specialists scurry about: his pathologist for his pathos, his psychologist for his psyche, his gastroenterologist, who needs some advice on Arizona real estate, and so on.[1] Playing off the famous hospital scene that opened *Catch-22* as it does, this first appearance by Yossarian is reassuring stuff. Heller the comic performer has picked up his hero where he left him thirty-three years earlier and unpacked him in perfect health. "[Y]ou might live forever," his doctors tell him (24). Almost seventy, Yossarian may be twice-divorced and more worldly worn, but his presence still sparks comic energy and vitality.

Alternately taking his readers behind the harlequin's mask and reassuming it again, Heller brings more of himself into a novel than he ever has before. Heller's presence is most noticeable to friends like Barbara Gelb, who can spot the author talking about himself as man: "a man who likes to be alone much of the time, thinks and daydreams a lot, doesn't really enjoy the give-and-take of companionship all that much, falls silent much of the time and broods and is indifferent to everything someone else might be talking about."[2] Of the many autobiographical details and observations, Heller himself says that they supply a factual dimension to an essentially fictional work. Indeed they do, but they also inextricably connect the novelist and the novel, making him simultaneously an embodied and a hovering presence in the novel. Heller calls *Closing Time* his summing-up, and, as in most summaries, the summarizer can never be wholly dispassionate and objective.[3] He or she is inextricably woven in.

The preeminent example of Joseph Heller's presence in the novel occurs in the scene in which Sammy Singer (Sammy is the unidentified airman in *Catch-22* who faints while Yossarian takes care of Snowden) and Yossarian meet by chance in the hospital for the first time since the war and talk about Snowden's death. Heller uses their conversation to reflect back upon *Catch-22*. Sammy's remarks about how Snowden has become an intimate friend in death serve as Heller's exegesis of the famous death scene and a comment about what he has himself made of experiences over Avignon:[4] "'But now I feel [Snowden] was one of my closest friends. . . . And I also feel,' Sammy persevered, 'he was one of the best things that ever happened to me. I almost hate to put it that way. It sounds immoral. But it gave me an episode, something dramatic to talk about, and something to make me remember the war was really real. People won't believe much of it; my children and grandchildren aren't interested in anything so old'" (356). Heller stresses that Snowden becomes a pal in death, not in life; the friendship exists in the fellowship with the dead crewmate remembered, not in any actual relationship. Snowden himself remains the barely known airman who whimpers "I'm cold, I'm cold." However, remembering him and subsequently telling his story accomplish a transformation, in Yossarian in *Catch-22*, in Sammy Singer in *Closing Time*, as well as in Joseph Heller their author. Like the grain of sand in an oyster, Snowden—or the wounded airman whom Heller attended over Avignon—rubs and irritates, wounds the consciousness until, against the irritation of mortality, a story comes into existence, complete and exquisite like a pearl.

Without the war, without the wounded airman to whom he himself ministered, Heller would not have written *Catch-22*, nor would he have had his dead-child masterplot, the germ for and stimulus to his imagination. As Sammy's reflections confirm, Snowden is the source of the narratable for Heller, the "episode" which he relates not only in "The Miracle of Danrossane," "Crippled Phoenix," and *Catch-22*, but also in each of his other novels as well. Snowden also serves as the differentiator, the point by which the real and the important can be distinguished from the unreal and the trivial. However, while Snowden himself can never be forgotten, the significance of his story can be. In fact, Yossarian himself has forgotten much of its import. "I would have used up all the morphine in the first-aid kit when I first saw him in such pain," he tells Singer. "That fucking Milo. I cursed him a lot. Now I work for him" (353). This work and its consequences constitute a principal thrust of the Yossarian plot. Yossarian wants to locate the import of this work outside himself. "Unreal city," he says alluding to Eliot's "The Waste Land," while watching the passersby near the Time-Life Building (now Milo's corporate headquarters). It does not occur to him to think that he may be one of those whom death has undone. As in *Catch-22*, Yossarian has mislocated the mortal wound.

In *Closing Time*, Heller wrings one more variation upon this story, extending what Kurt Vonnegut calls the mythic dimensions of *Catch-22* and *Something Happened*. In this extension, veterans like Yossarian found the peace that they so passionately wished for disappointing, even stultifying. And they frequently found themselves inadequate to protect the children to whom they claimed to dedicate their lives. Like latter-day Ivan Ilyches, these veterans found personal satisfaction and happiness transitory and elusive and discovered to their horror that they were dying without the consolation of rewarding lives or the promise of an afterlife. When they talked, as Sammy Singer does, about the one event in their lives whose excitement was undiminished—the war—they found their children uninterested, their spouses out of touch, their non-veteran friends bored. They came to doubt that their lives had any significance to anyone outside families. As Heller's myth has it, it is "closing time" not simply for these veterans but also for ourselves.

With *Closing Time*, Joseph Heller has cast his authorial die, risking part of the reputation that he secured with *Catch-22* and bidding, I think, for literary immortality. Unquestionably, *Catch-22* furnished one of the most influential visions of contemporary America, one that simultaneously imparted the atmosphere and values of the Cold War in the fifties and provided a vehicle for explaining the dilemmas of involvement in the Vietnam War in the sixties and seventies.[5] John Aldridge best speaks to the prophetic character of the novel: "with the seemingly eternal and mindless escalation of the war in Vietnam, history had at last caught up with the book and caused it to be more and more widely recognized as a deadly accurate metaphorical portrait of the nightmarish conditions in which the country appeared to be engulfed."[6] With *Closing Time*, has Joseph Heller achieved such currency of vision and such foresight again? Predictably, critics think not. While paying homage to Heller's past achievement, most reviewers found the novel wanting: not funny or inventive enough, a curious hybrid of the serious and comic, or a sign of diminishing talent.[7]

But are the critics right? Are the reviews more accurate this time than most were about *Catch-22*? About Heller's foresight, it is too soon to tell if he has succeeded in summing up his era and commenting upon its end. His vision is clear enough, for *Closing Time* primarily extends the pessimistic thesis of *Picture This*. Any victories portend future defeats. Contemporary America has not become the city on the hill that the Puritans envisioned, rather its benighted urban landscapes testify to values lost or abandoned. The mechanism for these things is capitalism, which, Heller believes, converts life into lifelessness and wastes spirit with no expense of shame. But what about comic achievement? An answer to this question depends upon looking at the novel in the terms that Heller announces, not, as tempting as it may be, upon measuring it against *Catch-22*. In order to appraise Heller's comic accomplishment, one wants to examine the way in which he has reconfigured Yossarian and redefined his story and not simply written its sequel. This difference is to be seen in the novel's complicated narrative structure, with its shuttlecock movement between omniscient and first-person points of view, the former providing the perspective of the satirist and the latter that of the memoirist. Heller's core story, his dead-child plot, propels *Closing Time* just as it has each of his previous novels. While the death of Kilroy, the disembodied omnipresent G.I. of World War II, seems a self-parodic version of his masterplot, this death in fact intensifies and extends its meaning. Heller accomplishes this amplification with the novel's hundreds and hundreds of allusions. In these allusions, particularly those to Mann, Dante, and Wagner, one glimpses Heller's own aspirations for the novel. In these allusions, one sees an artist aware of his limitations and attempting to defy them—one sees the author of *Catch-22*.

■

AGING AN ANTIHERO, CHANGING A CONCEPTION

In *Closing Time*, Yossarian—now Major John Yossarian, retired—has aged, entered human time in a way that he never did in *Catch-22*. Although set in 1944, time in *Catch-22* beat to the clock of the ever-escalating missions that the crews flew, and these missions were atemporal, as much about America of the fifties as about World War II. In such a world, Yossarian could "live forever or die in the attempt." Now he resides in Heller's old Manhattan neighborhood in an apartment on West End Avenue, divorced and lonely as Heller himself once was while in residence there.[8] *Closing Time* unfolds against the passing of the World War II generation as a historical actuality. With his hands inside Snowden's wound, Yossarian grasped the implications of another's mortality and, conceptually at least, had an image of his own. Together with the rest of the war generation, now he lives them, daily experiencing the proximity of his own death. When late in the novel McBride, a friend, observes "at least Yossarian is alive," he wants to know "for how long?" (439).[9]

To age Yossarian in this way and to transport him from Pianosa to Manhattan, Heller has had partially to reconfigure him. He is no longer quite the same character announced by the famous opening lines to *Catch-22*: "It was love at first sight. The first time Yossarian saw the chaplain he fell madly in love with him" (7). That Yossarian was defined by his fertile comic imagination, his resistance to authority, his sensitivity to the suffering of others, and—his fears notwithstanding—his naive, hopeful innocence. There was a sense in which Pianosa was his world, a realm that he, like Don Quixote, could transfigure with the vitality of his own imagination. However, in *Closing Time*, he is "Mr. Yossarian," "a fleeing figure wearing a businessman's chapeau and moving with a cane."[10] Although still defined by his comic vitality, this Yossarian has lost his innocence, has become more self-absorbed, and is more likely to cooperate with authority than to flout it. As Heller announces him, this Yossarian thinks about his mother and immediately worries that he might die. In this portrait, Heller admits what some astute readers realized when they first read *Something Happened*: Yossarian and Bob Slocum embody aspects of the same character, linked by their self-pity and their egoism. Slocum's suburbia and Yossarian's Manhattan are home, the inescapable reality that constricts the dreams of a Heller protagonist and deadens his desires. Home situates Yossarian—as it has situated returning quest heroes from Odysseus onward—rendering him a member of a generation whose time is passing.

The change of locale signifies the change of plot pattern, for Heller trades the initiation story for the marriage comedy, thereby redirecting Yossarian's quest. In *Catch-22*, Yossarian's story follows the traditional pattern of initiation: his pre-knowledge innocence, the knowledge gained over Avignon that destroys his innocence and psychically wounds him, and the discovery of Snowden's secret that enables him to live. In *Closing Time*, Heller undercuts the implications of Yossarian's initiation, revealing Sweden to have been an Edenic fantasy. There has been no place where Yossarian could be unburdened of his memories of guilt or where he could protect innocents like Nately's whore's kid sister. After the war, Yossarian returned home and began making deals again, only it is Milo rather than Colonels Cathcart and Korn that he agrees to like and to say nice things about. In *Closing Time* Yossarian must learn how to live again: how to enjoy life, to exercise humor without lapsing into cynical irony, and to hope. As in the comedies of Moss Hart and George S. Kaufman that Heller once aspired to write, a good woman can teach Yossarian these things. However, as Heller retools the pattern, a younger woman guides Yossarian toward what to remember—herself and the potentially redemptive power of love—and toward what to forget—his guilt about his failed marriages and his fatherhood.

He has a lot to learn. "[B]y preparing to die," Yossarian tells his favorite son Michael, "That's the only way to live" (33). He is joking when he says this, but the joke reveals what he cannot acknowledge to his son or himself. He indulges himself with visions that he has a stroke or seizure and fixates on Gustav Aschenbach and "his immortal death in Venice" (20). The pun upon immortal is Yossarian's, but it points to the life after death he cannot conceive for himself. It also signifies his failures to realize his ambitions for authorship. He has tried and failed to publish in *The New Yorker*; he concocts plots for novels that parody Dickens's *Christmas Carol* and Mann's *Dr. Faustus*, but never writes them. Alone and lonely, he checks himself into the hospital rather than endure the solitude, but even there with his favorite nurse Melissa MacIntosh by his side "he [finds] himself in dire need of something to need" (22). In such paradoxes, his life spirit remains, expressed by his comic imagination and his fondness for language as language. But it needs a mode of expression, a mission akin to that of *Catch-22*, in which he dedicated himself to living forever or dying in the attempt.

In this sense, Yossarian is, to borrow Wallace Stevens's phrase, an "emptiness that would be filled,"[11] an existential desire defining him and potentially offering him a direction. However, Yossarian himself misconstrues his predicament, believing that desire itself has failed him. In this, he has also fallen victim to his own cynical understanding of the world.[12] Working for Milo's M & ME & A, he has unconsciously assumed its outlook. He trades upon others' appetite for status, as in his scheme for the Maxon-Minderbinder marriage (have it in the Port Authority Bus Terminal with actors playing the parts of the prostitutes, pimps, pushers, and homeless who are usually in residence there), and sells Milo's schemes to the government, knowing full well that they won't work (in fact Yossarian gets $500,000 for his access to the presidential assistant G. Noodles Cook on behalf of Milo's Sub-Supersonic Invisible and Noiseless Defensive Second-Strike Offensive Attack Bomber). When his son Michael has ethical qualms about being the commercial artist for the sales proposal for the bomber, Yossarian angrily barks at him, "you're only being asked to draw a picture of the plane, not to fly the fucking thing or launch an attack. . . . [Milo and Associates] don't care now if it works or not. All they want is the money" (185). Money is what motivates Yossarian as well—and is what distracts him from the necessary urgencies of desire.

Fortunately, Yossarian's desire exists independently of his control and can redirect him, once it is aroused by a life-affirming partner. As Heller presents the matter, this will be accomplished by Melissa MacIntosh, the "attractive floor nurse with the pretty face and the magnificent ass who was openly drawn to Yossarian, despite his years" (20). The impediment to the romance plot is Yossarian himself. While openly attracted to this woman who seems "too good to be true" (22), he can flirt with Melissa, but cannot bring himself to assume the part of a lover. He jokingly wonders whether, once he leaves the hospital, "he would ever even remember to want to see her again" (36). Heller's point in this is more serious: memory reveals the plots by which one's life unfolds. In *Catch-22*, memory transfigured Snowden from crewman into pal, thereby making available the secret of his entrails, and it awakened Yossarian to the pangs of love forever lost in Luciana.[13] As the vehicle that creates expectations, memory also offers the tool by which Yossarian can plot a future.

So it is that Yossarian comes to conceive his relationship with Melissa in terms of the Wagnerian operas of which he is so fond: he will be Siegfried and she will be his Brünnhilde.[14] Or rather, after he and Melissa unexpectedly make love in the old Time-Life Building, memory refigures the experience in this way and projects what will follow accordingly. However, as in *Catch-22*, Yossarian envisions a plot that he cannot control and participates in ones that have meanings beyond his ken. His "Rhine Journey" in pursuit of Melissa is enacted within Heller's novel, enacted with

Wagnerian implications that Heller remembers and Yossarian partially forgets (291). Wagner's *The Ring* occurs without Siegfried's understanding the story of which he is part until it is too late; Siegfried does not know, for example, about the potion that makes him forget Brünnhilde or about Hagin's scheme that he marry Gutrunne. Wagner describes his intentions in composing the Siegfried plot in terms that are relevant to *Closing Time* and that define what Siegfried and Yossarian never realize: "Experience is everything. Siegfried alone (the male alone) is also not the complete 'man'; he is but one half. It is only with Brünnhilde that he becomes the redeemer. One alone cannot achieve everything; many are needed, and the suffering, self-sacrificing woman is the final knowing redeemer, for love is really the 'eternally feminine' itself."[15] Like Wagner, Heller places Yossarian's Siegfried fantasy in the context of what he has forgotten, of what he does not know, and within his own *Götterdämmerung*. Like Wagner, Heller stresses the importance of experience and locates love in the eternally feminine.

Nevertheless, as an expression of his comic spirit, Yossarian's Wagnerian imaginings are useful, helping to extricate him from his lassitude and loneliness. In order to assume the role of Siegfried, Yossarian must acknowledge the desire that he experiences in the presence of Melissa, he must differentiate its sexual and relational components, and he must come to terms with his past failures as a lover and husband. The first occurs because Melissa flirtatiously pursues him, reminding him of her presence and offering him the part of her lover. She reinstructs him in the rituals of courtship. The second two things occur via doubles for Melissa, Frances Beach, a companionable former lover who serves as a reminder of the temporality of erotic love, and Angela Moore, Melissa's roommate, who represents the self-extinguishing dimension of sexual desire. Each represents a relationship that Yossarian knows all too well and that has contributed to his malaise.

The Angela Moore plot—Angela Moorecock in Heller's regrettably adolescent joke—partakes of the Freudian logic that renders thanatos inextricable from eros. A Circe figure, Angela possesses sexuality that unmans those whose desire she provokes. Her elderly Jewish employers become tongue-tied when she describes her ideas for novelty erotic products; she entices business executives into dancing with her, then gives them the phone number of the city morgue instead of her own. Over a drink, Yossarian falls victim to her blandishments when she describes her idea for a bedroom clock with a luminous dial: its numbers are nude female figures in various stages of arousal, whose climax occurs at twelve; its hands are circumcised penises. They go off together and she performs fellatio on him (presumably at midnight), Heller's symbolic representation of desire that yields satiety. In the logic of the novel, their oral sex signifies the way in which Yossarian has been silenced. Interweaving this episode with Milo's bomber scheme in a chapter entitled "Tritium," Heller extends its symbolic implications, linking Yossarian's false feelings of potency with Angela (he has her feel the erection that occurs as he listens to her describe the clock) to the explosive nuclear power that Milo spuriously markets. Lest it follow this self-extinguishing path, Yossarian's desire must be redirected.[16]

Frances Beach offers Yossarian a more companionable relationship, but not one which affords the appropriate stimulus to desire and therefore to life. Like Yossarian, Frances has come to view love as a casual and temporary erotic phenomenon ("love seldom makes it through the second weekend," she says [81]). Her values are those of society, which Heller satirizes in the novel. For her, marriage is a means to social status and prestige, and she plays marriage and romance games well. In the past she and Yossarian shared an adulterous affair, which has resulted in a friendship that persists. Now they are comrades in arms. It is with Frances that Yossarian concocts his scheme for a Port Authority Bus Terminal wedding. Fittingly, at the wedding it is his dance with Frances that Yossarian sees on the PABT video screen, which "replay[s] . . . the event[s] taking place in the future" (411). Their dance testifies to his accommodation to the world of the Minderbinders and Maxons—to what he has become. Seeing the image of what will be, he has the "abstract belief that he ought to be ashamed," but cannot bring himself to feel any shame (420). Their companionability is symptomatic of Yossarian's emptiness, of his stunted emotions and ethical myopia.

While Yossarian luxuriates in transfiguring his relationship with Melissa into Wagnerian opera, he finds himself involved in a quite different drama, a much more quotidian one. After dating and having sex with him, she begins to fall in love with him and anticipates living with him, maybe marrying him. Melissa wants to listen to the *Ring* with Yossarian; she talks too much when they make love; and, worst of all from his point of view, she listens to the TV news: "There was no war, no national election, no race riot, no big fire, storm, earthquake, or airplane crash—there *was* no news, and she was listening to it on television" (298). Out of the TV noise emerges an uncomfortable truth: for Yossarian, his loneliness is preferable to the company of others.[17] His enjoyment of Melissa depends upon his recasting their relationship into the tempestuous passions of operatic love. The actual woman gets in the way of the life that he likes to lead. Yossarian's loneliness fuels and sustains the pleasures of his Siegfried fantasy. Alone, he can "put a complete *Lohengrin, Boris Godunov,* or *Die Meistersinger*, or four whole symphonies by Bruckner, and play them all through in an elysian milieu of music without hearing someone feminine intruding to say, 'What music is that?' or 'Do you really like that?' or 'Isn't that kind of heavy for the morning?' or 'Will you please make it lower? I am trying to watch the television news" (300). As the domestically happy Melissa makes breakfast and watches the news after a shared night, this Siegfried finds himself in a domestic marriage plot rather than in an operatic romance. Twice-divorced, he knows its costs, can script what will happen to him in daily contact with the woman of his dreams.

Faced with such unpleasant realities, Yossarian runs, just as he did in *Catch-22*. He flies to Kenosha, Wisconsin, to search for Chaplain Tappman; from there he goes to Washington, D.C., to try to secure the chaplain's release but instead earns $500,000 for brokering Milo's bomber deal; and finally he enters the hospital—still Yossarian's preferred refuge from actualities that discomfit him.[18] During each phase of this self-proclaimed Rhine Journey, he entertains himself with the contrasts between Siegfried's situation and his own, while still giving himself the part of the romantic quest hero, albeit a worldly wise one: Siegfried dies and Valhalla collapses, but Yossarian lives. In his Wagnerian scenarios, Yossarian's imagination runs ahead of him and enmeshes him in stories whose implications he wants to resist. The most symbolically important of these occurs when, thinking about Melissa in Kenosha, he actually hears the anvil chorus from *Das Rheingold* on the radio. The clinking anvils render Kenosha a Wagnerian underworld (a point that Heller underscores by making it part of the military's underground defense network) and align Yossarian more with Wotan and Alberich than with Siegfried.[19] Like them, Yossarian has forsaken love and, by choosing money, pursues power instead. Mrs. Tappman partially awakens Yossarian to these implications when she shows him the pictures of her husband, himself, Snowden, and Singer on Pianosa and tells about the miracle (i.e., the angel that the chaplain detected in the tree at Snowden's funeral).[20] Against his inclination, Yossarian resists explaining the miracle and commits himself to finding her husband for her.

The clinking anvils from *Das Rheingold* are followed by "a very different, lonely, lovely, angelic wail of a children's chorus in striking polyphonic lament," a musical motif that Heller links to the dead-child plot of *Closing Time* (309). Yossarian eventually places the unknown music as an excerpt from Adrian Leverkühn's *Apocalypse* in *Dr. Faustus*. But while Yossarian recognizes the chorus, he does not hear its theme or meanings: "the inner unity of the chorus of child angels and the hellish laughter of the damned."[21] Nor does Yossarian remember that the death of Leverkühn's beloved nephew Echo follows the composition of the *Apocalypse* and leads to his final masterpiece *The Lamentations of Faust*, his "Ode to Sorrow" that satirically and angrily reverses the harmony and themes of Beethoven's "Ode to Joy." Hearing a composition on the radio that he knows does not exist in actuality, Yossarian fears that he has lost his bearings, as indeed he has. As the signal fades out, only radio static breaks "the primeval void of human silence" (309).

Like Melissa, its loquacious opposite, this silence speaks to something very deep in Yossarian and his author. It betokens another story of which Yossarian is part. Heller objectifies this story in the Belgian patient, who has had his cancerous larynx removed, an operation that saves his life at the cost of his speech. "He was hyperalimentated through a tube stuck in his neck so that he would not starve to death. They fed water intravenously into the poor man so that he would not dehydrate, suctioned fluids from his lungs so that he would not drown" (34). This is the soldier-in-white plot from *Catch-22* redrawn on the basis of Heller's own experiences in Mount Sinai Hospital, where he also had a room adjacent to that of a Belgian patient with throat cancer. As in *Catch-22*, proximity to the silence of life-in-death moves Yossarian to action: "He could not stand the Belgian's pain. He was going . . . to leave her" (35). The "her" in this instance is, of course, Melissa, his nurse; the dialectic relationship between Melissa—the provocateur of flirtatious speech—and the Belgian—speechlessness—is Heller's doing.[22] Knowing that the risks of cancer are increased by stress and experiencing a sore throat and difficulty in swallowing, Yossarian knows what could lie ahead for him, just as he thought he knew what the soldier in white portended and fled the hospital on Pianosa.

The oscillation between Melissa and the Belgian patient recurs throughout the novel, with each serving to call up the other. Yossarian yo-yos between the two, impelled by desires toward life and death that he only partially glimpses. His emptiness remains. On the one hand, he anticipates the joys of intimacy and companionship with Melissa, even as he finds the resulting familiarity estranges him from her. On the other hand, Yossarian finds himself continually being reminded of the Belgian cancer patient and, once reminded, finds an imaginative kinship with him. In his own mind Yossarian becomes the silent patient, experiencing his pain and the terrors of speechlessness. Impelled by the fear that results, he flees Melissa as well as the Belgian.

However, events overtake Yossarian. During one of his flights to the hospital Melissa becomes pregnant by him—a parallel with the Siegfried/Brünnhilde story that Yossarian overlooks. Fatherhood would give Yossarian a mission and would reconfigure the dead-child story, whereas an abortion would give the masterplot a deadly new twist. As prospective father, Yossarian cannot insist upon the innocence that his flight to Sweden signified, nor can he claim to preserve innocence as he implicitly did by rescuing Nately's whore's kid sister. Like Abraham, the archetypal Jewish father, Yossarian must experience the ambiguity of fatherhood: its conjunctions of guilt and innocence, mortality and immortality, continuity and change. From the wounds that he has unintentionally inflicted upon his son Michael, Yossarian understands how a father's love and concern inevitably maim as well as comfort. Yet his desire will have yielded a son, an external manifestation of his love for Melissa and of his own life-spirit. Yossarian will have agreed to live in time, to acknowledge the significance of his seventy years. His self will be bound up with others' lives, never again to be fully free.[23]

■

NARRATIVE STRUCTURE, COMIC ENERGY, AND THE PRESERVATIONIST'S ART

Like a great stand-up comedian, the comic novelist performs just ahead of the audience's expectations, perpetually the hare in front of our tortoise-like selves. The whirling energy of *Catch-22* demonstrates as much: the nonsense, puns, paradoxes, and other verbal pyrotechnics work to keep us off balance; to stymie, defer, redefine, and overturn our expectations. Robert Polhemus might have been speaking of these aspects of *Catch-22* when he wrote: "One reason for the surge of liberation that comedy can stir in us is that so much gets covered so fast, and we must race our brains to keep up: we feel we are mentally flying. To follow, to stay on top of what's happening, to 'get it,' to 'get the joke,' we have to rivet our attention on the winging moment and focus on the particularity of what we are sensing, living fully and intensely in a speedy present."[24] In this, Polhemus also characterizes the demands of comic performance for its practitioners, the imperative to place the audience in a roller-coasterish world, a world often on the edge of veering off the tracks. But unless it is on the edge, its velocities intermittently hinting at disaster and holding out relief, comic novels like *Catch-22* become predictable, turn into situation comedy, the stable but ephemeral stuff of television and other mass audience media.

However, such comic performances cannot finally be sustained; they create a drag, a counterforce to their own frenetic energies. Among other things, this counterforce results from the comic novelist's own values, from what the novelist wants to attack, preserve, or defend. And in *Closing Time* Heller wants to preserve Yossarian and the Coney Island of his boyhood. He devises his complicated narrative structure to accomplish both ends, to energize the novel and to ensure that Yossarian and Coney Island live. The shifts among four narrators—three first-person narrators, Sammy Singer, Lew Rabinowitz, and his wife Claire, and an omniscient one—create a shuttlecock movement among viewpoints above and within the novel's world. They also set up contrasting narrative tempos, the hustle-bustle, carnivalesque rhythms of the omniscient narrator's sections featuring Yossarian and the more measured cadences of personal memoir in the first-person portions. Such a variety of tempos and perspectives unsettles readers, never allowing their expectations to fall into the predictable or the routine or to fix the relationship between the comic or the serious with any certainty. With respect to Yossarian himself, Sammy Singer's first-person viewpoint has just the opposite effect. It accommodates him to the reader's world, a world of childhood friends, army buddies, and office colleagues, a world in which Yossarian exists within a set of everyday associations and memories. It is not the realm of Siegfried and Brünnhilde, nor of Coney Island rendered as an inferno, but it is the one that Melissa MacIntosh invites him to share with her. In such a place, Yossarian is simply a man, paunchy and white-haired, but blessed with the comic spirit to impose himself upon his observers' memories.

The voices of Sammy, Lew, and Claire constitute a community of friends within a world in which such voices are under threat of extinction. They form a crucial connection between Heller and the authorial reader. Like Heller, Sammy and Lew grew up on Coney Island and have fond memories of their childhood and early adulthood, despite the hard times of the Depression and the wrenching uncertainties of the war; they know the people whom Heller knew and in Sammy's case read the authors that he read; they represent the kind of life Heller might have led, if he had not written *Catch-22* and become a world-reknowned author. With Sammy Singer's opening to the novel, Heller invites the reader to join them in looking upon their world:

> When people our age speak of the war it is not of Vietnam but of the one that broke out more than half a century ago and swept in almost all the world. It was raging more than two years before we even got into it. . . . Yet a million Americans were casualties of battle before it was over—three hundred thousand of us were killed in combat. Some twenty-three hundred alone died at Pearl Harbor on that single day of infamy almost half a century back—more than twenty-five hundred others were wounded—a greater number of military casualties on just that single day than the total in all but the longest, bloodiest engagements in the Pacific, more than on D day in France. (11)

Against such a backdrop, the dropping of the atomic bomb was, as Sammy Singer observes, an event to be rejoiced over, a reaction that temporarily united "the civilized Western world" in collective relief and joy. World War II is the defining experience for this generation, the magnitude of which is so great that all the rest of their lives are measured against it. And although their lives have been productive and happy, nothing else was ever to mean or has meant as much to them. In this way, they have aged prematurely, glancing back as many athletes do to the glories that have been and living with the regret that they will never come again.

Heller constructs the novel so that these voices enter, albeit indirectly, into conversation with each other, catching, as old friends' conversation does, the flavor of a shared past. Their talk has the quality of oral history. Each reminisces about the past, trying to convey by anecdote the texture of his or her experience. Together their narratives present a variegated tapestry in which evocatively memorable moments emerge out of ordinary lives. There are such stories as Sammy's sneaking his father's World War I gas mask out to play with, or Lew's triumph over an eighth-grade bully, or Claire's memories of working in a junk shop on MacDonald Avenue in Coney Island with Lew and his father. Their comradery sets Yossarian's loneliness in relief. Despite Lew's Hodgkin's disease or the suicide of Sammy's stepson, the enduring satisfactions of their lives present a striking contrast to Yossarian's unremitting desires. Although a comfortable world, it is hardly the one that readers coming to *Closing Time* from *Catch-22* expected to find. Its pace is more like a carousel than a roller coaster, its humor muted to sound like the jokes that can be heard over most middle-class kitchen tables.

Heller endows Sammy Singer, as he does Yossarian, with aspects of his own personality and experience, especially his memories of the past. Most evocative in this last respect is the anecdote about Singer learning after the fact that his mother broke down and cried after he left to join the army.[25] His entire narrative has the residue of this particular memory, a vague uneasiness about emotion and an undercurrent of unhappiness. Like Heller, Singer is bright and witty, possessed of an off-the-wall sense of humor. Although he taught composition at Penn State and worked successfully at *Time*—as Heller did—he never wrote the things that he wanted to write or fulfilled his dream of being published in *The New Yorker*.[26] Unlike Heller, he married a divorced shiksa, becoming father to her three children. It was a marriage of rare happiness, one depending upon the complementarity of opposite personalities, Glenda's warmth and brashness and his reticence. Aside from his verbal facility and bravado, Singer is shy, reserved with women, inexperienced with sex. He is a reader, a pedant according to Glenda and a bookish prick according to Yossarian. Singer's reading mediates experience for him, making his own more intelligible and bearable and keeping the world at a remove where it is less threatening.

In *Closing Time*, Singer speaks nostalgically of the world that is being lost. He is a preservationist who realizes the limitations of his efforts and a Wordsworthian who knows the world that is too much with us. He remembers and reverences the Concy Island in which he, Lew, and Heller grew up. His recollections are studded with particularities: the gong of the ocean buoy at the beach which the neighborhood kids called "bellboy," the Steinberg candy store on the corner of Surf Avenue, and the Norton's Point trolley tracks. He remembers when, for a nickel, you could get a MeloRol, an Eskimo Pie, or even a hotdog at Rosenberg's delicatessen. Like Heller, he laments the passing of the old neighborhoods, because they constitute the place of his youth and because their disappearance signals the loss of communal values and shared assumptions. He knows that Luna Park and Steeplechase were not the innocent pleasure palaces that he took them to be as a youth, yet he cannot forget the magic opened up to him when Robby Kleinline's father would give him a free pass to George Tilyou's Steeplechase. A few pennies and you could win a coconut in a pitch game there, once you learned how. No more. They are gone together with *The Bell Telephone Hour*, a block of Nestle's chocolate for two cents, and the New York where, as WNYC radio announcers would claim, "seven million people live in peace and harmony and enjoy the benefits of democracy" (207).

Among these losses, the passing of the World War II generation weighs upon Singer most heavily. "We don't look that beautiful now," he says. "We wear glasses and are growing hard of hearing, we sometimes talk too much, repeat ourselves, things grow on us, even the most minor bruises take longer to heal and leave telltale traces. And soon . . . there will be no more of us left" (13). And while he would like to believe that mementos and relics will preserve the presence of the war generation, he knows about the fragility of memory and has experienced firsthand its limits. Sammy's father, like Heller's, died soon after World War I, while he was still quite young, and as a result he can recall very little about him. Only the odd detail remains: his father's World War I gas mask, the smell of his cigars, or his fondness for sitting on the beach in the evenings. Sammy realizes that his own sergeant's stripes and gunner's wings face a similar fate. Their evocations will be so faint so as to be virtually indiscernible; in them, Howard Snowden, if remembered at all, will be only a name, his whimpering cries that he is cold only words.

Singer's memory affords a perspective on Yossarian that is quite different from the omniscient narrator's view. Although Singer is timid, slight, and Jewish, he identifies with the brash Armenian Yossarian, "who kept joking crazily that he was really an Assyrian and already practically extinct" (14). As he explains the connection, "My feelings lay with Yossarian, who was humorous and quick, a bit wild but, like me, a big-city boy, who would rather die than be killed" (14). Although separated since the war until they meet by chance in the hospital late in the novel, Singer believes two episodes bind them together for the rest of their lives, Snowden's death and a fight in which Yossarian intervened to protect Sammy (the latter an addition to the *Catch-22* story). As Singer views these incidents, Yossarian acted as he wishes he himself would have. In the first instance, he fainted, overwhelmed by the bloody wound, while Yossarian took care of Snowden. In the second, Singer wished he would have stood up for himself instead of being rendered helpless when a drunken private charged him. When Yossarian came to the rescue, he took the punch that Singer should have taken.

Such memories familiarize Yossarian and *Catch-22*. The second-sight that they proffer is as educative as the absurdist "seeing it twice" was in *Catch-22*. Singer's recollections have the grainy authenticity of a World War II newsreel: "Yossarian folding flesh back into a wound on the thigh, cutting bandages, retching, using the pearly cloth of Snowden's parachute as a blanket to warm him, and then as a shroud" (385–86). Over Avignon, Sammy fainted at these sights; now, he stares unblinkingly into them, as he has many times since. Through this re-vision, he can understand why he prayed on all his subsequent bombing missions and why he—as Heller did—promised himself not to fly again, until the travel required by a sales conference caused him to break his vow. In retrospect, he can say of the episode, "I saw death" (386). When he and Yossarian talk about the Avignon mission, they share the perspective of memory. Of such reunions and perspectives, Harry Paige, World War II veteran and novelist, has written: "After a half century we went back and discovered ourselves and the war that joined us to the skies. We got to know the people we became as well as the kids we were, a kind of looking both ways at the same time, a second chance at knowing and caring."[27] From this outlook, Singer confides in Yossarian, "now I feel [Snowden] was one of my closest friends" (356). This is another way of saying "man [is] matter," but it is gentler, the kind of thing one says to an old friend while remembering the beginning of a friendship and while almost glimpsing the end.

In *Closing Time*, Lew Rabinowitz is to Sammy Singer what Speed Vogel is to Joseph Heller in *No Laughing Matter*. As between Heller and Vogel, their complementary accounts depend upon badinage. Their gruff male bonding reveals itself in rivalry and unvoiced loyalty: "He was good at chess, I was good at pinochle. I stopped playing chess, he kept losing money to me at pinochle. Who was the smart one?" (39). This is Rabinowitz in a nutshell, avoiding losses by finding arenas where he can triumph, bulling his way through life. He opens his portion of the novel, "I was born strong and without fear" (39). He views neighborhood toughs like the Bartolinis or Palumbos or unethical business rivals in the same way: if he busts a few jaws, they'll stop. If he knew the Siegfried myth, he would know the precedent for this attitude, but, unlike Yossarian, he is too busy living his life to worry about what is or to invent what might be, let alone to go to the opera. Lew would still be the same person if it were not for the Hodgkin's disease.

While Sammy testifies to the world that is being lost, Lew speaks as one of its casualties. Much of Lew's narrative consists of tales of adversaries bested and circumstances confronted, but it has the undercurrent of the disease that is slowly killing him.[28] "I'm well into my sixties and we're into the nineties, and this time I'm beginning to feel . . . things are beginning to come to an end" (155). His narrative constitutes a holding action against this end. He is still Lew Rabinowitz, though, unafraid when it comes to threats from other human beings. His concerns are for his family's welfare, especially for that of his favorite son Michael. He worries that Michael will inherit his genetic predisposition to cancer. But financially and emotionally, he has made sure that they are all well provided for: "I feel better knowing they'll all be left okay when I'm gone. *At least for a start*" (emphasis added, 274). Indeed each of his four children has done well, and Claire is as emotionally tough as Lew himself. But he can do nothing to provide for their health and, in the hospital, ravaged by chemotherapy whose side effects are as physically debilitating as the disease itself, he knows what may lie ahead for them. And this weighs on his mind.

Lew has a personal code for talking about cancer and its effects, one partially anchored in denial. "It's those green apples I'm more afraid of now, all the time, those green apples in my mother's loony theory that green apples were what made people sick. Because more than anything else now, I'm afraid of nausea. I am sick of feeling nauseous" (152). The green apples were Lew's mother's explanation for an abscessed ear that he had as a child, and now it is his label for the physical sensations of illness, especially for the nausea associated with the Hodgkin's disease and chemotherapy. The green-apple taste imposes itself on him, coming when he least expects it. In what Lew comes to believe was the first manifestation of the disease, nausea interrupts a trip to the Caribbean when Lew, flush with confidence, invests in land on Saint Maarten that certainly will accrue value. After some celebratory Saint André cheese that he has particularly enjoyed, the green-apple taste overwhelms him, and he vomits uncontrollably through the night. The nausea and the illness of which it is symptomatic call into question Lew's self-definition of being strong and unafraid. For several years, he cannot even tell Claire about the Hodgkin's disease, and it is much longer before he learns how to live with its uncertainties and to acknowledge his vulnerability.

As his death nears, the tenor of Lew's narrative changes. His memories turn more insistently to the war. Ironically, it provided the time when he felt invulnerable. A sniper kills a corporal who was not a foot away from him, and he "felt it had to happen that way" (135). In his platoon, "[n]o one lasted long," but Lew survives uninjured (279).[29] During the Battle of the Bulge—in a scene that Heller casts as the infantryman's equivalent of Avignon—the same bullet kills one soldier next to Lew and wounds another, David Craig, in the thigh, and yet Lew is unfazed, in fact makes jokes about it.[30] Later in the battle, when he is captured and sent to Dresden together with Kurt Vonnegut and good soldier Schweik (the latter the protagonist of Jaroslav Hasek's novel by the name), he still laughs and jokes with the other prisoners of war, especially the Polish women who work with him. "Rabinowitz, you're crazy," Vonnegut tells him (285). One night in their barracks in the slaughterhouse meat locker, he hears the bombers flying overhead, but even this does not make him afraid. In the recollection, his tone is flat and unemotional, recording the dull thumps and thuds that he later learned were incendiary bombs. To his ears, the resulting roar was like a train in a tunnel or a roller coaster accelerating. It never occurred to him that he might die.

However, the mass death of Dresden irremediably changes Lew's outlook on life. The overwhelming destruction roused feelings of pity, pity for everyone, including the Germans. In the tears that follow, he realizes that "I didn't count. . . . I saw I made no difference. It all would have taken place without me and come out just the same" (287).[31] In recollection, he extends the implication of the insight to assert that "[t]he only place I've counted is at home, with Claire and the kids" (288). But even at home, Lew's Hodgkin's disease erodes what he can count on and has counted for. He likes to think that he can protect his family, slam potential assailants into the pavement as he did the purse snatcher at the Port Authority Terminal. But, as the disease spreads, the "sharpshooters" that he faces are the X-ray technologists who "take aim" at his cancer and in the process forever take away from himself. The cancer always reappears somewhere else. The mortal enemy resides within, and for Lew this fact confirms what he learned at Dresden.

After he dies, Claire's narrative picks up where Lew's leaves off, completing his story and erecting a memorial. As she tells it, when the cancer "reached his stomach again, he decided to give up and let himself pass away" (394). At this point, nausea—the green-apple taste—had become the condition of his existence. Yet he had fought on, not against death, but to ensure that Claire and their children would be provided for. The backgammon and Scrabble games that Claire and Lew shared were replaced by his quizzes about interest rates and multiplication tables—Lew wanted to be certain that Claire could manage the money that he has left her. He did not want visitors anymore, and he lost his appetite, although the smell of cheese would still bring a smile to him. Even at the end, some of the life spirit remained in Lew, embedded in details evoked by small pleasures like the cheese. Claire's voice—the first woman given narrative powers in a Heller novel—completes the love story, for that is what underlay Lew's account of his life. When all that remained for Lew was to lie silently in bed, she helped him pass the time by giving him manicures and pedicures. The contact, the intimacy of the marital rituals of a lifetime, confirms a lifetime of happiness.

"'He died laughing, you know,' I said to Sam" (405). Although Claire does not know this for sure, it is the way she tells the story, a way that fits Lew's as well as Heller's temperament. The cause for the laughter was Sammy's last letter, part of a series of luxuriously imagined accounts of a trip to New Zealand, Australia, and Singapore, with Hawaii, Fiji, Bali, and Tahiti thrown in. For Lew who, like Yossarian, passes the time by flirting with the nurses, the trip has been an extended joke—how can Singer make a trip like this if he still has not learned how to pick up a girl? Claire's account of the circumstances of Lew's death for Sammy is the last of the first-person sections. This is entirely fitting, signifying the gradual passing away of the war generation and providing one more meaning for "closing time," one that reflects back upon the ending of *Picture This*. Unlike Socrates or Asclepius, Lew can die laughing, his laughter transfiguring what must be into comic possibility.

The omniscient narrator provides a satiric vision of the America in which Yossarian, Sammy, Lew, and Claire live. He sees society as having become the military-industrial complex that President Eisenhower forecast and seeks to expose from the inside out the life-denying logic of capitalism that is responsible for this transformation. In particular, he wants to drive home the way in which capitalism victimizes the economically successful and the economically disadvantaged alike. By mocking the political, military, and business elites of contemporary America via the omniscient narrator, Heller wants to liberate authorial readers with scathing laughter, to make his readers spectators to their emperor's new clothes. The world may be under threat of nuclear annihilation; American cities may be so dangerous as to make daily life a hardship; and political and economic power elites may have as their principal agendas concentrating as much power as possible in their own hands. But when authorial readers see the characters responsible for all this insanity, they can only laugh. How can it be otherwise when the president wants friends and advisors to call him "The Little Prick" or one of the advisors wants to be known as G. Noodles Cook? When such characters' follies are blown up, as they might be in a political cartoon, the reader is freed from their thrall, just as the readers of political cartoons are by seeing the pretensions, foibles, and self-deceptions of their political leaders lampooned.

While the narrator seemingly stands above the world of *Closing Time*, his rhetorical stance frequently emerges from within the characters themselves. In this respect, his first chapter title, "The Little Prick," is not his angrily satiric title for the new president (although it is Heller's comment upon President Bush's choice of Dan Quayle as his vice president). Similarly, the secret that provides the plot complication of this chapter—why the President originally picked the Little Prick as his running mate—is that there is no secret. The President did exactly what he said he had done, exercised his best judgment! The political sections of the novel extend the principle: G. Noodles Cook qualifies as an eminent presidential advisor because he is self-serving, calculating, mendacious, and mercenary; Harold Strangelove prospers, in part, because he has the best business card ("Fine Contacts and . . . Secondhand Influence Bought and Sold [also] Bombast on Demand" [70]); Milo Minderbinder unabashedly markets his Sub-Supersonic Invisible and Noiseless Defensive Second-Strike Offensive Attack Bomber, knowing that it can fulfill none of its claims; and the Little Prick succeeds politically by spending all his time playing video games. In Heller's joke, these characters are one-dimensional because they want to be one-dimensional; his point—the same one that he made in *Good as Gold*—is that this outlook, in part, gives these people their political and economic power and prestige. If they were intelligent, humane, and thoughtful, they would fail.

Heller's omniscient narrator knows the world as intimately as a Dickensian narrator does. He guides the readers through the secret corridors of MASSPOB (Military Affairs Special Secrets Project Office Building) power and into the labyrinthine Port Authority sub-basements rather than through dilapidated London streets like Tom-all-Alone's or into Lady Dedlock's boudoir at Chesney Wold. But, like a Dickens narrator, the narrator of *Closing Time* insists that everything is connected: the Time-Life Building and the Port Authority sub-basements; the Pentagon (Heller's MASSPOB) and Kenosha, Wisconsin; the Coney Island on which Lew, Sammy, and Heller grew up and its infernoesque re-creation; the Port Authority Bus Terminal (PABT) homeless and Yossarian. The entire society is as interconnected as M & M Enterprises was in the famous coals-to-Newcastle section of *Catch-22*, in which Milo's syndicate spreads out to cover the globe. There is the secret underground network of nuclear weapons systems and of hideaways for the privileged in case of an attack; there are the economic connections symbolized by the Japanese purchase of Rockefeller Center; there are communications networks in which virtual reality becomes actuality, as in the PABT wedding scene. The narrator knows all this and the world of the afterlife as well. He sees Satan's respect for George C. Tilyou and knows why J. P. Morgan is "gimlet-eyed and eternally furious" (367). The omniscient narrator is like a god, and his sections of the novel are his revelation.

Conversely, the narrator is a powerful comic performer, so confident that he reveals the mechanisms of his own performance. He assumes a stance similar to the famous narrator of *Vanity Fair*: "Ah! *Vanitas Vanitatum!* Which of us is happy in this world? Which of us has his desire? or, having it, is satisfied?—Come children, let us shut up the box and the puppets, for our play is played out."[32] With such devices as chapter titles like "Entr'acte" and "Finale," he defines via his operatic analogies the terms under which his performance is to unfold, to be interpreted, and, finally, to be judged. (Heller uses the same technique in *Good As Gold* when he makes the titles of Bruce Gold's articles structural principles for his own chapter.) Once the workings of the narrator's blackly comic prose opera have been opened up for inspection, his performance is demystified. It is only a fiction. Yet when this unveiling takes place, the audience as well as the narrator is implicated in what has occurred. Recognizing the illusions upon which the narrator has hung his performances for what they are, the audience discovers its own compositional role, helping to transform "Entr'acte" into a novelistic "musical interlude" and a "Finale" into an operatic wrap-up. Having peered into the secret working of the military-industrial complex and shared the fictional enterprise that accomplished this inspection, Heller's late twentieth-century audience will find it as difficult as Thackeray's Victorian one did to separate themselves from the narrator's vision of the vanity of human endeavors.

Through the medium of the omniscient narrator's art, the "Finale" becomes a fictional apocalypse, a last revelatory gesture in which all perishes. The nuclear attack occurs because the Little Prick mistakes the nuclear attack apparatus for *Triage*, his favorite virtual reality video game. "Call [the bombers and missles] all back," he tells his aides when he finds out what he has done, "Say I am sorry. I didn't do it on purpose" (443).[33] Yossarian and Melissa are caught in the Armageddon that follows; so are Sammy and Claire, their narratives subsumed by the omniscient narrator's god-like performance. The dead—Lew Rabinowitz and Kid Sampson and McWatt from *Catch-22*—as well as the living have a part to play; Sampson and McWatt, for example, are resurrected as crewmen aboard the Sub-Supersonic Invisible and Noiseless Defensive Second-Strike Offensive Attack Bomber. The damned—Lucifer, Satan, Tilyou, and General Groves (who was the military commander of the Manhattan Project)—discover the temporality of underworld empires: "Even hell was not forever" (457). All the characters make their brief appearance on the narrator's stage, living out a choice that will be their last, a fulfillment as it were of what they have been, although they don't know this. Only the narrator perceives the unity of all this.[34] In this narrative apocalypse all is present and complete, poised for what will happen next.

▧

Death as Intermezzo: Kilroy Dies, but Yossarian Lives

With the death of Kilroy, the disembodied omnipresent G.I. of World War II, Joseph Heller reforges his dead-child story, even as he apparently debases it. After the wrenching deaths of Snowden in *Catch-22*, Slocum's son in *Something Happened*, and Absalom in *God Knows*, Kilroy's death seems, at first glance, a whimper, a comic anticlimax. Predictably, Heller situates the death in his penultimate chapter, a brief four-page chapter titled "Entr'acte." This maneuver, seemingly, reduces it to a narrative function, a means to get from here to there. In this self-parodic version of the dead-child story, it is death by natural causes: "It was cancer. Of the prostate, the bone, the lungs, and the brain" (439). Kilroy has simply gotten old and died; never mind that he never existed in the first place, even in the novel. However, Kilroy's death also comprises the story of *Closing Time*, providing both its narrative source and its Snowden-like secret. Like the tolling funeral bells of John Donne's famous "Meditation XVII," it announces all of our deaths, albeit in a fashion requiring self-reflexive laughter rather than funereal contemplation.[35]

Kilroy's death constitutes one of the paradoxes of which Heller is so fond: it is a death that is not a death. In linguistic terms, Kilroy is a sign with no actual referent and no acknowledged author. Heller emphasizes this point with a series of jokes. For example, Yossarian knows that Kilroy was alive because he had been in the stockade in which Yossarian himself was locked up and had been in the same college library stacks after the war as Yossarian. Or, as Yossarian explains to his son Michael, who has never heard of Kilroy, "Kilroy was everywhere you went in World War II —you saw it written on a wall. We don't know anything about him either. That's the only reason we still like him" (240). Despite the physical attribution of cancer as the cause, Kilroy's death is a verbal event. It occurs when his name disappears from the plaque beneath the New York Port Authority Terminal—the missing sign purportedly designating the "actual" death. Ever attuned to mortality, Yossarian has previously anticipated this passing when he hears the calliope in Tilyou's infernal Coney Island play the Siegfried funeral music from *Götterdämmerung*. Within the novel, Heller's Wagnerian joke, however, has serious implications, for the announcement of Kilroy's death coincides with the alarm bells signalling the nuclear apocalyse that closes the novel. As even this brief sketch suggests, Kilroy's death marks an immensely complicated textual event.

The chapter title "Entr'acte" directs attention to the role Kilroy's death plays in the novel's discourse. It is death as intermezzo, the musical analogy defining the narrative—and meta-operatic—work that the episode performs. Earlier, in another connection, Heller used Wagnerian analogies to set up this work: "Think of this episode as an entr'acte. . . . Like Wagner's music for Siegfried's Rhine Journey and Funeral Music in the *Götterdämmerung*, or that interlude of clinking anvils in *Das Rheingold*" (317). In *Götterdämmerung*, the Funeral Music recapitulates the various musical themes connected with the Siegfried story and distills their essence, conveying the loss of "a fearless human being . . . who never cease[d] to love."[36] The tragic music consoles as well as foreshadows the destruction ahead: Brünnhilde's suicide and the razing of Valhalla. As novelistic musical interlude, the chapter similarly forms a bridge; it connects Yossarian's self-proclaimed Rhine Journey, which culminates in the Minderbinder-Maxon marriage, with the nuclear apocalypse of the last chapter during which he is redeemed by his love for Melissa. Like the Funeral Music (or Snowden's death in *Catch-22*), it also compresses Yossarian's story, so that it can be re-heard, its meaning powerfully intensified. Heller's discourse succeeds where Yossarian has thus far failed; it transforms his pursuit of Melissa and of financial security into a Rhine Journey and him into one capable of love.

As a variant upon the dead-child story, Kilroy's death also constitutes the story of *Closing Time*, designating both its source and destination. Heller acknowledges as much when Yossarian and Sammy Singer talk about what Snowden's death has meant to them. As we have seen, Snowden is the source of the narratable, the dramatic element that gives each something to talk about: "It's funny about Snowden. . . . I didn't know him that well. . . . But now I feel he was one of my closest friends" (356). As in *Catch-22*, the friendship metaphor is absolutely crucial.[37] The barely known other becomes friend—is familiarized—when his story is perceived and related, a point that Heller underscores by giving Snowden the first name Howard in *Closing Time*. The relation—the telling—must also perforce manifest the identity of the teller, the teller's sense of what is real and crucially important, Snowden's secret being the premier example of this in Heller's fiction. As this reading suggests, the familiarization of the stranger occurs within the perceiver, thereby forging a companionability between teller and told. This process reconstitutes relationships, rendering

Snowden—whom Yossarian never noticed until he attended to his death and whom Singer barely noticed—the closest of friends. The companionability of teller and tale is crucial in Heller's fictional world, for his characters almost never have it with each other. Only the story itself—that of Snowden, Kilroy, and of all Heller's dead children—finally matters, for it makes possible the human intersections where meaning, albeit tentatively and incompletely, can be shared between army buddies, like Sammy and Yossarian; between fathers and sons, like Yossarian and Michael; between an author and his readers, like Heller and us.

If Kilroy serves as the figure in the carpet of *Closing Time*, his story is as varied as the carpet itself, its meaning as many-hued as an Isfahani carpet. The Kilroy story parodies Heller's masterplot by replacing the child with a sign, a signifier whose meaning depends upon its having no actual referent; it refigures Snowden's death as a memorial for the passing of the World War II generation; it unfolds variations on the core Heller plot pattern of fathers who injure or kill their sons or of fathers who are too ineffectual to protect them. The Kilroy story proclaims the finality of death, even as it asserts that "Yossarian lives." Out of Kilroy's death, as out of Snowden's viscera, the genetic coding for all of Heller's fiction emerges: "Man was matter; that was Snowden's secret" (*Catch-22* 429–30). In this cosmological moment, all of Heller's novels begin and end. With Kilroy's death, Heller insists that we readers experience the immanence of our mortality and that we acknowledge what he believes is virtually an apocalyptic certainty. Yet, paradoxically, he asserts that we, like Yossarian, should vow "to live forever or die in the attempt."

The self-parodic mode gives the masterplot a lighter tone. Kilroy is everywhere in the novel, as he indeed was for the war generation: in library stacks and on bus station walls, in Korea and Vietnam as well as wartime Europe, and most crucially on a plaque near the entrance to the sub-basements of the New York Port Authority Bus Terminal. Like Beckett in *Waiting for Godot*, Heller makes a name the object of expectation for characters and audience alike. The narrative audience believes in Kilroy's existence and senses his passing, just as Yossarian does. In narrative terms, Heller reworks the same pattern that he used in *Catch-22* with "where are the Snowdens of yesteryear," although placing, in this instance, the emphasis on the sign rather than upon the referent. Snowden's secret—of which his viscera is the bloody representation—is replaced by a word that has no corporeal manifestation and thus whose meaning is not easily encapsulated or conveyed. Of course, the famous World War II slogan—"Kilroy was here"—did not mean what it said either, affirming neither Kilroy's existence nor his past presence. His disappearance or death simply reverses the process, erasing what never was.

But, like most of Heller's jokes, the death of Kilroy conveys a serious point. Heller underscores its seriousness by placing its notice in the infernoesque underworld beneath the Port Authority. For Heller, Kilroy's death partakes of another order of experience from Snowden's, but one just as intimately bound up with human mortality. It connotes the passing of the World War II generation, the generation who know who Kilroy is and what he represents. Others may use the name Kilroy, as soldiers did in Korea and Vietnam, but the experience in which the name originated and became meaningful is passing out of existence with the war generation. Yossarian himself senses this when he intuits Kilroy's death: "Kilroy, immortal, was dead too, had died in Korea if not Vietnam" (340). The problem that Heller is getting at is one of history—not of its public events, not of its battles, its heroes or its villains, but of the private experience of its participants. As signified by details like Sammy Singer's father's gas mask, such experiences pass out of existence with their participants. Efforts to transmit them inevitably fall short, as does Yossarian's own attempt to explain Kilroy to his son Michael.

In Yossarian's explanation to Michael, Heller renders the Kilroy story a testimonial to the passing of the war generation. Lamenting his aging and a world in which "so many people like" Michael have never heard of Kilroy or, having heard, do not understand its meaning, Yossarian says (and Heller jokes), "I can't always remember what I meant to remember. I talk a lot and say things twice. I talk a lot and say things twice. My bladder a little, and my hair. . ." (240). Middle-aged and older readers will wince at this, even as they laugh. They experience time differently from the young, perceiving in its passage the insistent reminders of personal mortality. In such lines, there is also the beginnings of song, an elegy for what has been and for those who have lived it. Here again is the opening to the novel: "When people our age speak of the war it is not of Vietnam but of the one that broke out more than *half a century ago* and swept in almost all the world" (emphasis added, 11). With his opening, Heller defines the stance that the authorial reader must assume, simultaneously as part of the war generation that is passing and as one of its mourners.

For such deaths, elegies must be composed, and Sammy Singer—his name signifying his function—does the singing. His narrative mourns the deaths of his wife and his best friend Lew Rabinowitz and laments the passing of the Coney Island that he, Rabinowitz, Yossarian, and Heller all shared. It is narrative by indirection, for Singer has difficulty articulating the loss that he feels. "I am only marking time," he says, "I expect nothing much new and good to happen to me again" (377). In the face of such desolation, he remembers rather than anticipates, numbering the losses from the war, on Coney Island, and in his life, especially the suicide of his adopted son Michael. The opening of chapter 17, "Sammy," provides a paradigmatic instance of this: "Knee-action wheels. I doubt I know more than a dozen people from the old days who might remember those automobile ads" (205). In such cataloguings, Sammy Singer's narrative becomes dirge-like, "All that is gone" (205). Indeed. However, the significance of the losses lies less in the urban blight of Coney Island or in his dead wife and son than in himself. Singer's recollections convince him that he has been a bystander for much of his life and that life—the quality of living that he associates with Yossarian—has passed him by. "I've missed out on much, and now that I no longer have it, mere happiness was not enough" (393).

Although Singer cannot himself compose a formal elegy for such losses, he becomes Heller's vehicle for transmitting elegiac emotion. Just as *Closing Time* opens with Singer's announcing the passing of the war generation, it also closes with him. As the nuclear night sets in, a disaster of which he is unaware, Sammy settles back in his airline seat to listen to Mahler's Fifth Symphony and to read Thomas Mann's eight stories (almost certainly *Death in Venice*). In such activities, he does not pass gently into that good night: "Listening again, he discovered more new things he treasured. The remarkable symphony was infinite in its secrets and multiple satisfactions, ineffable in loveliness, sublime, and hauntingly mysterious in the secrets of its power and genius to so touch the human soul. He could hardly wait for the closing notes of the finale to speed jubilantly to their triumphant end, in order to start right back at the beginning and revel again in all of the engrossing movements in which he was basking now" (464). In this way, Heller ends the novel elegiacally, marking the passing of the war generation (and of the world in which he himself lives) and preserving life. Via Singer, Heller surely speaks personally as well, sharing his own sensations in listening to Mahler's Fifth Symphony. He uses the music to represent life: his, Singer's, other veterans', the Jewish people's, and finally all of ours. To adapt Walter Benjamin, Heller's "gift is the ability to relate his life; his distinction, to be able to tell his entire life. . . . The story teller is the figure in which the righteous man encounters himself."[38]

Heller recapitulates his various dead-child stories with Kilroy's death and comments upon their meaning. He is most concerned with the fathers' views of these deaths for, as he announced with "The Miracle of Danrossane" and "Crippled Phoenix," the father is always complicit in them. These aspects of the Kilroy plot become clear in the way that Heller uses the name Michael for the sons of Sammy Singer, Yossarian, and Lew Rabinowitz.[39] Just as Kilroy comes to stand for all World War II G.I.s, so do the Michaels come to represent all sons, with each Michael embodying an aspect of the dead-child story. Clinically depressed, Michael Singer commits suicide, despite his parents' efforts to combat his illness. He hangs himself on Fire Island, and Sammy cuts the corpse down so that neighbors will not have to share the grizzly sight. The death recalls that of Slocum's son in *Something Happened*, for Fire Island is where Heller, as he tells it, conceived the novel, including the ending. It also points to Absalom's death in *God Knows*, although there the son's own hair causes the hanging. As always, the effects of the death radiate outward: Glenda Singer soon dies of cancer, her death hastened by her broken spirit over her son's death. In the aftermath of these deaths, Sammy experiences the loneliness for which others' company provides little solace.

Michael Rabinowitz outlives his father, but in Heller's world, the loving father will nevertheless bear responsibility for his death. His birth was an accident, a diaphragm slipped and an unwanted pregnancy occurred after Lew knew that he had Hodgkin's disease. "[W]e . . . had our little Michael, I felt so good. It's a way we showed confidence. We named him after my father. Mikey, we called him, and still do when we're kidding around. I felt so vibrant I could have had a hundred more. His Jewish name is Moishe, which was the Jewish name of my father. . . . But now I worry about Michael, little Mikey, because apart from money, I don't know what I'm leaving him in the way of genes, and his 'natural biological destiny,' and the other kids too, and maybe even my grandchildren. Those fucking genes. They're mine and won't listen to me? I can't believe that" (152). Within the novel, such genes foretell the future, a future mapped out by Kilroy's cancer of the prostate, lungs, and brain. Lew's life furnishes the script for Michael's. Lew, the strongest character in the novel, dies physically and emotionally emaciated, the happiness and luck of life largely displaced by the desire to die. Heller's message in this is not unlike that of the chorus at the end of *Oedipus Rex*:

> Let every man in mankind's frailty
> Consider his last day; and let none
> Presume on his good fortune until he finds
> Life, at his death, a memory without pain.[40]

Michael Yossarian is another maimed son, damaged by his father's love for him. In a symbolically resonant moment, Yossarian intervenes to rescue Michael after he has been falsely arrested in the Port Authority Bus Terminal. Using the persona "Major John Yossarian, retired," he successfully bullies the Port Authority police into releasing Michael, but in the process psychologically disables him. The episode confirms Michael's sense that he is unable to solve his own problems.[41] Similarly, Yossarian ethically compromises and emotionally weakens Michael by securing for him the position as a commercial artist for M & ME & A. Overriding his son's objections to working the Noiseless Defensive Second-Strike Offensive Attack Bomber project, Yossarian provides a convenient fiction so that Michael can "put [his] conscience at rest" (185). However, the scheme backfires for, while Michael accepts the contract, he cannot accept the view of the future that his father holds out for him, one "in which he could flourish with . . . more security and satisfaction" (188). When the novel ends, Michael's pessimism is confirmed. With the alarms for the nuclear attack going off, Michael senses that either he or his father is dying; a Heller reader knows which one. In terms of Heller's masterplot, "the resurrection of optimism" that saves the father is purchased at the cost of the son's death (461).

Kilroy's death by cancer is symbolically resonant in another sense as well, for it provides a contemporary gloss to the secret of Snowden's entrails. Cancer is everywhere in the novel. Lew Rabinowitz dies of cancer, so does Glenda Singer, as do Betty Abrams and Lila Gross, actual friends of Heller. Cancer of the larynx silences the Belgian patient, but it also educates him to Heller's message of mortality: "this sick man of Europe shared an additional secret, his absolute belief that nothing he, his colleagues, or any organization of experts could do would have any enduring corrective effect" (447). Cancer can be resisted, as Lew Rabinowitz does for twenty-eight years. But the costs of the resistance, especially the effects of the chemotherapy, are frightful. In detailing Lew's nausea and vomiting, Heller relentlessly depicts the quality of life when food becomes like poison that must be spewed out. The refrain about the green-apple taste provides a stark demonstration of a sickness that makes the sufferer yearn for death. In the terms of the novel, cancer constitutes "the natural biological destiny" of humanity (152).

And so it is that Kilroy's death refigures and extends the signficance of Heller's core message—man is matter. If Kilroy is himself disembodied, his authors are not; they live the secret of Snowden's entrails. They are matter, and they are dying. And yet there is the "tock" to the "tick" of Heller's narrative clock, "Kilroy was dead."

> "It could be worse," said Gaffney, sympathizing. "At least Yossarian is alive."
> "Sure," said McBride, like a hearty fellow. "Yossarian still lives."
> (439)

While Heller discarded "Yossarian Lives" as the title for his sequel, he never changed the conception it signalled. Yossarian lives. Heller cannot have it otherwise: "Should I ever write another sequel," he says, "[Yossarian] would still be around at the end. Sooner or later, I must concede, Yossarian now 70, will have to pass away too. But it won't be by my hand."[42] Snowden's death begot Yossarian's Sweden. In his film, Mike Nichols captures this spirit with his final frames of Yossarian in the lifeboat. Heller approves, just as he appreciates the jaunty figure on the dust jacket for *Closing Time*. As Kilroy's death signifies, it may be "closing time" for the World War II generation, but Yossarian, the embodiment of its spirit, is again in motion as the novel ends.

This time he is bounding up an escalator in search of Melissa Mac-Intosh, "stimulated joyously by a resurrection of optimism more native to Melissa than himself, the innate—and inane—conviction that nothing harmful could happen to him, that nothing bad could happen to a just man" (461). In part, this ending takes its meaning from the ending of *Catch-22*, in which Yossarian jumps sideways to escape the knife of Nate-ly's whore. Yossarian races into the nuclear darkness to find Melissa and to assume responsibilities for their unborn child (surely a son). His inane conviction that goodness prevails bespeaks a triumph of the spirit, the obverse of the message of Snowden's entrails. In this moment, he is a comic Job, transfiguring the biblical hero's angry questions about justice into ironic humor. He recovers his goodness by asserting and acting upon it; he is Job and he provides his own voice from the whirlwind. Yossarian "had no doubt then that all three of them, he, Melissa, and the new baby, would survive, flourish, and live happily—forever after" (461). Yossarian has changed direction, committing himself to become a protagonist in a marriage.

"Forever after" replaces Sweden as Yossarian's and, by extension, Heller's destination. The fiction-making power of the comic hero is poised against the apocalyptic repercussions of society's fictions, figured by a bumbling president who initiates a nuclear attack because he cannot differentiate between a video game and the war-making machinery. Almost seventy, Yossarian defies the logic of mortality and personal circumstance by starting another family. Stepping out into the darkness for which there may be no dawn, he insists that the free individual is more powerful than social forces, even than atomic weapons. Such convictions scorn rational belief. Seemingly, they also ignore the secret of Snowden's entrails. However, in fact, Yossarian's convictions and the choices that they prompt preserve his life and confirm that "Yossarian lives." As in *Catch-22*, he eschews a choice affording personal safety for an impossibility. "[L]iving happily—forever after" is more grandiose than living forever or dying in the attempt; it is also more illusory. Yet, via Yossarian, Heller insists upon the necessity for such illusions; it is his comic version of the Socratic wisdom "that the really important thing is not to live, but to live well."[43]

Heller's aspirations show through in his Preface to the Special Edition of *Catch-22*. He quotes with approbation the opening to Richard Starnes's February 28, 1962, column in *The New York World-Telegram* about *Catch-22*: "Yossarian will, I think, live a very long time" (Preface 15). Such is also his author's deepest desire. With the publication of *Closing*

Time, Joseph Heller simultaneously furthers and places in jeopardy Mr. Starnes's prediction. He has brought Yossarian into human time and joined his fate to the World War II generation for whom it is now closing time. Therein lies a crucial element of the risk: Heller's Yossarian may pass away with this generation and its children, who made *Catch-22* a publishing sensation in the sixties and seventies. And yet, like great comic novelists from Cervantes onward, Heller seeks to create a character who remakes the world, who insists that imagination is more powerful than reality—and who lives on, enspiriting readers no longer familiar with the historical circumstances in which he came about.

ALLUSIONS: QUOTING EMOTION, PROJECTING A VISION, CONSTRUCTING A CONTEXT

Joseph Heller believes that he has little facility for "literary language," the language that he associates with Shakespeare, Dante, Mann, Faulkner, and Dickens, among others.[44] For him, such language concentrates emotion and meaning with arresting power. If he were a poet, he might say with Emily Dickinson: "If I read a book [and] it makes my whole body so cold no fire ever can warm me I know *that* is poetry. If I feel physically as if the top of my head were taken off, I know *that* is poetry."[45] As an author, Joseph Heller has never had any confidence that he could blow anyone's head off. In his novels, the necessary concentration of meaning and sentiment would discomfit him. In this, he is not unlike his protagonist King David, who cannot voice a simple "I love you" without embarrassment. Emotion articulated—a source of power for literary language—renders him uncertain. The effort to express it frequently translates in Heller's ears into sentimentality.[46] So previously Heller has suppressed emotion as in *Catch-22* or has rendered it as bathetic and suspicious as in *Something Happened* or has distanced it with ironic humor as in *God Knows*. Yet the events that energize his imagination—Snowden's death, Luciana's wounding, and so on—invite an emotional response. In *Closing Time* more than in any previous novel, Heller finds in allusions a narrative device that enables him to express emotion. These allusions simultaneously provide the vehicle for Heller's vision.

Heller has always been fond of allusions, including emotionally evocative ones, but he has chiefly used them for ironic and parodic effects, as,
for example, by punctuating the famous biblical elegy about the death of
Jonathan with David's crass commentary, or by fracturing them: "April
had been the best month of all for Milo. . . . April was spring, and in the
spring Milo Minderbinder's fancy had lightly turned to thoughts of tanger-
ines" (*Catch-22* 246). While still exploiting allusions for ironic effect,
Heller uses them in *Closing Time* to voice emotion, to insert the sensations
occasioned by such works as Dante's *Inferno*, Mann's novels, Mahler's
Fifth Symphony, and Wagner's *Ring Cycle* into his own text. For Heller,
music in particular evokes the sensations that seem to elude expression in
the language of all but the most gifted of writers. In *No Laughing Matter*,
he describes these effects and how the sensations can be elicited in others.
In the intensive care unit of Mount Sinai Hospital, Brahms concertos, Beethoven quartets, and "anything and everything by Bach" become the antidote to the frightened, lonely self-consciousness and self-absorption
induced by his physical paralysis (*Matter* 80). In this state, the choral music of Bach's Saint Matthew's Passion is as "soothing and sublime as anything ever conceived by the mind of man" (*Matter* 80). As importantly,
such sensations can be shared with others. He can loan the Passion to a
fellow patient or can persuade his nurses to play one of his cassettes on a
recorder at the nurses' station: "There followed an extraordinary ten minutes, both charmed and unreal, in which everyone present was brought to a
standstill by the bars of music flowing so melodic and ethereal, of a different world—everyone sentient, that is" (*Matter* 81).[47] By contrast, in his
previous writing the affective dimensions of music and art could be experienced by the protagonist, but the protagonist could never impart them to
others, even to intimates. The plots of "Make Room for Renoir," "'Catch-
22' Revisited," *God Knows*, and *Picture This* highlight the impossibility
of communities of feeling like the one in the Mount Sinai I.C.U. that De-
cember night in 1982. In *Closing Time*, he creates a world akin to that of
the hospital intensive care ward and into this world inserts via allusion the
music and language that produce the emotionally heightened consciousness that was shared there.

The allusions of *Closing Time* derive their force and vision from the
proximity of death. In this, they further the elegiac mood that pervades the
novel. Typically, Heller locates these allusions in characters, so that the
particular allusion draws its significance from the user as well as from the
work to which it refers. Heller's allusions to Mann, especially to *Death in
Venice* and *Dr. Faustus*, illustrate this process—the way that he locates
them in character and the effects that he derives from this. For Yossarian,
Mann's novels constitute a frame of reference, a way for him to interpret
his experience and to make it comprehensible to others. For Heller, Yos-

sarian's allusions become a device for making Yossarian's experiences representative, much as Mann's protagonists Aschenbach and Leverkühn are representative figures of different moments in twentieth-century German culture. Because the allusions both delineate the consciousness of characters within the novel and point to the state of culture outside it, they complicate the text, opening up a network of unexpected significances and meanings. Yossarian's noticing a red-haired man with a walking stick and green rucksack near Rockefeller Center is a case in point, for this man to Yossarian's mind is the same fellow who appeared near the mortuary chapel at the beginning of Mann's novella.

The unknown red-headed man serves Heller as he did Mann, occasioning a proleptic version of the story that follows. Before spying the stranger, Mann's artist hero, Gustav Aschenbach, had been contemplating the "mystical meanings" of the inscriptions on a mortuary chapel, an aesthetically detached and intellectualized way of contemplating death. The stranger awakens Aschenbach to his own dissatisfactions, although Aschenbach is unable to decipher if it is the stranger's pilgrim-like air or his physical attractiveness that has such an epiphanic effect on him. In any case, Aschenbach experiences an overpowering desire to travel and immediately has a hallucinatory vision of the world such travel would open up to him: "He beheld a landscape, a tropical marshland, beneath a reeking sky, steaming, monstrous, rank—a kind of primeval wilderness-world of islands, morasses, and alluvial channels" (Mann 5). In nightmare form, this is the Venice in which Aschenbach finds the Polish youth Tadzio whose beauty transfixes him, and it is the city where he dies, as he lived, contemplating a world in which he could never bring himself to participate. Although Aschenbach never realizes it, he has been impelled all his life by an attraction to death; the red-haired stranger personifies this attraction.

By his own admission, Yossarian identifies with Aschenbach much more closely than he cares to admit (243). Thus, not surprisingly, when Yossarian spies Mann's red-headed stranger at the Rockefeller Center it initiates a more complicated story than he realizes, one in which his own attraction to death is revealed. Like Aschenbach, Yossarian has been contemplating the signs of death before his attention is arrested by the stranger. Death—in his glib allusive joke to "The Waste Land"—is personified by New York City middle-class subway riders: "He had not thought American-free market capitalism had undone so many of its disciples" (234). Of course, chief among the casualties is Yossarian himself, although he does not apprehend this. His sexual desire—Heller's representation of Yossarian's vitality—is gone. He can tell Melissa that he would like to make love to her each day, but he knows that this is a lie. "Desire is starting to fail me," he tells his son Michael, and unable to get Michael to understand what he means, he summarizes *Death in Venice* for him. "Aschenbach too had run out of interests. . . . He was an artist of the intellect, who had tired of working on projects that would no longer yield to even his most patient effort, and knew he now was faking it. But he did not know that his creative life was over and that he and his era were coming to a close" (242–43). This describes Yossarian as well, save for his self-awareness. Self-consciousness can rescue Yossarian from Aschenbach's fate, but it cannot reveal to him that he, like Mann's hero, has a deep attraction to death. His joke about the Port Authority Bus Terminal— "Is that my Venice?"—is Heller's version of Aschenbach's hallucination. It is, as we shall see, simultaneously Heller's (and Yossarian's) version of Dante's *Inferno* and Wagner's *Götterdämmerung*.

In his plot summary of *Death in Venice*, Yossarian communicates much more to Heller's authorial reader than he does to Michael, who has read the novel but remembers little about it. His recounting is another of the stories about the secrets of mortality that fathers try and fail to relate to their sons. It is connected to Heller and the Frenchman's desire to explain to their sons the perils of war in "'Catch-22' Revisited," to Starkey's task of apprising each son who appears on stage that he will die in a bombing raid in *We Bombed in New Haven*, to Slocum's efforts to warn his son about the dangers of pristine innocence in *Something Happened*, and to David's ineffectual responses to Amnon, Absalom, and Solomon in *God Knows*. However, the truth of mortality can be understood only when death is proximate, and paradoxically, as we have seen, in Heller's fictional world the sons embody its proximity. Like his predecessors, Michael can hear the story but cannot understand its import. He responds to Yossarian's retelling: "you might be trying to make it sound better than it really is" (243). Yossarian's own poignant but futile observation—"But it remains unforgettable"—highlights what Michael has forgotten and will never understand (242). With the nuclear bombers and missiles in the air at the novel's end, Michael has "the listless, desolate feeling" of impending death, but he does not recall his father's story about the locus of this feeling. And now it is too late for him re-read *Death in Venice*.

Yossarian's précis functions as a *mis en abyme* for Joseph Heller, the acclaimed author of *Catch-22*, in particular its account of a writer whose "true creative life was over." Reviewers claim to find evidence of this decline in *Closing Time*, as many have ever since *Catch-22*. With Yossarian's musings, Heller, however, anticipates and parries such reviews and criticisms—not because he can be certain that his creativity is undiminished; he can't. But he can use his most famous protagonist's ruminations upon *Death in Venice* to share and to comment upon his own dilemma as the author of *Catch-22* and to lampoon critics who are too easily and unreflectively dismissive of *Closing Time*. Chances are such readers are like

Michael Yossarian with respect to Mann's novella. They have read without understanding, including what his novel says about them and their situation during "closing time." They have not heard Heller define his own aspirations for the novel in his allusions to Mann, Dante, and Wagner. Most simply, he hopes that Yossarian's Aschenbach-like state has begotten his own Mann-like novel, one that encapsulates an era and self-consciously reflects and comments on its end. If he fails in this, so be it, but he has succeeded far beyond the expectations of many of his critics, because they never saw what he attempted. In this, reviewers who commented upon the flagging of Heller's comic energies missed the joke that was on them.

PABT—the Port Authority Bus Terminal and Yossarian's Venice—is where many of Heller's allusions intersect. There are too many references to explore here, and so I will concentrate on the ones to Dante, for they can explain how Heller can simultaneously have PABT signify such disparate phenomena as Yossarian's Venice and his own Coney Island childhood. With his allusions to the *Inferno*, Heller follows the epic poet's lead in constructing a vision of the world in which he himself lives. Or as Michael Yossarian puts the matter, "But each time I think of that bus terminal, I imagine it's what Dante's *Inferno* might represent" (231). However, the two infernos are worlds apart. Dante's vision—his *Divine Comedy*—has its anchors in Aristotelian ethical beliefs, in which humans construct their characters by their own free choices, and in his reading of Catholic doctrine, in which God guarantees absolute justice. Heller can affirm neither belief system. His inferno—PABT and Steeplechase, George C. Tilyou's reconstructed amusement park underneath it—testifies to human victimization and to what is, for Heller, the hidden, hellish logic of capitalism.

Like Dante, Heller seeks to have his protagonist and, by extension, his readers see in a way that reeducates them to the significance of phenomena that can be observed but are almost always missed in daily life. Thus, when McBride, the Vergil figure, guides Yossarian to the locked entrance to Tilyou's domain, he points out and explains the significance of the sinned against, rather than of the sinners. McBride serves as the appropriate guide to this world because "he had never been able to outgrow the sympathy he suffered for every type of victim he encountered" (93). And there are plenty of victims among the terminal's pimps, prostitutes, petty criminals, and drug users; but most important for Heller's symbolic purposes are the three women who function like the three Fates: the one-legged woman, the brown-skinned woman in a pink chemise, and the skinny blonde with the bruised eye. In Heller's ironic reconfiguration, the Fates have become fated victims, the victims who mirror what society has already become. Dante's hell works upon the principle of symbolic retribution: the sinner's punishment is the symbolic representation of the choices he or she made in life, as for example the gluttons who lie in fetid slush while being chewed upon by Cerberus, the hound of Hell. By contrast, Heller's hell testifies to rapacious capitalism, social indifference, and the victimization that results. For example, each time the one-legged woman gets a wheelchair it is stolen from her, and when the reader first sees her, she is being raped by a "man with scrawny blanched buttocks and a livid scrotum" (97). McBride and Yossarian walk on past, as if not wanting to disturb the lovers. In order to learn what he needs to learn, Yossarian must look unflinchingly at such sights as this rape or at the nearby woman in the pink chemise with the dark, bushy armpits and an exposed vagina.[48] However, unlike the character Dante in the *Inferno*, Yossarian resists the knowledge available in these victims. "He did not know who [the woman in the chemise] was, but he knew he had not one thing he wanted to talk to her about" (97). And it does *not* occur to him, as it did to Dante, to ask the residents of hell what they could tell him.

Heller uses the character of George C. Tilyou to represent his vision of capitalism, in which each transaction victimizes. Historically, Tilyou was the entrepreneur most responsible for what Coney Island became. Like P. T. Barnum, he was a consummate showman who believed there was a sucker born every minute, and he knew how to make money off these suckers. He imported a carousel built for William II of Germany, purchased the ferris wheel from the Chicago Exposition, invented the Steeplechase (a mechanical horse race that spectators could bet on) and other attractions that have become standard amusement-park fare, and, when his amusement park burned down, charged ten cents admission to see the ruins. Heller's Tilyou has satanic power; in Heller's joke: "Even Satan called him Mr. Tilyou" (113). Playing off the inscription over the gate of Dante's Inferno—"Abandon hope all you who enter here"—the inscription on Tilyou's tombstone memorializes what he has achieved with his earthly and underworld Coney Islands: "MANY HOPES LIE BURIED HERE" (110). Among the hopes that lie buried beneath this tombstone are those of John D. Rockefeller, who comes to cadge dimes, and J. P. Morgan, who regularly needs favors. Hemingway, Faulkner, Kafka, Woolf, O'Neill, and other great Modernists also reside in Tilyou's underworld amusement park, although it is their imitators' hopes that lie buried there together with those of writers, such as Saroyan, who are no longer read.[49] The hopes of many lesser- knowns have come to rest under the tombstone as well; most notably, these include the thousands who paid nickles and dimes for the pleasures of Tilyou's Steeplechase. Ironically, however, Tilyou's own hopes perish here as well.

Like Dante's Satan, Tilyou ultimately becomes the victim of what he hoped to create. He made his fortune by supplying immediate and cheap

gratification—his amusement park was the pleasure emporium for temporary excitement and illusory satisfaction. "He had triumphed with symbols, was used to illusions. His Steeplechase ride was not really a
steeplechase, his park was not a park. His gifts were in collaborative pretense" (368). His ability to capitalize upon others' appetites blinds him to
the implications of his own greed. He locates his amusement park below
PABT and above a lake of ice, a dark woods, a desert of burning sand, and
rivers of boiling blood and pitch, never recognizing his location as that of
Dante's Inferno. The man who has counted upon his commercial imagination to turn a catastrophic fire into an opportunity for profit cannot understand why he can think of nothing to do with these surroundings. With his
eyes upon the immediately profitable, he is bewildered by Dante's symbols for eternal values and truths—the leopards, lion, dog with three
heads, and so on. With such details, Heller follows Dante's reasoning: the
damned never apprehend their damnation. They are damned because they
choose what American capitalism offers and what human nature invites,
and such choices are inevitably self-blinding.

Unlike Dante's *Divine Comedy* with its God who redeems and transfigures human tragedy, Heller's "Comedy" is an entirely humanized one,
one that exposes and entraps people in their most basic instincts. Tilyou's
reflection upon the workings of his amusement park also describes the
workings of Heller's comedy: "Mr. Tilyou relished things that surprised,
threw people into confusion, annihilated dignity, blew boy and girl clum-
sily into each other's arms, and, with luck, flashed a glimpse of calf and
petticoat, sometimes even feminine underpants, to a delighted audience
just like them who viewed the comedy of their utter, ludicrous helplessness with gaiety and laughter" (110). This description of the delights of
Tilyou's earthly and infernal Coney Island speaks to what enticed "Joey
Heller" (the character who represents his author's youth) and hundreds of
thousands of others to Steeplechase and Luna Park and to the sensations
that Heller hopes to create in the narrative audience.[50] Like many a comedian, Heller hopes to unmask his audience by exposing them as victims of
the very phenomena at which they laugh.

Yossarian is Heller's tool for accomplishing this reversal; his entrapment is the figure for that of the authorial audience. On his journey
through Tilyou's inferno, Yossarian confronts himself in every image he
sees. In Heller's Dantean logic, Tilyou's funhouse mirrors do not distort
Yossarian's image, but rather reveal his disfigured humanity. Like the residents of Dante's *Inferno*, he has become the sum of his choices; most crucially, he has become the willing, well-paid employee of M & ME & A
Enterprises, a man without qualities. Like Tilyou himself, he has cynically
cashed in on the self-deceptive greed that capitalism inspires. Looking at
image after deformed image of himself, he discovers that his "authentic

appearance, his objective structure, was no longer absolute. He had to wonder what he truly looked like" (342). He explains to himself that this disorientation must result from the funhouse illusions. But when the grotesque images resolve into clarity, he confronts the self that he resisted seeing in the one-legged woman, the woman with the exposed vagina, or the skinny blonde: "he almost swooned at a hideous glimpse of himself as homeless, abominable, filthy, and depraved" (343). He runs away from this image, only to discover other visionary manifestations, most notably of himself as Gregor Samsa encased in his own brown carapace. After many other images, one last mirror remains, one in which "he was still himself," albeit his pre-thirty self "with a blooming outlook, an optimistic figure no less comely and immortal than the lordliest divinity that ever was" (343). Like a latter-day Narcissus he moves to embrace the image, and when he does he finds himself tumbling down Tilyou's Barrel of Fun, and thus he is revealed as one more willing victim of Tilyou's enticingly tawdry delights.

In exposing his protagonist in this way, Heller follows Dante's lead in constructing a double version of himself as a man whose inner drives and desires are revealed and as the author who unfolds the story of this man. It is a remarkably daring and self-revelatory authorial maneuver, particularly for an author who feels handicapped by his lack of facility with literary language. As Yossarian enters the circle of writers, the jokes function on both narrative planes. In this scene, Yossarian is the figure for Heller, the youthful writer, and the implied author stands in for the actual writer fully aware of the risks he takes with his parodic imitation of Dante. The joke about Irving Faust—"good reviews, but never a best seller"—whom Yossarian mistakes for Dr. Faustus is typical of Heller's multi-layered comedy. With the name Irving Faust together with his unknown companion William Saroyan, Heller plays off his Irving Washington, Washington Irving jokes in *Catch-22* and pays homage to one of his authorial models, Saroyan, as he subsequently will to Hemingway as well. Yossarian's mistaken identification also serves as Heller's own comment upon his own ambitions and choices. Money—not knowledge, experience, or artistic creativity as in, respectively, Marlow's, Goethe's, and Mann's retellings of the Faust myth—may have provided the source for the Faustian bargain Heller may have made, including his well-publicized advance for *Closing Time*.[51] As revealed by Heller's portraits of the other writers in Tilyou's underworld, authorship entails many Faustian bargains: excess drinking for Hemingway and Faulkner, late-life personality disorders for James, Conrad, and Dickens; suicide for Kosinski, Woolf, Koestler, and Plath.

So it is that Yossarian strides through a world where Heller has been, the figures of his world pointing to those of his author: his mother and father, his brother Lee (Heller has a brother by this name), his Aunt Ida and

Uncle Sam (also Heller relatives), La Guardia and FDR, Joseph Kaye and good soldier Schweik, and finally the Angel of Death and Snowden.[52] With this last pair, Heller works one last turn on one of the most famous joke sequences from *Catch-22*, for Yossarian "was seeing them twice" (347). This second sight, so crucial to making sense of the *Catch-22* paradox, will eventually serve Yossarian well. But not yet. For now his double vision serves to call back McBride, who in Virgilian fashion reaches out his hand to steady the stumbling, staggering protagonist. Thus reoriented, Yossarian flees to the hospital for safety where he meets and talks with Sammy Singer about Snowden. From there, he returns to PABT for the Minderbinder-Maxon wedding he has orchestrated and during which he will find his Venice, his *Götterdämmerung*, and his way out of the Inferno.

In the PABT marriage phantasmagoria, Heller's allusive art conflates illusion and reality. As one would predict, Yossarian, who conceived the PABT wedding spectacle in the first place, becomes disoriented, unable to differentiate the past from the future or the imaginary from the purportedly real. Like Tilyou, Yossarian becomes the victim of his own artifice. He again hears Adrian Leverkühn's children's chorus from Mann's *Dr. Faustus* and almost involuntarily joins in the climax to the wedding festivities that it signals. The chorus functions as a musical version of Heller's masterplot and foreshadows Kilroy's death.

> As the dying harmonies ending *Götterdämmerung* neared conclusion, a tender children's chorus Yossarian could not remember having heard before came stealing ethereally, at first a breath, a hint, then rose gradually into an essence of its own, into a celestial premonition of pathetic heartbreak. And next, when the sweet, painful, and saddening foreshadowing was almost unbearable, there smashed in, with no warning, the shattering, unfamiliar toneless scales of unrelenting masculine voices in crashing choirs of ruthless laughter, of laughter, laughter, laughter, and this produced in the listeners a reaction of amazed relief and tremendous, mounting jollity. The audience quickly joined in with laughter of its own. (419)

Overwhelmed by the emotional power of this auditory dead-child story, Yossarian laughs, adding his voice to the raucous, masculine laughter of Leverkühn's piece. Mann's account of this laughter describes Heller's intentions in the scene: "that pandemonium of laughter, of hellish merriment. . . . beginning with the chuckle of a single voice and rapidly gaining ground, embracing choir and orchestra, frightfully swelling in rhythmic upheavals and contrary motions to a fortissimo tutti, an overwhelming, sardonically yelling, bawling, bleating, howling, piping, whinnying salvo, the mocking, exulting laughter of the Pit."[53] Although Yossarian laughs with the rest of the celebrants, he simultaneously wants to assert his detachment from the scene that he watches on the PABT Communications Center video screen, for unlike anyone else he recognizes the music as Adrian Leverkühn's *Apocalypse* and furthermore knows that it exists only in Mann's novel.[54] But he is also mesmerized by what he hears and sees, especially himself dancing in white tie and tails. Yossarian has an "abstract belief that he ought to be ashamed" but does not actually feel shame for what he has orchestrated; his conscience has been dulled by his work with M & ME & A (420). And yet the power of his imaginative response to Mann's novel—his ability to hear and recognize the music from Leverkühn's *Apocalyse*—redeems him, at least partially. He glimpses what the others do not, the coming of the end. This imaginative sensitivity will be confirmed in the "Entr'acte" when Kilroy dies. Like Snowden's, Kilroy's death turns Yossarian toward the possibilities afforded by life, life with Melissa and their unborn child.

Using the allusions to Mann's *Dr. Faustus* as well as those to the *Inferno* and the *Ring Cycle*, Heller depicts the "realities" to which the characters themselves are blind and affirms the constitutive power of art. Language, perception, and the artistic medium constitute reality; they do not simply reflect it. Heller underscores this point by making Yossarian and the others hear the *Apocalypse* coincidentally with the beginning of the nuclear attack. All of the novel's characters, including Yossarian, are responsible for this apocalypse, not just the president and the military. With its actors and actresses and its piped in diesel fumes, the PABT wedding is symptomatic of the illusions with which American society refigures actuality. Everything has been reduced to appearance, everything has become bogus and factitious: love, friendship, virtue.[55] The Minderbinders and Maxons are surrounded by their "thirty-five hundred very close friends" (409). In such a context, the "Redemption through Love" theme from *Götterdämmerung*, which plays during the nuptials, signifies the disappearance of love and the twilight of a society in which it has become such a sham.

In the PABT scenes as well as many other places in the novel, Heller borrows some literary language, but he requires the authorial reader to hear much more. To understand Yossarian's laughter in a way that he himself cannot, this reader must recall Mann's triumph in *Dr. Faustus*, constructing language so powerful that it produces music—or at least the illusion of music that Heller and other readers have heard. Yet, recognizing the allusion is not enough, for that may too easily confine it to the world of art. For unless we hear Leverkühn's *Apocalypse*—hear its story and recognize Mann's account of the Third Reich as culmination and downfall of German culture—we will neither understand the passing of the World War II generation nor understand what it portends for ourselves. Denis Diderot has observed that one should tell stories because then time passes swiftly and the story of life comes to an end unnoticed.[56] Joseph Heller would disagree. He tells stories so that he, his protagonists, and his readers can see the swift passage of time and glance noticingly to an end. One might say analogously of Heller and Yossarian what Robert Alter says of Cervantes and Don Quixote: "so Cervantes is not merely mocking chivalric romances through the Don's adventures but contemplating, in the most oblique and searching way, the unthinkable prospect posed by his own imminent end" (*Partial Magic* 244). But Heller does not possess the power of Cervantes's language.

Without such powers, Heller must educe them. So it is that Heller returns to Mann's *Death in Venice* in the novel's last paragraph, as well as to Mahler's Fifth Symphony. From Yossarian's conversations with his son and all the other allusions to Mann, the authorial reader knows what Sammy Singer will discover in these works. Unlike Yossarian, Singer has not heard Leverkühn's *Apocalypse* in PABT, nor does he know about the impending nuclear disaster. But in Mann's prose and Mahler's symphony, he hears music akin to that which Heller heard in Mount Sinai Hospital's I.C.U. "The small adagio movement later was as beautiful as beautiful melodic music could ever be. Mostly of late he preferred the melancholy to the heroic. His biggest fear now in the apartment in which he dwelt alone was a horror of decomposing there. The book he was holding in his lap when he settled back to read was a paperback edition of eight stories by Thomas Mann" (464). These are intimations only. Yet with them, Heller invites the reader to supply the music beyond, "ineffable in loveliness . . . hauntingly mysterious in the secrets of its powers and genius to so touch the human soul" (464). In this moment, the reader through the power of Heller's fabulation hears both Yossarian's Venice and Mann's novella, which Singer himself is just about to read. The "narrative amplitude and richness" reminds us that our world is "ruled by chance and given over to death" (*Partial Magic* 244–45). Yet the art that we hear accommodates us to such contingencies, those of *Closing Time* and our own lives: "The yellow moon turned orange and soon was as red as a setting sun" (464).

AFTERWORD

> This last phrase seems familiar, suddenly I
> seem to have written it somewhere before,
> or spoken it word for word. . . . [T]he plan
> I had formed, to live, and cause to live, at
> last, to play at last and die alive, was going
> the way of all my other plans.
>
> SAMUEL BECKETT, *Malone Dies*

"A free man thinks of death least of all things; and his wisdom is a meditation not of death but of life."[1] In the biography of her friend, the painter Roger Fry, Virginia Woolf quotes this line from Spinoza with approbation, and its attitude toward death might serve as an account of Woolf's own artistic aims. While it does not describe Heller's, the contrast between his point of view and hers may be instructive. As Avrom Fleishman formulates Woolf's perspective on mortality, "[s]he makes no effort to imagine post-existence, with or without memory of preexistence, presumably because even a transfer of life is an unmaking of the individual identity, and no other self can be the same. The firmness of Woolf's acceptance of the fact of death . . . is equalled only by the firmness of the attachment to the value of life" (Fleishman 178). While Heller shares Woolf's attachment to the value of life, in his fiction he never accepts death. The endings to his novels virtually shriek about its inevitability, but death remains an opponent to be grappled with, even though it cannot be overcome. To accept one's death would be tantamount to acknowledging the rightness of a bully's conquest. The rambunctious, frequently angry humor expresses Heller's own point of view; Yossarian's cry "to live forever or die in the attempt" is also Heller's. Over time, the humor darkens, becomes more scathing. "Mankind is resilient: the atrocities that horrified us a week ago become acceptable tomorrow" (*Picture This* 350).

Unlike Heller, Woolf can maintain a dual vision, which accepts death and values life, because she holds "to an ideal of a timeless life in apparent time, the transcendence to where we already are, an identity composed of relationships with others" (Fleishman 178). Heller can neither affirm a transcendence within time, nor an identity begotten and maintained by relationships. For him, time is corrosive. He cannot embrace the Platonism that Fleishman detects in Woolf, a factor that explains his choice of Aristotle, not Plato, as protagonist of *Picture This*. Heller protagonists live by struggle, their identity defined by their opponents: Yossarian's by the missions that he must fly (the missions embodying American values of the fifties); Slocum by an opponent that he will not acknowledge, himself (this self, in fact, constructed by its context, Madison Avenue and suburban America); Gold by American political attitudes of the Nixon years and by his personal aspirations; King David by a God who sanctions the death of children; and Aristotle by Platonic thought as well as by human nature, especially its willful greed and blindness. Opponents are never vanquished. Yossarian flees to Sweden or later runs to find Melissa, and Gold leaves Washington. The mortal enemy within remains: because man is matter, death is immanent. Although unconquerable, it must be resisted. Only in resistance does life in time have meaning and can individual identity be maintained. Slocum fails because he cooperates with "the company in which he works"; his son's death is the horrifying objectification of the life that he has chosen.

However, as Heller makes clear in *Closing Time*, "Yossarian lives" because he and his author defy. Like Beckett's Malone, Yossarian acknowledges that his plan to "die alive" will fail. When the novel opens, circumstance confines him: old age, family, a flagging spirit, work with M & ME & A, loss of desire, as well as impending death. Yossarian himself supplies, albeit half parodically, the analogue for his situation in the plight of Gustav Aschenbach, the protagonist of Thomas Mann's *Death in Venice*. Like Aschenbach, he has run out of interests and believes that his creative life is over. With his talent for self-pity and self-absorption, Yossarian luxuriates in the comparison. Fortunately, his imagination is also reanimated by the power of Mann's vision, as it is by his recollections of Wagner, Eliot, and Dante. Similarly, Melissa MacIntosh's engaging presence rekindles Yossarian's desire and restores his spirit. Out of living texts and a living woman, Yossarian finds the illusions necessary to rediscover a sense of purpose. He refigures Melissa as Brünnhilde and conceives their romance as operatic love. Such fictions push back circumstance by focusing on what might be or may come, thus by imbuing the present with the possible. In this attitude toward time, Yossarian embodies the comic spirit, that intensity of experience that makes the present hold the illusion of timelessness.[2] With full knowledge of the nuclear apocalypse underway, Yossarian has "no doubt . . . [that] he, Melissa, and the new baby, would survive, flourish, and live happily—forever after" (461).

Such a comic affirmation is more difficult for Joseph Heller, the author of *Closing Time*. As he describes the novel's thesis, "things are coming to an end."[3] Like the novel's characters, Heller has observed the transformation of Coney Island from a wonderfully exciting amusement park and neighborhood into the tawdry, crime-ridden remnants of what once was. As Heller portrays the change, the Edenic world of his youth has given way to an urban hell; it has become PABT, the infernoesque world of pimps, prostitutes, homeless, drug addicts, and panhandlers. Similarly, like his characters, Heller participates in the passing of the war generation. Cancer, senility, depression—these are among the late-life manifestations of Snowden's secret. Man is matter, but in old age, this truth does not slide dramatically out onto a bomber floor as it did during the war. Rather it is a more quotidian reality, embodied in arthritic aches, sagging flesh, and insistent worries. In old age time wears, making minutes seem like hours, days like months, and months like years. At such times, the need for comedy is never greater, occasioning the hope for the laughter and the release that the comic moment affords. In *Closing Time* as in *Catch-22*, such a moment is, paradoxically, embodied in Snowden's entrails. Speaking for Heller, Sammy Singer reflects back upon the meaning of Snowden's death: "But it gave me an episode, something dramatic to talk about, and something to make me remember that the war was really real" (356). Like *Catch-22*, *Closing Time* has its genesis in an intense awareness of personal mortality, and, as in *Catch-22*, its humor originates in Snowden's viscera. From such auguries, Heller follows the steps of seers of old and unlocks stories, whether those stories be the liver and tomato episodes of *Catch-22* or the extended Kilroy joke of *Closing Time*.

As *Closing Time* decisively demonstrates, Heller has never left the territory of *Catch-22*, never stopped writing its story, even during his journeys to biblical Judea in *God Knows* and to Rembrandt's seventeenth-century studio in *Picture This*. The territory of human mortality has always provided the catalyst to his imagination. His vision of it is unchanging, although its articulation varies: "Man was matter," he says in *Catch-22*, "Set fire to him and he'll burn" (429–30); or in *God Knows* David speaks for him, "I hate God and I hate life. And the closer I come to death, the more I hate life" (9). Or in *Picture This*, he asserts that Plato is wrong about the death of Socrates—"Death by hemlock is not as peaceful and painless as he portrays: there is retching, slurring of speech, convulsions, and uncontrollable vomiting" (350). For Heller, death situates human life, the grave controlling existence as inexorably as gravity controls motion.

Each of Heller's novels, however, resists this truth, as if re-enacting Yossarian's rebellion. In this resistance, Heller descends from Shahrazad, the heroine of *The Thousand Nights and a Night*, and his novels from its 1001 stories.[4] Shahrazad spins her stories in order to save herself from a king who would kill her after sleeping with her. As long as the king remains enchanted by them, life will outwit death. The stories of *The Thousand Nights and a Night* follow a similar logic; one can remake the conditions of life, circumventing even death. Story after story implicitly articulates the claim that reality can be transformed to accommodate human wishes. Like Shahrazad, Heller believes that while telling his stories he cannot die. While "Yossarian lives," so must he.[5]

Like the king, we readers anticipate the coming installment of Heller's masterplot. However, our hopes for the story differ from his; they are more like Yossarian's with respect to Snowden and to his dying words, "I'm cold" (429). Like Yossarian, we believe the meaning of life is revealed in death. Speaking to this, Walter Benjamin observes: "The novel is significant, therefore, not because it presents someone else's fate to us, perhaps didactically, but because this stranger's fate by virtue of the flame which consumes it yields us the warmth which we never draw from our own fate. What draws the reader to the novel is the hope of warming his shivering life with a death he reads about."[6] Benjamin's analogies—the reader and the shivering human being, the novel and the burning log, the reader's mortality and that which he or she reads about—insist that readers consume that which sustains their interest. Applied to *Catch-22* and *Closing Time*, this means that our warmth is gained at the expense of the novel and of Snowden's death. It follows that our expectations exact their cost on authors as well. Like the rapacious king of *The Thousand Nights and a Night*, we can dispatch the storyteller—at least figuratively—if we become dissatisfied with the tale. (Arguably, many reviewers, readers, and critics have done this to Heller by measuring each subsequent novel against *Catch-22*.) But then again, renewal is possible. At the end of each story, Shahrazad begins anew, forestalling the time when the king's interest will fade, fulfilling his expectations by stymieing or recreating or deferring them. Similarly Heller, by narrating afresh his resistance to his mortality, enables our accommodation to our own.

Heller is not, of course, the only modern author to write out of such a sensibility. Samuel Beckett's conclusion to *The Unnamable* perhaps provides the most memorable formulation for this viewpoint. Beckett's narrator confirms his existence by narrating, even as his novel lapses into silence: "I can't go on, you must go on, I'll go on, you must say words, as long as there are any . . . it will be the silence, where I am, I don't know, I'll never know, in the silence you don't know, you must go on, I can't go on, I'll go on."[7] This formulation, its halting cadences and uneven rhythms, might stand for the trajectory of Heller's career. Thirteen years pass between the publication of most of his stories and *Catch-22*; thirteen more before *Something Happened* appears, then after a five-year hiatus his next four novels appear within a fifteen-year span. Beckett's formulation also approximates the rhythms of the novels themselves—Gold's delay in taking up his pen to write his book on the contemporary Jewish experience; the pell-mell narrative of *Picture This* with its jumps among Periclean Athens, Cold War America, and Golden Age Holland; or the shuttlecock movement among the narrators of *Closing Time*. Having flown over Avignon, Heller knows the silence that *The Unnamable* denominates and the nothingness that it foretells. He writes. Each novel emerges as another gesture of comic defiance, each constituting a strident, insistent, angry, sometimes eloquent protest against mortality.

APPENDIX A
SUMMARIES OF UNPUBLISHED SHORT STORIES

At first glance, one does not find the author of *Catch-22* in Joseph Heller's unpublished stories. Many are moralistic and didactic. Most frequently, their protagonists fail as result of lack of courage or intellectual tenacity. There is little humor in them, except for the farcical. They are the product of a very young writer's imagination and, thus, may inspire young writers who find their own efforts falling short of their aspirations. Yet, in these stories lie some of the origins of Heller's novels.

Copies of all these stories can be found in the Brandeis University Libraries, Special Collections Department. Below I list the stories that are discussed within the text and summarize those that are not. For cases in which there are versions of the same story with different titles, I note this fact.

STORIES DISCUSSED IN THE TEXT

"The Coward" (discussed in chapter 1)
"Crippled Phoenix" (discussed in chapter 2)
"A Day in the Country" (discussed in chapter 1)
"The Death of the Dying Swan" or "Swan Song" (discussed in chapter 1)
"Early Frost" (discussed in chapter 1)
"Jephthah's Daughter" (discussed in chapter 5)
"To Laugh in the Morning" or "The Merry Dance" (discussed chapter 1)

"Lot's Wife" (discussed in chapter 1)
"The Man Who Came Looking for Moses Richmond (discussed in chapter 4)
"The Miracle of Danrossane" (discussed in chapter 2)
"The Polar Bear in the Ice Box" (discussed in chapter 1)
"A Scientific Fact" (discussed in chapter 4)
"Young Girl on a Train" or "Slow Train to New York" (discussed in chapter 1)

INTERPRETIVE SUMMARIES OF OTHER STORIES

"The Art of Keeping Your Mouth Shut"

Like "Bookies, Beware!" (*Esquire*, May 1947), "The Art of Keeping Your Mouth Shut" works as an extended joke: the art of conversation has disappeared because people have nothing to say and yet persist in talking continuously. The story takes the form of a magazine or newspaper feature that purports to explain the causes, effects, and varieties of the purposeless—but noisy—conversation. The narrator quotes liberally from Professor Marvin B. Winkler of the Bansakani Institute of Des Moines, Iowa, in analyzing this phenomenon. According to Winkler, the few interesting conversationalists include pickpockets, sandhogs, smugglers, Mexican harlots, peeping Toms, and men who have lived with Mexican harlots. This list provides Heller with his jokingly advisory conclusion to the story: "When you find yourself with a Peeping Tom, keep your mouth shut and let *him* do the talking." In addition to using Winkler again, Heller makes another childhood friend, Dan Rosoff, a character in the story; Rosoff is credited with the "remarkable" insight that neither birds nor women can utter sounds that please the ear.

"From Dusk to Dawn" or "The First Touch of Winter"

Like such stories as "Young Girl on a Train" and "World Full of Great Cities," "From Dusk to Dawn" tells about writer who is unable to write. Andy, the frustrated writer, and his girlfriend, Esther, walk through New York talking about his writing and their relationship. However, Andy has already decided how to handle his problems: "It was the job, of course, writing copy when you should be writing plays, but you couldn't get rid of the job because the job was bread and alcohol, so you got rid of the girl instead." Andy justifies this choice to himself as the price he must pay for his aspirations, the price of grabbing "something permanent." Later, Andy and Esther walk through New York again, with Andy feeling ambivalent about his decision to dump her and Esther pondering whether to accept the invitation of another writer, Harry Proust, to move in with him. In a scene with symbolic overtones, Andy and Esther stop in a pet store and buy canaries that they plan to release in Central Park. Andy deliberately chooses a young canary that he knows will die with the onset of winter—a choice Heller makes emblematic of Andy's pessimism and blighted hopes.

Heller first wrote the story as an undergraduate. Calling the piece something that a small magazine might publish, his professor praised Heller for getting language under better control, for using dialogue as a means of plot development, and for handling the symbolism of the canary episode. Like other Heller stories about aspiring writers, "From Dusk to Dawn" opposes writing and desire, art and commercial writing, and aspirations and achievement. And Andy, like Heller's other aspirants, waits and hopes without doing the writing that would extricate him from his problems. "Shame, futility, disillusionment, despair. The whole Thesaurus," Andy says of the guilt his inactivity causes.

"I Don't Know Why"

In its portrait of paralysis of will in the face of danger, "I Don't Know Why" is similar to Heller's other stories about low life. Harry, the protagonist, sits in a bar worrying because he has heard that a sometime patron of the bar is wanted by the police. Eventually, he decides to share his concerns with Mac the bartender, urging him to call the police, but Mac resists. Harry's anxieties mount when Glynn, the patron in question, comes into the bar and claims to know Harry. The story ends with Harry still wondering what to do. As in accounts of low life such as "Nothing to Be Done," the world and its perceived violence is more powerful than the individual.

"Part by Part" or "Almost Like Christmas"

Heller explores mob violence and an idealistic teacher's moral cowardice. Jess Calgary, an African-American youth, has killed a white teenager, thus inflaming the passions of the town. Carter, the schoolteacher protagonist, is persuaded by the police to go after Calgary to ask him to turn himself in, because the teenager likes and trusts his teacher. Carter locates Calgary, only to learn that he is innocent. Calgary was attacked by three whites and the killing occurred in self-defense. "I tried not to fight," Calgary explains to Carter; "I thought if I kept my hands down they'd stop hitting me, but they kept after me like they'd beat me to death." Having seen the lynch mob forming, Carter urges his student to flee, but Calgary tells him that his family has already decided that he must turn himself in in order to protect the African-American community from mob violence. The decision frustrates the teacher, who tells Calgary, "I'm washing my hands of the whole thing." As Heller's ending makes clear, the well-meaning Carter has become morally lost: "He had put the car in gear and was rolling forward, and [the scene] vanished slowly behind him part by part. Like the murky macrocosm of a turbulent dream. He crawled aimlessly ahead, wondering dully where to go, and then turned in the direction of his house. It was too late for school, he realized, too late for anything now but sleep."

Like "The Man Who Came Looking for Moses Richmond," Heller's account of anti-Semitism in a small Southern town, "Part by Part" is didactic and moralistic. The townspeople turn to mob violence because they want to feel important: "Respectability. . . . They want to be respectable, and joining a mob is the easiest way." As the crowd grows and the excitement builds, the town streets are ironically described as almost like Christmas. Against this backdrop, Carter finds that his values—equality, justice, and moral responsibility—are irrelevant. He is the outsider, blamed by some for putting "smart, college ideas" in the heads of students like Calgary. In Heller's world, such values enfeeble.

"Room for Renoir"

"Room for Renoir" anticipates themes of Heller's novels, notably the evocative power of great art and the prudishness of middle-class values. George Baker, a lawyer on his lunch break, takes a fancy to a print of a Renoir nude that he sees in a bookstore window. The usually cautious Baker acts upon his impulse to buy the painting and looks forward to taking it home to his wife. Her response to his find, however, disappoints him. His wife objects to every spot that he proposes hanging the print, finally telling him: "you can't hang a nude in the living room." Stymied, George takes it to the office where he finds himself the subject of jokes about dirty pictures. Feeling rather heroic, Baker stands his ground amidst the jokes and criticism, that is, until his boss tells him to take it down. Baker reluctantly takes his Renoir nude home again. His wife tells him that she was afraid the office uproar would occur, but to salve his feelings offers to let him hang the picture over the living room fireplace. George, however, has learned his lesson; "think of the comments we'd have to put up with every time we entertained," he replies. So, the Renoir nude goes into the closet along with the rusty golf clubs that were the product of George's last impulse. He decides that he'd better take up golf again.

The ending and portrait of middle-class marriage foreshadow *Something Happened*. The return to golf signals that George and, later, Slocum stifle their individuality. In purchasing the nude, Baker tried to seize what he finds absent in his life—he was attracted by the play of light upon the woman's skin and "the definite expectancy of the fleshy arm captured in mid-motion." But, like Heller's other married protagonists, George finds that marriage restricts rather than occasions desire and possibility, and like the others he succumbs.

"A Simple Mission"

"A Simple Mission" turns upon an ethical choice and its consequences. Hallie Adams, an empathetic, idealistic, twenty-three-year-old teacher at a women's boarding school, sees one of her students, Christine Ruarke, steal another student's purse. The well-meaning Hallie tries to handle the theft in a way that will minimize the disruption, but instead ends up angering everyone involved. Her critical error is agreeing to contact Christine's father on her behalf, a choice that is explicitly against school policies. In the conversation with Mr. Ruarke, Hallie repeatedly tries to explain that the theft was Christine's cry for her parents' attention. However, Mr. Ruarke is not at all shocked by the account of his daughter's theft and offers Hallie money to take care of the problems that have resulted. When Hallie persists in trying to interest Ruarke in his daughter's plight, he assures Hallie that he fully understands the whole situation; then he seizes her, kisses her, and grabs her breast. The story ends after the interview with Hallie leaning against the wall sobbing, "he didn't understand; he didn't understand."

Among Heller's stories, "A Simple Mission" is unusual for featuring a female protagonist. As the irony of Heller's title suggests, there is little simple about innocence, guilt, and evil, or about ethical choices. The innocent Hallie ends up feeling more guilty than either Christine or her father. Hallie's quest to act fairly and empathetically results in actions in which her good intentions are taken advantage of, she has been sexually victimized, and she transgresses school policies. Like the idealists of Heller's other stories, Hallie finds herself alone, disillusioned, and misunderstood.

"The Sound of Asthma"

Exploring the loss of idealism and purpose, "The Sound of Asthma" has thematic affinities with many other Heller stories. However, its subject, American communism in the forties, sets the story apart. Heller represents the Party members and their meeting hall with the same gritty detail that he uses in pool hall and drug stories. The story opens with protagonist Peter Winkler daydreaming as he talks with his friend Alex in a Party recreation hall. Heller sets the tone with sounds of Alex's asthmatic breathing and of the monotonous echoes of a nearby Ping-Pong game. While Alex drones on about faith and the future, Peter grows increasingly "depressed because he felt that [the organization] had all dropped dead some time ago and he had been living with a corpse without knowing it." Their conversation is interrupted by the arrival of Crawford, a young, callow Party activist who tells Peter that Max Hirsch, an old friend, has returned. Peter immediately leaves to find Max's apartment, discovering when he does that Max is married and has no interest in Party affairs. Peter tries to persuade Max to attend an upcoming Party meeting, eventually calling him a coward and hinting at violence. Peter would have succeeded in convincing his old friend if Max's wife had not intervened and called him back to the dinner table. Heller ends the story with a reversal: Peter begs for a dinner invitation (he can dress up if necessary, he tells Max). Walking away from the apartment, Peter realizes that he will never see Max again; he wishes that he, like his former friend, would find someone to love.

In contrast to much of Heller's early fiction, "The Sound of Asthma" portrays marriage in a positive light. Max's wife keeps him living a proletarian life, rather than theorizing about it. Her tears counteract Peter's arguments and threats, and keep Max from returning to the emotional and political sterility of Party life. As for Peter, like other Heller protagonists, he dreams of possibilities to which he will not allow himself to commit and of romantic relationships upon which he will not act. Heller's portrait of American communism emphasizes the Party's tyranny over its members as well as the members' tyranny over each other. His thematic counterbalance is Max's newly adopted bourgeois life, which prompts such a sentimental reaction from Peter. Although Heller's portrayal of Party life is not entirely convincing, his evocation of menace is; it is a world of power and barely suppressed violence.

CHRONOLOGY		YOSSARIAN	DUNBAR / MCWATT
	CIVILIANS	URBAN. ASSYRIAN	
	ENLISTED MAN	STATIONED IN COLORADO → MEETS WINTERGREEN → DISCOVERS HOSPITAL	
EARLY 1944	AVIATION CADET	EPISODE OF "SOLDIER WHO SAW EVERYTHING TWICE" STATIONED AT SANTA ANA, CALIFORNIA; BOMBARDIER MEETS CLEVINGER. SCHEISSKOPF WINS PARADES. SLEEPS WITH SCHEISSKOPF'S WIFE.	
25 MISSIONS REQUIRED	SHIPPED OVERSEAS TO PIANOSA	FLIES AS A LEAD BOMBARDIER. LATER HE IS DEMOTED TO WING BOMBARDIER, THEN REINSTATED, THEN DEMOTED AGAIN	MCWATT IS YOSSARIAN'S PILOT DUNBAR A LEAD BOMBARDIER IN ANOTHER SQUADRON
	CATHCART ARRIVES AS GROUP COMMANDER	YOSSARIAN HAS 23 MISSIONS WHEN CATHCART ARRIVES AND RAISES THE MISSIONS TO 30.	
30 MISSIONS	RAISES MISSIONS		
MARCH	FERRARA	GOES OVER THE TARGET TWICE, DESTROYS THE BRIDGE. IS REPRIMANDED BECAUSE KRAFT'S PLANE IS SHOT DOWN THE SECOND TIME AROUND. TO AVERT CRITICISM, YOSSARIAN IS GIVEN A MEDAL AND PROMOTED TO CAPTAIN	MCWATT IS YOSSARIAN'S PILOT ON THIS MISSION
APRIL	MILO FORMS HIS CARTEL (APRIL)		
35 MISSIONS			
JUNE Allies enter ROME	ROME CAPTURED (JUNE 4)	YOSSARIAN ACCOMPANYS NATELY TO HIS GIRL FRIEND'S WHOREHOUSE	DUNBAR GOES TO THE WHOREHOUSE
LATE JUNE	BOLOGNA	1. MISSION IS POSTPONED AND EVERYONE IS TERRIFIED 2. YOSSARIAN CAUSES ONE DELAY BY "POISONING" FOOD, ANOTHER BY MOVING THE BOMBLINE. HAS 32 MISSIONS 3. HAS A DRUNKEN RUN AT THE OFFICERS CLUB WITH COLONEL KORN. 4. SABOTAGES INTERCOM AND MAKES PILOT TURN BACK. MISSION IS A MILK RUN. 5. YOSSARIAN GOES BACK AS A LEAD BOMBARDIER THE NEXT DAY, TAKES NO EVASIVE ACTION, RUNS INTO FLAK. 6. AFTER THE MISSION, HE GOES TO ROME ON A REST LEAVE AND MEETS	MCWATT IS YOSSARIAN'S PILOT ON THIS MISSION
40 MISSIONS 45 MISSIONS	BETWEEN BOLOGNA AND AVIGNON	LUCIANA. 7. WHILE HE IS AWAY, COLONEL RAISES MISSIONS TO 40, AND YOSSARIAN RUNS INTO THE HOSPITAL WHEN HE RETURNS. 8. LEAVES HOSPITAL, FLIES SIX MORE MISSIONS, + GOES BACK IN WHEN MISSIONS ARE RAISED TO 45. HE NOW HAS 38 MISSIONS	DUNBAR MOANS BACK
JULY	AVIGNON	1. YOSSARIAN MOANS IN THE BRIEFING ROOM. NATELY TRIES TO PROTECT HIM. 2. SNOWDEN IS SHOT THROUGH THE MIDDLE AND DIES. YOSSARIAN TREATS HIM FOR THE WRONG WOUND.	
	SNOWDEN'S FUNERAL	1. YOSSARIAN EMERGES FROM THE PLANE NAKED. 2. GOES NAKED TO CEMETERY AND SITS IN A TREE 3. STANDS IN FORMATION NAKED TO RECEIVE THE MEDAL HE WON FOR FERRARA.	MCWATT HELPS CARE FOR YOSSARIAN WHEN HE EMERGES FROM THE PLANE
50 MISSIONS	CLEVINGER DISAPPEARS IN A CLOUD	SHORTLY BEFORE CLEVINGER IS LOST, YOSSARIAN ARGUES WITH HIM AT THE OFFICERS CLUB ABOUT WHICH ONE IS CRAZY.	DUNBAR ARGUES WITH CLEVINGER THAT LIFE IS ALL
AUGUST	YOSSARIAN ENTERS HOSPITAL	YOSSARIAN ENTERS THE HOSPITAL IN DESPAIR OVER CLEVINGER'S DEATH. FAKES A LIVER AILMENT, CENSORS LETTERS WITH WASHINGTON IRVING'S NAME	DUNBAR IS IN HOSPITAL AS A FRIEND AND FELLOW MALINGERER
MISSIONS	YOSSARIAN LEAVES HOSPITAL	HE NOW HAS 44 MISSIONS	

Appendix B
JOSEPH HELLER'S SCHEMATIC OUTLINE FOR *CATCH-22*

During the composition of *Catch-22*, Joseph Heller did two overviews of the novel on desk blotters, both of which are preserved in the Brandeis University Libraries Special Collections Department. A portion of one original is shown here. Subsequently, a typescript of one of the blotters was prepared. The overviews illustrate Heller's passion for order and detail. Viewed through the lens of the blotter, *Catch-22* has as many interrelated plot strands as a Victorian novel does, each possessing its own developmental logic and integrity. Together with the novel, the blotter provides compelling evidence of Heller's concern with and mastery of his craft. The full text of the blotter is reproduced on the following pages and on an oversized sheet in the pocket attached to the inside cover of this volume. Grateful acknowledgment is made to Joseph Heller and to the Brandeis University Libraries, Special Collections Department, for permission to reproduce the blotters here.

CHRONOLOGY	YOSSARIAN	DUNBAR — MCWATT	CLEVINGER — NATELY	HUNGRY JOE — DOBBS	ORR	MILO	AARFY — CAPT. BLACK	CHAPLAIN
Civilians	Urban Assyrian		Nately Rich — Clevinger an Idealistic Student	Hungry Joe — A Photographer	Poor and Rustic	Married: A Faithful Husband	Aarfy: A College Alumnus	Married: With young Children
Enlisted man	Stationed in Colorado. Meets Wintergreen. Discovers Hospital Episode of " Soldier Who Saw Everything Twice"							
Early 1944 / Aviation Cadet	Stationed in Santa Ana, California: Bombardier: meets Clevinger. Scheisskopf wins parades. Sleeps with Scheisskopf's wife.		Clevinger faces trial as Cadet & found guilty			Milo is A Pilot		
25 Missions Required / Shipped Overseas to Pianosa	Flies as a lead bombardier. Later he is demoted to wing bombardier, then reinstated, then demoted again.	McWatt is Yossarian's Pilot. — Dunbar a Lead Bombardier in another squadron	Nately is A Co-Pilot. — Clevinger a Bombardier	Hungry Joe and Dunbar are Both Pilots	Orr is a Pilot in a Wing Plane & is always being shot down	Volunteers for Mess Officer as soon as he arrives overseas	Aarfy is Yossarian's Navigator. Black is the Squadron Intelligence Officer.	Chaplain does not fit in and has no friends.
Cathcart arrives as Group Commander Raises Missions	Yossarian has 23 Missions when Cathcart arrives and raises the missions to 30.			Hungry Joe has 25 Missions & is waiting to go home. He is put back on combat duty		He produces Fresh Eggs and begins organizing his Buying Syndicate		He fears both Colonels and is bullied by them
30 Missions March / Ferrara	Goes over the target twice. Destroys the bridge. Is reprimanded because Kraft's plane is shot down the second time around. To avert criticism, Yossarian is given a medal and promoted to Captain.	McWatt is Yossarian's Pilot on this mission		Hungry Joe has wrecked a plane because he was given a medal to cover up his mistake			Aarfy misleads Yossarian, making it necessary for them to go around twice	
April / Milo forms his Cartel (April)					Orr goes along on the trip to Egypt to buy Cotton.	Milo flies to Egypt and buys whole cotton crop	Black starts his loyalty oath crusade against Major Major	He loves his wife and misses her
35 Missions June 4 Allies enter Rome / Rome Captured (June 4)	Yossarian accompanies Nately to his girl friend's whorehouse.	Dunbar Goes to the whorehouse	1. Nately falls in love. 2. Nately finds his girl again 3.They go to her apartment	Hungry Joe is amazed by all the naked girls in the apartment		Milo arranges the mission to Orvieto as a business deal, working for both sides	Aarfy speaks of Nately's girl with smug contempt	
Late June / Bologna	1. Mission is postponed and everyone is terrified. 2. Yossarian causes one delay by 'poisoning' food, another by moving the bombline. Has 32 Missions. 3. Has a drunken row at the Officers' Club with Colonel Korn. 4. Sabotages intercom and makes pilot turn back. Mission is a Milk Run. 5. Yossarian goes back as a lead bombardier the next day, takes no evasive action, runs into flak. 6. After the mission he goes to Rome on a rest leave and meets Luciana. 7. While he is away, Colonel raises Missions to 40, and Yossarian 'runs' into the hospital when he returns.	McWatt is Yossarian's Pilot on this mission	Clevinger argues that Yossarian has no right to save his own life — Nately is in Rome courting his whore and runs out of money	Hungry Joe has nightmares because he is not scheduled for mission to Bologna — Hungry Joe tries to take pictures of Yossarian in bed with Luciana	Orr has an engine and his landing gear shot out but crash lands safely.	Milo has disapproved of the loyalty oath crusade because it disrupted business — Aarfy gets everything wrong on the Bologna mission and doesn't hear when Yossarian shouts at him to get out of the nose	Black rejoices that men are going to Bologna and hangs morbid signs on the closed medical tent — Black sleeps with Nately's girl just to taunt him	
40 Missions / Between Bologna and Avignon / 45 Missions	8. Leaves hospital, flies six more Missions and goes back in when Missions are raised to 45. He now has 38 Missions.					Milo bombs his own squadron when paid to do so by Germans		He worries constantly about health & safety of his wife and children
July / Avignon	1. Yossarian moans in the briefing room. Nately tries to protect him. 2. Snowden is shot through the middle and dies. Yossarian treats him for the wrong wound.	Dunbar moans back	Nately succumbs to Yossarian's mischief and moans in the briefing room	Dobbs panics, siezes controls, and plunges plane down into flak		Milo has removed the morphine from the first aid kit, & there is nothing to ease Snowden's pain		
Snowden's Funeral	1. Yossarian emerges from the plane naked. 2. Goes naked to cemetery and sits in a tree. 3. Stands in formation naked to receive the medal he won for Ferrara.	McWatt helps care for Yossarian when he emerges from plane				Milo seeks Yossarian out during Snowden's funeral for help in disposing of cotton		Chaplain spies Yossarian naked in a tree and thinks it is a mystical vision
50 Missions / Clevinger Disappears in a cloud / August	Shortly before Clevinger is lost, Yossarian argues with him at the Officers' Club about which one is crazy.	Dunbar argues with Clevinger that life is all.	Clevinger argues that Yossarian is crazy just before he is killed.					
First Chapter Begins here / Yossarian enters Hospital	Yossarian enters the hospital in despair over Clevinger's death. Fakes a liver ailment. Censors letters with Washington Irving's name.	Dunbar is in hospital as a friend and fellow malingerer.	Clevinger's plane has disappeared in a cloud. He is given up for dead.	Hungry Joe keeps finishing missions and keeps being returned to combat duty.	Orr is Yossarian's roommate and keeps improving tent.	Milo trusts Yossarian because he will not steal from country he loves.	Aarfy is Yossarian's incompetent lead navigator	Chaplain meets Yossarian in hospital
50 Missions / Yossarian leaves Hospital	He now has 44 Missions.		Nately is away in Rome courting his whore		Orr started to winterize the tent while Yossarian was in the hospital.	Milo is away buying figs.		
Yossarian tries to be Grounded	1. Goes to Daneeka for help and is turned down 2. Flies three more missions and has 47. 3. Goes to Chaplain for help.							Chaplain has authority to help but they become friends
September 55 Missions / Missions raised to 55	1. Yossarian goes to Daneeka with the idea of being judged crazy, but is turned down. He now has 48 missions. 2. Goes to Wintergreen and is turned down. Missions are raised to 55 while he is away.		Nately is away in Rome courting his whore			Milo advises him to fly the 55 Missions like a good soldier.		

DOC DANEEKA — DR. STUBBS	OTHER COMBAT OFFICERS	ENLISTED MEN	MAJOR MAJOR — MAJOR DANBY	COL. CATHCART — COL. KORN	GEN. DREEDLE — GEN. PECKEM	ITALIANS	NURSES & OTHER AMERICAN WOMEN	CASUALTIES	NOTES	THE WAR IN EUROPE
Daneeka: profitable practice before war. Kickbacks abortions			Major Major looks like Henry Fonda	Cathcart: A Harvard graduate with a cigarette holder						1943 / 6/11 Sicily Landings
		Wintergreen: Advises Yossarian to do his duty.	Promoted by an IBM machine					Soldier who sees everything twice dies of some mysterious disease	Family of dead soldier visits Yossarian instead of their son.	9/9 American forces land at Salerno
		Trained at Cadet School as a Pilot					Scheisskopf's wife has affair with Yossarian		Scheisskopf has a mania for parades.	
				Becomes a full Colonel at age 36. Longs to be a general	Dreedle has taken his son-in law, Col. Moodus, into the business			Col. Nevers, Previous Group Commander is killed over Arezzo	Cathcart's predecessor was, presumably, a satisfactory officer who did not shirk his combat duties.	1944 / 1/22 Anzio Landings
			Finds true happiness as a combat pilot, where he finally fits in	Arrives as the New Group Commander and raises missions to 30					Cathcart arrives as the new Commander and immediately raises the missions to 30	Jan.-Mar. Cassino Battles
	Kraft is killed on Yossarian's second bomb run			Reprimands Yossarian, then decides to promote him and give him a medal				Kraft His plane blows up right above Yossarian's the second time around	Cathcart has volunteered his men for Ferrara to make a good impression for himself. Yossarian feels responsible for Kraft's death	5/12 Anzio and Cassino breakthrough
			Major Major is appointed Sqd. Commander when predecessor is killed over Perugia	Disapproves of Black's Loyalty Oath campaign but afraid to intervene				Maj. Duluth Previous squadron commander is killed in action over Perugia	Major Major's predecessor, like Col. Cathcart's, is killed in combat.	
	Mudd, the dead man in Yossarian's tent, is killed over Orvieto the day he arrives.		As Sqd. Commander he is ostracized and abused and made victim of Black's Loyalty Oath Crusade			Nately's whore sits naked in a room full of enlisted men who ignore her		Mudd The dead man in Yossarian's tent is killed over Orvieto	Milo organizes the mission to Orvieto as a sound business venture and does not feel guilty over Mudd's death.	6/4 Rome entered
Stubbs is sorry for the men and feels Yossarian might be the only sane person left.		Wintergreen refuses to help and lectures Yossarian on his duty to be killed.	After he is beaten up on the basketball court, he turns himself into a recluse and sees no one	Korn closes the Medical Tents while the men are waiting to fly to Bologna	Peckem receives a medal and begins recommending that bombing activities be placed under his own special service command	The old man in the whore house baits Nately. Girl gets bored with argument and abandons Nately				6/6 Normandy landings
		Wintergreen's own duty as he sees it is to make a profit on his black market operations			Peckem is a smooth politician. Dreedle is a blunt outspoken man who drinks heavily and knows he is losing out because he does not make the right contacts	Yossarian meets Luciana. Throws away her address. Sleeps with maid in lime-colored panties when he cannot find her again		Anonymous Planes are shot down on the mission to Bologna	Yossarian throws away Luciana's address and spends the rest of the book looking and longing for her	
Daneeka behaves with courage when Milo bombs the squadron									Milo justifies bombing the squadron in terms of free enterprise and the large profit he has made.	
Daneeka takes care of Yossarian when he emerges from plane in state of shock		Snowden is shot through the middle and dies	Danby moans while conducting briefing and is ordered taken outside and shot	Korn grandstands for Gen. Dreedle but earns his contempt	Gen. Dreedle brings his girl friend to the Avignon briefing	Nately's whore Black and gives him some of the money Natley pays her		Snowden "Freezes to death" while Yossarian attends him		
			Both Majors attend Snowden's funeral	Cathcart vows to punish Yossarian for standing naked in formation	Dreedle awards medals and sides with Yossarian when Cathcart offers to punish him					
								Clevinger Plane flies into cloud and is never seen again		8/12 Florence captured
										8/15 Invasion of Southern France
Daneeka is a self-pitying hypochondriac with whom Yossarian is friendly	The soldier in white appears in hospital ward and is judged dead	Snowden has already been killed. Wintergreen as mail clerk is already influential	Major Major is sent CID man and begins to sign papers "Washington Irving"	Cathcart has raised missions from 25 to 50	Dreedle and Peckem are feuding and vying for power	Nately's whore is bored with him and pays him little attention	Yossarian has no relationship with Nurse Duckett yet	Soldier in White Pronounced dead in the hospital	First chapter begins here.	8/23 Paris liberated
				Cathcart strives to impress both Generals favorably	Neither General takes enough notice of Cathcart to intervene either way				Men have to fly 50 missions, although headquarters requires only 40.	8/23 Russia occupies Rumania
Daneeka refuses to help but says headquarters wants only 40 missions			Major Major visited by second CID man and puts him on trail of the first							9/11 Allied forces move into Germany
Explains Catch-22 in terms of Orr		Wintergreen refuses to help and will turn against him if he gets into trouble.								

CHRONOLOGY	YOSSARIAN	DUNBAR / MCWATT	CLEVINGER / NATELY	HUNGRY JOE / DOBBS	ORR	MILO	AARFY / CAPT. BLACK	CHAPLAIN
September 55 Missions Missions raised to 55	1. Yossarian goes to Daneeka with the idea of being judged crazy, but is turned down. He now has 48 Missions. 2. Goes to Wintergreen and is turned down. Missions are raised to 55 while he is away.					Milo advises him to fly the 55 Missions like a good soldier.		
Yossarian keeps Flying	Goes to Major Major for help, but is turned down. He tackles Major Major in a ditch in order to see him. He now has 51 missions.			Dobbs is no longer fit to pilot a plane, but can't get grounded.				
60 Missions Missions raised to 60	1. Yossarian tries Doc Daneeka again to no avail. He still has 51 missions when missions are raised to 60. 2. Yossarian protects the Chaplain when the Colonel tries to throw him out.			Dobbs comes to Yossarian with plot to murder Colonel. Yossarian declines.			Black taunts Nately at the Officers Club about screwing his girl	Summoned by Colonel to say prayers in the briefing room. Complains in vain about 60 missions
Yossarian Wounded	He is wounded in the leg on a milk run when AARFY gets lost and leads the planes over the flak.	McWatt is the pilot and administers first aid.	Nately is the co-pilot on the mission.				Aarfy is unable to hear Yossarian's screams or see his blood	Tries to see Major on Yossarian's behalf
Yossarian in the Hospital	1. Yossarian gooses Nurse Duckett and a love affair starts between them. 2. Refuses again to join Dobbs in the plot to murder the Colonel, because he's sure he will be sent home. 3. A psychiatrist finds him insane, but he is returned to combat and a different man is sent home in his place.	Dunbar goes in to the hospital just to keep Yossarian company.		Dobbs still wants to kill the Colonel even though he has only two more missions to fly	Orr has to ditch on second mission to Avignon, but everyone survives without injury.	Milo has removed the gas cylinders from the Mae Wests to make ice cream sodas for the officers.		Chaplain sees Daneeka on Yossarian's behalf & is going to try Wintergreen next
Orr lost in Combat	Yossarian continues flying missions; when Colonel volunteers for Bologna again, Yosssarian goes to Dobbs and agrees to the murder plot.			Dobbs has finished his 60 Missions and is now repelled by the idea of murdering the Colonel	Orr invites Yossarian to fly with him. He is shot down on the mission to Bologna and given up for lost, although everyone else in the plane survives			
Between Orr and Kid Sampson	1. Yossarian is distressed by the assignment to destroy a whole village in order to create a road block. 2. Yossarian is ready to kill McWatt when McWatt buzzes with Yossarian in the plane.	McWatt forgives Yossarian. Dunbar turns surly and starts to crack up.					Black's taunts cause Chaplain to doubt his wife's fidelity	
65 Missions 70 Missions Kid Sampson Killed. McWatt commits suicide	Yossarian is on the beach with Nurse Duckett when McWatt's plane cuts Kid Sampson in half.	McWatt lets the others bail out, then flies into a mountain.						
Mid-October Nately Gets His Girl	1. In Rome he looks for Luciana and is ready to fall in love with Nurse Duckett. He is lonely and does not know what to do with himself. 2. He helps Nately rescue his girl from the higher-ranking Officers.	Dunbar goes along to help Nately.	Nately rescues his girl and guards her while she sleeps.	Dobbs and Hungry Joe go to help Nately. Dobbs threatens violence.			Aarfy does not go along because he does not want to get in bad with anyone	
November (Thanksgiving Day) Yossarian Breaks Nately's Nose	After Milo's Thanksgiving Day party, Yossarian is awakened in terror by machine gun fire and so angry he grabs his gun to go after the man who fired the gun as a joke. When Nately tries to restrain him, he punches Nately so savagely that Nately is taken to the hospital.	Dunbar goes berserk in the hospital and is disappeared.	Nately's friends come to the hospital as patients to be with him.	Hungry Joe's camera hoping to take pictures of Yossarian and Nurse Duckett.		Milo gives a huge banquet at which everyone gives thanks to him.		Even the Chaplain enters the ward, pleased he has at least had the courage to sin.
70 Missions Finished Nately killed	Has 70 Missions. Yossarian pleads with Nately not to offer to fly more missions to remain overseas with his girl. Appeals to Milo to help Nately.		Nately is killed in mid-air crash over LaSpezia	Dobbs causes mid-air collision with Nately's plane and is also killed.		Milo persuades Cathcart to raise missions to 80, knowing Nately will fly them.		The Chaplain is taken to a cellar, tried, and found guilty. Angrily he decides to go directly to Gen. Dreedle
80 Missions Yossarian Refuses to Fly More Missions	Yossarian is sent to Rome on a rest leave. Tells Nately's whore about his death. She tries to kill him. He escapes back to Corsica.			Hungry Joe Flies Yossarian back and forth			Black laughs when whorehouse is raided and girls are chased out	
Goes AWOL to "The Eternal City"	Yossarian goes back to Rome to find and help the kid sister. He is arrested for being in Rome without a pass and returned.					Milo urges him piously to do his duty. Deserts him to smuggle tobacco.	Aarfy rapes and murders the maid but is allowed to go free	
Accepts Korn's Deal. Is stabbed.	Yossarian accepts the chance to become "One of the boys" in return for being allowed to go home a hero.							
In hospital he repudiates the deal	Yossarian cannot go along with the deal even though it will mean his life will be saved. Does not know what he will do.			Hungry Joe dies in his sleep.				Chaplain does not know what Yossarian should do
December 1944 Yossarian runs away joyously when he learns Orr is safe	Heads for Rome to try to save Nately's kid sister, and then for Sweden, but does not expect to get there. Has 71 missions				Orr rows to Sweden and gives Yossarian the hope that anything is possible.			Chaplain is delighted and encouraged by Yossarian's decision

DR. DANEEKA — DR. STUBBS	OTHER COMBAT OFFICERS	ENLISTED MEN	MAJOR MAJOR — MAJOR DANBY	COL. CATHCART — COL. KORN	GEN. DREEDLE — GEN. PECKEM	ITALIANS	NURSES & OTHER AMERICAN WOMEN	CASUALTIES	NOTES	THE WAR IN EUROPE
Explains Catch-22 in terms of Orr		Wintergreen refuses to help and will trun against him if he gets into trouble.								
Daneeka shares Yossarian's fear of death & will take no chances of any kind.			Major Major is sorry for Yossarian but there is nothing he can do	Both Colonels are involved in "Plum Tomato" deals with Milo						9/21 Allies push past Pisa
Dr. Stubbs does ground the men in his squadron, even though Korn puts them right back on combat duty				Col. wants prayers in the briefing room in order to get into Saturday Evening Post						10/2 Sigfried Line collapses. Russia occupies Bulgaria.
Daneeka again refuses to ground Yossarian, even though he has been judged crazy				Col. is terrified by mention of Yossarian's name						
		Wintergreen sends the Chaplain away without seeing him					Yossarian gooses Nurse Duckett			
	Scheisskopf is shipped overseas to General Peckem			Cathcart volunteers for Bologna again	Peckem steps up campaign against Dreedle		They become lovers	Orr Ditches and is given up for lost		10/26 Americans approach Bologna
				Colonels are not concerned with the road block. They want a good aerial photo			She tries to reform him.			
Daneeka is officially "dead" when McWatt's plane crashes.				Uses these deaths as an excuse to raise missions to 70			She is on the beach with him when Kid Sampson is killed	Kid Sampson Cut in half McWatt Flies into mountain	Daneeka, by refusing to get involved in anything, has been "dead" all the time	
Dr. Stubbs is defying group & Korn wants to get rid of all flight surgeons						Nately's whore gets a good night's sleep and falls in love with him			As soon as Nately gets his girl he turns insufferably bourgeoise and tries to reform everybody.	
		Sgt. Knight fires a machine gun at night and shouts "Happy New Year!"				Nately's whore is furious with Yossarian for hitting him	Warns Yossarian that they are going to disappear Dunbar	Dunbar He is disappeared	Nurse Duckett has begun to think of her future. She wants to marry a doctor and has begun to disassociate herself from Yossarian, whom she does not regard as a suitable husband.	
Dr. Stubbs is transferred to the Pacific	Scheisskopf finds himself in charge of everything	Wintergreen blames Peckem when Scheisskopf is put in charge of them all.			Peckem replaces Dreedle. Then his own recommendation is adopted and he finds himself under Scheisskopf			Nately Dobbs Killed in mid-air crash	Milo and Cathcart have each flown no more than 5 missions.	
	The other men side with Yossarian secretly but none will join him				Peckem sends the Chaplain away without seeing him	Nately's whore tries to stab Yossarian and begins her chase after him	Nurse Duckett is embarrassed by Yossarian's stand		Natley's whore becomes a symbol of his guilt and responsibility for never intervening in the injustices he knows exist everywhere.	
						Kid sister is adrift in Rome with no one to help her		Old Man He dies of old age. Maid Murdered by Aarfy.		
	The other men would be tricked by Yossarian's decision and induced to continue flying			Colonel must deal with Yossarian or punish him		Nately's whore stabs Yossarian as he leaves the office				
		Yossarian has treated Snowden for the "wrong wound".	Danby comes to persuade Yossarian to go through with the deal but is converted to Yossarian's point of view					Hungry Joe Dies in his sleep		12/16 – 1/20 1945 Battle of The Bulge
			Danby aids him in escape and offers money & advice			Nately's whore is right behind Yossarian with a knife	Nurse Duckett helps him escape because she is eager to be rid of him.		In making the decision to desert, Yossarian accepts the responsibility he now knows he has to the other men. As he says, he is not running away from his responsibilities, but to them.	3/7 Remagen Bridge Captured 4/1 Russians enter Austria 5/3 Berlin falls

NOTES

PREFACE

1. See Sam Merrill, "*Playboy* Interview: Joseph Heller," *Playboy* (June 1975): 76. In the same interview, Heller admits that "[a]lmost all of Slocum's dreams are [his] own" (76), which is also suggestive because many of Slocum's dreams have to do with silent threats.

2. Valerie Humphries (then his nurse, now his wife) confirms the importance conversation had to the bedridden Heller: "I knew right away that, if I were to help him recover, I had to keep him talking. . . . Because he was completely incapacitated, conversation was his only stimulation. For anyone as vital as Joe, talking to a responsive, communicative person can be akin to therapy." See Joseph Heller, Speed Vogel, and Valerie Humphries, "In the Hospital: Crisis and Recovery," *McCall's* (Aug. 1986): 92.

3. Joseph Heller is a famous verbal performer, especially in the dinner gatherings of the Gourmet Club, which includes Heller, Mel Brooks, Mario Puzo, George Mandel, Joe Stein, Julius Green, Ngoot Lee, Speed Vogel, and sometimes Rob Reiner. His friend Mel Brooks says, "Joe plays the best verbal Ping-Pong of anyone I know. The ball will be returned with a spin on it, always. He has a Talmudic tenacity in argument" (quoted in Barbara Gelb, "Catching Joseph Heller," *The New York Times Magazine* [4 Mar. 1979]: 42). For a sample of the group's conversation, see "Eating with Their Mouths Open" (*The New York Times Magazine* [3 Nov. 1985]: 62–63, 93–94). A piece that Heller did for *The New York Times Magazine*, "Oslo: Meet Me at the Cafe," reveals another side of Heller's oral life ([17 Mar. 1985]: 38, 121–22). Ostensibly a mood piece on the Oslo cafe The Theatercafeen, Heller's article discloses his method of dealing with foreign climes by going to a place where there is good talk.

4. Whitney Balliett, review of *Catch-22*, *The New Yorker* (9 Dec. 1961): 247.

5. A. Alvarez, "Working in the Dark," *The New York Review of Books* (11 Apr. 1985): 17.

6. See Walter Ong, *Orality and Literacy* (London and New York: Methuen, 1982), 177. Ong's description of the way in which speech functions in oral cultures—"speech is more performance-oriented, more a way of doing something to someone" (177)—could also serve to describe Heller's approach to fiction. Heller's compositional habits also have an oral dimension; since working on *Something Happened*, he has taken notes and sketched out ideas with a dictating machine (Alden Whitman, "Something Always Happens on the Way to the Office: An Interview with Joseph Heller," in *Pages: The World of Books, Writers, and Writing*, vol. 1, ed. M. J. Bruccoli [Detroit: Gale, 1976], 77–78).

7. Charles Ruas, "Joseph Heller," interview, in *Conversations with American Writers* (New York: Alfred A. Knopf, 1985), 171.

8. One of Heller's unpublished stories, "The Art of Keeping Your Mouth Shut," humorously explores "the rapidly disappearing art of conversation." Its tone and details are suggestive of the value Heller places on good talk: "Statistics published recently by the Bansakani Institute in Des Moines, Iowa, reveal that the average person today spends more time squirming in his chair than at any other time since man first unfortunately discovered a means for communicating with his neighbors." Heller papers, Brandeis University Library.

9. Laurence Sterne, *The Life and Opinions of Tristram Shandy* (Baltimore: Penguin, 1967), 615.

10. T. S. Eliot, "Burnt Norton," in *Collected Poems* (New York: Harcourt, Brace & World, 1954), 180.

11. See, respectively: Robert Merrill, *Joseph Heller* (Boston: Twayne Publishers, 1987); David Seed, *The Fiction of Joseph Heller* (New York: St. Martin's Press, 1989); Sanford Pinsker, *Understanding Joseph Heller* (Columbia: Univ. of South Carolina Press, 1991); Judith Ruderman, *Joseph Heller* (New York: Continuum, 1991); Stephen Potts, *Catch-22* (Boston: Twayne Publishers, 1989); and James Nagel, ed., *Critical Essays on Joseph Heller* (Boston: G. K. Hall, 1984).

12. Sam Merrill interview, 73.

13. Robert M. Polhemus's account of what is revealed by studying comedy is relevant to Joseph Heller's fiction: "Our comic sense—like our linguistic capability, our habits of reflection, our emotionally complicated love life, and our preparation of food—seems to be one of those elementary characteristics of our species that define us as human. When we discover the comic motive and understanding in great works of art, we go straight to the heart of civilization" (*Comic Faith* [Univ. of Chicago Press, 1980], 6). See the Introduction for an explanation of the comic sensibility.

Chapter 1

1. Not surprisingly, criticism of the stories is limited, primarily consisting of brief overviews in James J. Martine, "The Courage to Defy," in *Critical Essays on Catch-22*, ed. James Nagel (Encino, Ca.: Dickenson, 1974), 142–49; Robert Merrill, *Joseph Heller*, 2; and David Seed, *The Fiction of Joseph Heller*, 14–21).

2. Extending structuralist thought, Seymour Chatman uses the distinction, story and discourse, to differentiate narrative content from the means by which this content is transmitted; see *Story and Discourse* (Ithaca: Cornell Univ. Press, 1978).

3. The unpublished stories are included in the Brandeis University Library collection of Heller manuscripts; see Appendix A.

4. The play is included in the Joseph Heller papers, Brandeis University Library.

5. Heller came to regret his involvement with *McHale's Navy* and asked that his name be replaced with a pseudonym in the credits, which after arbitration was done. Explaining his reasons, he wrote: "It is no longer a funny show but a show based on a funny situation, and that is something different entirely." Letter to Jay Sanford, 20 July 1962, Heller papers, Brandeis University Library.

6. *Story* recently republished "I Don't Love You Any More," and, in an interview done for the occasion, Heller described the circumstances of its composition. He wrote the story on his tent mate's portable typewriter in Corsica, while waiting to go home because he had finished his mission (*Story* [spring 1992]: 116).

7. Ruas interview, 148.

8. Ibid.

9. Melanie M. S. Young, "Joseph Heller: A Critical Introduction," (Ph.D. diss., Rice Univ. 1981), 12.

10. In its presentation of the bleakness of marriage, "The Death of the Dying Swan" anticipates *Something Happened*, while the humor of "The Polar Bear in the Ice Box" prefigures the exchanges between David and Bathsheba in *God Knows*.

11. Heller makes the Hemingwayesque mood explicit by linking Cooper's longings to Hemingway: "Byron had already died in Greece, but there was a man named Hemingway who wrote a book he understood and a man named Wagner who wrote music that almost made him cry."

12. The unpublished story, "Room for Renoir," turns upon a related conception. A man, who has bought a print of a Renoir nude, finds that his wife won't let him hang it up, because of comments that the nude would occasion when they entertained. When the protagonist then tries to put it up at the office, his boss has similar objections. See Appendix A.

13. Heller says that he realized the correspondence between the two stories after the fact. See Ruas interview, 149.

14. The poolroom serves as setting for several unpublished stories as well, including "A Day in the Country" and "To Laugh in the Morning" (another version is called "The Merry Dance").

15. Heller acknowledges that his friend also serves as a partial model for Milo Minderbinder in *Catch-22* (see Barbara Gelb, "Catching Joseph Heller," 51). The most notable similarities among these "Winkler" characters are their pseudo-expertise and their predilection for money and money-making schemes. Heller also frequently refers to Winkler when he talks about his Coney Island boyhood; a favorite story tells of Winkler and he sharing and wetting the same baby carriage (Gelb 51). In *Closing Time*, Winkler appears as a character in his own right and tries to sell shoes to Milo, and Heller thanks Winkler for his long friendship in the acknowledgments.

16. The term "authorial audience" is Peter Rabinowitz's, and he distinguishes it from narrative audience. The authorial audience is the ideal reader posited by an author, the reader who completely attends to authorial intentionality. By contrast, the narrative audience is the reader implied by the text itself, by its narrative and rhetorical structure; this reader participates in the illusion that the text is real, that it constitutes a world. See "Truth in Fiction: A Reexamination of Audiences," *Critical Inquiry* 4 (1977): 121–41. My examination of the reader's role in Heller's fiction is an exercise in authorial reading; for a theoretical examination of the workings of such readings, see Peter Rabinowitz, *Before Reading: Narrative Conventions and the Politics of Interpretation* (Ithaca, N.Y.: Cornell Univ. Press, 1987) and James Phelan, *Reading People, Reading Plots* (Chicago: Univ. of Chicago Press, 1989).

17. Gerard Genette introduces the concept of focalization in order to distinguish among the possibilities for "seeing" the action of a story and would call Heller's use of Murdock an instance of internal focalization (the narrator reports only what the character sees and knows). This will become a standard tool in Heller's narrative repertoire, notably for deaths

like Snowden's or Slocum's son's. Heller uses this technique in order to place the narrative audience in the character's position so that they experience the death as the character does. For the authorial audience, Heller uses this technique variously: for instance, so they come to understand Snowden's death by much the process by which Yossarian does or so they discern what Slocum cannot. More recently, Seymour Chatman criticizes the term because it does not discriminate precisely enough between "telling" and "seeing" and the meaning that results from the two complementary processes. See, respectively: *Narrative Discourse* (Ithaca: Cornell Univ. Press, 1980) 189–94 and "A New Point of View on 'Point of View,'" in *Coming to Terms: The Rhetoric of Narrative in Fiction and Film* (Ithaca: Cornell Univ. Press, 1990) 139–60.

18. James Martine praises the realism of Heller's stories and argues that "Heller's very real understanding of this world [specifically, the poolroom society of "Nothing to Be Done"], of its morals and its codes, leads one to believe that if Joseph Heller is to give us a really permanent work, he must return to the social milieu of 'Castle of Snow,' 'A Man Named Flute,' and 'Nothing to Be Done'" (144). Martine's realist orientation is evident in this assessment, and his judgment is not born out by Heller's career. Heller's most realistic novel, *Good as Gold*, is by critical consensus also one of his weakest, and as he himself admits: "My strength as a writer is not as a realist" (Ruas interview, 151).

19. See Ruas interview, 149.

20. Ian Watt uses the term "delayed decoding" to describe this kind of narrative method; for Watt, this narrative technique "combines the forward temporal progression of the mind . . . with the much slower reflexive process of making out . . . meaning," the latter of which must move backward and well as forward in time (175). See *Conrad in the Nineteenth Century* (Berkeley and Los Angeles: Univ. of California Press, 1979), 175–79.

21. The chart below summarizes these transformations:

Actual Event	Voyage or Ship	Transformation or Event
Gastritis attack	*Washington*	Stormy passage that makes Captain seasick
Reads about Europe in guidebooks	*Queen Elizabeth*	Unnarrated journeys to Europe's historical past
Dispute over the oil well game	*Niew Amsterdam*	Unnarrated enjoyable voyage
War years and series of gastritis attacks	Murmansk runs	Torpedoed and indisposed as of swallowed seawater, awarded D.S.M.O.
Meets Mr. Simpson, ship's officer	Simpson's ship	Unnarrated voyages on actual Simpson's ship
Cynthia's abortion recovery	Simpson's ship	Gets tour of the engine room
Argument about location of the Blue Grotto	Simpson's ship	Learns Simpson has been arrested
Aftermath of confessing voyages are fictions	Planned voyage	Voyage to visit sister

22. Heller admits this: "'The Girl from Greenwich' was about a literary party, and I had never been to a literary party in my life" (Ruas interview, 149). He sets the party at

Sidney and Louise Cooper's, the protagonists of "The Death of a Dying Swan" and "Lot's Wife." Heller characterizes the Coopers by their unreflective attachment to middle-class values and morals.

23. In the unpublished "From Dusk to Dawn" (an undergraduate version of the same story is called "The First Touch of Winter"), Heller works a variant of this plot. In it, Andy, an aspiring playwright, dumps his girlfriend, rather than his job writing copy; the job provides "bread and alcohol," but she is dispensable. The manuscript is interesting because it contains Heller's professor's comment. This comment anticipated the critical appraisal of Heller's authorial strengths and weaknesses: commending him for having better control of language, in part, because the story relies so heavily on dialogue. The professor also liked the story's symbolic ending and advised him to try to publish it in a small magazine.

24. The detail of Sidney being a Western Union messenger has an interesting resonance. As a teenager, Heller was himself a Western Union messenger, and he makes Slocum one also in *Something Happened*. As in this story, the Western Union episodes are highly sexual, although it is Penny, a slightly older co-worker, who is the object of the protagonist's desires.

25. Edward Said, *Beginnings: Intention and Method* (New York: Basic Books, 1975), 205.

CHAPTER 2

1. Heller's interviews continually address the issue of correspondence between his war experience and *Catch-22*, with Heller giving a variety of answers, some contradictory. For a representative selection of interviews, readers should see: "*Catch-22* and After," *Gentlemen's Quarterly* (Mar. 1963): 95, 26, 28, 33, 40–41 46, 64–65; Sam Merrill interview; W. J. Weatherby, "The Joy Catcher," *The Guardian* (20 Nov. 1962): 7; and Joseph Heller, "On Translating *Catch-22* into a Movie," in *A "Catch-22" Casebook*, eds. Frederick Kiley and Walter McDonald, (New York: Crowell, 1973), 356–57; Ken Barnard, "Joseph Heller Tells How *Catch-22* Became *Catch-22* and Why He Was Afraid of Airplanes," *Detroit News* (13 Sep. 1970): 19–19, 24, 27–28, 30, 65: rpt., "Interview with Joseph Heller," in Kiley and McDonald, 294–301. The Brandeis University Library Heller collection allows a deeper exploration of his time in the service, for among its materials are: a list of events from his time on Corsica, including the missions that he flew, pictures of his unit, and accounts of the 488th Squadron, 340th Bombardment Group in which he served.

2. "The Miracle of Danrossane" and "Crippled Phoenix" (three versions of the latter), Joseph Heller papers, Brandeis University Library.

3. James Nagel has done the seminal work on the manuscript and other working papers for *Catch-22*, but much more study remains to be done. Nagel isolates important changes in documenting Heller's meticulous planning and analysis during the composition process. See: "The *Catch-22* Note Cards," *Studies in the Novel* 8 (1976): 394–405; rpt. in *Critical Essays on Joseph Heller*, ed. Nagel (Boston: G. K. Hall, 1984), 51–61; and "Two Brief Manuscript Sketches: Heller's *Catch-22*," *Modern Fiction Studies* 20 (1974): 221–24.

4. Said, *Beginnings*, 196.

5. Each of these sites has personal significance to Heller: Rome, which Heller visited shortly after it was liberated, afforded him his most memorable wartime leave; Île Rousse was an army rest camp on Corsica near where he was based; Poggibonsi was the destination for his first bombing mission, a mission on which he got bored and dropped his bombs too late; and Ferrara was the first mission on which Heller's squadron lost a plane.

6. "Chronology 2/13/66," Heller papers, Brandeis University Library.

7. Heller, "On Translating *Catch-22* into a Movie," 357.

8. Notably, Robert Merrill, among others, agrees with Heller: "the fact that *Catch-22* appeared sixteen years after the end of World War II suggests that its author was not primarily interested in recapturing the intensity of his own experiences" (*Joseph Heller*, 4).

9. See, for example, Barnard interview, 297; Heller, "On Translating *Catch-22* into a Movie," 357; and Joseph Heller, " 'Catch-22' Revisited," *Holiday* 41 (Apr. 1967): 56; rpt. in Kiley and McDonald, 316–32.

10. See Sam Merrill interview, 68; and Barnard interview, 298.

11. Heller, "Revisited," 142.

12. Barnard interview, 298.

13. As *Catch-22* readers know, the detail about bombs being dropped early also figures prominently in the novel. Evidently, it also has significance to Heller the man because in " 'Catch-22' Revisited" he jokes about visiting a hole in a mountainside where he dropped his bomb load too soon.

14. Luciana apparently is an early version of the Luciana of *Catch-22*. As Cramer remembers her: "Luciana was best. Tall, young, and graceful, she was a novice at love, and he remembered her smile as she came to him, her ingenuous astonishment at the sudden force of her passion, and the fumbling manner" ("Crippled Phoenix"). The Luciana episodes in *Catch-22* are also based upon personal experience, including the details about asking for her address, then tearing it up: "Luciana was Yossarian's vision of a perfect relationship. That's why he saw her only once, and perhaps that's why I saw her only once. If he examined perfection too closely, imperfections would show up" (Sam Merrill interview, 64). For other details of Heller's actual experience with Luciana, see Joseph Heller, "What Did You Eat in the War, Daddy?" *Forbes FYI* (11 Mar. 1996): 104.

Catch-22 reveals, however, that the Luciana plot is more closely tied to Heller's core authorial concerns than his remarks about his own personal experience would indicate. In the novel, Luciana's "perfection" is already impaired, for she has been wounded in an air raid and wears a pink chemise to hide her scar even while making love with Yossarian. However, he is fascinated by it, runs his hands over it, and insists that she relate its story. Later, after he has torn up the slip of paper with her address on it, Yossarian's search for her leads him into symbolic encounters with death: death in his nightmares about the Bologna mission and proleptic death when he looks for her in Snowden's room.

15. Heller derives much of the power of his novels from the protagonist's struggle to confront, understand, and finally relate his story. However, as in the case of "Crippled Phoenix," the protagonist never entirely succeeds in his efforts to disclose his story, and the relative successes and failures in this regard can be surprising. For example, in *Closing Time*, Yossarian—seemingly the most honest of all Heller heroes—partially evades the implications of his own story, that is, what Snowden's death has meant to him. Heller leaves it to Sammy Singer to divulge the meaning of Snowden's death. By contrast, although he can never publicly take responsibility for his son's death, Slocum can say to himself, knowing full well what he means: "I hug him tightly with both my arms. I squeeze" (562).

16. Joseph Heller papers, Brandeis University Library.

17. The notecards to *Catch-22* reveal the extensive role literary allusions played in the planning of the novel. Shakespearian allusions and connections particularly interested Heller; in fact, his play *We Bombed in New Haven* had its origin in Heller's idea for a dramatic tour in which actors would intersperse readings from *Catch-22* and Shakespeare. See Susan Braudy, "Laughing All the Way to the Truth," *New York* 1 (14 Oct. 1968): 44; rpt. in *Critical Essays on Joseph Heller*, ed. James Nagel (Boston: G. K. Hall, 1984), 215–21.

Several articles have been written on the the Shakespearean allusions in *Catch-22*: see Michael J. Larson, "Shakespearean Echoes in *Catch-22*," *American Notes and Queries* 17

(1979): 76–78, and James R. Aubrey and William E. McCarron, "More Shakespearean Echoes in *Catch-22*," *American Notes and Queries* 3 (Jan. 1990): 25–27.

18. Sam Merrill interview, 68.

19. Ruas interview, 151.

20. David Seed shows how war novels like James Jones's *From Here to Eternity* and Norman Mailer's *The Naked and the Dead* also contributed to Heller's evolving conception of *Catch-22* (see *The Fiction of Joseph Heller*, 23–33). *Catch-22* has frequently been examined as a novel in the war novel tradition; for a representative sample of such treatments, see: Robert Merrill, *Joseph Heller*, 10–16; John M. Muste, "Better to Die Laughing: The War Novels of Joseph Heller and John Ashmead," *Critique* 5 (fall 1962): 16–27; J. P. Stern, "War and the Comic Muse: *The Good Soldier Schweik* and *Catch-22*," *Comparative Literature* 20 (summer 1968): 193–216; Eric Solomon, "From Christ in Flanders to *Catch-22*: An Approach to War Fiction," *Texas Studies in Literature and Language* 11 (spring 1969): 851–66; Wayne Charles Miller, *An Armed America* (New York: New York Univ. Press, 1970), 205–244; and Jeffrey Walsh, *American War Literature: 1914 to Vietnam* (New York: St. Martin's Press, 1982), 190–95.

21. John W. Aldridge provides one of the best descriptions of the place that *Catch-22* has come to occupy on the American literary scene: "it has passed from relatively modest initial success . . . through massive best-sellerdom and early canonization as a youth-cult sacred text to its current status as a monumental artifact of contemporary American literature, almost as assured of longevity as the statues on Easter Island" ("The Loony Horror of It All —'Catch-22' Turns 25," *The New York Times Book Review* [26 Oct. 1986]: 3). Obviously, Aldridge is a fan of Heller's; equally influential detractors could be cited. But his sketch furnishes a useful account of the evolution in the novel's influence and reputation. Its modest initial success is little known today. It sold thirty thousand copies the first year and was a best-seller in Great Britain before it received much recognition in America. As a cult text, *Catch-22* attracted unusually diverse admirers. For example, Thomas Pynchon wrote Candida Donadio, the literary agent whom he and Heller shared, to praise it, and NBC newsman John Chancellor had buttons made up that he distributed, proclaiming "Better Yossarian than Rotarian." Actor Tony Curtis wrote a fan letter, the outcome of which was an intense friendship as well as Heller's becoming his creative consultant. (The letters between Heller and Curtis are part of the Brandeis University Library collection, as is Pynchon's letter to Donadio.) Despite the reputation of *Catch-22*, Heller has not achieved the acclaim of many well-known contemporary American writers. For mastery of craft and for extending the realist tradition, novelists like John Updike and Norman Mailer are better known. While Heller is recognized for his formal innovations, Thomas Pynchon, John Hawkes, and John Barth would probably be among the writers critics would mention first. Philip Roth, Bernard Malamud, and Saul Bellow come more readily to mind as writing out of the American Jewish tradition. And, unlike most of these writers, Heller has never won a major literary prize in America. More than anything else, for most readers and critics, he is known as the author of *Catch-22*—and some other novels which are not all that good.

22. Patrick O'Neill insightfully demonstrates the way in which humor in modern and postmodern texts depends upon privileging discourse over story. In particular, he is interested in what he calls entropic comedy, comedy that is aware of the fictionality of all discourse and "of the element of play" that is involved in the production of any meaning (23). O'Neill's discussion of *Catch-22* as an example of entropic satire is also valuable, although I disagree with his conclusion that the novel's discourse undercuts the implications of the story: "Heller's narrator is a showman who spreads before us in a comedian's patter an absurd and appalling world of viciousness, hypocrisy, and stupidity, and leaves us to draw whatever conclusions we may choose (or not choose) to draw" (172). Calling the narrator a showman or, alternatively, characterizing him as an omniscient and omnipotent narrative

God (172) is misleading, more appropriate to nineteenth-century novels like *Vanity Fair*. Heller does not personify the narrator in the way that O'Neill suggests. Similarly, as the Snowden death scene makes clear, Heller endeavors to control the meaning that the authorial audience will draw from his novel. See *The Comedy of Entropy: Humour/Narrative/Reading* (Toronto: Univ. of Toronto Press, 1990).

23. I borrow the notion of a synthetic element of narrative from James Phelan's *Reading People, Reading Plots*, though I am modifying his definition. Phelan explores the relationship between character and narrative progression, and he conceives of three aspects of character, which in turn contribute to narrative progression: thematic (as conveyer of narrative and authorial meaning), mimetic (as designation for a "person," albeit a textual one), and synthetic (as linguistic construct). I use the concept of synthetic component of narrative progression, without attaching it to character.

24. In describing Cervantes's achievement in *Don Quixote*, Robert Polhemus delineates a tradition of which *Catch-22* is a part; his account also might be taken to describe Heller's authorial intentions: "the comic imagination can change reality. [Cervantes] makes us respect the pluralism of life and the shifting nature of appearance and reality; most originally, he manages to give readers an option of respecting and loving a truly . . . eccentric character—that is, an option of *embracing the humorous*. He contradicts himself . . . but he opens a whole new range of possibilities for the comic imagination" (*Comic Faith* 15).

25. There are several ways in which Heller's imagination links death and women. In the short stories, women occasion symbolic, if not literal, deaths. In the marriage stories, women are obstacles to male authenticity, identified as they are with middle-class—and for Heller inauthentic—values. Thus, when Sidney Cooper returns home in "The Death of the Dying Swan," he gives up his quest for life and, in effect, accepts death: "He longed for people who were real, people who lived with honest passions and found vigorous pleasure in the mere event of existing, people for whom death came too soon." In the artist stories, women play a similar role, except it is the writer's creativity that is lost. A more interesting and complicated relationship (though one that perforce must remain speculative) is suggested by the original closing line to *Something Happened*: "I'm a cow" (Sam Merrill interview, 70). All the references to cows in the novel are to Slocum's mother, as in: "I can see myself all mapped out inanimately in stages around that dining room table, from mute beginning (Derek) to mute, fatal, bovine end (Mother), passive and submissive as a cow, and even beyond through my missing father (Dad)" (401). In rejecting the line, "I'm a cow" for "Everyone seems pleased with the way I've taken command," Heller may be refiguring the nature of, if not the effect of, Slocum's symbolic death. His mother dies in a nursing home, all her mental faculties gone. Rather than have Slocum identify himself with her and by extension with such a death, Heller has him handle the secretary Martha's nervous breakdown and fire his friend Andy Kagle. The "take charge" ending still signifies Slocum's symbolic death, one in which his identity independent from the company is extinguished. However, it connects death with what are in the novel masculine attitudes.

26. George Plimpton, "The Art of Fiction LI: Joseph Heller," interview, *The Paris Review* 15.60 (winter 1974): 129–30.

27. Ruas interview, 157.

28. Quoted by Susan R. Horton, *Interpreting Interpreting* (Baltimore: The Johns Hopkins Univ. Press, 1979), 28; from Said, 196.

29. The original manuscript shows the copy editor's excision and Heller's restoration of the line. Joseph Heller papers, Brandeis University Library.

30. David Seed astutely characterizes the workings of death in *Catch-22* as "a conversion process whereby human beings become mere matter and are assimilated into the non-human" (41).

31. Aeschylus, *Prometheus Bound* (Harmondsworth, England: Penguin Books, 1961). Further quotations from *Prometheus Bound* will be identified by page number in the text.

32. David Adams Leeming, *Mythology* (Philadelphia and New York: J. B. Lippincott Company, 1973), 186.

33. A colleague, John N. Serio, pointed out the Promethean correspondences to me.

34. The tripartite structure of Yossarian's story corresponds to the tripartite structure of the romance hero's quest. See, for example, Northrop Frye, who uses the terms *agon* (conflict), *pathos* (death struggle), and *anagnorisis* (discovery), or Joseph Campbell, whose terms are separation, initiation, and return. While Frye's and Campbell's categories are equally appropriate to Yossarian as "romance hero," I choose my own in order to emphasize the progress of Yossarian's knowledge. See Frye, *Anatomy of Criticism* (Princeton: Princeton Univ. Press, 1957), 187; and Campbell, *The Hero with a Thousand Faces* (Princeton: Princeton Univ. Press, 1968), 30.

Constance Denniston believes that Heller parodies romance structures and that the third stage of Yossarian's quest affords no illumination. See "The American Romance-Parody: A Study of Heller's *Catch-22*," *Emporia State Research Studies* 14 (1965): 42–59; rpt. in *Critical Essays on "Catch-22,"* ed. James Nagel (Encino, Ca.: Dickenson, 1973), 64–77.

35. Critics have used various schemas to characterize the structure of the novel; see, for example, Robert Merrill and Clinton Burhans, who also use a tripartite division; also Stephen W. Potts, who divides the novel into five sections. For Merrill, the divisions are chapters 1–16, 17–34, and 35–42 (see *Joseph Heller*, 48–49), and for Burhans, the divisions are 1–29, 29–39, and 40–42. Potts locates the divisions as chapters 1–9, 10–18, 19–25, 26–37, and 38–42. See Burhans, "Spindrift and the Sea: Structural Patterns and Unifying Elements in *Catch-22*," *Twentieth Century Literature* 19 (1973): 239–50; rpt. in Nagel, *Critical Essays on Joseph Heller*, 40–51; and Potts, *Catch-22*, 27–32.

In addition to these studies, three early, but still valuable studies dealing with the structure of *Catch-22* are: James L. McDonald, "I See Everything Twice: The Structure of Joseph Heller's *Catch-22*," *University Review* 34 (spring 1968): 175–80; James M. Mellard, "*Catch-22*: *Deja vu* and the Labyrinth of Memory," *Bucknell Review* 16.2 (1968): 29–44; and Jan Solomon, "The Structure of *Catch-22*," *Critique* 9 (1967): 46–57. All three essays are reprinted in Kiley and McDonald.

36. The working papers to *Catch-22* reveal Heller's own concern with the chronology of Yossarian's experience. For example, he outlines the order of events for the three crucial missions, Ferrara, Bologna, and Avignon. See Appendix B, which reproduces the desk blotter on which Heller laid out the chronology of the novel. Joseph Heller papers, Brandeis University Library.

37. Robert Merrill, Clinton Burhans, Stephen W. Potts, and Doug Gaukroger argue that there are several errors in Heller's chronology. See Merrill, *Joseph Heller*; Burhans; Potts, *Catch-22*; and Gaukroger, "Time Structure in *Catch-22*," *Critique* 12.2 (1970): 70–85; rpt. in Kiley and McDonald, 132–44; rpt. in Nagel, *Critical Essays on Catch-22*, 89–101.

Using internal evidence, Burhans constructs his own elaborate chronology for the events of the novel. His chronology differs from that of Heller's working papers. For example, in Heller's notes on the bombing missions, he dates Ferrara as "sometime in March," Bologna as "late June," and Avignon as "about July," while Burhans dates these missions as May, May, and June respectively. While Heller's notes are meticulous in recording what happens on the crucial missions, he is less exact in other matters; for example, his notes say: when "the book opens, he [Yossarian] has forty-four [missions]. And one of these has been the Avignon mission on which S[nowden] was killed." Joseph Heller papers, Brandeis University Library.

38. Robert M. Torrance's account of the comic hero applies to Heller's representation of Yossarian:

He is most completely a hero when most intentionally comic, and at the peak of his prowess is audaciously conscious both of the ridicule he provokes and of the challenge he poses. Although the odds are always against him he never shrinks from the contest, and by countless contrivances of wit and imagination he most often emerges not as the victim of fate but as the virtuoso of fortune—wary or cunning, prudent or forward as befits the occasion, but forever adaptable and inventive. He assimilates each of his multiple roles to his own comprehensive and pliable nature and magnifies himself by the stratagems that belittle his baffled opponents. He spurns a world bridled by an alien law and substitutes in its stead, to the best of his ample powers, a realm of bodily and spiritual freedom fabricated by fantasy in the shape of desire. By exalting his stubbornly animal nature to the jubilance of the divine he testifies to the multifarious wholeness of his battered humanity, and thereby achieves his most indelible triumph. (*The Comic Hero* [Cambridge: Harvard Univ. Press, 1978], 274–75)

39. Daniel Walden shows how the life-affirming values that Yossarian embodies grow out of Jewish writing. See "'Therefore Choose Life': A Jewish Interpretation of Heller's *Catch-22*," in Nagel, *Critical Essays on Catch-22*, 57–63.

40. For an exploration of the parallels with the Genesis story, see Marcus K. Billson, III, "The Un-Minderbinding of Yossarian: Genesis Inverted in *Catch-22*," *Arizona Quarterly* 36 (1980): 315–29.

41. Minna Doskow, "The Night Journey in *Catch-22*," *Twentieth Century Literature* 12 (1967), 186–93; rpt. in Kiley and McDonald, 165–73; rpt. in Nagel, *Critical Essays on Catch-22*, 155–63; rpt. in *Catch-22: A Critical Edition*, ed. Robert M. Scotto (New York: Delta, 1973), 491–500.

42. For a more extensive examination of the old man's role in the novel, see James Nagel, "Yossarian, the Old Man, and the Ending of *Catch-22*," in Nagel, *Critical Essays on Catch-22*, 164–74.

43. Yossarian's inspection of Snowden's viscera accomplishes another kind of education as well, one that undercuts the typical military education and reproduces the experience of combat veterans. As an aside, it bears attention that Heller satirically treats military education throughout *Catch-22*, for example, in such episodes as Lieutenant Scheisskopf's parades and the many briefing sessions. As described by John Keegan in his classic study *The Face of Battle* (New York: Viking Press, 1976), the aim of such an education "is to reduce the conduct of war to a set of rules and a system of procedures—and thereby to make orderly and rational what is essentially chaotic and instinctive. It is an aim analogous to that . . . pursued by medical schools in their fostering among their students a detached attitude to pain and distress in their patients, particularly victims of accidents" (20). Yossarian has long recognized the insanity of war, but he has not, even while treating the wounded Snowden, taken the next step of recognizing his complicity in this insanity. Nor has he yet comprehended the effects of a "military" education. As his subsequent actions demonstrate, his studied recollection of Snowden's death occasions these recognitions.

The death scene also serves as a brilliant representation of the sensations of the combat veteran. Again, to draw upon John Keegan, in battle the combatants experience a "sense of littleness, almost of nothingness, of their abandonment in a physical wilderness, dominated by vast impersonal forces, from which even the passage of time had been eliminated. The dimensions of the battlefield (in this instance the inside of combat aircraft) . . . reduced [the combatant's] subjective role, objectively vital though it was, to that of a mere victim" (322). Keegan's account closely parallels Yossarian's sensations in the Snowden scene and defines what Yossarian—and by extension the reader—must be reeducated to reject.

44. Denis de Rougement, *Love in the Western World*, trans. Montgomery Belgion (New York: Pantheon, 1956), 51.

45. For a representative reading that is critical of Yossarian's choices at the end of the novel, see Howard J. Stark, "*Catch-22*: The Ultimate Irony," in Nagel, *Critical Essays on Catch-22*, 130–41.

46. Critics have interpreted Sweden variously. For example, James Nagel believes Heller's "Sweden is less a place than a possibility, a state of mind which allows for hope and aspiration" ("Yossarian, the Old Man, and the Ending of *Catch-22*," 173); while Mike Frank argues, "the Sweden [Yossarian] aims for is located, perhaps, not so much in the real world as in the geography of the moral imagination" ("Eros and Thanatos in *Catch-22*," *Canadian Review of American Studies* 7 [spring 1976]: 86).

Of his many remarks about the ending to *Catch-22*, Heller's most suggestive come in his interview with Paul Krassner:

> I don't think Sweden is paradise. Sweden was important to me as a *goal*, or an objective, a kind of Nirvana. It's important, if you're in a situation which is imperfect, uncomfortable, or painful, that you have some *objective* to move toward to change that situation.
>
> Now, in Yossarian's situation—his environment, the world itself—the monolithic society closes off every conventional area of protest or corrective action, and the only choice that's left to him is one of ignoble acceptance in which he can profit and live very comfortably—but nevertheless ignoble—or *flight*, a renunciation of that condition, of that society, that set of circumstances. (Krassner, "An Impolite Interview with Joseph Heller," *The Realist* 39 [Nov. 1962]: 30; rpt. in Kiley and McDonald, 273–93)

47. In a scathing early review of *Catch-22*, Roger H. Smith uses Heller's style, particularly his self-negating sentences, to support his view that "its author cannot write." See "A Review: *Catch-22*," *Daedalus* 92 (winter 1963): 156; rpt. in Nagel, *Critical Essays on "Catch-22*," 21–33; and Kiley and McDonald, 27–39.

48. Tony Tanner, *City of Words: American Fiction, 1950–1970* (New York: Harper & Row, Publishers, 1971), 20. Tanner also writes about *Catch-22*, including Heller's use of language (72–84); his thesis is that: "Joseph Heller's brilliant dark comedy is less about the tactical struggle of two armies than the struggle for survival of the individual within his own society" (72). Similarly, Gary W. Davis argues that *Catch-22* reveals the problematic nature of language itself; more specifically, he contends that the novel "becomes a medium which reminds us of our longings for a language of continuity and referentiality at the very same time it exposes the dangerous, closed discourses to which such desires may lead"; see "*Catch-22* and the Language of Discontinuity," *Novel* 12 (1978): 66–77; rpt. in Nagel, *Critical Essays on Joseph Heller*, 62–75. Like Davis, Judith Ruderman believes that *Catch-22* reveals the limitation of language itself: "In *Catch-22*, Heller uses a language of deficiency to expose not only gaping holes in the fabric of society but also the inability of language to give voice to outrage at the human condition" (30); see "'Words Cannot Express. . . .': *Catch-22* and the Language of Deficiency," in her *Joseph Heller*, 30–48.

49. David Lodge identifies foregrounding as one of the defining characteristics of postmodernist fiction and describes six of its characteristics: contradiction, permutation, discontinuity, randomness, excess, and short circuit. *Catch-22* contains examples of all of

these devices except randomness. *The Modes of Modern Writing* (1977, rpt. Chicago: Univ. of Chicago Press, 1988), 220–45.

50. In *Reading People, Reading Plots*, James Phelan uses the concept of narrative instability in order to account for narrative progression. He identifies two kinds of instabilities, those occurring within stories ("instabilities between characters, created by situations, and complicated and resolved by actions" [15]) and those created by discourse ("instabilities—of value, belief, opinion, knowledge, expectation—between authors and/or narrators, one the one hand, and the authorial audience on the other" [15]).

51. For representative reading of this type, see Jean Kennard, "Joseph Heller: At War with Absurdity," *Mosaic* 4.3 (spring 1971): 75–87; rpt. in Kiley and McDonald, 255–69; Sanford Pinsker, "Heller's *Catch-22*: The Protest of a *Puer Eternis*," *Critique* 7 (1965): 150–62; and Brian Way, "Formal Experiment and Social Discontent: Joseph Heller's *Catch-22*," *Journal of American Studies* 2 (1968): 253–70.

52. Self-negating sentences remain a Heller stylistic preference, although his use of them and the effects he derives from them change. In *Something Happened*, the sentences illustrate Slocum's cast of mind, particularly his capacity for self-deception: "I'm bored with my work very often now. . . . Actually, I enjoy my work" (28); "(I know so many things I'm afraid to find out)" (158); or "[The salesmen] are a vigorous, fun-loving bunch when they are not suffering abdominal cramps or brooding miserably over the future" (22). Such sentences work ironically, with Slocum unaware of the ironies he authors. In *Good as Gold*, Heller locates such sentences in a number of characters, most notably in Ralph Newsome: "We'll want to move ahead with this as speedily as possible, although we'll have to go slowly. . . . We'll want to build this up into an important public announcement, although we'll have to be completely secret" (53). Here the sentences function satirically, revealing the contradictory expedience of the novel's politicians and, by extension, of such satiric targets as Henry Kissinger. In *Picture This*, Heller makes self-negating sentences part of the narrator's vision: "The strategy of Pericles was flawless. The strategy failed" (153); "The motion in the Athenian Assembly to invade Syracuse to restore order in Sicily was deceitful, corrupt, stupid, chauvinistic, irrational, and suicidal. It carried by a huge majority" (211); "In the *Jewish Bride*, almost everything seems wrong in a picture that is absolutely right" (251). These sentences point out the darkening of Heller's vision; tonally, they are less playful and more sarcastic. They serve to illuminate human obtuseness; even Rembrandt's great painting succeeds because the artist did not get it right.

53. Douglas Hofstadter, *Godel, Escher, Bach* (New York: Basic Books, 1979), 702.

54. Characterizing the difficulties that Heller's paradoxes pose for the reader, David Seed says, "Paradox induces a state of uncertainty in the reader comparable to that of many characters, denying an overview of actions" (52).

55. For a particularly useful discussion of repetition, see J. Hillis Miller, "Two Forms of Repetition," chap. 1 in his *Fiction and Repetition* (Cambridge: Harvard Univ. Press, 1982), 1–21. For a psychological account, see Peter Brooks, *Reading for the Plot* (New York: Vintage Books, 1985) and for one of the first extensive treatments of the concept, see Bruce F. Kawin, *Telling It Again and Again* (Ithaca and London: Cornell Univ. Press, 1972).

56. An early manuscript version of the *Catch-22* passage not only is significantly longer, but also makes *Catch-22* a rule that is actually written down. In an early version recorded in Heller's handwriting, the conversation between Doc Daneeka and Yossarian continues. To illustrate Heller's compositional process, I include sections that he crossed out, placing the crossed out words in parentheses. It should also be noted that *Catch-22* is called Catch-18; Heller changed the number when Leon Uris's *Mila-18* was to be published at the same time his novel was to appear.

"That's some catch, that Catch-18," he [Yossarian] observed with (sardonic rueful) awe.

"It's the best there is," Doc Daneeka agreed.

"I've got a copy lying around here somewhere," (Doc Daneeka said.) "I've never read it all the way through, but I'll let you borrow it if I can find it and you promise to give it back."

Dunbar was (even more deeply) moved and (let out a softer, lower, more solemn whistle or still more profound respect).

"That's some catch, that Catch-18," he murmured gravely (with even more rueful awe).

"Doc Daneeka says it's the best there is," Yossarian agreed (spiritlessly). (Joseph Heller papers, Brandeis University Library)

Working with his editor, Robert Gottleib, who subsequently became the editor of *The New Yorker*, Heller substantially cut the manuscript from the 800 typewritten pages originally submitted, to about 625 pages. As in the excerpt above, dialogue was shortened and language tightened, but incidents were not usually cut. For Heller's account of this process, see Krassner's interview, 28.

57. While many critics discuss Heller's use of repetition, two of the most illuminating treatments are those of David H. Richter, "The Achievement of Shape in the Twentieth-Century Fable," in his *Fable's End: Completeness and Closure in Rhetorical Fiction* (Chicago: Univ. of Chicago Press, 1974), 136–65) and Robert Merrill, *Joseph Heller*. For Richter, repetition is a vehicle for Heller's absurdist humor: "Instead of going from incident to incident, with each successive event darker in tone than the last . . . incidents and situations are repeated frequently, with few factual changes, but with detail added to bring out the grotesque horror that underlies their absurd comedy" (141). Merrill sees the repeated elements as "a kind of trap, [in which] the reader is encouraged to laugh at characters and events which ultimately seem quite serious" (47).

58. For a discussion of this passage, see Caroline Gordon and Jeanne Richardson, "Flies in Their Eyes? A Note on Joseph Heller's *Catch-22*," *Southern Review* 3 (winter 1967): 96–105; rpt. in Nagel *Critical Essays on "Catch-22*," 117–24.

59. J. Hillis Miller would consider such transformations a second kind of repetition. Defining repetition based on disparity, Miller says, "The other, the Nietzschean mode of repetition posits a world based on difference. Each thing, this other theory would assume, is unique, intrinsically different from every other thing. Similarity arises against the background of this 'disparité du fond.' It is a world not of copies but of what Deleuze calls 'simulacra' or 'phantasms' " (*Fiction and Repetition*, 6).

60. Robert Merrill points out that the "hot tomato" is a reference to the pumpkin in the Alger Hiss case. Whittaker Chambers claimed to have found documents demonstrating Hiss's disloyalty in a pumpkin (*Joseph Heller*, 25).

61. For a discussion of the chaplain as character and the lens that he affords on Heller's methods, see David Seed, 33–39.

62. Tony Tanner argues that one of the defining characteristics of contemporary American writers is the way in which they employ the tranformation of language. See his introduction to *City of Words*, especially pages 20–21.

63. David Lodge calls such pairing of alternatives a special kind of permutation and uses Heller to illustrate its effects: "When reduced to only two variables, permutation becomes simply alternation and expresses the hopelessness of the human condition" (231).

64. Quoted by Richard Rhodes, *The Making of the Bomb* (New York: Simon and Schuster, 1986), 77.

65. Weatherby interview, 7.

66. In its use of Plato's *Symposium*, *Picture This* makes explicit the connection Heller sees between tragedy and comedy: "Socrates was busy compelling these two prize-winning playwrights [Aristophanes and Agathon] to acknowledge that a man who could write a comedy could also write a tragedy, and that the true artist in tragedy was an artist in comedy too" (91).

67. A number of critics explore the "gradual darkening of tone" of *Catch-22* (Merrill, *Joseph Heller*, 49). See, for example, Richter and Burhans in addition to Merrill. While true in a large sense, such arguments do not take into account "the *sequence* of modes of presentation" (Horton 44) or that one mode of presentation—comic, tragic, ironic, descriptive, etc.—seldom controls an entire episode. As Susan Horton shows, taking into account these elements allows much more finely tuned interpretations. See chapter 3, "Questioning the Interpretive Unit," of Horton's *Interpreting*, 42–55.

The need for finer interpretations becomes clear in the argument that Merrill makes: that the novel's narrative "sequences . . . invariably move from the comic to the tragic" (*Joseph Heller*, 49). As I will show, the way in which the tragic and comic impinge on each other is much more complicated than this, and, even at the novel's darkest moments, comedy emerges out of tragedy.

68. Mathew Winston, "*Humour noir* and Black Humor," *Harvard English Studies* 3 (1972): 273. Among the many perspectives on black humor, Winston provides a particularly clear and sound approach, tracing the history of the term and identifying its characteristics. See also his "Black Humor: To Weep with Laughing," in *Comedy: New Perspectives*, ed. Maurice Charney (New York: New York Literary Forum, 1978), 31–43. For a broader perspective on humor in contemporary literature that includes black humor, see Sarah Blacher Cohen, *Comic Relief* (Urbana, Chicago, and London: Univ. of Illinois Press, 1978).

69. Randall Craig's account of tragicomedy can be usefully applied to this aspect of Heller's art. See *The Tragicomic Novel* (Newark: Univ. of Delaware Press, 1989).

70. Burhans and Robert Merrill believe that Heller has made an error in chronology in chapter 17 and in this mistaken belief they miss the way in which he locates crucial aspects of the chapter, including the soldier-in-white scene, in Yossarian's memory. The error affects Merrill's interpretation of the scene, which he sees as an "exact" repetition (*Joseph Heller*, 42) of the scene in chapter 1. Rather, Yossarian *recalls* the scene, just as he recalls the deaths of Kraft, Snowden, and Clevinger, which precede the soldier in white's death.

71. Taking his departure point from Kierkegaard and Pirandello, Randall Craig (38–39) shows that while people are seen as primarily tragic or comic, to the tragicomic novelist "the proportions are equal." In this regard, he quotes Søren Kierkegaard: "The relative difference which exists for immediate consciousness between the comic and the tragic, vanishes in the doubly reflected consciousness. . . . What lies at the root of both the comic and the tragic in this connection, is the discrepancy, between the infinite and the finite, the eternal and that which becomes" (*Concluding Unscientific Postscript*, trans. David F. Swenson [Princeton: Princeton Univ. Press, 1941], 82–83). For the tragicomic artist then: "a thought cannot originate without the opposite or contrary thought originating at the same time, . . . for each reason he has to say *yes*, there arise one or more that compel him to say *no*" (Luigi Pirandello, *On Humor*, trans. Antonio Illiana and Daniel P. Testa, [Chapel Hill: Univ. of North Carolina Press, 1960], 132).

72. Alvin Kernan sees such intensification as intrinsic to the satiric plot: "Whenever satire does have a plot which eventuates in a shift from the original condition, it is not a true change but simply an intensification of the original situation" (*Modern Satire*, [New York: Harcourt, Brace & World, 1962], 177).

73. See Leslie Fiedler, *Love and Death in the American Novel* (New York: Criterion Books, 1960).

74. This phrase occurs in the outline that Heller made of the Ferrara, Bologna, and Avignon missions. Joseph Heller papers, Brandeis University Library.

75. See E. H. Gombrich, *Art and Illusion* (Princeton: Princeton Univ. Press, 1960), 220.

76. M. M. Bakhtin, "Epic and Novel," *The Dialogic Imagination*, ed. Michael Holquist, trans. Carl Emerson and Michael Holquist (Austin: Univ. of Texas Press, 1981), 23.

77. Heller, quoted in Medwick, 702.

78. Chet Flippo, "Checking in with Joseph Heller," interview, *Rolling Stone* (16 Apr. 1981): 57; see also Ruas interview, 163–64.

CHAPTER 3

1. Particularly at its inception, *Something Happened* had affinities with *Catch-22*. Like Yossarian, Slocum was a bombardier flying missions over Italy and France, but as David Seed indicates, Slocum's war experiences get attentuated between a preliminary version (which appeared in *Esquire*) and the published novel (Seed, *The Fiction of Joseph Heller*, 96). In talking about the relationship between the two works, Heller himself quotes a line from *Something Happened*: "It was after the war that the struggle began" (Plimpton interview, 142).

2. Heller says of his representation of American life in *Something Happened*, "I am trying very hard to *keep* the context of our society, not only familiar but with nothing extraordinary in it and yet maybe as horrifying as Kafka does in his world. Now you see consciously I know this is my object. I'm trying to get the same sense of imprisonment, of intimidation, of psychological paralysis and enslavement, but without using any symbolism other than the society being a symbol of itself" (James Shapiro, "Work in Progress/Joseph Heller," interview, *Intellectual Digest* 2 [Dec. 1971]: 8).

3. Andre Furlani makes the same point, showing how Slocum uses Socratic devices (specifically, the elenchus) to avoid self-knowledge rather to achieve it; see "'Brisk Socratic Dialogues': Elenctic Rhetoric in Joseph Heller's *Something Happened*," *Narrative* 3.3 (Oct. 1995): 252–70.

4. As a novel confronting readers with considerable difficulties, *Something Happened*, unsurprisingly, received mixed reviews. For readers today looking for guidance, the reviews of Kurt Vonnegut, "*Something Happened*: Joseph Heller's Extraordinary Novel about an Ordinary Man," *New York Times Book Review* (6 Oct. 1974): 1–3, rpt. in Nagel, *Critical Essays on Joseph Heller*, 93–97; William Kennedy, "Endlessly Honest Confession," *The New Republic* (Oct. 1974): 17–19; and John W. Aldridge, "Vision of Man Raging in a Vacuum," *Saturday Review World* (19 Oct. 1974): 18–21, hold the most value. Picturing Heller as a man building a novel with a million taps of a ball peen hammer, Vonnegut provides a particularly useful vantage point for approaching the novel. "As far as I know," Vonnegut says, "Joseph Heller is the first major novelist to deal with unrelieved misery at novel length. Even more rashly, he leaves the major character, Slocum, essentially unchanged at the end" (2). Aldridge and Kennedy use Slocum's character as entry point to the novel. For Aldridge, Slocum is a descendant of Dostoevski's underground man, "a man raging in a vacuum, and the character of his raging identifies him as squarely belonging in the anti-heroic tradition" (19), while for Kennedy, Slocum is much more ordinary—"a woefully lost figure with a profound emptiness, a sad, absurd, vicious, grasping, climbing, womanizing . . . fearful victim of the indecipherable, indescribable malady of being born human" (17).

For representative negative reviews, see Nelson Algren, "*Something Happened* by Joseph Heller," *Critic* 33.1 (1974): 90–91; and Pearl K. Bell, "Heller's Trial by Tedium," *New Leader* (28 Oct. 1974): 17–18. Bell voices the most frequent complaint about the novel by focusing on the tedium of Slocum's monologue: "Throughout its almost 600 pages we are forced to listen to the turgid, self-pitying, unintelligent, scandalously repetitive, childishly narcissistic, suffocatingly tedious monologue of a faceless organization man named Bob Slocum" (18).

5. Heller's accounts of the genesis of *Something Happened* imply a correspondence between his own concerns and those of the novel: "In 1962 I was sitting on the deck of a house on Fire Island. I was frightened. I was worried because I had lost interest in my job then—which was writing advertising and promotion copy. . . . As I sat there worrying and wondering what to do, one of those first lines suddenly came to mind: 'In the office in which I work, there are four people of whom I am afraid. Each of these four people is afraid of five people.' Immediately, the lines presented a whole explosion of possibilities and choices— characters (working in a corporation), a tone, a mood of anxiety, or insecurity" (Plimpton interview, 128–29). Out of Heller's boredom and anxiousness comes a novel about anxiety and virtually unrelieved boredom. As in *Catch-22*, there are also biographical correspondences between his life and the novel: both Slocum and Heller work in marketing; Heller models Slocum's company on Time, Inc., where he himself worked; and Heller's daughter recognizes aspects of her life in Heller's portrait of Slocum's daughter. Describing the relationship between his experience and the novel, Heller himself says, "I used plenty of my own experience in it, but the mind the book is about is not my mind" ("Joseph Heller in Conversation with Martin Amis," interview, *New Review* 2 [Nov. 1975]: 59).

6. Describing the relationship between Slocum's progressive loss of control and the design of his novel, Heller says: "In the last two sections, preceding the end, I did have in mind a man having a breakdown. And there, too, the syntax, the language, is intended to correspond to that. So whereas in the earlier portions he was punctilious about grammar and sentence structure, in those last sections he does have run-on sentences, the use of parentheses, he loses his logic, and he even begins having what amount to auditory hallucinations" (Ruas interview, 159). Robert Merrill calls Heller's technique in this novel psychological realism and believes that it "enable[s] Heller to render his protagonist's extraordinary contradictions" (*Joseph Heller*, 94).

7. C. E. Reilly and Carol Villei, "An Interview with Joseph Heller," *Delaware Literary Review* (spring 1975): 21.

8. Of the relationship that he intends between Slocum and the reader, Heller says: "It was meant to be a first person, present tense, uncomfortably intimate book" (Ruas interview, 160).

9. See Robert Langbaum, *The Poetry of Experience* (New York: Norton, 1963).

10. Thomas LeClair, "Joseph Heller, *Something Happened*, and the Art of Excess," *Studies in American Fiction* 9 (autumn 1981): 255; rpt. in Nagel, *Critical Essays on Joseph Heller*, 114–27; see also Furlani, 266.

11. Evan Carton insightfully shows how Heller uses Slocum's monologue to implicate his authorial audience in the novel's vision of American middle-class life:

To the extent that Slocum is a powerful stereotype . . . he implicates the reader, who shares, perhaps more fully than he cares to admit, Slocum's white middle class, masculinist America. If Slocum's confession resolves itself into a form of detachment, the reader's initial resistance to Slocum gives way to a confessional form of engagement. . . . *Something Happened* personalizes its reader precisely when it breaks down his privacy through the medium of its narrator's voice—a voice whose indivisibility from a dominant American ideology accounts both for Slocum's sense of its self-estrangement and for our sense of its haunting familiarity. ("The Politics of Selfhood: Bob Slocum, T. S. Garp and Auto-American-Biography," *Novel* 20 [fall 1986]: 50.

12. Numerous critics have found the length of *Something Happened* problematic. Robert Merrill gives a concise account of this position: "Heller stretches the structure to the reader's breaking point by rendering digression after digression, each reported at great length and with unrelenting realism. What is harrowing in *Something Happened* is also what becomes tedious. . . . At something like four hundred pages *Something Happened* would have been a much better book" (*Joseph Heller*, 94–95). Extending the point, Joseph Epstein argues that *Something Happened* "demonstrat[es] that fiction written under the assumptions of the post-Modernist sensibility cannot sustain itself over the length of a large novel. A Donald Barthelme can float a story or sketch under these same assumptions for eight or ten pages on sheer brilliance. But at greater length, things tend to flatten out—the literature of exhaustion itself in the end proves exhausting to read" ("Joseph Heller's Milk Train: Nothing More to Express," *Washington Post Book World* [6 Oct. 1974]: 3); rpt. in Nagel, *Critical Essays on Joseph Heller*, 97–101.

13. For studies of the amount or repetitiveness of information, see Thomas LeClair, 245–60; Lindsey Tucker, "Entropy and Information Theory in Heller's *Something Happened*," *Contemporary Literature* 25.3 (1984): 323–40; and Patricia Merivale, "'One Endless Round': *Something Happened* and the Purgatorial Novel," *English Studies in Canada* 6.4 (Dec. 1985): 438–39; Judith Ruderman, "*Something Happened* and the Compulsion to Repeat," in her *Joseph Heller*, 49–67.

14. Roland Barthes's account of a text can be applied to the reader's role in *Something Happened*: "a text is made of multiple writings, drawn from many cultures and entering into mutual relations of dialogue, parody, contestation, but there is one place where this multiplicity is focused and that place is the reader, not as was hitherto said, the author. The reader is the space on which all the quotations that make up a writing are inscribed without any of them being lost; a text's unity lies not in its origin but in its destination" ("The Death of the Author," in *Image-Music-Text* [New York: Hill and Wang, 1977], 148).

15. James Phelan's concept of narrative and discourse instabilities (the latter designated by the term "tensions") can be used to describe the dual narrative progression of *Something Happened*—Slocum's story and his telling of this story. My examination of narrative form in the fourth section of this chapter ("The Logic of Emptiness") examines what Phelan calls narrative tension in his *Reading People, Reading Plots*.

16. Heller himself mentions the way in which limitations provide the ground for artistic accomplishment: "It may have something to do with the discipline of writing advertising copy (which I did for a number of years) where the limitations provide a considerable spur to the imagination. There's an essay of T. S. Eliot's in which he praises the disciplines of writing, claiming that if one is forced to write within a certain framework the imagination is taxed to its utmost and will produce the richest ideas" (Plimpton interview, 130).

17. Robert Merrill compares Slocum's monologue to the Jason section of *The Sound and the Fury* (*Joseph Heller*, 87–90), and Slocum himself calls Derek "Benjy."

18. Vonnegut, 2.

19. Vonnegut associates the mythic dimensions of novels like *Something Happened* with the resistance of critics and readers to such narratives: "This, in my opinion, is why critics often condemn our most significant books and poems and plays when they first appear, while praising feebler creations. The birth of a new myth fills them with primitive dread for myths are so effective" (ibid.).

20. David Seed also describes Slocum as a myth maker but in a more limited sense than I do: "By implying a singular cause [for his problems] Slocum almost composes a personal mythology where he falls from happiness through some primal wrongdoing" (109).

21. J. Hillis Miller, "The Ontological Basis of Form," in his *The Form of Victorian Fiction* (Notre Dame, Ind.: Univ. of Notre Dame Press, 1968), 31–32.

22. Wallace Stevens, "Notes toward a Supreme Fiction," in his *The Collected Poetry of Wallace Stevens* (New York: Alfred A. Knopf, 1971), 383.

23. Of Slocum's formulation of the child self, Evan Carton observes, "[l]ike both Bartleby and his biographer, Slocum privileges origins and equates originality and selfhood. It is an equation that the model of an institutional and foundational identity alone will satisfy" (46).

24. Injured feet and legs are one of the tropes of Heller's imagination. In *Something Happened*, in addition to this reference, there are Kagle's deformed leg and the Oedipus-like ankles of Slocum's son. In *Catch-22*, Yossarian mistakenly treats Snowden for a thigh injury, and in *Good as Gold*, Gold receives the fortune cookie message, "You will hurt your foot." As this brief survey suggests, references to injured feet convey menace. In his other writings, feet are associated with humor as well, as for instance in his account of the onset of Guillain-Barré syndrome: "I was never totally paralyzed. The word they use is 'quadraparetic.' . . . I could not move at all after eight to ten days. They told me I'd be weak, but I didn't know what weak meant. The only thing left intact by the disease was my sense of humor—and my feet" (Joseph Heller, "Something Happened," *People* [23 Aug. 1982] 26).

25. Norman Holland's discussion of the repetition compulsion, a concept that he borrows from Freud, can be applied to this aspect of *Something Happened*; see *The Dynamics of Literary Response* (New York: Columbia Univ. Press, 1989), 44–45.

26. See R. W. B. Lewis, *The American Adam: Innocence, Tragedy and Tradition in the Nineteenth Century* (Chicago: Univ. of Chicago Press, 1955). Much of Lewis's discussion of the way American writers use the myth of Adamic innocence could be applied to *Something Happened*.

27. Describing the relationship between Slocum and Derek, Heller says, "The damaged [autistic] child is a reflection of himself, symbolically" (Barbara A. Bannon, "PW Interviews: Joseph Heller," *Publishers Weekly* [30 Sept. 1974]: 6).

28. The psychological dimensions of *Something Happened* have received comparatively little attention; for psychological readings of the novel, see Joan DelFattore, "The Dark Stranger in Heller's *Something Happened*," in Nagel, *Critical Essays on Joseph Heller*, 127–38 and James M. Mellard, "*Something Happened*: The Imaginary, The Symbolic, and the Discourse of the Family," in Nagel, *Critical Essays on Joseph Heller*, 138–55; also see Ruderman, *Joseph Heller*.

29. My reading of *Oedipus Rex* is indebted to E. R. Dodds, "On Misunderstanding Oedipus," in his *The Ancient Concept of Progress* (Oxford: The Clarendon Press, 1973), 64–77.

30. In a Lacanian reading James Mellard argues that "[t]hough the psychological dimensions of *Something Happened* are evident from the outset, readers are perhaps thrown off the track by an overt invocation of the Oedipus complex as an explanation of those psychological disturbances suggested in the narrator's—Bob Slocum's—fear of closed doors and other features of behavior. Slocum seems to imply that since he actually invokes an outmoded Freudian etiology, one must look elsewhere for the 'real' causes of his neurotic behavior" (138). Mellard takes the linguistic and semiotic approach of Lacan to explicate Slocum's complicity in his son's death.

31. J. Hillis Miller, *Form of Victorian Fiction*, 35.

32. See Joseph Campbell, "Myth and the Modern World," in his *The Power of Myth* (New York: Doubleday, 1988), 3–36.

33. Soren Kierkegaard, *Fear and Trembling* (Princeton, N.J.: Princeton Univ. Press, 1941), 10–15.

34. David Seed (107–9) provides the best account of Slocum's obsession with time.

35. Slocum's character has attracted a great deal of attention; see, for instance, George J. Searles, *"Something Happened*: A New Direction for Joseph Heller," *Critique* 18.3 (1977): 74–81; Richard Hauer Costa, "Notes from a Dark Heller: Bob Slocum and the Underground Man," *Texas Studies in Literature and Language* 23 (1981): 159–82; and David Seed, 96–128.

36. Of the connection between Slocum telling his story and fixing his identity, David Seed observes, "Slocum tries constantly to assemble continuous sequences because only in this way can he find his identity. His narrative should thus be seen as a series of attempts to construct a continuous sequence, to bridge over the gaps . . ." (108).

37. For a study of the satire in *Something Happened*, see Wayne D. McGinnis, "The Anarchic Impulse in Two Recent Novels," *Publications of the Arkansas Philological Association* 5 (1979): 36–40.

38. William Kennedy, 18.

39. See, for example, the reviews of Pearl K. Bell ("Trial by Tedium," 17), Joseph Epstein (3), and Caroline Blackwood, "The Horrors of Peace," *Times Literary Supplement* (25 Oct. 1974): 1183.

40. This defense was particularly prevalent among the early critics of *Catch-22*; see, for example, Jean Kennard, who argues that "the novel itself becomes an object which provides the reader with the experience of the absurd" (87). For a more recent formulation, see John W. Aldridge, "The Loony Horror of It All": "It has also been demonstrated that the tangled, excessively repetitive structure is a perfectly convincing formal statement of the novel's theme, even of the reiterated double bind of the central symbol, Catch-22" (55).

41. As a way of announcing his new novel, Heller published a preliminary version of this chapter ("Something Happened," *Esquire* 66 [Sept. 1966]: 136–41, 212–13). In the published novel, the *Esquire* material was revised, becoming parts of chapters 1 and 2. Israel Shenker attributes the changes to the suggestions of Heller's editor Robert Gottlieb ("2nd Heller Book Due 13 Years After First," *New York Times* [18 Feb. 1974]: 30).

42. Patricia Merivale shows why a second reading is necessary to perceive this structure; in her words, "[o]nly thus [by rereading the novel] can these pages take their true shape and sense from the mortal event which not only ends but begins them" (" 'One Endless Round,' " 449).

43. Mike Frank discusses the Freudian concept of thanatos in *Catch-22* and much of what he says can be applied to *Something Happened*. See his "Eros and Thanatos in *Catch-22*."

44. Of the importance of an ending, Heller says, "I've never begun a book that I didn't finish, because I haven't started writing until I knew the beginning and the ending, felt they matched, and felt they associated enough with the middle. The journey from the opening paragraph to the end would have to make interesting fiction" (quoted in Michael Schumacher, "Heller," *Writer's Digest* [Mar. 1987]: 24). Of the novel's climactic moment itself, Heller says that it came to him along with the moment of inspiration while he was "sitting on that deck in Fire Island" (Plimpton interview, 142).

45. Accounting for the title *Something Happened*, Heller says, "I was on Fifth Avenue and there was the sound of two automobiles colliding. Two kids who were there said, 'Come on, something happened.' As soon as I heard it I thought, [t]hat's a good title. Then I began using the phrase, which is what happened with *Catch-22*—once I decided on the title, then I began using it in the text a great deal" (Ruas interview, 158).

46. Susan Strehle first explores the pattern of mind that prompts Slocum to kill his son; see her insightful essay " 'A Permanent Game of Excuses': Determinism in *Something*

Happened," Modern Fiction Studies 24 (1978–79): 550–56; rpt. in Nagel, *Critical Essays on Joseph Heller*, 106–14. Like Strehle, James Mellard sees a psychological inevitability to the killing: "It *had* to happen, if Slocum was going to come to terms with his life—the Oedipus structure—within his culture" (*Something Happened*, 153). Judith Ruderman provides a psychologically plausible explanation for the killing: "Perhaps by getting rid of the little boy he kills those inadequacies in himself (the 'timid little boy' hiding inside himself), gains control and therefore—this is his equation—gains maturity" (*Joseph Heller*, 60). See also George Sebouhian, "From Abraham and Isaac to Bob Slocum and My Boy: Why Fathers Kill Their Sons," *Twentieth Century Literature* 27 (1981): 43–52.

47. Heller says that he became aware of the possibility that Slocum acted willfully in his son's death retrospectively: "Shortly after the book came out, Bruno Bettelheim wrote my editor a letter about the validity of the death—the father willfully, deliberately killed his son because he had no choice. When I read that I started getting chills, because I had not thought of that. . . . Now, it could be that in terms of drawing on recesses of my mind, with which I'm not in touch, what Bruno Bettelheim said was there" (Ruas interview, 163–64).

48. Evan Carton provides an alternative but complementary account of Slocum's loss of identity: "Slocum's narrative, finally, enacts the production, packaging and sale of his identity, an identity that, like the unnamed product that has made the company 'the leader in the field,' is nothing but that which America demands. . . . His ultimate success is that of the trade name which becomes a generic name and, in cornering the market, loses it" (48).

49. Heller originally had chosen quite a different, but equally bleak, closing line— "I'm a cow" (Sam Merrill interview, 70).

CHAPTER 4

1. Sam Merrill interview, 73.

2. *Good as Gold* received mixed reviews. Leonard Michaels ("Bruce Gold's American Experience," *New York Times Book Review* [11 Mar. 1979]: 1, 24–25]; rpt. in Nagel, *Critical Essays on Joseph Heller*, 167–72, and John W. Aldridge ("The Deceits of Black Humor," *Harper's Magazine* 258 [Mar. 1979]: 115–18; rpt. in his *The American Novel and the Way We Live Now*, 42–46) provide two of the most laudatory assessments of Heller's achievement. For Michaels, *Good as Gold* is Heller's successful attempt to explore the life of "some American Jews, their bastardized existence, their sense of congenital inauthenticity" (1). Aldridge sees more flaws than Michaels but praises the novel as "a comedy of the bleakest and blackest kind . . . about a society that is fast going insane, that is learning to accept chaos as order, and unreality as normal" (46). The critical voices are equally strong and are sometimes stridently insistent in their criticisms. Never a fan of Heller, Pearl Bell ("Heller and Malamud, Then and Now," *Commentary* 67 [June 1979]: 71–72) gives the most lacerating critique of the novel: "Heller's present targets—the Jewish family, Washington politics—demand the kind of complex understanding and moral courage that are beyond his grasp, and they have stubbornly resisted his glib antics and crude literary tricks" (72). While seeing more merit than Bell, Benjamin DeMott ("Heller's Gold and a Silver Sax," *The Atlantic Monthly* 243.3 [Mar. 1979]: 129–31); rpt. in Nagel, *Critical Essays on Joseph Heller*, 172–75 finds the novel "unsatisfying," because Heller fails to control his portrait of Gold.

Looking back on the novel, Heller himself is critical of it, observing that "*Good as Gold* is not a book with that much depth" (Ruas interview, 172). One suspects, however, that this is more the view of the 1984 Heller who endured the criticism of the novel than it is of the man who originally wrote it.

3. Not surprisingly, most critics have focused on Heller's portrayal of Jewish life. See Wayne C. Miller, "Ethnic Identity as Moral Focus: A Reading of Joseph Heller's *Good as Gold*," *MELUS* 6.3 (1979): 3–17; rpt. in Nagel, *Critical Essays on Joseph Heller*, 183–95; Melvin J. Friedman, "Something Jewish Happened: Some Thoughts about Joseph Heller's *Good as Gold*," in Nagel, *Critical Essays on Joseph Heller*, 183–95; Judith Ruderman, "Upside-Down in *Good as Gold*: Moishe Kapoyer as Muse," *Yiddish* 5.4 (1984): 55–63; Joseph Lowin, "The Jewish Art of Joseph Heller," *Jewish Book Annual* 43 (1985–86): 141–53; Robert Merrill, "Heller's Jewish Novels: *Good as Gold* and *God Knows*," in his *Joseph Heller*, 198–122; Frederick C. Stern, "Heller's Hell: Heller's Later Fiction, Jewishness, and the Liberal Imagination," *MELUS* 15.4 (winter 1988): 15–37, and David Seed, "*Good as Gold*," in his *The Fiction of Joseph Heller*, 129–57.

4. With each novel, Heller becomes more interested in what James Phelan calls the synthetic component of narrative (i.e., characters as artificial constructs, who exist as linguistic entities), in this case by calling attention to Gold's authorship of his own character. This self-authorship creates a continual interplay between the mimetic and synthetic aspects of character—Bruce Gold the college professor delineating his own life as a way to represent the Jewish experience. For Phelan, there are three aspects of character: mimetic, thematic, and synthetic; for this theory of character and its relation to narrative progression, see *Reading People, Reading Plots*.

Heller consistently foregrounds the synthetic dimension of character in the novel. For example, when the governor lectures Gold about the role he is expected to play, he simultaneously describes the workings of Heller's narrative at that moment: "Now, Gold. Everybody here is a somebody, and I don't know why you're being so captious about who it is you are. He is the Spade, she is the Widow, I am the Governor, and you're the . . ." (197).

5. Heller himself variously describes the Jewish heritage he shares with Gold. The sense that Gold and Heller have not lived a particularly "Jewish" life comes across in the interview with Charles Reilly, "Talking with Joseph Heller," *Inquiry Magazine* (1 May 1979): 22–26; rpt. in Nagel, *Critical Essays on Joseph Heller*, 176–82: "*Good as Gold* does focus upon the Jewish experience, but ultimately Bruce Gold finds his experience is not particularly more Jewish than, well, mine. I feel that many people my age, people who went to college after the war and became involved in academic or literary activities, have had experiences that are not materially different from those of people who aren't Jewish" (23).

6. Quoted in Rita Christopher, "On the Train from Wilmington," *Macleans* 92 (16 Apr. 1979): 46.

7. For Heller's account of his Coney Island childhood, see: "Coney Island: The Fun Is Over," *Show* (July 1962): 50–54, 102–3. Heller's conclusion suggests the tenor of the article: "Almost everyone I know from Coney Island has moved somewhere else. No one I know who has lived there wants to move back. It is almost as though we all share a common revulsion, and this in a way is strange, for we spent what I'm sure were happy childhoods there" (103).

8. In a July 1995 letter to me, Heller confirmed that the murder of Raymie Rubin's mother is based upon an actual incident that took place in his Coney Island neighborhood.

9. "The Man Who Came Looking for Moses Richmond" and "A Scientific Fact," Joseph Heller papers, Brandeis University Library.

10. As these early stories demonstrate, Heller's concern with Jewish subjects is long-standing and hardly "belated" as Robert Merrill has suggested (*Joseph Heller*, 99).

11. References to Jews and Jewish life are virtually absent in each novel; what references there are anticipate the anti-Semitism of political Washington in *Good as Gold*:

Yossarian had done his best to warn him [Clevinger] the night before. "You haven't got a chance, kid," he had told him glumly. "They hate Jews."

"But I'm not Jewish," answered Clevinger.

"It will make no difference," Yossarian promised, and Yossarian was right. "They're after everybody." (*Catch-22*, 80)

[Slocum:] "Settle down, will you? Control Brown and cooperate with Green, and why don't you hire a Negro and a Jew?" . . .

"What would I do with a coon?" he asks finally, as though thinking aloud, his mind wandering.

"I don't know."

"I could use a Jew."

"Don't be too sure." (*Something Happpened*, 64–65)

12. Joseph Heller papers, Brandeis University Library. For a discussion of these two notecards, see James Nagel, "Two Brief Manuscript Sketches: Heller's *Catch-22*," *Modern Fiction Studies* 20 (1974): 221–24.

13. James Nagel discusses Heller's early plans for making Yossarian Jewish, in "Two Brief Manuscript Sketches," 222–23.

14. Krassner interview, 22.

15. Ruas interview, 158.

16. Plimpton interview, 134.

17. Reviews first explored Heller's appropriation of the device of the book within a book technique; see Morris Dickstein, "Something Didn't Happen," *Saturday Review* 6 (31 Mar. 1979): 49–52; and Leonard Michaels, "Bruce Gold's American Experience."

18. Heller's demands upon the reader are in accord with Peter Brooks's account of the workings of plot: "Plot in this view belongs to the reader's 'competence,' and in his 'performance'—reading the narrative—it animates the sense-making process: it is a key component of that 'passion of [for] meaning' that, Barthes says, lights us afire when we read" (*Reading for the Plot*, 37).

19. Reilly interview, 24.

20. For a sample of such pieces, see: Heller, "Joseph Heller on America's 'Inhuman Callousness,'" *U.S. News and World Report* (9 Apr. 1979): 73; Sam Merrill interview, 68; Heller, "Moths at a Dark Bulb," *New York Times* (24 May 1976): 29; and Chet Flippo interview.

21. The concept of the implied author has been widely used since Wayne Booth's *The Rhetoric of Fiction* (Chicago: Univ. of Chicago Press, 1961); for a more recent exploration and pragmatic defense of its utility, see Seymour Chatman, "In Defense of the Implied Author" and "The Implied Author at Work," both in his *Coming to Terms: The Rhetoric of Narrative in Fiction and Film* (Ithaca: Cornell Univ. Press, 1990), 74–108.

22. Heller acknowledges his satiric refutation of criticisms of his previous novels; see Schumacher, 24, and Reilly interview, 24.

23. According to Barbara Gelb, at the time of *Good as Gold*, Heller "command[ed] royalty advances in the high six figures" ("Catching Joseph Heller," 15). In 1987, Edwin McDowell reported that Heller signed a contract for two novels, including a sequel to *Catch-22*, with G. P. Putnam's Sons for four million dollars ("'Catch-22' Sequel by Heller," *New York Times* [8 Apr. 1987]: C19).

24. I am using my own experience as reader as the basis for this remark (a colleague, Peter Freitag, first called these lines to my attention), as well as to explain the relative absence of commentary about this self-reflexiveness in early reviews and criticism.

25. In the process of composition, Heller began to worry about the self-reflexiveness of the novel: "I began to worry that the effect might be too precious—I have even conceived at one point of having dialogues between a character and 'me'—and I was worried it would

prove too jarring upon the reader. What I ultimately decided to do was include a number of lines here and there that would have the same effect but would not stand out" (Reilly interview, 24).

26. Heller's interview comments suggest that he did not conceive the ending of *Good as Gold* at the same time he imagined the beginning—as he did for *Catch-22* and *Something Happened*. Usually the novel as pre-formed structure is important for Heller, for as he says, "I have a beginning, and I sometimes have an end, and I work towards that pattern, but in between there has to be something" (Ruas interview, 155). Perhaps for *Good as Gold*, the narrator's self-reflexive description is furnishing an account of how Heller actually plotted an ending for the novel. Possible evidence for this also comes in Heller's *Playboy* interview with Sam Merrill, in which he talks of going to Mexico "with the hope of achieving perfect boredom" (70).

27. Ruas interview, 157.

28. Heller explicates the allusion to Dickens as follows: "I don't know if you noticed the way the allusions to Dickens operate. On one occasion the phrase occurs, and it's a borrowed simile, 'as solitary as an oyster.' In the ensuing passages there are a number of criticisms that seem to apply to Charles Dickens but have also been applied to *Something Happened* and *Catch-22*: too long, too many characters, too many improbable events" (Reilly interview, 24).

29. Nancy Crampton, "Writing under the Influence," *Writer's Digest* (Aug. 1979): 15.

30. Melanie Young makes this point in a most perceptive chapter on *Good as Gold* in her Ph.D. dissertation, "Joseph Heller: A Critical Introduction."

31. Of his use of Gold's titles, Heller himself says, "I thought that one of the unifying structures for the novel would be to have—ideally—every section deal with something Gold was going to write or had written and use that as a title for that section or the following section" ("Mel Brooks Meets Joseph Heller," interview, *Washington Post Book World* [19 Mar. 1979]: F4). David Seed shows how two of these chapter titles function, "Every Change Is for the Worse," and "Nothing Succeeds as Planned" (155).

32. Heller admits that the *Tristram Shandy* references are deliberate: "I had *Tristram Shandy* very much in mind for this book. That's the reason I refer to it so often" (Reilly interview, 24).

33. Plimpton interview, 131.

34. Ernst Cassirer, *Language and Myth*, trans. Susanne K. Langer (1946; rpt. New York: Dover Publications Inc., 1953), 89.

35. Both Wayne C. Miller and Judith Ruderman show that Heller's depiction of Gussie, especially as instructress to Gold, is important to his Jewish theme; see Miller, "Ethnic Identity as Moral Focus," 14, and Ruderman, *Joseph Heller*, 57–58.

36. There may be a correspondence between this account of Gold's mother and Heller's own mother. Publicly, he has said little about her; however, one of his most poignant memories is related by Barbara Gelb. It concerns how surprised and touched Heller was to learn that "his mother had collapsed into heartbroken sobs" when he left for the army. In *Closing Time* Heller gives this memory to Sammy Singer ("Catching Joseph Heller," 54).

37. Miller, "Ethnic Identity as Moral Focus," 16. David Seed reaches exactly the opposite conclusion from Miller, contending: "Since the question of ethnicity relates primarily to the past it becomes impossible to argue plausibly that Gold regains contact with his roots since he cannot even come to terms with his individual past" (135). The difficulty with this formulation is that Seed fails to consider Gold's purported authorship of the novel *Good as Good*, a novel which is explicitly about Gold's reassessment of his past.

38. Judith Ruderman argues that this scene "sums up the Jewish experience that Gold has come to appreciate in his [family]" ("Upside-Down," 62).

39. Robert Merrill interprets the ending scenes as more secularized than I do: "I take this spirit to be far more humanistic than sectarian, and I doubt very much that Heller means to recommend ethnicity for its ritualistic sake" (*Joseph Heller*, 111).

40. Ian Watt calls this method formal realism, and he still provides the most usefully compact description of its workings. See chapter 1 of his *The Rise of the Novel* (1957; rpt. Berkeley and Los Angeles: Univ. of California Press, 1959), 9–34.

41. Wayne C. Miller puts the matter this way: "It is the contention of this essay that the notion of ethnicity, particularly as alternative to the values of the corporate order of the modern nation-state, is at the heart of the moral vision of *Good as Gold* and that the hero finds a salvation of sorts in the personal commitment to the family, to friends, and, finally, to the composite of values that grow out of the American Jewish experience as he accepts his personal past" ("Ethnic Identity as Moral Focus," 5).

42. David Seed discusses some of the repetitive elements of family scenes, but reaches a different conclusion about their function with respect to Gold. He characterizes the Gold story as "a study in self-deception" (137).

43. In the extraordinary attention given to food in the family chapters—to the cheese blintzes, chopped liver, and smoked salmon—the reader sees a bit of Joseph Heller as well. As the Golds savor the various dishes, the relish that Heller took in writing the scenes becomes apparent. Heller loves good food. Barbara Gelb recounts an incident that took place at the house of Craig Claiborne, the food critic for the *New York Times*, in which Heller, in his enthusiasm for the meal Claiborne had prepared, began eating off the pewter underplate before the meal was formally served. In the weekly meals with George Mandel, Mel Brooks, Mario Puzo, and other friends, Heller gained the nickname Wolfman for his voracious appetite for and enjoyment of food. The value placed on good food is woven into all Heller's novels, as Heller describes and differentiates his characters according to their attitudes toward food: for example, Milo's chocolate covered cotton in *Catch-22* or Andrea's failure to appreciate Gold's Jewish delicacies point to their moral failings. See Gelb, "Catching Joseph Heller."

44. Charles Berryman shows the way the comedy of the meals and family scenes "depends upon outrageous multiplication" (111). In this sense, the novel's family scenes are related to the way in which Heller uses repetition and transformation in *Catch-22*. See "Heller's Gold," *Chicago Review* 32.4 (1981): 108–18.

45. Judith Ruderman also examines this scene, arguing that "[i]n actuality the world is turned upside-down and something has happened: going to Washington will be a step up for Gold in status and prestige; this elevation of politics and denigration of family are subversive in ways that Gold refuses to see" ("Upside-Down," 57).

46. Heller will again use Shoot the Chutes as a symbol for social dissolution in *Closing Time*.

47. Such lines are strikingly similar to Heller's social and political opinions.

Much that happens in society is of a savage nature. There's a kind of inhuman callousness in the country. On the highest level, the world of finance dominates the world of government, and nobody is trying to solve the problems of this nation as a community. Nobody is trying to deal with unemployment and inflation at the same time.

I deal with disintegration in American society in my books because disintegration appears to be a continuing process. . . .

But cities *are* decaying. I don't believe there's ever going to be a way to solve our economic problems. I think the era of easy national prosperity is over for this country. (Heller, "Joseph Heller on America's 'Inhuman Callousness,'" 73)

48. Again, there is a parallel with Heller's personal political opinions. "Every recent change in American politics has been for the worse and Ford will not prove an exception. A year ago, it was hard for me to imagine anyone worse than Nixon. But Nixon, because of the self-knowledge of his own small nature, may prove to have been less dangerous than Ford, who lacks that self-knowledge. Ford is a lot like Milo Minderbinder. Thinks of himself as a good guy, and God knows what devastation may result from that misconception" (Sam Merrill interview, 66).

49. Melvin Friedman sees the connection between politics and language somewhat differently, arguing "[p]olitical chicanery is revealed in *Good as Gold* through language, especially through its abuse" (202).

50. Quite rightly, David Seed sees such sentences "repeating a rhetorical pattern set in *Catch-22*—actually block[ing] off progression and deny[ing] access to information" (143).

51. Heller makes this point when he talks about the novel: "Look at the way Kissinger talks about Vietnam—as if to disassociate himself from his own failures, he talks about having served at a time when the country was close to civil war, and how it was impossible to get the support of Congress—ignoring the fact that he was the cause of most of the dissension. That's like Herbert Hoover saying he had the misfortune of serving when the market collapsed, or Hitler saying unfortunately he was in power when the war broke out" (quoted in Debra Rae Cohen, "Washington Gold Digging: Joseph Heller vs. Henry K.," *Feature* [Apr. 1979]: 16).

52. Heller's handling of Gold's change of heart has been frequently criticized; see, for example: Robert Merrill, *Joseph Heller*, 109–10; and Malcolm Bradbury, *The Modern American Novel* (New York: Oxford Univ. Press, 1984), 167.

53. The criteria established by the American Psychiatric Association's Task Force on Nomenclature and Statistics for diagnosing the narcissistic personality are as follows:

A. Grandiose sense of self-importance and uniqueness, e.g., exaggerates achievements and talents, focuses on how special one's problems are.
B. Preoccupation with fantasies of unlimited success, power, brilliance, beauty, or love.
C. Exhibitionistic: requires constant attention and admiration.
D. Responds to criticism, indifference of others, or defeat with either cool indifference, or with marked feelings of rage, inferiority, shame, humiliation, or emptiness.
E. At least two of the following characteristics of disturbances in interpersonal relationships:

    1. Lack of empathy: inability to recognize how others feel, e.g., unable to appreciate the distress of someone who is seriously ill.
    2. Entitlement: expectation of special favors without assuming reciprocal responsibilities, e.g., surprise or anger that people won't do what he wants.
    3. Interpersonal exploitiveness: takes advantage of others to indulge his own desires for self-aggrandizement, with disregard for the personal integrity and rights of others.
    4. Relationships characteristically vacillate between extremes of over-idealization and devaluation.

Quoted by Carol Strongin Tufts, "A Psychoanalytic Reading of Nora," *Comparative Drama* (summer 1986): 141–42, originally, Task Force on Nomenclature and Statistics, American Psychiatric Association, *DSM-III: Diagnostic Criteria Draft* (New York: American Psychiatric Association, 1978), 103–4.

54. Heller acknowledges the exhibitionistic impulses of his own writing in connection with *No Laughing Matter*, and I suspect the same attitude would apply to *Good*

as Gold: "People don't write books to benefit humanity; they're doing it to satisfy, I believe, an exhibitionistic . . ." (quoted in Schumacher, 24).

CHAPTER 5

1. David's boast provided the seminal lines for the novel; see Walter Goodman, "Heller Talks of Illness and King David Book," interview, *New York Times* (24 Sept. 1984): C13.

2. While Shakespeare's Henry cycle probably did not directly influence Heller, he does know it, as evidenced by his allusions to Henry's lines in *We Bombed in New Haven*. It is also noteworthy that the play had its genesis in an idea Heller had for combining readings from *Catch-22* and Shakespeare for public performance. At Oxford University, Heller took a course in Shakespeare and his account of Shakespeare and Shakespeare criticism casts an interesting light on *God Knows*: "Way back, when I read a lot of Shakespeare criticism, I read a critic. . . . Others have said that Shakespeare went through periods of depression when he wrote *Hamlet, King Lear* and *Macbeth*. . . . and the depressed person doesn't work. Imagine Shakespeare writing: he's thinking of the crowds—what will make the scene, what will make them laugh, what will make them cheer" (quoted in Schumacher, 24).

3. Robert Merrill makes a similar point, describing *God Knows* as: "a decidedly humanistic subtext, the kind that makes sense to Heller. The David who founded a dynasty and built a home for the ark of God does not seem to interest Heller much. The David who did these things while finding and losing love does interest him. *God Knows* is the story of that man, a story as mixed with joy and sorrow as any to be found within the biblical covers Heller has ransacked like a Jewish Shakespeare making his way through the world of his historical sources" (*Joseph Heller*, 118–19).

In discussing the way in which Heller humanizes David, Sanford Pinsker links this to Heller and George Mandel, his boyhood friend, reading biblical stories together and "punch[ing] up the narrative lines" (*Understanding Joseph Heller*, 108).

4. D. A. Traversi, *An Approach to Shakespeare* (New York: Doubleday & Company, 1956), 36.

5. Quoted in Medwick, 701.

6. Walter Benjamin, "The Storyteller," in his *Illuminations*, ed. Hannah Arendt, trans. Harry Zohn (New York: Schocken Books, 1969), 108–9.

7. Describing this, Heller says, "I hid from myself the fact that I was seriously ill. I did it by denying the amount of anxiety I felt in intensive care. The first night I was there, the man next to me died, and every few days somebody would die. . . . After three or four days, I was scared stiff without realizing it. I was afraid to go to sleep, but I was dying for sleep. My eyes kept falling shut, but I kept snapping my head up. I felt if I fell asleep I would never wake up" (Heller, "Something Happened," *People*, 26).

8. Goodman interview, C13.

9. For Heller's account of this illness, see *No Laughing Matter*, which he wrote with Speed Vogel (New York: G. P. Putnam's Sons, 1986).

10. Heller describes the way he used his own experiences in the novel to Charles Ruas while he was still working on the novel; see Ruas interview, 178.

11. *God Knows* received more negative than positive reviews; for a representative sample see: Leon Wieseltier, "Schlock of Recognition," *The New Republic* (29 Oct. 1984): 31–33; A. Alvarez, "Working in the Dark," *The New York Review of Books* (11 Apr. 1985): 15–17; Joel Wells, "A Psaltery of One Liners," *Commonweal* 111 (19 Oct. 1984): 561–62; and Paul Gray, "The 3000-Year-Old Man," *Time* (24 Sept. 1984): 74–75. Reviews that find

more merit in Heller's achievement include: Frances Gussenhoven, "'Fiction is fact distorted into truth,'" *America* (17 Nov. 1984): 325; Galen Strawson, "Saith the King Already," *Times Literary Supplement* (23 Nov. 1984): 1330; and Mordecai Richler, "He Who Laughs Last," *New York Times Books Review* (23 Sept. 1984): 1, 36. Richler makes the insightful comparison between Heller's method of storytelling and peeling an onion: "He doesn't so much tell a story as peel it like an onion—returning to the same event again and again, only to strip another layer of meaning from it, saving the last skin for the moving final pages, which is to say that, like all truly grand comic novels, 'God Knows' is ultimately sad" (36).

The novel did gain important critical recognition abroad; it won the 1986 Medici Prize, a French award for the best fiction not written in French.

12. Ruas interview, 168.

13. Walter Benjamin, 94. Benjamin's idea of the authority of death is also relevant to Heller: "Death is the sanction of everything that the storyteller can tell. He has borrowed his authority from death" (94).

14. For James Phelan, David directly addressing the reader represents a variant of Peter Rabinowitz's narrative audience, the characterized audience; in the case of *God Knows*, the characterized audience is assumed to know both the Kings and Chronicles accounts of the David story in some detail. While I do not pursue the implications of the characterized audience here, much of Heller's humor depends upon playing off the expectations of the characterized audience. See Phelan, *Reading People, Reading Plots*, 135–41.

15. Judith Ruderman explores the complementary pattern of David's relationship with a series of father figures: Jesse, Saul, and God; see her *Joseph Heller*, 115–16.

16. David Seed argues that David fails to achieve self-understanding in either the past or the present and that a crucial narrative strategy is to portray himself as victim: "The implication of David's narrative tactics is that he is minimizing his own responsibility so as to throw God's punishment of Bathsheba's child into maximum prominence as an unjust act" (164). I differ from Seed in believing that, as retrospective, David's narrative occasions self-awareness, particularly of his own responsibility for his sons' deaths.

17. The phrase "multiple identity" comes from the title of a Kenneth Gergen essay, "Multiple Identity: The Healthy, Happy Human Being Wears Many Masks" (*Psychology Today* [May 1972]: 31–35, 64–66), but Gergen, like many other theorists of an open-ended identity, looks back to Erving Goffman's classic study, *The Presentation of the Self in Everyday Life* (New York: Doubleday Anchor, 1959). Amidst the multitude of material dealing with the identity of the self, Kenneth Gergen and Chad Gordon's *The Self in Social Interaction* (New York: John Wiley & Sons, 1968) provides a particularly useful introduction and survey.

18. For a discussion of the protean self in contemporary literature, see Tony Tanner, *City of Words*, especially "Appendix Five" (432–38).

19. See Northrop Frye, *The Great Code* (New York: A Harvest/HBJ Book, 1982), 222.

20. See Alvin B. Kernan, Peter Brooks, and J. Michael Holquist, *Man and His Fictions* (New York: Harcourt Brace Jovanovich, 1973), 403–10. Kernan, Brooks, and Holquist define this emergent sense of character this way: "Identity is in this view a continuing and dynamic compromise between what we feel is the essence of ourselves and the essence of the roles we are called upon to assume in encounters with each other and the world. Somewhere in the dialectic between the two senses is located our 'character'" (407).

21. See Norman Holland, "How Can Dr. Johnson's Remarks on Cordelia's Death Add to My Own Response?" in *Psychoanalysis and the Question of the Text*, ed. Geoffrey H. Hartman (Baltimore: The Johns Hopkins Univ. Press, 1978), 21.

22. David Seed also explores the performative nature of *God Knows*, especially the theatricality of the text. In an insightful interpretation, which aligns Heller's method with that

he used in *We Bombed in New Haven*, Seed argues: "It is repeatedly implied in *God Knows* that Biblical characters are performers rehearsing their lines. In this way Heller draws attention to the familiarity of the narratives he is using" (167).

23. Drawing upon the example of Proust, Philip Weinstein explores a performative model of identity, which may serve to illuminate Heller's practice: "[T]he Proustean model . . . focuses attention less on [protagonists'] intrinsic properties than on their mode of relations with the world they inhabit. Freedom and identity emerge in the subject's transactions, in his capacity, not to create new conditions, but to realize himself by accepting and energizing his given conditions. Throughout, of course, these given conditions are nature and culture, bodily desire and societal constraint" (*The Semantics of Desire* [Princeton: Princeton Univ. Press, 1984], 10).

24. This interplay between role and circumstance recalls Heller's use of the same motif in *We Bombed in New Haven*. Typical of Heller's handling of the principle of necessity is an exchange between Henderson and Starkey that occurs late in the play, just before Henderson's death:

> Henderson: I'm quitting.
> Starkey: What do you mean you're quitting? Right now? Right in the middle? Right —
>
> Henderson: Right before I have to fly to Minnesota and be killed! Why should I if I don't want to? (163)

25. David Seed sees the relationship between David's narrative presence and his character differently: "David maintains a constant distance between his narrating and his earlier experiences—a distance expressed as a difference between then and now, belief and scepticism, etc.—so that he and the implied reader can enjoy the latter as spectacle" (176).

26. Northrop Frye argues that the metonymic period of language makes this ability to resolve inconsistency possible: "In continuous prose, if A and B seem to be inconsistent, one can always insert intermediary verbal formulas, or rephrase them in a commentary, in a way that will 'reconcile' them: if only we write enough of such intermediate sentences, any statement whatever can eventually be reconciled with any other statement" (*Anatomy of Criticism*, 10).

27. In answering the question about whether female readers will be offended by the novel's portrayal of women, Heller himself attributes his presentation of his women characters to their biblical sources; "[t]hose quotations in my book that make slighting or critical reference to women do come from the Old Testament" (quoted in Medwick, 701). Sanford Pinsker extends the point, arguing that "Heller explores the discrepancy between biblical quotation . . . and the more rounded, more humanly interesting, women Heller creates when he allows them to speak" (*Understanding Joseph Heller*, 122). I suspect that a number of readers—male as well as female—will find the novel's presentation of women limited, unsatisfying, or offensive.

28. One of the few exceptions to these types tends to fall into another counter-type exemplified by Mrs. Yerger in *Something Happened*. Hulking and androgynous, these women are threats to men. In part their danger comes because they render men silent, as Mrs. Yerger does the young Slocum of the insurance office. A related type is best represented by Slocum's mother. As her judgment about Slocum, "you're just no good," exemplifies, these women menace the male's sense of self.

29. Denis de Rougement, *Love in the Western World*, 21.

30. Yossarian also reaches out for Nurse Duckett in this scene in order to ward off death: "He wondered mournfully, as Nurse Duckett buffed her nails, about all the people who had died under water" (331). More specifically, he remembers the first dead person that

he saw, recalls watching "a tufted round log that was drifting toward him on the tide turn unexpectedly into the bloated face of a drowned man" (331). The psychological resonance in this cannot be avoided, in the inextricable linkage between love and death outlined in different ways by Sigmund Freud, Leslie Fiedler, and Denis de Rougement, the latter of whose arguments I will draw upon in more detail.

31. In exploring the opacity of desire, Tony Tanner quotes Jacques Lacan: "Man's ignorance (*nescience*) of his desire is 'less ignorance of what he demands, which can after all be defined or limited, than ignorance of *whence* he desires'" (87). For a more complete discussion of this issue see: *Adultery in the Novel* (Baltimore and London: Johns Hopkins Univ. Press, 1979), 87–100; as well as Lacan himself, *The Language of the Self*, trans. Anthony Wilden (Baltimore: Johns Hopkins Univ. Press, 1968).

32. Tony Tanner's (72–79) analysis of Tolstoy's *The Kreutzer Sonata* could be applied to the way in which Heller's men treat women. For example, his account of the way Pozdnyshev views his wife as a commodity could equally describe the views of Yossarian, Slocum, and Gold, as well as David: "He [Pozdnyshev] has lived his whole life in estrangement from his real condition and the reality of other people, regarding her as a commodity or a positive or negative intoxicant—as though marriage had become another kind of factory for the reification of people" (77).

33. Heller made this admission in a talk that he gave at SUNY Albany on February 4, 1986. Sanford Pinsker makes the interesting argument that David's language provides "the vehicle" for his discovery of his own love story (*Understanding Joseph Heller*, 122).

34. Heller himself would undoubtedly reject the homoerotic suggestiveness of this opening line; however, it would be possible to argue that there is a homoerotic dimension to the relationship between Yossarian and the chaplain. Similarly, the Slocum/Kagle relationship in *Something Happened* and David/Jonathan relationship in this novel could read as the rejection of a homoerotic attraction, homophobically so in the former and comically so in the latter. Finally, Yossarian self-consciously identifies Gustav Aschenbach, the protagonist of Thomas Mann's *Death in Venice*.

35. For a brilliant discussion of adultery in the novel, see Tony Tanner, *Adultery in the Novel*, 3–112.

36. Of the relationship among marriage, transgression, and desire, Tony Tanner says: "One of the basic problems about marriage is that its security depends upon repetition—'le marriage implique l'habitude'—and that repetition and habit diminish the feelings, particularly the erotic intensity, upon which the marriage was founded. Hence, and only apparently, paradoxically, marriage can breed the need for 'irregularité,' 'des explosions capricieuses,' 'désordre et l'infraction.'" The quotations are from Georges Bataille's book *L'Erotisme*, in which he also writes:

> What makes it difficult to speak about the forbidden is not only the variability of its objects, but also its illogical character. With reference to the same object, it is never impossible to make a directly contrary proposition. There is nothing that is forbidden that may not be transgressed. *Often transgression is admitted, often it is prescribed* [Tanner's emphasis]. . . . In the realm of the irrational, where our reflections effectively enclose us, we must say: "Occasionally an intangible prohibition is violated—that doesn't mean it has ceased to be intangible." We could even go so far as to putting forward the absurd proposition: "*the forbidden is there to be violated.*" This proposition is not, as it at first seems, outrageously risky, but *the correct statement of an inevitable relation between emotions pulling us in contrary directions.* [Tanner's emphasis] (*Adultery in the Novel* 375)

See also Georges Bataille, *L'Erotisme* (Paris: Union Générale d'Editions, 1965).

37. Heller's handling of this episode is closely related to *Catch-22*, stylistically as well in the entangling of blood, guilt, and death. In this instance, this entanglement is at first hidden by the sexual humor:

> "It's really possible?" I asked naively. "During your period?"
> "Would there be a law against it if it weren't?"
> "It isn't gross?"
> "It isn't gross."
> "You've done it before?"
> "Is everyone squeamish?"
> "Suppose your flowers be upon me?"
> "You'll wash."
> "I'd be unclean for seven days."
> "Don't noise it around."
> "And all of the bed on which I lay would be unclean."
> "Don't noise that around either." (278)

38. See René Girard, *Deceit, Desire, and the Novel* (Baltimore: Johns Hopkins Univ. Press, 1965), 1–52.

39. Borrowing from Paul Ricoeur, Philip Weinstein argues that accounts of desire, whether by characters or their authors, are systematically suspect. "A man of desires is opaque—to himself, to others. To be understood, he must be subjected to a hermeneutical scrutiny that will unravel its utterance by locating the kernel of unacknowledged desire that is serving at its orientations" (10).

40. René Girard shows how desire for God begins with and collapses back into the self: "The impulse of the soul toward God is inseparable from a retreat into the self" (58).

41. This pattern of desire recurs in Heller's fiction: most notably in Luciana of "Crippled Phoenix" and *Catch-22* who has been wounded in an air raid and Virginia of *Something Happened* who was raped by her football player boyfriend and his friends. These wounded innocents would seem to be the female counterparts to Heller's dead-child story. In each situation, the Heller protagonist seeks to be reunited with the lost innocent.

42. Throughout this section, I am greatly indebted to the suggestions of Linda Van Buskirk, particularly for her idea that love constitutes a split between mind and body similar to that embodied in the Snowden death scene.

43. Sigmund Freud, *Beyond the Pleasure Principle*, trans. and ed. by James Strachey (New York: Norton, 1961), 23.

44. Peter Brooks's account of the working of desire in Rousseau's *Emile* can be refigured to describe David's narrative: "What, ultimately, does [David] as narrator of his life's story have to tell? The story of the insistence of a desire as persistent as it is incoherent, a desire whose lack of satisfaction gives death as the only alternative, but whose satisfaction also would be death. Here we have figured the contradictory desire of narrative, driving toward the end which would be both its destruction and its meaning, suspended on the metonymic rails which tend toward that end without ever being able quite to say the terminus" (57–58).

45. Ruas interview, 173.

46. See Sam Merrill interview, 74, and Charles Reilly interview, 25. Specifically, Heller says of these protagonists: "I've said many times Slocum was perhaps the most contemptible character in all literature" (Merrill, 74) and "Morally, Gold is an ignominious person. He wound up the way Bob Slocum of *Something Happened* started out to be" (Reilly, 25).

47. Joseph Lowin sees Heller's use of the Bible as "crucial for a serious reading of *God Knows*, for reading it as a specifically Jewish novel, and not a Greek one" (143). See also Robert Merrill, *Joseph Heller*, and David Seed for other examinations of the Jewish character of *God Knows*.

48. Two versions of "Jephthah's Daughter" are included among Heller's papers in the Brandeis University Library.

49. In explaining the novel's relationship to the Bible, David Seed argues: "Heller has demonstrated a constant awareness of the values embedded in the King James Bible and it is these values which his own narrative works against through burlesque, ribald mockery and anachronism. . . . Instead of using the biblical story as an occasion for pious retelling as did Sholem Asch, Heller produces a running commentary on it where the recurring main event is the bizarre clash between two kinds of discourse—that of the Authorised Version, and a modern and irreverent speech idiom" (171).

50. For investigations of Heller's biblical language, see Seed (171–72) and Lowin (143).

51. John R. Searle, *Speech Acts: An Essay in the Philosophy of Language* (Cambridge: Cambridge Univ. Press, 1969), 22–53.

52. See, for example, the reviews by Leon Wieselter, Paul Gray, A. Alvarez, and Joel Wells.

53. The notecard on Major Major reads: "Had been warned by a tattered old drunk at the MLA convention never to trust a man who said he'd finished a book by Henry James. If he said he did and didn't he was a liar. If he said he did and did, he would lie about having enjoyed it" (Joseph Heller papers, Brandeis University Library).

Heller also acknowledges that he parodies criticisms that he has received, as for example, when Bathsheba comments that some of David's psalms are "flawed by excessive length" (quoted in Schumacher, 25).

54. John Barth, "The Literature of Exhaustion," *Atlantic Monthly* 220 (Aug. 1967): 29–39.

55. Quoted in Medwick, 702.

56. See Wojcik, "Transformations of the Myth of David," in *The David Myth in Western Culture*, eds. Raymond-Jean Frontain and Jan Wojcik (West Lafayette, Ind.: Purdue Univ. Press, 1980), 1–10.

57. See Goodman interview, C13.

58. When Heller's notecards to *God Knows* become available to scholars, it will be possible to trace the evolution of the novel.

59. Rougement, 53.

60. Sarah Blacher Cohen describes Jewish humor in a way that can be usefully applied to *God Knows*. Cohen argues that Jewish humor is born out of the discrepancy between the destiny promised in the Bible and the circumstance in which Jews in the modern age often find themselves. Her account of the value of such humor fits both Heller and David: "It has helped the Jewish people to survive, to confront the indifferent, often hostile universe, to endure the painful ambiguities of life and to retain a sense of internal power" (*Jewish Wry: Essays on Jewish Humor* [Bloomington and Indianapolis: Indiana Univ. Press, 1987], 13.

61. Of the biblical outlook, Heller says: "There are such musical, soothing phrases in the King James translation, being 'full of years and full of days.' I think implicit in that was a resignation that if one did live to the point where he was full of days, it was time to go" (quoted in Medwick, 702).

CHAPTER 6

1. Gary Michael Dault makes this connection in his book review of *Picture This*. See "Heller's Self-Satisfied Iconoclasm Is a Flimsy Excuse for a Novel," *Toronto Star* (26 Nov. 1988): M8.

2. McDowell, C19.

3. Quoted in Bill Moyers, *A World of Ideas* (New York: Doubleday, 1989), 31.

4. In his interview with Bill Moyers, Heller makes explicit these analogues: "I went back to ancient Greece because I was interested in writing about American life and Western civilization. In ancient Greece I found striking—and grim—parallels. . . . In the war between Sparta and Athens, the Peloponnesian War, I could see a prototype for the Cold War between this country and Russia" (30).

5. Heller did not always view the novel as being so pessimistic; in fact, during its composition he called it a departure from the dark tone of *Good as Gold* and *God Knows*. See "Heller Unbound," *U.S. News and World Report* (13 Oct. 1986): 68.

6. It is worth recalling that in his earlier novels his "villains" are, in part, defined by their blindness to history—such characters as Milo, Aarfy, Cathcart, Newsome, and the governor. Without historical understanding these characters might say, as Ralph Newsome does, "Let's build some death camps" (*Good as Gold*, 127).

7. Heller bases his Rembrandt on Gary Schwartz's *Rembrandt: His Life, His Paintings* (New York: Viking, 1985). Schwartz writes a revisionist account of Rembrandt's life and art, attempting to avoid, as he puts it, "the art historian's sin of trying to interpret [the] artist's character on the basis of his work" (348). As Schwartz sums up his portrait, "Rembrandt had a nasty disposition and an untrustworthy character" (363).

8. Steiner, "Books: Master Class," *New Yorker* 64 (30 May 1988): 99.

9. "Room for Renoir" also embodies what, for Heller, is the complementary truth about art. Failure to respond to its emotion betokens a deadness of spirit. Thus, when George, the story's protagonist, accedes to his wife's and his boss's wishes not to hang the print, he simultaneously loses his identity as an individual. The golf clubs that George finds in the closet when he goes to put the Renoir print away presage the ending of *Something Happened*, in which Slocum's irretrievable loss of self is represented by his taking up golf.

10. For a representative sample of reviews, see: Walter Goodman, "Heller Contemplating Rembrandt," *New York Times* (1 Sept. 1988): 14; Christopher Hitchens, "The Rise of Bunk," *Times Literary Supplement* (14–20 Oct. 1988): 1155; Robert M. Adams, "History Is a Bust," *New York Times Book Review* (11 Sept. 1988): 9; Paul Taylor, "History Lessons from a Canvas Prison," *Sunday Times* (16 Oct. 1988): G6; Anne Smith, "Nothing Works," *The Listener* 120 (27 Oct. 1988): 32; Adrian Dannatt, "Aristotle Meets Rembrandt," *The Spectator* 261.5 (5 Nov. 1988): 45; as well as Dault.

11. Ruas interview, 172.

12. Goodman, "Heller Contemplating Rembrandt," 14.

13. David Seed lists Heller's classical sources and the chapter from the novel based on each source (216).

14. Heller's materialist conception of history has affinities with Karl Marx's vision of history:

> Men make their own history, but they do not make it just as they please; they do not make it under circumstances chosen by themselves, but under circumstances directly found, given, and transmitted from the past. The tradition of all the dead generations weighs like a nightmare on the brain of the living. And just when they seem engaged in revolutionising themselves and things, in creating something entirely new, precisely in such epochs of revolutionary crisis they anxiously conjure up the spirits

of the past to their service and borrow from them names, battle slogans and costumes in order to present the new scene of world history in this time-honoured disguise and this borrowed language. . . . In like manner the beginner who has learnt a new language always translates it back into his mother tongue, but he has assimilated the spirit of the new language and can produce freely in it only when he moves in it without remembering the old and forgets in it his ancestral tongue. ("The Eighteenth Brumaire of Louis Bonaparte," in *The Marx-Engels Reader*, ed. Robert C. Tucker (New York: W. W. Norton & Co., 1978), 595.

15. See Schwartz, 12–15.

16. Heller's technique is also related to that used in the autobiographical *No Laughing Matter*, in which he includes excerpts from the court transcript of his divorce proceedings and from the attorneys' briefs and letters.

17. Sanford Pinsker makes a related point: "*Picture This* is an extended exercise in deconstruction—that is, a self-conscious effort which calls determinant meanings into question and which regards the text as a closed verbal system"; see *Understanding Joseph Heller*, 157–58.

18. Quoted in Richard Rhodes, *The Making of the Bomb* (New York: Simon and Schuster, 1986), 130.

19. Judith Ruderman sees Heller's protrait of artists rather differently: "Because *Picture This* is itself a work of art—or, at least aspires to be—the novel is not in fact cynical about art and artists per se" (*Joseph Heller*, 127).

20. My discussion of Heller's use of catachresis is heavily indebted to J. Hillis Miller, "Reading Writing: Eliot," in *The Ethics of Reading* (New York: Columbia Univ. Press, 1987), 61–80. I take my departure point from Miller's ideas about the role figurative language plays in representation, especially the performative nature of such language.

21. Joseph Heller papers, Brandeis University Library. Other stories in which writers play a significant role include: "World Full of Great Cities," "The Death of the Dying Swan," "From Dawn to Dusk," "Lot's Wife," "To Laugh in the Morning" (in which the drug addict protagonist, Nathan Schwoll, does not actually write but thinks of writing as something he could do, if he could stay straight), "The Sound of Asthma," "Early Frost," and "The Polar Bear in the Ice Box."

22. In his representation of artists, Heller becomes increasingly metafictional: Slocum's monologue provides a lens upon the composition of *Something Happened*; Gold's articles function as design principles in *Good as Gold* and the narrator talks explicitly about his novelistic choices; David purportly both composes and comments upon the plot of *God Knows*; and Rembrandt's character-creating art corresponds to Heller's own task in *Picture This*.

23. See, for example, the reviews by Dault, Hitchens, and Taylor.

24. "Aristotle contemplating" provided the generative lines for the novel: "Aristotle, contemplating the bust of Homer, was thinking of Socrates, while Rembrandt dressed him in Medieval garments and surrounded him in shadows" ("Heller Unbound," 68).

25. In his observations about Rembrandt's paintings, Heller draws upon the interpretations of art historians. His account of the role the spectator plays in *The Syndics* is a case in point; it parallels such interpretations as: "It cannot be denied that the rising man adds substantially to the illusion that the group is reacting spontaneously to somebody in front of them. And since this object of attention cannot be somebody in an imaginary assembly, it must be the entering spectator. So Rembrandt was not only concerned with giving an ordinary illusion of gathering, but dramatizes it slightly by aiming at the very moment of the spectator's appearance" (Jakob Rosenberg, Seymour Slive, and E. H. ter Kuile, *Dutch Art and Architecture 1600–1800* [New York: Penguin, 1966], 126).

26. Sanford Pinsker argues that *"Picture This* virtually abandons the usual expectations about character, plot, and setting. What readers get instead is the process of painterly composition: a survey of histories ancient, post-Renaissance, and modern; and most of all, a meditation on what art and life eventually come to" (*Understanding Joseph Heller*, 160).

27. It should also be noted that, although chronological, none of Heller's fiction from "MacAdam's Log" onward uses a straightforward linear plot and that each counterpoises public and private chronologies. For example, while the fictional clock of *Catch-22* beats to the number of missions flown, Heller moves freely back and forth along this time line, thereby constructing a textual chronology for the reader that is different from that of Yossarian's experience. Also crucially, he allows Yossarian to escape the imperatives of public time when he flees to Sweden and to replace it with a personal time in which he "can live forever or die in the attempt." Yet for all these chronological manipulations, the novel follows the developmental logic of an initiation novel, as unscrambling the sequence of bombing missions demonstrates.

28. There are noteworthy synchronic impulses in Heller's previous fiction. The "fish" scene between Yossarian and Dr. Sanderson exemplifies them. No matter how hard Dr. Sanderson endeavors to interpret Yossarian's fish dream or to advance the conversation, Yossarian manages to return the focus to fish. The network of associations that Heller develops in the scene eventually connects Yossarian's fish to Catch-22, and in this the scene participates in the narrative development of the novel as a whole.

29. See Frank Kermode, *The Sense of an Ending* (New York: Oxford Univ. Press, 1966).

30. "Heller Unbound," 68.

31. The phrase "contextual integration" is Alexander Gelley's, in "Metonymy, Schematism, and the Space of Literature," *New Literary History* 11 (spring 1980): 476.

32. Drawing upon the insights of Kuhn, Nietzche, and Vico, Edward Said makes a distinction between texts that act as obstructions and those that act as pathways to the reality which they represent. "When writing is considered to be not the solitary act of an individual, nor the imprisonment of sense in graphological inscription, but rather an act that constitutes participation in various cultural processes, then the text as obstruction becomes a text as pathway to new texts." In a similar sense, Heller designs *Picture This* as a pathway to Western history, to open up relationships, to resist the "didactic simplicity"—to borrow Said's phrase—with which historical narration is often cast (*Beginnnings*, 205).

33. In his nonfiction, Heller's bout with Guillain-Barré syndrome has prompted, not surprisingly, some of his most direct personal reflections about death: "I knows it sounds like Catch-22. I'd listen to the respirators for 24 hours every day, and without realizing it, I was aware of every breath I took. Consciously, I was not afraid of dying or permanent paralysis. Unconsciously, I suppose I was scared stiff. I don't think I ever slept more than two hours at a time—even when I got a private room" (Heller, "Something Happened," *People*, 26).

34. David Seed interprets the ending differently, but in a way that relates to my own: "By undermining the plausibility of a key scene in his own book and the authenticity of its central point (*Aristotle* may, after all, not be by Rembrandt) Heller denies a final resolving certainty to his own text" (216).

35. Judith Ruderman interprets the ending differently; she argues that Heller subverts his own narrative strategies: "The skepticism of the ending subverts the narrative method of the book, that is, the telling of a story by marshalling historical facts gleaned from the wealth of material cited in Heller's acknowledgments" (*Joseph Heller*, 133).

CHAPTER 7

1. Heller has recycled these details from chapter 1 of *Catch-22* in which it was the dying colonel who was so attended. The colonel is noteworthy, because he provides a proleptic version of the Snowden death scene and of the message of his entrails: "he was kept busy day and night transmitting glutinous messages from the interior into square pads of gauze" (*Catch-22*, 14). Heller's substitution of Yossarian for the colonel as the patient under the care of all the specialists has a suggestive resonance. In this instance, Yossarian's dream about his mother constitutes the "message from the interior," a comic version of the secret of Snowden's entrails.

2. "Catch-22 Plus: A Conversation with Joseph Heller," interview, *New York Times Book Review* (28 Aug. 1994): 18. Heller dramatizes aspects of his personality and experience in Sammy Singer and Yossarian. The Coney Island childhood, immigrant parents, the war and Avignon, and college on the G.I. Bill are common to Heller, Yossarian, and Singer. Yossarian's relationship with his son Michael and with his nurse Melissa MacIntosh are fictional versions of Heller's relationships with his son and wife. Similarly, Heller uses his own experiences as the basis for those of Sammy working at *Time* magazine and teaching at Penn State. Singer and Yossarian's emotional reactions to music and literature originate in Heller's own responses.

Closing Time also has aspects of a roman à clef: Heller's friends Marvin Winkler, Mario Puzo, Betty Abrams, and Lila Gross, among many others, appear in the novel. Sammy Singer is based upon Gerald Broidy (as well as upon Heller himself), who worked in the advertising department of *Time* with Heller, and Lou and Marion Berkman provide the models for Lew and Claire Rabinowitz. In fact, Marion Berkman lent Heller her husband's letters to her, and the Rabinowitz plot is essentially a fictional transcription of an actual relationship. Heller's reworking of factual material, especially with respect to Sammy, Lew, and Claire, gives the novel a "different sensibility" from Heller's other work, one that celebrates an ethnic past, family life, and "marriage as an optimum, desirable state" (Gelb interview, 3).

3. Heller tells Barbara Gelb that *Closing Time* represents a summing-up of his career, but not his swan song as a novelist (Gelb interview, 18).

4. Heller is speaking personally through Singer and Yossarian in this conversation. Heller confirmed the personal basis for this scene on 22 February 1995, in a conversation that we had during his visit to the New York State Writers Institute.

5. While *Catch-22* (1961) became a vehicle for understanding the Vietnam War, it is inaccurate to claim, as Jerome Klinkowitz does, that the novel is "as much about Vietnam as . . . about the European theater two decades before" (*Structuring the Void* [Durham: Duke Univ. Press, 1992], 136). Klinkowitz's mistake does, however, testify to the novel's influence.

6. Aldridge, "The Loony Horror of It All," 55.

7. For readers seeking guidance to *Closing Time*, William H. Pritchard and Thomas R. Edwards provide the most helpful reviews; see, respectively, "Yossarian Redux," *New York Times Book Review* (25 Sept. 1994): 1, 36–37, and "Catch-23," *New York Review of Books* (20 Oct. 1994): 20, 22–23. Pritchard calls the novel "an independent creation" rather than a sequel "in whose best parts the serious and the joking are inseparable as they should be in art" (37). Edwards believes that Heller "has trouble managing [the novel's] mixed moods," but argues that it "deserves respect and attention" (23).

For reviews portraying *Closing Time* as a curious or a flawed hybrid of the comic and serious, see: Paul Gray, "Catch-23," *Time* (3 Oct. 1994): 78; Christopher Lehmann-Haupt, "For an Aging Yossarian, the Catch Is Cosmic," *New York Times* (22 Sept. 1994): C21; Christopher Buckley, "Götterdämmerung-22," *The New Yorker* (10 Oct. 1994): 104–9, and

NOTES TO CHAPTER SEVEN 303

Robert Pinsky, "After 'Catch-22' Updated Insanity," *Washington Post* (29 Sept. 1994): D1–D2. For reviews portraying *Closing Time* as a failure, see: Merle Rubin, "A New Satire in 'Catch-22' Sequel," *The Christian Science Monitor* (4 Oct. 1994): 14, and Malcolm Jones, "*Closing Time*: The Sequel to *Catch-22*," *Newsweek* (3 Oct. 1994): 66.

8. For descriptions of Heller's West End Avenue apartment and of his life there, see *No Laughing Matter*.

9. McBride is modeled upon Heller's acquaintance Jerry McQueen, a "soft-hearted ex-homicide cop" (Gelb interview, 18). McQueen helped Heller during his recuperation from Guillain-Barré, taking him on a number of social outings, including one to Coney Island. Of one such occasion, Barbara Gelb said to Heller: "Jerry rolled his car over to the curb and pulled it to a stop on the sidewalk, only inches from the restaurant's front door, sprang out, seized you in his arms and whisked you inside. I've never seen you so ebullient, so purely joyful" (18). Heller endows McBride with McQueen's helpfulness and makes Yossarian its chief recipient.

10. Preface to the Special Edition of *Catch-22*, (New York: Simon and Schuster, 1994), 15.

11. "An Ordinary Evening in New Haven," in *The Collected Poems of Wallace Stevens* (New York: Alfred A. Knopf, 1971), 467.

12. Heller's portrait of Yossarian is ethically ambiguous. On the one hand, Milo rightly remarks, "I'm not sure I trust [Yossarian]. I'm afraid he's still honest" (73). On the other hand, Yossarian himself cannot think of a product or cause that he will not support if the money is right, and indeed his career with M & ME & A demonstrates the ethical compromises that he has made.

13. In some ways, Melissa is Luciana's descendant: like Luciana, she is too good to be true, initiates the relationship, insists that Yossarian court her like a lady, and thoroughly enjoys sex.

14. Heller distinguishes Yossarian's Siegfried fantasy from his own Wagnerian allusions. Heller says that Yossarian is just "kidding around" with his Wagnerian imaginings, but believes that his own allusions to the cataclysmic atmosphere of Götterdämmerung reinforce the point of the novel: "If there is one thesis to this novel, it's that things are coming to an end" (Gelb interview, 18).

15. Charles Osborne, *The Complete Operas of Richard Wagner* (North Pomfret, Vt.: Trafalgar Square Publishing, 1990), 185.

16. Yossarian eventually sees his own self-destructive erotic desire externalized in the hideously old and young prostitutes in the Port Authority Bus Terminal who offer to perform fellatio on him for $5. He is so repulsed by them that he does not stop to consider his kinship with them. This kinship is revealed not only in his oral sex with Angela, but also in his Coney Island nightmare in which, looking in a mirror, he sees the prostitutes' images as his own.

17. In responding to Melissa, Yossarian uses the description of himself as a man who enjoys being alone that Barbara Gelb recognizes as Heller talking about himself (Gelb interview, 19).

18. As in *Catch-22*, while the hospital seems to be a refuge from actuality, in fact it is not. For example, while Yossarian thinks that he can enjoy his dalliance with Melissa without consequence, she becomes pregnant during one of their hospital-room trysts. Similarly, Yossarian and Singer meet and talk in the hospital; it is there they share their recollections of Snowden's death and its significance.

19. Heller connects Yossarian's pursuit of money with Alberich's and Woton's schemes to secure the Nibelung's gold. According to Wagner, such a pursuit of power constitutes "a poison that is fatal to love" and destructive to their own characters (Wagner, letter to August Röckel, quoted in Osborne, 261).

20. According to Mrs. Tappman, when the chaplain sees the nude figure in the tree during Snowden's funeral, it caused a change of heart. Before the vision the chaplain had been on the verge of renouncing "any belief in God, or religion, or justice, or morality, or mercy"; after the vision, his faith is reaffirmed (307). While Yossarian is tempted to explain the miracle to her, he resists on the grounds that, "even a naive conviction, was in the last analysis more nourishing than the wasteland of none" (308).

21. Thomas Mann, *Dr. Faustus* (New York: Vintage Books, 1992), 486.

22. In *No Laughing Matter*, Heller juxtaposes an account of Valerie Humphries first becoming his nurse with one of the Belgian cancer patient's arrival. This juxtaposition anticipates dialectical relationship between the Belgian cancer patient and Melissa; see *No Laughing Matter*, 147.

23. In his acknowledgment of his dependence upon others and theirs upon him, Yossarian is no longer the antihero who seeks to transcend time and to recover his innocence. His is no longer a self in recoil from the world and against itself. By reconfiguring his protagonist in this way, Heller distances himself from the mode of fiction that Ihab Hassan characterizes in *Radical Innocence* (Princeton: Princeton Univ. Press, 1961): the protagonist of such fiction—including the Yossarian of *Catch-22*—"is the anti-hero who, instead of turning dreams into history, converts history into dreams" (328).

24. Polhemus, *Comic Faith*, 275.

25. Barbara Gelb recounts this episode in her 1979 *New York Times Magazine* biographical profile of Heller ("Catching Joseph Heller"). She recognizes the fictional retelling in *Closing Time* and confirms that Heller is using his own experience as the basis for Singer's (Gelb interview, 18).

26. The disappointment of not publishing in *The New Yorker* that Singer and Yossarian share probably comes from Heller himself. When his friend and former editor Robert Gottlieb was appointed *New Yorker* editor, Heller would have had every reason to believe that Gottlieb, who had worked so hard on *Catch-22*, would find space in the magazine for one of his most famous authors. But Heller was never published the *New Yorker*.

27. Paige, "Discovery a Life-Long Process for All," *North Country This Week* (2–8 Nov. 1994): 1.

28. In order to envelop Lew's narrative with the atmosphere of his disease, Heller uses the technique of delayed decoding that he first developed in his short stories. From early in his narrative, Lew alludes to his symptoms and his chemotherapy without explaining them. For the reader, the effect of this information which can be only partially understood is rather like being on the verge of a cold or flu—Heller's text mirrors the nagging vagueness of the symptoms in oneself that makes one sense the onset of an illness.

29. By making Lew's story parallel Sammy's and Yossarian's in this way, Heller provides a contrapuntal variation on the dead-child story. Unlike Yossarian and Singer, Lew is externally unscarred by the Snowden-like death of a comrade. However, when Lew contracts Hodgkin's disease, it is as if he has internalized the secret of Snowden's entrails; his own vital organs are one by one attacked by the cancer.

30. David Craig is a World War II veteran whom Heller met through Kurt Vonnegut; the details of this episode correspond to what actually happened to Craig during the Battle of the Bulge. Joseph Heller volunteered this information to the author in a letter dated 17 Feb. 1995.

31. Just as the Yossarian and Singer plots constitute as much a reflection upon *Catch-22* as its sequel, so too the Rabinowitz plot seems Heller's meditation upon *Slaughterhouse-Five*. Like Sammy's accounts of Avignon, Lew's description of Dresden have the verisimilitude of a veteran's memoir.

32. William Thackeray, *Vanity Fair* (Boston: Houghton Mifflin Company, 1963), 666.

33. Heller is satirizing President Reagan's much-quoted comment about being able to re-call nuclear missiles once they have been launched. However, his point is a more general one: politicians succeed by misunderstanding, misrepresenting, or obfuscating the facts rather than by accurately reporting them.

34. Heller's narrative technique is reminiscent of Dickens's in *Bleak House*: in each case the omniscient narrator maintains a view of life that seemingly undermines that of the first person narrator/s. However, both Dickens and Heller insist upon the validity of their first-person narrator's point of view.

35. Robert Alter argues that self-conscious fiction and a comic response to mortality go hand-in-hand (*Partial Magic* [Berkeley, Los Angeles, and London: Univ. of California Press, 1975]).

36. Osborne, 261.

37. In *Catch-22*, the friendship with Snowden operates metaphorically, while in *Closing Time* it works metonymically. In *Catch-22*, Yossarian unravels the dream-like message, "we've got your pal," by substituting his memories of Snowden's viscera for a missing, living friend. By contrast, in *Closing Time*, the little-known fellow crewman Snowden becomes a friend through a series of metonymic relationships: memories of Snowden lead to memories of Avignon that, in turn, evoke thoughts of the reality of war, and so on. The distinction between metaphoric and metonymic fictional modes originates with Roman Jakobson, *Fundamentals of Language* (The Hague: Mouton, 1956).

38. Benjamin, "The Storyteller," in his *Illuminations*, 108–9

39. Heller says that he uses the same name for each son in order to "suggest an effect of shared experience" (Gelb interview, 18).

40. Sophocles, *The Oedipus Cycle* (New York: Harcourt Brace Jovanovich, 1967), 78.

41. The motif of the father who unwittingly hurts his son while attempting to aid him runs throughout Heller's fiction, figuring most prominently in "The Miracle of Danrossane," "The Crippled Phoenix," *Something Happened, We Bombed in New Haven*, and *God Knows*.

42. Preface to the Special Edition of *Catch-22*, (New York: Simon and Schuster, 1994), 15.

43. Plato, *The Last Days of Socrates*, trans. Hugh Tredennick (Harmondsworth: Penguin, 1954), 87.

44. Ruas interview, 150.

45. Emily Dickinson, *The Letters of Emily Dickinson*, eds. Thomas H. Johnson and Theodora Ward (Cambridge: Belknap Press of Harvard Univ. Press, 1958), 473–74.

46. Heller makes the same point on the level of character: "Slocum lets himself go and often does become maudlin, because he has these defects of nature or character," while Yossarian "fights against letting himself feel emotion." Interestingly, in describing himself, Heller compares himself to Slocum rather than to Yossarian. See Ruas interview, 172.

47. Heller continues the mordant joke: "The other three patients in the unit with me that evening were on their backs unconscious (they indeed did seem part of a different world), and one or two of them, perhaps all three, were attached to the mechanical respirators or to other pieces of pumping and suctioning equipment that huffed and puffed in the background night and day" (*Matter* 81–82). Heller's joke is typical of his allusions to art and music, with art being associated with life, spirit, and consciousness; and insensitivity to art being linked to lifelessness, malaise, and ethical blindness.

48. The pink chemise connects the homeless woman to Luciana in *Catch-22*. In each case, the pink chemise comes to signify a wounded woman victimized by forces she cannot

control: Luciana by the war and the air raid in which she was wounded and the homeless woman by American capitalism and by her life in the PABT.

49. The scene also functions as a *mis en abyme* for Heller's own authorial hopes, anxieties, and wonderings about his position place in the literary pantheon.

50. Norman Rosten's description of the attractions of Coney Island can, by way of analogy, serve as an account of Heller's comic method, of the way in which his readers come to participate in a spectacle that they thought they were only observing:

> Steeplechase started an era of mass entertainment. A couple would enter the Park, rent "clown" suits to protect their clothes, and frolic with ten of thousands. To this day, one of the great draws is Steeplechase's public stage. Innocent visitors walk out from the wings into a series of sharp surprises: falling scenery, moving floors, electrically-wired railings, compressed-air tricks (woe to the lady without firm undergarments!)—all to the delight of the seated audience. Coney Island invited you to see the clowns—yourself and others. The trick mirrors showed you fat, lean, crooked, stunted, baloon-headed, pin-headed—and you laughed. You came to laugh and it gave you what you came for. (88)

See "Coney Island," *Holiday* (Sept. 1955): 86, 88–89.

51. Heller originally signed a contract with the Putnam Publishing Group for $4 million for two novels, for *Picture This* and the proposed sequel for *Catch-22*. After *Picture This* had weak reviews and poor sales, the contract was cancelled by mutual agreement. In the aftermath, other publishers, reportedly, had considerably less interest in *Closing Time*. Eventually, Heller signed a contract with Simon & Schuster reportedly for a $750,000 advance. See David Streitfeld, "Catch-23," *New York* (12 Sept. 1994) for these and other financial and publication details.

52. This linkage between the Angel of Death and Snowden functions as a nightmare version of Avignon, in which Snowden is the Angel of Death announcing Yossarian's death. Viewed in another way, this linkage makes Yossarian the Angel of Death, for at Snowden's funeral it is Yossarian who is seen as an angel, at least by the Chaplain. Yossarian's "angelic" appearance is illusory, but is inextricably connected to the death whose memorial he observes.

53. Mann, *Dr. Faustus*, 378.

54. For Heller, to recognize an allusion is to participate, in fact, to be complicit in the fictional realm in which the allusion occurs. Thus, while Yossarian wants to insists that he is an observer and auditor to Leverkühn's *Apocalypse*, the act of recognition signifies his role in the marriage phantasmagoria and the "apocalypse" that follows. For Heller, the reader's act of recognition has a similar effect, actively involving him or her in the text. Heller's point in this is not unlike that of Schrödinger's famous physics thought experiment. In Schrödinger's experiment, an observer determines the fate of a cat that is caged in a box with a radiation source even though the observer tries to avoid such a determination by conducting the experiment in a way which prevents him or her from observing the experiment or its outcome.

55. Heller's social analysis is reminscent of Rousseau's in *Discourse on the Origins of Inequality*: both stress that appearance becomes more important than reality, that humans in society live their lives in accordance to the opinions of others, that there are vast disparities in economic power and privilege, and that virtues have been emptied of content. See Jean-Jacques Rousseau, *The Basic Political Writings* (Indianapolis: Hackett Publishing Company, 1987), 80–81.

56. Alter, *Partial Magic*, 244.

AFTERWORD

1. Quoted by Avrom Fleishman, *Fiction and the Ways of Knowing* (Austin: Univ. of Texas Press, 1987), 167; originally in *Roger Fry: A Biography* (New York: 1940), 298. Fleishman documents, in part, the importance of the attitude toward death expressed by Spinoza to Woolf by showing how she corrects Frye's own misquotation of the line.

2. Robert Polhemus articulates the way in which comedy can refigure time: "Potentially the greatest effects available in comic art would seem to be attainable by combining the intensity of the comic moment—the mood of laughter and release—with the promise of some form of enduring life in which we have a part, and that is what the best modern comic fiction achieves" (18–19).

3. Gelb interview, 18.

4. This intepretation of *The Thousand Nights and a Night* had its genesis in Alvin B. Kernan, Peter Brooks, and J. Michael Holquist, *Man and His Fictions*.

5. Another authorial survival strategy is suggested by Walter Kendrick's account of Anthony Trollope; its implications cast a suggestive light on Heller's own possible hopes: "In 1871, when Trollope set out for Australia, he had left three finished novels, so that if the *Great Britain* sank 'there would be new novels ready to come out under my name for years to come' ([Autobiography] 297). *An Autobiography* joined an *An Old Man's Love* as a similar provision against departure for death's further shore. The end of Trollope's life would not mean the end of his writing; fiction and autobiography would share in keeping the narrator alive, though the man was dead" (*The Novel Machine: The Theory and Fiction of Anthony Trollope* [Baltimore: John Hopkins Univ. Press, 1980], 14).

6. Benjamin, "The Storyteller," in his *Illuminations*, 101.

7. Samuel Beckett, *Three Novels* (New York: Grove Press, 1965), 414.

BIBLIOGRAPHY

WORKS BY HELLER

Books

Catch-22. New York: Simon & Schuster, 1961.
We Bombed New Haven. New York: Alfred A. Knopf, 1968.
Catch-22: A Dramatization. New York: Samuel French, 1971 (acting edition).
Catch-22: A Dramatization. New York: Delacorte Press, 1973.
Clevinger's Trial (from Catch-22): *A Play in One Act*. New York: Samuel French, 1973.
Something Happened. New York: Alfred A. Knopf, 1974.
Good as Gold. New York: Simon & Schuster, 1979.
God Knows. New York: Alfred A. Knopf, 1984.
With Speed Vogel. *No Laughing Matter*. New York: G. P. Putnam's Sons, 1986.
Picture This. New York: G. P. Putnam's Sons, 1988.
Closing Time. New York: Simon & Schuster, 1994.

Stories

"I Don't Love You Any More." *Story* 27 (Sept.–Oct. 1945): 40–44.
"Castle of Snow." *Atlantic Monthly* 181 (Mar. 1948): 52–55.
"Girl from Greenwich." *Esquire* 29 (June 1948): 40–41, 142–43.
"A Man Named Flute." *Atlantic Monthly* 182 (Aug. 1948): 66–70.
"Nothing to Be Done." *Esquire* 30 (Aug. 1948): 73, 129–30.
"MacAdam's Log." *Gentlemen's Quarterly* 29 (Dec. 1959): 112, 166–76, 178.
"World Full of Great Cities." In *Nelson Algren's Own Book of Lonesome Monsters*, edited by Bernard Geis Associates, 7–19. New York: Lancer Books, 1962.

Excerpts, Articles, Etc.

"Bookies, Beware!" *Esquire* 27 (May 1947): 98.

"Catch-18." *New World Writing* 7 (Apr. 1955): 204–14.

"Middle-Aged Innocence." *The Nation* 194 (20 Jan. 1962): 62–63.

"Coney Island: The Fun Is Over." *Show* 2 (July 1962): 50–54, 102–3.

"Too Timid to Damn, Too Stingy to Applaud." *New Republic* 147 (30 July 1962): 23–24, 26.

"Irving Is Everywhere." *Show* 3 (Apr. 1963): 104–5, 126–27.

"Something Happened." *Esquire* 66 (Sept. 1966): 136–41, 212–13.

"Letters." *New York Times Magazine* (12 Mar. 1967): sec. 1, pp. 12, 22.

" 'Catch-22' Revisited." *Holiday* 41 (Apr. 1967): 44–61, 120, 141–42, 145.

"How I Found James Bond, Lost My Self-Respect, and Almost Made $150,000 in My Spare Time." *Holiday* 41 (June 1967): 123–25, 128, 130.

"Love, Dad." *Playboy* (Dec. 1969): 181–82, 348.

"On Translating *Catch-22* into a Movie." In *A "Catch-22" Casebook*, edited by Frederick Kiley and Walter McDonald, 346–62. New York: Crowell, 1973.

"From Sea to Shining Sea, Junk." *New York Times* (30 Sept. 1974): 35.

"This Is Called National Defense." *New York Times* (24 Nov. 1975): 35.

"Moths at a Dark Bulb." *New York Times* (24 May 1976): 29.

"Joseph Heller on America's 'Inhuman Callousness.' " *U.S. News and World Report* (9 Apr. 1979): 73.

"Something Happened." *People* (23 Aug. 1982): 24–29.

"Humor and the Ability to Create It Cannot Be Taught." *U.S. News and World Report* 97.20 (12 Nov. 1984): 71.

"Oslo: Meet Me at the Cafe." *New York Times* (17 Mar. 1985): sec. 6, pp. 38, 121–22.

"Joseph Heller: The Road Back." *New York Times Magazine* (12 Jan. 1986): 30, 34, 36–37, 50, 52.

With Speed Vogel and Valerie Humphries. "In the Hospital: Crisis and Recovery." *McCall's* (Aug. 1986): 85–92.

"Yossarian Lives." *Smart* (May 1990): 81–96.

"The Day Bush Left." *The Nation* (4 June 1990): 779–85.

" 'I *am* the Bombardier!' " *New York Times Magazine* (7 May 1995): 61.

"What Did You Eat in the War, Daddy?" *Forbes FYI* (11 Mar. 1996): 98–100, 103–4, 106.

Interviews

———. "*Catch-22* and After." *Gentlemen's Quarterly* 33.2 (Mar. 1963): 95, 26, 28, 33, 40–41, 46, 64–65.

———. "Fiction: The Personal Dimension." In *The Writer's World*, ed. Elizabeth Janeway, 137–74. New York: McGraw-Hill, 1969.

———. "Heller, in Sweden, Says Why He Likes Living in New York." *New York Times* (9 Nov. 1974): 22.

———. "Joseph Heller in Conversation with Martin Amis." *The New Review* 2.2 (Nov. 1975): 55–56, 58–59.

———. "Mel Brooks Meets Joseph Heller." *Washington Post Book World* (19 Mar. 1979): F1, 4.

———. "So They Say: Guest Editors Interview Six Creative People." *Mademoiselle* 57 (Aug. 1963): 234–35.

Bannon, Barbara A. "PW Interviews: Joseph Heller." *Publishers Weekly* (30 Sept. 1974): 6.

Barnard, Ken. "Joseph Heller Tells How *Catch-18* Became *Catch-22* and Why He Was Afraid of Airplanes." *Detroit News* (13 Sept. 1970): 18–19, 24, 27–28, 30, 65. Rpt.,

"Interview with Joseph Heller," in *A "Catch-22" Casebook*, edited by Frederick Kiley and Walter McDonald, 294-301. New York: Crowell, 1973.

Braudy, Susan. "'C'mon, Joe,' they would say to him . . ." *The New Journal* (26 Nov. 1967): 7, 9–10.

Charles, Gerda. "Catch 22 minus Seven." *Jewish Chronicle* (6 June 1980): 10.

Flippo, Chet. "Checking in with Joseph Heller." *Rolling Stone* (16 Apr. 1981): 50–52, 57, 59–60.

Frymer, Murry. "He Adds Another Catch to List." *Newsday* (14 Oct. 1968): 40A.

Gelb, Barbara. "Catch-22 Plus: A Conversation with Joseph Heller." *The New York Times Book Review* (28 Aug. 1994): 3, 18.

Gold, Dale. "Portrait of a Man Reading." *Washington Post Book World* (27 July 1969): 2.

Gonzales, Bro. Alexis. "Notes on the Next Novel: An Interview with Joseph Heller." *New Orleans Review* 2.3 (1971): 216–19.

Goodman, Walter. "Heller Talks of Illness and King David Book." *New York Times* (24 Sept. 1984): C13.

Keough, William T. "*Something Happened* after *Catch-22*." *Philadelphia Evening Bulletin* (3 Oct. 1974): 8, 11.

Krassner, Paul. "An Impolite Interview with Joseph Heller." *The Realist* 39 (Nov. 1962): 18–31. Rpt. in *A "Catch-22" Casebook*, edited by Frederick Kiley and Walter McDonald, 273–93. New York: Crowell, 1973.

Kustow, Michael. "Joseph Heller." London: ICA, 1985. Video recording.

Lennon, Peter. "Heller's New Gospel." *The Times* (9 Nov. 1984): 10.

Mandel, George. "Dialogue with Joseph Heller." *Penthouse* (May 1971): 54–56, 59, 60, 98.

Merrill, Sam. "*Playboy* Interview: Joseph Heller." *Playboy* (June 1975): 59–61, 64–66, 68, 70, 72–74, 76.

Moorehead, Caroline. "Writing Novels Slowly but with Hardly a Catch." *The Times* (17 Oct. 1975): 10.

Moyers, Bill. "Joseph Heller." In *A World of Ideas*. New York: Doubleday, 1989.

Plimpton, George. "The Art of Fiction LI: Joseph Heller." *The Paris Review* 15.60 (winter 1974): 126–47.

Powers, Charles T. "Joe Heller, Author on Top of the World." *Los Angeles Times* (30 Mar. 1975): sec. 7, pp. 1, 12.

Raidy, William A. "Meet Joseph Heller: Man against War." *Long Island Press* (6 Oct. 1968): 34.

Reilly, C. E., and Carol Villei. "An Interview with Joseph Heller." *Delaware Literary Review* (spring 1975): 19–21.

Reilly, Charles. "Talking with Joseph Heller." *Inquiry Magazine* (1 May 1979): 22–26.

Robinson, Robert. "Thirteen Years after *Catch-22*—An Interview with Joseph Heller." *The Listener* (24 Oct. 1972): 550.

Rothbardt, Helen. "First Play Discussed by Author." *Philadelphia Enquirer* (11 Sept. 1968): 51.

Ruas, Charles. "Joseph Heller." In *Conversations with American Writers*. New York: Alfred A. Knopf, 1985.

Rubin, Con. "*Catch-22* Author Hopes He Won't Bomb in New Haven." *New Haven Register* (26 Nov. 1967): sec. 4, pp. 1, 7.

Sale, Roger B. "An Interview in New York with Joseph Heller." *Studies in the Novel* 4 (1972): 63–74.

Schnedler, Jack. "*Catch-22*'s Joe Heller: He's Back after 13 Years . . ." *Chicago Daily News* (5–6 Oct. 1974): 2.

Shapiro, James. "Work in Progress/Joseph Heller." *Intellectual Digest* 2 (1971): 6, 8, 10–11.

Shenker, Israel. "Did Heller Bomb on Broadway?" *New York Times* (29 Dec. 1968): sec. 2, pp. 1, 3.

———. "Joseph Heller Draws Dead Bead on the Politics of Gloom." *New York Times* (10 Sept. 1968): 49.

Sinclair, Clive. Interview with Joseph Heller. *Jewish Chronicle* (16 Nov. 1984): 12.

Span, Paula. "Catch-23: For Joseph Heller, a Late-Life Summing Up." *The Washington Post* (29 Sept. 1994): D1, D2.

Strafford, Peter. "Mr. Heller Catches the Spirit of a Generation." *The Times* (19 Oct. 1974): 12.

Swindell, Larry. "What Happened to Heller after *Catch-22*?" *Philadelphia Enquirer* (22 Sept. 1974): G1, 10.

Waldron, Ann. "Writing Technique Can Be Taught, Says Joseph Heller." *Houston Chronicle* (Mar. 1975): 2.

Weatherby, W. J. "The Joy Catcher." *Guardian* (20 Nov. 1962): 7.

Whitman, Alden. "Something Always Happens on the Way to the Office: An Interview with Joseph Heller." In *Pages: The World of Books, Writers, and Writing*, vol. 1, edited by M. J. Bruccoli, 74–81. Detroit: Gale, 1976.

SELECTED WORKS ABOUT HELLER

———. "Eating With Their Mouths Open." *The New York Times Magazine* (3 Nov. 1985): 62, 93–94.

———. "Heller Unbound." *U.S. News and World Report* (13 Oct. 1986): 68.

———. "Joseph Heller." *A Writer's Yearbook*, no. 34 (1963): 46–49.

———. "Pre-*Catch-22* Heller." *New York Times* (3 May 1979): C16.

———. "Rembrandt Revised." *The Economist* 309 (22 Oct. 1988): 100–101.

Adams, Robert M. "History Is a Bust." *New York Times Book Review* (11 Sept. 1988): 9.

Aldridge, John W. *The American Novel and the Way We Live Now*, 35–46. New York: Oxford Univ. Press, 1983.

———. "The Loony Horror of It All—*Catch-22* Turns 25." *New York Times Book Review* 91 (26 Oct. 1986): 3, 55.

———. "Vision of Man Raging in a Vacuum." *Saturday Review World* (19 Oct. 1974): 18–21.

Algren, Nelson. "*Something Happened* by Joseph Heller." *Critic* 33.1 (1974): 90–91.

Alvarez, A. "Working in the Dark." *New York Review of Books* (11 April 1985): 16–17.

Aubrey, James R. "Major ——— de Coverley's Name in *Catch-22*." *Notes on Contemporary Literature* 18 (Jan. 1988): 2–3.

Aubrey, James R., and William E. McCarron. "More Shakespearean Echoes in *Catch-22*." *American Notes and Queries* 3.1 (Jan. 1990): 25–27.

Balliett, Whitney. Review of *Catch-22*. *New Yorker* (9 Dec. 1961): 247–48.

Beatty, Jack. "*Good as Gold* by Joseph Heller." *The New Republic* 180.10 (10 Mar. 1979): 42–44. Rpt. in *Critical Essays on Joseph Heller*, edited by James Nagel, 163–67. Boston: G. K. Hall, 1984.

Bell, Pearl K. "Heller and Malamud, Then and Now." *Commentary* 67 (June 1979): 71–72.

———. "Heller's Trial by Tedium." *New Leader* (28 Oct. 1974): 17–18.

Bernard, Bina. "The Author of *Catch-22* Brings Forth Another Novel." *People* (7 Oct. 1979): 47–49.

Berryman, Charles. "Heller's Gold." *Chicago Review* 32.4 (1981): 108–18.

Billson, Marcus K., III. "The Un-Minderbinding of Yossarian: Genesis Inverted in *Catch-22*." *Arizona Quarterly* 36 (1980): 315–29.

Blackwood, Caroline. "The Horrors of Peace." *Times Literary Supplement* (25 Oct. 1974): 1183.

Blues, Thomas. "The Moral Structure of *Catch-22*." *Studies in the Novel* 3 (spring 1971): 64–79.

Braudy, Susan. "Laughing All the Way to the Truth," *New York* 1 (14 Oct. 1968): 42–45. Rpt. in *Critical Essays on Joseph Heller*, edited by James Nagel, 215–21. Boston: G. K. Hall, 1984.

Bronson, Daniel Ross. "Man on a String: *Catch-22*." *Notes on Contemporary Literature* 7 (1977): 8–9.

Buckley, Christopher. "Götterdämmerung-22." *New Yorker* (10 Oct. 1994): 104–9.

Buckman, Rob. "Images of Illness." *The Sunday Times* (7 Oct. 1986): 48.

Burgess, Anthony. "With a Lot of Help from His Friends." *New York Times Book Review* (16 Feb. 1986): 8.

Burhans, Clinton S., Jr. "Spindrift and the Sea: Structural Patterns and Unifying Elements in *Catch-22*." *Twentieth Century Literature* 19 (1973): 239–50. Rpt. in *Critical Essays on Joseph Heller*, edited by James Nagel, 40–51. Boston: G. K. Hall, 1984.

Canaday, Nicholas. "Joseph Heller: Something Happened to the American Dream." *CEA Critic* 40 (1977): 34–38.

Carton, Evan. "The Politics of Selfhood: Bob Slocum, T. S. Garp and Auto-American-Biography." *Novel* 20 (fall 1986): 41–61.

Cheuse, Alan. "Laughing on the Outside." *Studies on the Left* 3 (1963): 81–87.

Christopher, Rita. "On the Train from Wilmington." *Macleans* 92 (16 Apr. 1979): 46.

Cockburn, Alex. "*Catch-22*." *New Left Review*, nos. 13–14 (Jan.–Apr. 1962): 87–92.

Cohen, Debra Rae. "Washington Gold Digging: Joseph Heller vs. Henry K." *Feature* (Apr. 1979): 16.

Costa, Richard Hauer. "Notes from a Dark Heller: Bob Slocum and the Underground Man." *Texas Studies in Literature and Language* 23.2 (1981): 159–82.

Crampton, Nancy. "Writing under the Influence." *Writer's Digest* (Aug. 1979): 15.

Dannatt, Adrian. "Aristotle Meets Rembrandt." *Spectator* 261.5 (5 Nov. 1988): 45.

Dault, Gary Michael. "Heller's Self-Satisfied Iconoclasm Is a Flimsy Excuse for a Novel." *The Toronto Star* (26 Nov. 1988): M8.

Davis, Gary W. "*Catch-22* and the Language of Discontinuity." *Novel* 12 (1978): 66–77. Rpt in *Critical Essays on Joseph Heller*, edited by James Nagel, 62–75. Boston: G. K. Hall, 1984.

Day, Douglas. "*Catch-22*: A Manifesto for Anarchists." *Carolina Quarterly* 15 (summer 1963): 86–92.

DelFattore, Joan. "The Dark Stranger in Heller's *Something Happened*." In *Critical Essays on Joseph Heller*, edited by James Nagel, 127–38. Boston: G. K. Hall, 1984.

DeMott, Benjamin. "Heller's Gold and a Silver Sax." *Atlantic Monthly* 243.3 (Mar. 1979): 129–31. Rpt. in *Critical Essays on Joseph Heller*, edited by James Nagel, 172–75. Boston: G. K. Hall, 1984.

Denniston, Constance. "The American Romance-Parody: A Study of Heller's *Catch-22*." *Emporia State Research Studies* 14 (1965): 42–59. Rpt. in *Critical Essays on "Catch-22,"* edited by James Nagel, 64–77. Encino, Ca.: Dickenson, 1974.

Dickstein, Morris. "Something Didn't Happen." *Saturday Review* 6 (31 Mar. 1979): 49–52.

Diliberto, Gioia. "Only God Knows How Joseph Heller Survived a Mysterious Disease to Tell His Tale of the Biblical King David." *People* (15 Oct. 1984): 139–40, 142.

Doskow, Minna. "The Night Journey in *Catch-22*." *Twentieth Century Literature* 12 (1967): 186–93. Rpt. in *Critical Essays on "Catch-22,"* edited by James Nagel, 155–62. Encino, Ca.: Dickenson, 1974. Rpt. in *Catch-22: A Critical Edition*, edited by Robert M. Scotto, 491–500. New York: Delta, 1973.

Edwards, Thomas R. "Catch-23." *New York Review of Books* (20 Oct. 1994): 20, 22–23.

Epstein, Joseph. "Joseph Heller's Milk Train: Nothing More to Express." *Washington Post Book World* (6 Oct. 1974): 1–3. Rpt. in *Critical Essays on Joseph Heller*, edited by James Nagel, 97–101. Boston: G. K. Hall, 1984.

Fetrow, Fred M. "Joseph Heller's Use of Names in *Catch-22*." *Studies in Contemporary Satire* 1 (1975): 28–38.

Frank, Mike. "Eros and Thanatos in *Catch-22*." *Canadian Review of American Studies* 7 (spring 1976): 77–87.

Fremont-Smith, Eliot. "Kvetch-22." *Voice* (5 Mar. 1979): 74–75.

Friedman, Melvin J. "Something Jewish Happened: Some Thoughts about Joseph Heller's *Good as Gold*." In *Critical Essays on Joseph Heller*, edited by James Nagel, 196–204. Boston: G. K. Hall, 1984.

Frost, Lucy. "Violence in the Eternal City: *Catch-22* as a Critique of American Culture." *Meanjin Quarterly* 30 (Dec. 1971): 447–53.

Furlani, Andre. "'Brisk Socratic Dialogues': Elenctic Rhetoric in Joseph Heller's *Something Happened*." *Narrative* 3.3 (Oct. 1995): 252–70.

Gaukroger, Doug. "Time Structure in *Catch-22*." *Critique* 12.2 (1970): 70–85. Rpt. in *Critical Essays on "Catch-22,"* edited by James Nagel, 89–101. Encino, Ca.: Dickenson, 1974.

Gelb, Barbara. "Catching Joseph Heller." *New York Times Magazine*, 4 March 1979, 14–16, 42, 44, 46, 48, 51–52, 54–55.

Glass, Peyton, III. "Heller's *Catch-22*." *Explicator* 36 (1978): 25–26.

Goldstein, William. "Story behind the Book: Joe and Speed Spend a Summer Day Laughing about *No Laughing Matter*." *Publishers Weekly* 228 (1 Nov. 1985): 32–33.

Goodman, Walter. "Heller Contemplating Rembrandt." *New York Times* (1 Sept. 1988): C23.

Gordon, Caroline, and Jeanne Richardson. "Flies in Their Eyes? A Note on Joseph Heller's *Catch-22*." *Southern Review* 3 (winter 1967): 96–105. Rpt. in *Critical Essays on "Catch-22,"* edited by James Nagel, 117–24. Encino, Ca.: Dickenson, 1974.

Gray, Paul. "Catch-23." *Time* (3 Oct. 1994): 78.

———. "The 3000-Year-Old Man." *Time* (24 Sept. 1984): 74–75.

Greenfeld, Josh. "22 Was Funnier than 14." *New York Times Book Review* (3 Mar. 1968): 1, 49–51, 53.

Gross, Beverly. "'Insanity Is Contagious': The Mad World of *Catch-22*." *The Centennial Review* 26 (1982): 86–113.

Gross, Ken. "Catch-2; Author Joe Heller Remarries; This Time It's the Nurse Who Brought Him Back to Health." *People* (27 Apr. 1987): 42, 45.

Grossman, Edward. "Yossarian Lives." *Commentary* 58 (Nov. 1974): 78, 80, 82–84.

Gussenhoven, Frances. "'Fiction is fact distorted into truth.'" *America* (17 Nov. 1984): 325.

Haberman, Clyde, and David Bird. "Pre-*Catch-22* Heller." *New York Times* (3 May 1979): C16.

Harris, Charles B. "*Catch-22*: A Radical Protest against Absurdity." In *Contemporary American Novelists of the Absurd*, 33–50. New Haven: College & University Press, 1971.

Hartshorne, Thomas L. "From *Catch-22* to *Slaughterhouse-V*: The Decline of the Political Mode." *South Atlantic Quarterly* 78 (1979): 17–33.

Hasley, Louis. "Dramatic Tension in *Catch-22*." *Midwest Quarterly* 15 (1974): 190–97.

Hays, Pelter L. "Yossarian and Gilgamesh." *Notes on Modern American Literature* (1980): Item 9.

Heller, Terry. "Notes on Technique in Black Humor." *Thalia: Studies in Literary Humor* 2.3 (1979): 15–21.

Henry, G. B. Mck. "Significant Corn: *Catch-22*." *Melbourne Critical Review* 9 (1966): 133–44.

Hitchens, Christopher. "The Facts of Strife." *Harper's Bazaar* (Sept. 1988): 260–61, 378.

———. "The Rise of Bunk." *Times Literary Supplement* (14–20 Oct. 1988): 1155.

Hoeber, Daniel R. "Joseph Heller's Corporate Catcher." *Notes on Contemporary Literature* 8 (1978): 10–11.

Houston, Gary. "Joseph Heller: A Novelist Who Knows He Cannot Be Rushed." *Chicago Sunday Sun-Times* (6 Oct. 1974): 1, 8.

Jensen, George H. "The Theatre and the Publishing House: Joseph Heller's *We Bombed in New Haven*." *Proof* 5 (1977): 183–216.

Jones, Malcolm. "Say It Ain't So, Joe, Books: Catch–00," *Newsweek* (3 Oct. 1994): 66.

Kaplan, Roger. "Heller's Last Gag." *Commentary* 79 (Feb. 1985): 59–61.

Karl, Frederick R. "Joseph Heller's *Catch-22*: Only Fools Walk in Darkness." In *Contemporary American Novelists*, edited by Harry T. Moore, 134–42. Carbondale: Southern Illinois Univ. Press, 1965.

Keegan, Brenda M. *Joseph Heller: A Reference Guide.* Boston: G. K. Hall, 1978.

Kennard, Jean. "Joseph Heller: At War with Absurdity." *Mosaic* 4:3 (1971): 75–87. Rpt. in *A "Catch-22" Casebook*, edited by Frederick Kiley and Walter McDonald, 255–69. New York: Crowell, 1973.

Kennedy, William. "Endlessly Honest Confession." *The New Republic* 171 (Oct. 1974): 17–19.

Kiley, Frederick, and Walter McDonald, eds. *A "Catch-22" Casebook*. New York: Crowell, 1973.

Kirsch, Robert. "Heller's Catch-23: The Entrapment of Everyman." *Los Angeles Times Calendar* (13 Oct. 1974): 1, 68.

Klemtner, Susan Strehle. "'A Permanent Game of Excuses': Determinism in Heller's *Something Happened*." *Modern Fiction Studies* 24.4 (1978–79): 550–56.

LaBelle, Maurice M. "Brains, Guts, and Luck in the Novels of Celine and Heller." In *Explorations: Essays in Comparative Literature*, edited by Makoto Ueda, 100–117. Lanham, Md.: University Press of America, 1986.

Larson, Michael J. "Shakespearian Echoes in *Catch-22*." *American Notes and Queries* 17 (1979): 76–78.

LeClair, Thomas. "Joseph Heller, *Something Happened*, and the Art of Excess." *Studies in American Fiction* 9 (autumn 1981): 245–60. Rpt. in *Critical Essays on Joseph Heller*, edited by James Nagel, 114–27. Boston: G. K. Hall, 1984.

Lehan, Richard, and Jerry Patch. "*Catch-22*: The Making of a Novel." *Minnesota Review* 7 (1967): 238–44.

Lehmann-Haupt, Christopher. "Review of *God Knows*." *New York Times* (19 Sept. 1984): C25.

———. "For Aging Yossarian, the Catch Is Cosmic." *New York Times* (22 Sept. 1994): C21.

Lenhart, Maria. "Wielding Humor's Two-Edged Sword." *Christian Science Monitor* (9 Apr. 1979): B3, B9.

Loukides, Paul. "The Radical Vision." *The Michigan Academician* 5 (spring 1973): 497–503.

Lowenkopf, Shelly. "When God Backs Off and Won't Apologize." *National Catholic Reporter* 21.4 (16 Nov. 1984): 12.

Lowin, Joseph. "The Jewish Art of Joseph Heller." *Jewish Book Annual* 43 (1985–86): 141–53.

Lyall, Sarah. "In 'Catch-22' Sequel, Heller Brings Back Yossarian, Milo, et al." *New York Times* (16 Feb. 1994): C13, C18.

Lyons, Gene. "Contradictory Judaism." *The Nation* 228 (16 June 1979): 727–28.

Martin, Robert A. "Joseph Heller's *Something Happened.*" *Notes on Contemporary Literature* 22.3 (May 1992): 11–12.

Martine, James J. "The Courage to Defy." In *Critical Essays on "Catch-22,"* edited by James Nagel, 142–49. Encino, Ca.: Dickenson, 1974.

McDonald, James L. "I See Everything Twice: The Structure of Joseph Heller's *Catch-22.*" *University Review* 34 (1968): 175–80.

McDonald, W. R. "He Took Off: Yossarian and the Different Drummer." *The CEA Critic* 36 (Nov. 1973): 14–16.

McDowell, Edwin. " 'Catch-22' Sequel by Heller." *New York Times* (8 Apr. 1987): C19.

McGinnis, Wayne D. "The Anarchic Impulse in Two Recent Novels." *Publications of the Arkansas Philological Association* 5 (1979): 36–40.

McNamara, Eugene. "The Absurd Style in Contemporary American Literature." *Bulletin de L'Association Canadienne des Humanites* 19 (1968): 44–49.

Medwick, Cathleen. "Man Bites God." *Vogue* 174 (Oct. 1984): 637, 701–2.

Mellard, James M. "*Catch-22: Deja vu* and the Labyrinth of Memory." *Bucknell Review* 16:2 (1968): 29–44.

_____. "Heller's *Catch-22.*" In *The Exploded Form: The Modernist Novel in America,* 108–24. Urbana: Univ. of Illinois Press, 1980.

_____. "*Something Happened*: The Imaginary, the Symbolic, and the Discourse of the Family." In *Critical Essays on Joseph Heller,* edited by James Nagel, 138–55. Boston: G. K. Hall, 1984.

Meltzer, Jay I. "Long Island Books." *East Hampton Star* 2 (3 July 1986): 22, 19.

Merivale, Patricia. "*Catch-22* and *The Secret Agent*: Mechanical Man, the Hole in the Centre, and the Principle of Inbuilt Chaos." *English Studies in Canada* 7 (Dec. 1981): 426–37.

_____. " 'One Endless Round': *Something Happened* and the Purgatorial Novel." *English Studies in Canada* 6.4 (Dec. 1985): 438–49.

Merkin, Daphne. "Jewish Jokester." *The New Leader* 62 (26 Mar. 1979): 12–13.

Merrill, Robert. *Joseph Heller.* Boston: Twayne, 1987.

_____. "The Rhetorical Structure of *Catch-22.*" *Notes on Contemporary Literature* 8 (1978): 9–11.

_____. "The Structure and Meaning of *Catch-22.*" *Studies in American Fiction* 14 (fall 1986): 139–52.

Michaels, Leonard. "Bruce Gold's American Experience." *New York Times Book Review* (11 Mar. 1979): 1, 24–25. Rpt. in *Critical Essays on Joseph Heller,* edited by James Nagel, 167–72. Boston: G. K. Hall, 1984.

Micheli, Linda McJ. "In No-Man's Land: The Plays of Joseph Heller." In *Critical Essays on Joseph Heller,* edited by James Nagel, 232–44. Boston: G. K. Hall, 1984.

Miller, Wayne Charles. "Ethnic Identity as Moral Focus: A Reading of Joseph Heller's *Good as Gold.*" *MELUS* 6.3 (1979): 3–17. Rpt. in *Critical Essays on Joseph Heller,* edited by James Nagel, 183–95. Boston: G. K. Hall, 1984.

_____. "Joseph Heller's *Catch-22*: Satire Sums up a Tradition." In *An Armed America: Its Face in Fiction,* chap. 7. New York: New York Univ. Press, 1970.

Mills, Russell. "Multiple Characterizations in *Catch-22.*" *Notes on Contemporary Literature* 9 (1979): 6–7.

Milne, Victor J. "Heller's 'Bologniad': A Theological Perspective on *Catch-22.*" *Critique* 12.2 (1970): 50–69.

Monk, Donald. "An Experiment in Therapy: A Study of *Catch-22.*" *The London Review* 2 (autumn 1967): 12–19.

Mullican, James S. "A Burkean Approach to *Catch-22.*" *College Literature* 8 (winter 1981): 42–52.

Muste, John M. "Better to Die Laughing: The War Novels of Joseph Heller and John Ash-mead." *Critique* 5 (fall 1962): 16–27.

Nagel, James. "*Catch-22* and Angry Humor: A Study of the Normative Values of Satire." *Studies in American Humor* 1 (1974): 99–106.

———. "The *Catch-22* Note Cards." *Studies in the Novel* 8 (1976): 394–405. Rpt. in *Critical Essays on Joseph Heller,* edited by Nagel, 51–61. Boston: G. K. Hall, 1984.

———, ed. *Critical Essays on "Catch-22."* Encino, Ca.: Dickenson, 1974.

———. *Critical Essays on Joseph Heller.* Boston: G. K. Hall, 1984.

———. "Joseph Heller." In *Contemporary Authors Bibliographical Series: American Novelists,* vol. 1, edited by James J. Martine, 193–218. Detroit: Gale, 1986.

———. "Joseph Heller and the University." *College Literature* 10 (1983): 16–27.

———. "Two Brief Manuscript Sketches: Heller's *Catch-22.*" *Modern Fiction Studies* 20 (1974): 221–24.

———. "Yossarian, the Old Man, and the Ending of *Catch-22.*" In *Critical Essays on "Catch-22,"* edited by Nagel, 164–74. Encino, Ca.: Dickenson, 1974.

Nelson, Gerald B. "Yossarian and Friends." In *Ten Versions of America,* 163–82. New York: Alfred A. Knopf, 1972.

Nelson, Thomas Allen. "Theme and Structure in *Catch-22.*" *Renascence* 23 (summer 1971): 173–82.

Nordell, Roderick. "Heller's Black Comedy of Society's Errors." *Christian Science Monitor* (28 Mar. 1979): 17.

Oetgen, George R. "The Twenty-Two of Heller's Catch." *American Notes and Queries* 15 (1981): 160.

Olderman, Raymond M. "The Grail Knight Departs." In *Beyond the Waste Land: The American Novel in the Nineteen-Sixties,* 94–116. New Haven: Yale Univ. Press, 1972.

Oldsey, Bernard. "Another Joe from Brooklyn: Heller in Happy Valley." *Town & Gown* (Nov. 1984): 24–26, 28, 30, 32.

Parr, Susan Resneck. "Everything Green Looked Black: *Catch-22* as Inverted Eden." *Notes on Modern American Literature* 4 (1980): Item 27.

Pearson, Carol. "*Catch-22* and the Debasement of Language." *CEA Critic* 38 (1976): 30–35.

Pinsker, Sanford. "Heller's *Catch-22*: The Protest of a *Puer Eternis.*" *Critique* 7 (1965): 150–62.

———. *Understanding Joseph Heller.* Columbia: Univ. of South Carolina Press, 1991.

Pinsky, Robert. "After '*Catch-22,*' Updated Insanity." *The Washington Post* (29 Sept. 1994): D1–D2.

Podhoretz, Norman. "The Best Catch There Is." In *Doings and Undoings,* 228–35. New York: Farrar, Straus & Giroux, 1964.

Potts, Stephen W. *Catch-22.* Boston: Twayne Publishers, 1989.

———. *From Here to Absurdity: The Moral Battlefields of Joseph Heller.* San Bernardino, Ca.: Borgo Press, 1982.

Prentice, Thomson. "Author Who Was Nearly Written Off." *The Times* (19 Nov. 1985): 14.

Pritchard, William H. "Yossarian Redux." *New York Times Book Review* (25 Sept. 1994): 1, 36–37.

Proffitt, Edward. "Slocum's Accident: An American Tragedy." *Notes on Contemporary Literature* 7 (1977): 7–8.

Protherough, Robert. "The Sanity of *Catch-22.*" *The Human World* 3 (May 1971): 59–70.

Ramsey, Vance. "From Here to Absurdity: Heller's *Catch-22.*" In *Seven Contemporary Authors: Essays on Cozzens, Miller, West, Golding, Heller, Albee, and Powers,* edited by Thomas B. Whitbread, 97–118. Austin: Univ. of Texas Press, 1966.

Richler, Mordecai. "He Who Laughs Last." *New York Times Book Review* (23 Sept. 1984): 1, 36.

Richter, David H. "The Achievement of Shape in the Twentieth-Century Fable: Joseph Heller's *Catch-22*." In *Fable's End: Completeness and Closure in Rhetorical Fiction*, 136–65. Chicago: Univ. of Chicago Press, 1974.

Robertson, Joan. "They're after Everyone: Heller's *Catch-22* and the Cold War." *CLIO* 19.1 (fall 1989): 41–50.

Rubin, Merle. "A New Satire in *'Catch-22'* Sequel." *Christian Science Monitor* (4 Oct. 1994): 14.

Ruderman, Judith. *Joseph Heller*. New York: Continuum, 1991.

_____. "Upside-Down in *Good as Gold*: Moishe Kapoyer as Muse." *Yiddish* 5.4 (1984): 55–63.

Scleier, Curt. "Joseph Heller on World War II: It Was 'pure pleasure.'" *A & E Monthly* (Oct. 1994): 37–40.

Schroth, Raymond A. "I Wonder Who's Kissinger Now?" *Commonweal* 106 (11 May 1979): 284–85.

Schumacher, Michael. "Heller." *Writer's Digest* (Mar. 1987): 20–25.

Scotto, Robert M., ed. *Catch-22: A Critical Edition*. New York: Delta, 1973.

_____. *Three Contemporary Novelists: An Annotated Bibliography of Works by and about John Hawkes, Joseph Heller, and Thomas Pynchon*. New York: Garland, 1977.

Searles, George J. "Joseph Heller." In *Dictionary of Literary Biography: Twentieth-Century American-Jewish Fiction Writers*, edited by Daniel Walden, 28, 101–7. Detroit: Gale, 1984.

_____. "*Something Happened*: A New Direction for Joseph Heller." *Critique* 18.3 (1977): 74–81.

Sebouhian, George. "From Abraham and Isaac to Bob Slocum and My Boy: Why Fathers Kill Their Sons." *Twentieth Century Literature* 27 (1981): 43–52.

Seed, David. *The Fiction of Joseph Heller*. New York: St. Martin's Press, 1989.

Seltzer, Leon F. "Milo's 'Culpable Innocence': Absurdity as Moral Insanity in *Catch-22*." *Papers on Language and Literature* 15 (1979): 290–310.

Shenker, Israel. "2nd Heller Book Due 13 Years after First." *New York Times* (18 Feb. 1974): sec. 1, p. 30.

Smith, Anne. "Nothing Works." *The Listener* 120 (27 Oct. 1988): 32.

Smith, Roger H. "A Review: *Catch-22*." *Daedalus* 92 (winter 1963): 155–65. Rpt. in *Critical Essays on "Catch-22,"* edited by James Nagel, 21–33. Encino, Ca.: Dickenson, 1974. Rpt. in *A "Catch-22" Casebook*, edited by Frederick Kiley and Walter McDonald, 27–39. New York: Crowell, 1973.

Sniderman, Stephen L. "'It Was All Yossarian's Fault': Power and Responsibility in *Catch-22*." *Twentieth Century Literature* 19 (1973): 251–58.

Solomon, Eric. "From *Christ in Flanders* to *Catch-22*: An Approach to War Fiction." *Texas Studies in Language and Literature* 11 (spring 1969): 851–66.

Solomon, Jan. "The Structure of *Catch-22*." *Critique* 9 (1967): 46–57.

Stanford, Les. "Novels into Film: *Catch-22* as Watershed." *Southern Humanities Review* 8 (1974): 19–25.

Stark, Howard J. "*Catch-22*: The Ultimate Irony." In *Critical Essays on "Catch-22,"* edited by James Nagel, 130–41. Encino, Ca.: Dickenson, 1974.

Stern, Frederick C. "Heller's Hell: Heller's Later Fiction, Jewishness, and the Liberal Imagination." *MELUS* 15.4 (winter 1988): 15–37.

Stern, J. P. "War and the Comic Muse: *The Good Soldier Schweik* and *Catch-22*." *Comparative Literature* 20 (summer 1968): 193–216.

Strawson, Galen. "Saith the King Already." *Times Literary Supplement* (23 Nov. 1984): 1330.

Strehle, Susan. "A Permanent Game of Excuses: Determinism in Heller's *Something Happened*." *Modern Fiction Studies*, 24 (1978–79, 550–56. Rpt. in *Critical Essays on Joseph Heller*, edited by James Nagel, 106–14. Boston: G. K. Hall, 1984.

———. "Slocum's Parenthetical Tic: Style as Metaphor in *Something Happened*." *Notes on Contemporary Literature* 7 (1977): 9–10.

Streitfeld, David, "Catch-23," *New York* (12 Sept. 1994): 100–5.

Swardson, H. R. "Sentimentality and the Academic Tradition." *College English* 37.8 (Apr. 1976): 747–66.

Taylor, Paul. "History Lessons from a Canvas Prison." *The Sunday Times* (16 Oct. 1988): G6.

Thomas, W. K. "The Mythic Dimension of *Catch-22*." *Texas Studies in Literature and Language* 15 (1973): 189–98.

———. "What Difference Does It Make." *The Dalhousie Review* 50 (winter 1970–71): 488–95.

Tucker, Lindsey. "Entropy and Information Theory in Heller's *Something Happened*." *Contemporary Literature* 25.3 (1984): 323–40.

Tyson, Lois. "Joseph Heller's *Something Happened*: The Commodification of Consciousness." *CEA Critic* 54.2 (1992 winter): 37–51.

Vogel, Speed. "Helping a Convalescent Friend (in Style)." *New York Times* (28 July 1982): C16.

Vonnegut, Kurt. "*Something Happened*: Joseph Heller's Extraordinary Novel about an Ordinary Man." *New York Times Book Review* (6 Oct. 1974): 1–2. Rpt. in *Critical Essays on Joseph Heller*, edited by James Nagel, 93–97. Boston: G. K. Hall, 1984.

Waldmeir, Joseph J. *American Novels of the Second World War*, 160–65. The Hague: Mouton, 1969.

———. "Two Novelists of the Absurd: Heller and Kesey." *Wisconsin Studies in Contemporary Literature* 5 (1964): 192–204.

Way, Brian. "Formal Experiment and Social Discontent: Joseph Heller's *Catch-22*." *Journal of American Studies* 2 (1968): 253–70.

Weixlmann, Joseph. "A Bibliography of Joseph Heller's *Catch-22*." *Bulletin of Bibliography* 31 (1974): 32–37.

Wells, Joel. "A psaltery of one liners." *Commonweal* 111 (19 Oct. 1984): 561–62.

Wershba, Joseph. "A Novelist in Search of Sanity in a World He Sees as Insane." *New York Post* (15 Mar. 1962): 54.

Wieseltier, Leon. "Schlock of Recognition." *New Republic* (29 Oct. 1984): 31–33.

Williams, Melvin G. "*Catch-22*: What the Movie Audiences Missed." *Christianity & Literature* 9 (1974): 21–25.

Young, Melanie M. S. "Joseph Heller: A Critical Introduction." Ph.D. diss., Rice University, 1981.

OTHER MATERIAL CONSULTED

Aeschylus. *Prometheus Bound*. Harmondsworth, England: Penguin Books, 1961.

Alpers, Svetlana. *Rembrandt's Enterprise: The Studio and the Market*. Chicago: Univ. of Chicago Press, 1988.

Alter, Robert. "The Apocalyptic Temper." *Commentary* 41 (June 1966): 61–66.

———. *Motives for Metaphor*. Cambridge, Mass: Harvard Univ. Press, 1984.

———. *Partial Magic*. Berkeley and Los Angeles: Univ. of California Press, 1975.

———. *The Pleasures of Reading in an Ideological Age*. New York: Touchstone, 1989.

Anderson, Chris. *Style as Argument: Contemporary American Nonfiction.* Carbondale: Southern Illinois Univ. Press, 1987.

Arendt, Hannah. *Eichmann in Jerusalem.* New York: The Viking Press, 1963.

Bakhtin, M. M. *The Dialogic Imagination,* edited by Michael Holquist, trans. by Carl Emerson and Michael Holquist. Austin: Univ. of Texas Press, 1981.

Barth, John. "The Literature of Exhaustion." *Atlantic Monthly* 220 (Aug. 1967): 29–39.

Barthes, Roland. *Image-Music-Text.* New York: Hill and Wang, 1977.

Bataille, Georges. *L'Erotisme.* Paris: Union Générale d'Editions, 1965.

Becker, Ernest. *The Denial of Death.* New York: Basic Books, 1973.

Beckett, Samuel. *Three Novels.* New York: Grove Press, 1965.

Bellow, Saul. *Mr. Sammler's Planet.* Greenwich, Conn.: A Fawcett Crest Book, 1971.

Benjamin, Walter. *Illuminations,* edited by Hannah Arendt, trans. by Harry Zohn. New York: Schocken Books, 1969.

Berendsohn, Walter E. *Thomas Mann: Artist and Partisan Trouble Times,* trans. by George C. Buck. Tuscaloosa: Univ. of Alabama Press, 1975.

Berger, John. *Ways of Seeing.* Harmondsworth: Penguin, 1976.

Bleich, David. *Subjective Criticism.* Baltimore: The Johns Hopkins Univ. Press, 1978.

Bogart, Michelle H. "Barking Architecture: The Sculpture of Coney Island." *Smithsonian Studies in American Art* 15.1 (1988): 3–17.

Boone, Joseph Allen. *Counter Tradition: Love and the Form of Fiction.* Chicago: Univ. of Chicago Press, 1987.

Booth, Wayne C. *The Company We Keep: An Ethics of Fiction.* Berkeley: Univ. of California Press, 1988.

———. *The Rhetoric of Fiction.* Chicago: Univ. of Chicago Press, 1961.

———. *A Rhetoric of Irony.* Chicago: Univ. of Chicago Press, 1974.

Bradbury, Malcolm. *The Modern American Novel.* New York: Oxford Univ. Press, 1984.

Brooks, Peter. *Reading for the Plot.* New York: Vintage Books, 1985.

Brustein, Robert. *Making Scenes: A Personal History of the Turbulent Years at Yale, 1966–1979.* New York: Random House, 1981.

Byrd, Scott. "A Separate War: Camp and Black Humor in Recent American Fiction." *Language Quarterly* 7.1, 2 (fall–winter 1968): 7–10.

Campbell, Joseph. *The Hero with a Thousand Faces.* Princeton: Princeton Univ. Press, 1968.

———. "Myth and the Modern World." In *The Power of Myth,* 3–36. New York: Doubleday, 1988.

Cassirer, Ernst. *Language and Myth,* trans. by Susanne K. Langer, 1946. New York: Dover Publications, 1953.

Chatman, Seymour. *Coming to Terms: The Rhetoric of Narrative in Fiction and Film.* Ithaca, N.Y.: Cornell Univ. Press, 1990.

———. *Story and Discourse: Narrative Structure in Fiction and Film.* Ithaca, N.Y.: Cornell Univ. Press, 1978.

Cohen, Sarah Blacher, ed. *Comic Relief.* Urbana, Chicago, and London: Univ. of Illinois Press, 1978.

———, ed. *Jewish Wry: Essays on Jewish Humor.* Bloomington: Indiana Univ. Press, 1987.

Cousins, Norman. *Anatomy of an Illness as Perceived by the Patient: Reflections on Healing and Regeneration.* New York: Norton, 1979.

Craig, Randall. *The Tragicomic Novel.* Newark: Univ. of Delaware, 1989.

Dodds, E. R. "On Misunderstanding Oedipus." In *The Ancient Concept of Progress,* 64–77. Oxford: The Clarendon Press, 1973.

Fiedler, Leslie. *Love and Death in the American Novel.* New York: Criterion Books, 1960.

Fish, Stanley. *Is There a Text in This Class? The Authority of Interpretive Communities.* Cambridge, Mass.: Harvard Univ. Press, 1980.

Fishkin, Shelley Fischer. *From Fact to Fiction: Journalism and Imaginative Writing in America.* Baltimore: Johns Hopkins Univ. Press, 1985.

Fleishman, Avrom. *Fiction and the Ways of Knowing.* Austin: Univ. of Texas Press, 1987.

Freud, Sigmund. *Civilization and Its Discontents*, trans. and edited by James Strachey. New York and London: W. W. Norton, 1961.

_____. *The Future of an Illusion*, translated and edited by James Strachey. New York: W. W. Norton, 1961.

Frontain, Raymond-Jean, and Jan Wojcik, eds. *The David Myth in Western Culture.* West Lafayette, Ind.: Purdue Univ. Press, 1980.

Frye, Northrop. *Anatomy of Criticism.* Princeton: Princeton Univ. Press, 1957.

_____. *The Great Code.* New York: A Harvest/HBJ Book, 1982.

Galloway, David D. "Clown and Saint: The Hero in Current American Fiction." *Critique* 7 (1965): 46–65.

Garten, H. F. *Wagner.* London: John Calder, 1977.

Gelley, Alexander. "Metonymy, Schematism, and the Space of Literature." *New Literary History* 11 (spring 1980): 469–86.

Genette, Gérard. *Narrative Discourse: An Essay on Method*, translated by Jane Lewis. Ithaca: Cornell Univ. Press, 1981.

Gergen, Kenneth. "Multiple Identity: The Healthy, Happy Human Being Wears Many Masks." *Psychology Today* (May 1972): 31–35, 64–66.

Gergen, Kenneth, and Chad Gordon. *The Self in Social Interaction.* New York: John Wiley & Sons, 1968.

Girard, René. *Deceit, Desire, and the Novel.* Baltimore: Johns Hopkins Univ. Press, 1965.

Girgus, Sam B. *The New Covenant: Jewish Writers and the American Idea.* Chapel Hill: Univ. of North Carolina Press, 1984.

Goffman, Erving. *The Presentation of the Self in Everyday Life.* New York: Doubleday Anchor, 1959.

Gombrich, E. H. *Art and Illusion.* Princeton: Princeton Univ. Press, 1960.

Greenberg, Alvin. "The Novel of Disintegration: Paradoxical Impossibility in Contemporary Fiction." *Contemporary Literature* 7 (1966): 103–24.

Guerard, Albert J. *The Triumph of the Novel: Dickens, Dostoevsky, Faulkner.* New York: Oxford Univ. Press, 1976.

Guthke, Karl S. *Modern Tragicomedy: An Investigation into the Nature of the Genre.* New York: Random House, 1966.

Harvey, W. J. *Character and the Novel.* Ithaca, N.Y.: Cornell Univ. Press, 1965.

Hassan, Ihab. "Laughter in the Dark: The New Voice in American Fiction." *The American Scholar* 33 (autumn 1964): 636–39.

_____. *Radical Innocence.* Princeton: Princeton Univ. Press, 1961.

Hill, Hamlin. "Black Humor: Its Cause and Cure." *Colorado Quarterly* 17 (summer 1968): 57–64.

Hofstadter, Douglas. *Godel, Escher, Bach.* New York: Basic Books, 1979.

Holland, Norman. *The Dynamics of Literary Response.* New York: Columbia Univ. Press, 1989.

_____. "How Can Dr. Johnson's Remarks on Cordelia's Death Add to My Own Response?" In *Psychoanalysis & the Question of the Text*, edited by Geoffrey H. Hartman. Baltimore: Johns Hopkins Univ. Press, 1978.

Horton, Susan R. *Interpreting Interpreting.* Baltimore: Johns Hopkins Univ. Press, 1979.

House, Humphrey. *Aristotle's Poetics.* Englewood Cliffs, N.J.: Prentice-Hall, Inc., 1968.

Howe, Irving. *Politics and the Novel.* Cleveland, Oh.: The World Publishing Company, 1957.

Iser, Wolfgang. *The Act of Reading.* Baltimore: Johns Hopkins Univ. Press, 1978.

_____. *The Implied Reader: Patterns of Communication in Prose Fiction from Bunyan to Beckett*. Baltimore: Johns Hopkins Univ. Press, 1974.

Jakobson, Roman, and Morris Halle. *Fundamentals of Language*. The Hague: Mouton, 1956.

Janoff, Bruce. "Black Humor, Existentialism, and Absurdity: A Generic Confusion." *Arizona Quarterly* 30 (1974): 293–304.

Johnson, Barbara. *The Critical Difference: Essays in the Contemporary Rhetoric of Reading*. Baltimore: Johns Hopkins Univ. Press, 1980.

Karl, Frederick R. *American Fictions 1940–1980*. New York: Harper & Row, 1983.

Kawin, Bruce F. *Telling It Again and Again*. Ithaca: Cornell Univ. Press, 1972.

Kazin, Alfred. "The War Novel from Mailer to Vonnegut." *Saturday Review* (6 Feb. 1971): 14–15.

Keegan, John. *The Face of Battle*. New York: Viking Press, 1976.

Kendrick, Walter M. *The Novel Machine: The Theory and Fiction of Anthony Trollope*. Baltimore: Johns Hopkins Univ. Press, 1980.

Kermode, Frank. *The Art of Telling: Essays on Fiction*. Cambridge, Mass.: Harvard Univ. Press, 1983.

_____. *The Classic: Literary Images of Permanence and Change*. Cambridge, Mass.: Harvard Univ. Press, 1983.

_____. *History and Value*. Oxford: Clarendon Press, 1989.

_____. *The Sense of an Ending*. New York: Oxford Univ. Press, 1966.

Kernan, Alvin. *Modern Satire*. New York: Harcourt, Brace & World, 1962.

Kernan, Alvin B., Peter Brooks, and J. Michael Holquist. *Man and His Fictions*. New York: Harcourt Brace Jovanovich, 1973.

Kierkegaard, Søren. *Concluding Unscientific Postscript*, trans. by David F. Swenson. Princeton: Princeton Univ. Press, 1941.

_____. *Fear and Trembling*. Princeton: Princeton Univ. Press, 1941.

_____. *Repetition*. Princeton: Princeton Univ. Press, 1941.

Klinkowitz, Jerome. *Structuring the Void*. Durham: Duke Univ. Press, 1992.

Lacan, Jacques. *The Language of the Self,* trans. with notes and commentary by Anthony Wilden. Baltimore: Johns Hopkins Univ. Press, 1968.

Langbaum, Robert. *The Poetry of Experience*. New York: W. W. Norton & Co., 1963.

Lasch, Christopher. *The Culture of Narcissism: American Life in an Age of Diminishing Expectations*. New York: Warner Books, 1979.

Leeming, David Adams. *Mythology*. Philadelphia and New York: J. B. Lippincott Company, 1973.

Lewis, R. W. B. *The American Adam: Innocence, Tragedy and Tradition in the Nineteenth Century*. Chicago: Univ. of Chicago Press, 1955.

_____. "Days of Wrath and Laughter." In *Trials of the Word*, 184–85, 226–27. New Haven: Yale Univ. Press, 1965.

Littlejohn, David. "The Anti-Realists." *Daedalus* 92 (spring 1963): 250–64.

Lodge, David. *The Modes of Modern Writing*. 1977. Rpt. Chicago: Univ. of Chicago Press, 1988.

Long, Elizabeth. *The American Dream and the Popular Novel*. London: Routledge & Kegan Paul, 1985.

Mann, Thomas. *Death in Venice and Seven Other Stories*. New York: Vintage Books, 1930.

_____. *Doctor Faustus*. New York: Vintage Books, 1992.

Marx, Karl. "The Eighteenth Brumaire of Louis Bonaparte." In *The Marx-Engels Reader*, edited by Robert C. Tucker. New York: W. W. Norton & Co., 1978.

Miller, J. Hillis. *The Ethics of Reading*. New York: Columbia Univ. Press, 1987.

_____. *Fiction and Repetition*. Cambridge, Mass.: Harvard Univ. Press, 1982.

_____. *The Form of Victorian Fiction*. Notre Dame, Ind.: Univ. of Notre Dame, 1968.

Milligan, Barry. *The Master Musicians: Wagner.* London & Melbourne: J. M. Dent & Sons Ltd, 1984.

Moore, Deborah Dash. *At Home in America: Second Generation New York Jews.* New York: Columbia Univ. Press, 1981.

Moyers, Bill. *A World of Ideas.* New York: Doubleday, 1989.

Nash, Walter. *The Language of Humour.* New York: Longman, 1985.

O'Neill, Patrick. *The Comedy of Entropy: Humour/Narrative/Reading.* Toronto: Univ. of Toronto Press, 1990.

Ong, Walter. *Orality and Literacy.* London and New York: Methuen, 1982.

Osborne, Charles. *The Complete Operas of Richard Wagner.* North Pomfret, Vt.: Trafalgar Square Publishing, 1990.

Paige, Harry. "Discovery a Life-Long Process for All." *North Country This Week* (2–8 Nov. 1994): 1.

Percy, Walter. "The State of the Novel: Dying Art or New Science?" *Michigan Quarterly Review* 16:4 (1977): 359–73.

Phelan, James. *Reading People, Reading Plots.* Chicago: Univ. of Chicago Press, 1989.

_____. *Worlds from Words: A Theory of Language in Fiction.* Chicago: Univ. of Chicago Press, 1981.

Pirandello, Luigi. *On Humor,* trans. by Antonio Illiana and Daniel P. Testa. Chapel Hill: Univ. of North Carolina Press, 1960.

Plato. *The Last Days of Socrates,* trans. by Hugh Tredennick. Harmondsworth: Penguin, 1954.

Polhemus, Robert M. *Comic Faith.* Chicago: Univ. of Chicago Press, 1980.

Prescott, Peter S. *Never in Doubt: Critical Essays on American Books, 1972–1985.* New York: Arbor House, 1986.

Rabinowitz, Peter. *Before Reading: Narrative Conventions and the Politics of Interpretation.* Ithaca, N.Y.: Cornell Univ. Press, 1987.

_____. "Truth in Fiction: A Reexamination of Audiences." *Critical Inquiry* 4 (1977): 121–41.

Rank, Otto. *Beyond Psychology.* New York: Dover, 1958.

Raphael, Robert. *Richard Wagner.* Twayne's World Authors Series. New York: Twayne Publishers, Inc., 1969.

Rhodes, Richard. *The Making of the Bomb.* New York: Simon and Schuster, 1986.

Ricoeur, Paul. "Narrative Time." *Critical Inquiry* 7 (1980): 169–90.

Rosenberg, Jakob. *Rembrandt: Life and Work,* rev. ed. New York: Phaidon Press, 1964.

Rosenberg, Jakob, Seymour Slive, and E. H. ter Kuile. *Dutch Art and Architecture, 1600–1800.* New York: Penguin, 1966.

Rosten, Norman. "Coney Island." *Holiday* (Sept. 1955): 86, 88–89.

Rougement, Denis de. *Love in the Western World,* trans. Montgomery Belgion. New York: Pantheon, 1956.

Rousseau, Jean-Jacques. *The Basic Political Writings.* Indianapolis: Hackett Publishing, 1987.

Rousseau, Theodore. "Aristotle Contemplating the Bust of Homer." *Metropolitan Museum of Art Bulletin* 20 (1962): 149–56.

Said, Edward. *Beginnings: Intention and Method.* New York: Basic Books, 1975.

_____. *The World, the Text, and the Critic.* Cambridge, Mass.: Harvard Univ. Press, 1983.

Schama, Simon. *The Embarrassment of Riches.* New York: Alfred A. Knopf, 1987.

Schulz, Max F. "Pop, Op, and Black Humor: The Aesthetics of Anxiety." *College English* 30.3 (Dec. 1968): 230–41.

Schwartz, Gary. *Rembrandt: His Life, His Paintings.* New York: Viking Press, 1985.

Searle, John R. *Speech Acts: An Essay in the Philosophy of Language.* Cambridge: Cambridge Univ. Press, 1969.

Shapiro, Stephen A. "The Ambivalent Animal: Man in the Contemporary British and American Novel." *Centennial Review* 12 (1968): 1–22.

Sophocles. *The Oedipus Cycle,* trans. by Dudley Fitts and Robert Fitzgerald. New York: Harcourt Brace, 1967.

Steiner, George. "Books: Master Class." *New Yorker* 64 (30 May 1988): 97–99.

Sternberg, Meir. *Expositional Modes and Temporal Ordering in Fiction.* Baltimore: Johns Hopkins Univ. Press, 1978.

Stevens, Wallace. "Notes toward a Supreme Fiction." In *The Collected Poetry of Wallace Stevens.* New York: Alfred A. Knopf, 1971.

Tanner, Tony. *Adultery in the Novel.* Baltimore: Johns Hopkins Univ. Press, 1979.

_____. *City of Words: American Fiction, 1950–1970.* New York: Harper & Row, 1971.

Thackeray, William Makepeace. *English Humorists of the Eighteenth Century.* Vol. 13. Boston: Houghton Mifflin, 1889.

_____. *Vanity Fair.* Boston: Houghton Mifflin, 1963.

Thucydides. *The Peloponnesian War,* trans. by Rex Warner. Harmondsworth: Penguin, 1974.

Torrance, Robert M. *The Comic Hero.* Cambridge, Mass.: Harvard Univ. Press, 1978.

Traversi, D. A. *An Approach to Shakespeare.* New York: Doubleday, 1956.

Wallace, Ronald. "Never Mind that the Nag's a Pile of Bones: The Contemporary American Comic Novel and the Comic Tradition." In *The Last Laugh,* 1–25. Columbia: Univ. of Missouri Press, 1979.

Walsh, Jeffrey. *American War Literature: 1914 to Vietnam.* New York: St. Martin's Press, 1982.

Watt, Ian. *Conrad in the Nineteenth Century.* 1957. Rpt. Berkeley and Los Angeles: Univ. of California Press, 1979.

_____. *The Rise of the Novel.* Berkeley and Los Angeles: Univ. of California Press, 1959.

Waugh, Patricia. *Metafiction: The Theory and Practice of Self-Conscious Fiction.* New York and London: Methuen, 1984.

Weinstein, Philip. *The Semantics of Desire.* Princeton: Princeton Univ. Press, 1984.

Winston, Mathew. "Black Humor: To Weep with Laughing." In *Comedy: New Perspectives,* edited by Maurice Charney, 31–43. New York: New York Literary Forum, 1978.

_____. *"Humour noir* and Black Humor." *Harvard English Studies* 3 (1972): 273.

Wisse, Ruth R. *The Schlemiel as Modern Hero.* Chicago: Univ. of Chicago Press, 1971.

Zumthor, Paul. *Daily Life in Rembrandt's Holland.* London: Weidenfeld and Nicolson, 1962.

INDEX

BOOKS
IN THE HUMOR IN LIFE AND LETTERS SERIES

The Contemporary American Comic Epic: The Novels of Barth, Pynchon, Gaddis, and Kesey,
BY ELAINE B. SAFER, 1988

The Mocking of the President: A History of Campaign Humor from Ike to Ronnie,
BY GERALD GARDNER, 1988

Circus of the Mind in Motion: Postmodernism and the Comic Vision,
BY LANCE OLSEN, 1990

Jewish Wry: Essays on Jewish Humor,
EDITED BY SARAH BLACHER COHEN, 1991 (reprint)

Horsing Around: Contemporary Cowboy Humor,
EDITED BY LAWRENCE CLAYTON AND KENNETH DAVIS, 1991

Women's Comic Visions,
EDITED BY JUNE SOCHEN, 1991

Never Try to Teach a Pig to Sing: Still More Urban Folklore from the Paperwork Empire,
BY ALAN DUNDES AND CARL R. PAGTER, 1991

Comic Relief: Humor in Contemporary American Literature,
EDITED BY SARAH BLACHER COHEN, 1992 (reprint)

Untamed and Unabashed: Essays on Women and Humor in British Literature,
BY REGINA BARRECA, 1993

Campaign Comedy: Political Humor from Clinton to Kennedy,
BY GERALD GARDNER, 1994

The Ironic Temper and the Comic Imagination,
BY MORTON GUREWITCH, 1994

The Comedian as Confidence Man: Studies in Irony Fatigue,
BY WILL KAUFMAN, 1997

Tilting at Mortality: Narrative Strategies in Joseph Heller's Fiction,
BY DAVID M. CRAIG, 1997